Violence and Public Memory

Violence and Public Memory assesses the relationship between these two subjects by examining their interconnections in varied case studies across the United States, South America, Europe, the Middle East, and Africa.

Those responsible for the violence discussed in this volume are varied, and the political ideologies and structures range from apartheid to fascism to homophobia to military dictatorships but also democracy. Racism and state terrorism have played central roles in many of the case studies examined in this book, and multiple chapters also engage with the recent rise of the Black Lives Matter movement. The sites and history represented in this volume address a range of issues, including mass displacement, genocide, political repression, forced disappearances, massacres, and slavery. Across the world there are preserved historic sites, memorials, and museums that mark places of significant violence and human rights abuse, which organizations and activists have specifically worked to preserve and provide a place to face history and its continuing legacy today and chapters across this volume directly engage with the questions and issues that surround these sometimes controversial sites.

Including photographs of many of the sites and events covered across the volume, this is an important book for readers interested in the complex and often difficult history of the relationship between violence and the way it is publicly remembered.

Martin Henry Blatt served as Professor of the Practice and Director of the Public History Program at Northeastern University, USA. He has served as President of the National Council on Public History (NCPH), on the Executive Board of the Organization of American Historians, and on the Board of MASS Humanities. Museum credits include a traveling exhibit on the Gulag, produced by the National Park Service, the Gulag Museum, and Amnesty International. He received the NCPH Robert Kelley Award for outstanding achievement in public history.

Violence and Public Memory

Edited by Martin Henry Blatt

LONDON AND NEW YORK

Cover image: ©Tony Webster

First published 2023
by Routledge
4 Park Square, Milton Park, Abingdon, Oxon OX14 4RN

and by Routledge
605 Third Avenue, New York, NY 10158

Routledge is an imprint of the Taylor & Francis Group, an informa business

© 2023 selection and editorial matter, Martin Henry Blatt; individual chapters, the contributors

The right of Martin Henry Blatt to be identified as the author of the editorial material, and of the authors for their individual chapters, has been asserted in accordance with sections 77 and 78 of the Copyright, Designs and Patents Act 1988.

All rights reserved. No part of this book may be reprinted or reproduced or utilised in any form or by any electronic, mechanical, or other means, now known or hereafter invented, including photocopying and recording, or in any information storage or retrieval system, without permission in writing from the publishers.

Trademark notice: Product or corporate names may be trademarks or registered trademarks, and are used only for identification and explanation without intent to infringe.

British Library Cataloguing-in-Publication Data
A catalogue record for this book is available from the British Library

ISBN: 978-1-032-10948-0 (hbk)
ISBN: 978-1-032-10947-3 (pbk)
ISBN: 978-1-003-21784-8 (ebk)

DOI: 10.4324/9781003217848

Typeset in Bembo
by Apex CoVantage, LLC

I dedicate this book to the memory of Jim Green, my close friend and colleague. I will always remember Jim – as a public historian, a labor historian, a fighter for social justice, a great intellect. But most importantly, I cherished his friendship. He was a wonderful friend from the time I first met him on a United Farm Workers picket line in the late 1970s until his untimely death in 2016. I truly miss him today and every day. When Jim gave me a copy of his last book, *The Devil Is Here in These Hills*, he wrote me the following dedication: "Dear old loyal friend, political comrade, fellow sports fan, and fellow seeker of past moments that inspire us to find social justice in our own time." To him I say the same.

Contents

List of Contributors	x
List of Illustrations	xv
Acknowledgments	xvii

Introduction 1
MARTIN HENRY BLATT

PART I
Genocide 17

1 **A Model Way of Coming to Terms With the Past?: On the Relevance and Future Tasks of Historical–Political Education in (German) Memorial Sites** 19
ELKE GRYGLEWSKI AND KATRIN UNGER

2 **The Holocaust in American Public Memory** 35
BARRY TRACHTENBERG

3 **Memorializing Violence as a Political Tool: Public Memory and the Genocide of the Tutsi in Rwanda** 57
TIMOTHY LONGMAN

PART II
Slavery 77

4 **From Rumblings to Roar: Racial Violence, Historical Justice, and the Changing Public History of Slavery in the United States** 79
RENEE C. ROMANO

viii *Contents*

5 **From a Culture of Abolition to a Culture War: Remembering Transatlantic Enslavement in Britain, 1807–2021** 102

JESSICA MOODY

PART III
Racial and Sexual Hatred in the United States 127

6 **Myths, Mascots, Monuments, and Massacres: Rethinking Native American History in the Public Sphere** 129

MARIA JOHN

7 **Creating the Conditions for Repair: Representation, Memorialization, and Commemoration** 153

KARLOS K. HILL AND KAREN MURPHY

8 **What Is Owed?: Reparations, an Indictment of Public Memory** 172

CALEB GAYLE

9 **Remembering Pulse** 193

LISA ARELLANO

PART IV
Apartheid 209

10 **The Art of Memory: Echoes of Apartheid Police Brutality in the 2012 Marikana Massacre** 211

LEAH NASSON, SIHLE-ISIPHO NONTSHOKWENI, AND DYLAN WRAY

11 **The Land of Milk and Honey (and Palestinians)** 231

EITAN BRONSTEIN APARICIO AND ELEONORE MERZA BRONSTEIN

PART V
Fascism and War 245

12 **Public Commemorations of Argentina's Histories of Violence** 247

MARISA LERER

Contents ix

**13 The Violence of the Vietnam War in the
Memorialized American Landscape** 267

ELISE LEMIRE

Index 285

Contributors

Eitan Bronstein Aparicio is an Israeli educator who received his MA in Hermeneutics from Bar Ilan University. After serving for over ten years as the coordinator of encounters and projects between Jews and Arabs at the School for Peace at Neve Shalom – Wahat al-Salam, he founded the NGO Zochrot and served as director until 2011. He is the co-author of *Nakba – The Struggle to Decolonize Israel* (2021). Among his many articles, he authored "The Nakba in Hebrew: Israeli-Jewish Awareness of the Palestinian Catastrophe and Internal Refugees," in Nur Masalha, ed., *Catastrophe Remembered: Palestine, Israel, and the Internal Refugees* (2005). In 2015, he co-founded De-Colonizer and is its current co-director. He is also a video director and editor.

Lisa Arellano, formerly an associate professor at Colby College, is a Berkeley-based historian and digital editor. She is the co-editor of *Queer Pasts* and a Visiting Professor of Women's, Gender, and Sexuality Studies at Mills College. Her research and teaching focus on comparative social movements, critical historiography, and violence studies. Her first book is *Vigilantes and Lynch Mobs: Community, Nation and Narrative* (2012). She is co-editor, with Amanda Frisken and Erica Ball, of the Fall 2016 issue of the *Radical History Review*, titled "Reconsidering Gender, Violence and the State." Arellano's current book manuscript, *Disarming Imagination: Violence and the American Political Left*, addresses high-profile rape revenge cases, anti-violence activism, militant political movements, and dis/utopian political literature.

Martin Henry Blatt, Emeritus Professor of Public History, Northeastern University, was director of the public history program and previously worked for the National Park Service in Massachusetts in Boston and Lowell for 24 years. The National Council on Public History awarded him the Robert Kelley Memorial Award for outstanding achievement in public history in 2020. The National Park Service presented him in 2013 with the Director's Award for Excellence in Cultural Resource Management. He was the co-editor of *Hope and Glory: Essays on the Legacy of the Fifty-fourth Massachusetts Regiment* and the author of *Free Love and Anarchism: The Biography of Ezra Heywood*. He is the author of many articles and reviews and has presented talks at a number of conferences. Also, he has been instrumental in the production of several exhibits, public programs, and documentaries. He served in elected leadership positions with the National Council on Public History and the Organization of American Historians and was appointed to the board of Massachusetts Humanities. Blatt received his PhD from Boston University.

Eleonore Merza Bronstein is a political anthropologist and associated researcher at the CNRS (the French National Scientific Research Council). She earned her PhD at the Ecoles des Hautes Etudes en Sciences Sociales (EHESS) in Paris; her work focused on analysis of the settings of non-Jewish citizenship in Israel and the political power games/relations between minorities and the state as well as political collective mobilizations. She had a postdoctoral position at the French Center of Research in Jerusalem. She is the co-author of *Nakba – The Struggle to Decolonize Israel* (2021). Her main fields of research are social protests, political mobilizations, gender and feminism, and memory activism. In 2015, she co-founded De-Colonizer and is its current co-director. She is also a photographer and writer.

Caleb Gayle is an award-winning journalist who writes about race and identity. A professor at Northeastern University's School of Journalism, he is a fellow at New America, PEN America, Harvard's Radcliffe Institute of Advanced Studies, and a visiting scholar at New York University. His writing has appeared in *The New York Times Magazine*, *The Atlantic*, *The Guardian*, *Guernica*, and other publications. The son of Jamaican immigrants, he is a graduate of the University of Oklahoma, the University of Oxford, and has an MBA and a master's in public policy, both from Harvard University. He lives in Boston.

Elke Gryglewski is the director of the Lower Saxony Memorials Foundation and the Bergen-Belsen Memorial. Previously, she worked as senior educator, head of the educational department, and deputy director of the House of the Wannsee Conference Memorial and Educational Site in Berlin. She wrote her PhD thesis on the relationship of young Berliners of Turkish and Palestinian backgrounds toward National Socialism and the Holocaust. She has published several books and articles on pedagogics in Memorial Sites and remembrance in diverse societies. She has been working for decades on the question of how societies deal with violent pasts, comparing mainly the German experience with the South American experience.

Karlos K. Hill is Regents' Professor and Chair of the Clara Luper Department of African and African American Studies at the University of Oklahoma. He is the author of three books: *Beyond The Rope: The Impact of Lynching on Black Culture and Memory*, *The Murder of Emmett Till: A Graphic History*, and *The 1921 Tulsa Race Massacre: A Photographic History*. He founded the Tulsa Race Massacre Oklahoma Teachers' Institute to support teaching the history of the race massacre to thousands of middle school and high school students.

xii   *Contributors*

He also serves on the boards of the Clara Luper Legacy Committee and the Board of Scholars for Facing History and Ourselves, and is actively engaged in other community initiatives working toward racial justice.

Maria John received her PhD in History from Columbia University. Before joining UMass Boston as an Assistant Professor of Native American History, she was an Indigenous Studies Mellon Postdoctoral Fellow in the American Studies Department at Wesleyan University. Her research interests include twentieth-century urban Indigenous histories, comparative histories of settler colonialism, social and political histories of health and healthcare, histories of health activism, the history of Indigenous sovereignty, and the politics of public history. Her book-in-progress compares health struggles and Indigenous health activism among urban Indigenous communities in Australia and the United States from the mid-twentieth century to the present. At UMass Boston, she teaches undergraduate and graduate classes on Native American history, Indigenous Studies, comparative colonialisms and decolonization, Native American health, Oral History, and Public History. She currently serves as the Director of the Native American and Indigenous Studies Program at UMass Boston.

Elise Lemire is Professor of Literature at Purchase College, SUNY, and the author of three books: *Black Walden: Slavery and Its Aftermath in Concord, Massachusetts*, *"Miscegenation": Making Race in America*, and most recently *Battle Green Vietnam: The 1971 March on Concord, Lexington, and Boston*. Educated at Yale and Rutgers, she is a two-time recipient of fellowships from the National Endowment for the Humanities.

Marisa Lerer is an associate professor of Modern and Contemporary art history at Manhattan College in the Bronx. She specializes in Latin American and Latinx art, public art, and memorials. Her interest in art and social justice movements is reflected in both the content of her courses and publications, which have appeared in journals such as *Public Art Dialogue*, *Visual Resources*, and *Latin American and Latinx Visual Culture* and in books including *A Companion to Public Art*, among others. She is co-editor of the journal *Public Art Dialogue*, which serves as a forum for critical discourse and commentary about the practice of public art.

Timothy Longman is Professor of political science and international relations at Boston University. He is the director of CURA: the Institute on Culture Religion and World Affairs and previously served as director of the African Studies Center for nine years. His research focuses on state and society in Africa, particularly human rights, transitional justice, the politics of race, ethnicity, and gender, and religion and politics. He has published two books on Rwanda, *Christianity and Genocide in Rwanda* and *Memory and Justice in Post-Genocide Rwanda*, co-authored a textbook on South Africa, *Confronting Apartheid*, and is currently writing a book on church-state relations across Africa. He has previously held teaching or research appointments at Vassar

College, the University of California, Berkeley, Columbia University, the National University of Rwanda, and the University of the Witwatersrand, and he has served as a consultant for USAID, the International Center for Transitional Justice, the Justice Department, and Human Rights Watch in Rwanda, Burundi, Uganda, and the Democratic Republic of Congo.

Jessica Moody is Senior Lecturer in Public History at the University of Bristol, UK. She has previously worked at the Universities of Portsmouth and York and for National Museums Liverpool. She is the author of *The Persistence of Memory: Remembering Slavery in Liverpool, 'slaving capital of the world'* (2020), which maps the public memory of enslavement in the city of Liverpool, the largest slave-trading port city in Europe, from the end of the eighteenth century through the twenty-first century. Her research concerns public history and public memory, especially the representation, historically and in the present day, of difficult, dissonant and contested histories of race, enslavement, empire and warfare, and decolonial approaches to public memory.

Karen Murphy is the CEO of the Human Responsibility Accelerator and the Chief Learning Officer for the High Resolves Group. Prior to these positions, she led Facing History and Ourselves global programs. She has developed and managed programs in countries around the world, including Colombia, Mexico, Northern Ireland, France, and South Africa. She has a deep interest in the role of education in countries emerging from mass violence, in divided societies with identity-based conflicts, and in the period of transition in the development of democracy and democratic stability. She has a PhD in American Studies and has researched and taught about the role of race and racial violence in the development of the United States as a modern nation.

Leah Nasson is a History curriculum specialist based in Cape Town. She holds an MA in Italian Literature, the focus of which was the intersection of literature and history during the era of Italian colonialism in Africa. She has published a number of articles in peer-reviewed academic journals and serves on the editorial board of *Yesterday and Today*, a journal which focuses on teaching history in South Africa. She has a specialist interest in teacher identity in post-apartheid South Africa and issues of social justice in the classroom.

Sihle-isipho Nontshokweni is the author of the award-winning Wanda children's book series. She has traveled to numerous countries, including Tibet, China, Australia, Finland, and 25 European countries. She lived in Beijing, completing a master's at Peking University. Her interest in schools stems from her lived experience across 12 schooling institutions, including KU Leuven, University of Cape Town, and Universitat de Barcelona. From this vast world experience, Sihle tells stories that explore how hierarchical and racialized contexts affect identity, aspirations, and opportunities.

xiv *Contributors*

Renee C. Romano is the Robert S. Danforth Professor of History and Professor of Comparative American Studies and Africana Studies at Oberlin College in Ohio. A specialist in recent American cultural and political history and in the field of historical memory, she is the author of *Racial Reckoning; Reopening America's Civil Rights Trials* (2014) and the co-editor of *Historians on Hamilton: How a Blockbuster Musical Is Restaging America's Past* (2018) and *Doing Recent History* (2012). She leads Oberlin's Public Humanities initiative and has been involved in numerous public history projects. She served as consultant for the May 4th Visitor's Center at Kent State University and recently earned a certificate in Museum Studies from Northwestern University.

Barry Trachtenberg is a historian of modern Jewry and holds the Rubin Presidential Chair of Jewish history at Wake Forest University in North Carolina. He is the author of *The Holocaust & the Exile of Yiddish: A History of the Algemeyne Entsiklopedye* (2022) and *The United States and the Holocaust: Race, Refuge, and Remembrance* (2018). His work has been supported by grants from the National Endowment for the Humanities, the Memorial Foundation for Jewish Culture, the National Foundation for Jewish Culture, the YIVO Institute for Jewish Research, and the United States Holocaust Memorial Museum. From 2015 to 2021, he served on the Academic Council of the Holocaust Education Foundation of Northwestern University. Since 2016, he has served on the Board of Scholars of Facing History and Ourselves. He also writes occasional pieces on the topics of Zionism, anti-semitism, and United States support for Israel.

Katrin Unger is the Head of the Educational Department at the Bergen-Belsen Memorial, where she has worked for many years as Senior Educator. She worked as a member of the educational staff at the Max Mannheimer Study Center Dachau related to the Memorial Site at the former Dachau Concentration Camp. She is a member of the Federal Working Group Pedagogics in Memorial Sites and has published articles. Due to her biographical experience, she has specialized in the aftermath of National Socialism in the German Democratic Republic.

Dylan Wray is the executive director and co-founder of Shikaya – a nonprofit organization that supports teachers and school leaders to ensure young people leave school thinking critically, and engaging as compassionate, active, and democratic citizens. He co-authored *A School Where I Belong – Creating Transformed and Inclusive South African Schools*. He has created workshops and school transformation programs for schools across South Africa. Since 2003 he has been managing and implementing the Facing History and Ourselves program in South Africa and has trained and supported thousands of teachers in South Africa to use lessons of history to challenge them and their students to stand up to bigotry and hate. He works globally training teachers and education leaders across Africa, South America, Asia, and the Middle East.

Illustrations

1.1	The first monuments in Bergen–Belsen were initiated and inaugurated by survivors – years before official commemoration signs were established by German authorities. On the first anniversary of the liberation, April 15, 1946, the first stone monument commemorating the Jewish victims was inaugurated by survivors living in the Displaced Persons camp nearby	21
2.1	Anti-Nazis hold demonstration, March 15, 1937	39
2.2	US Holocaust Memorial Museum, Washington, DC, 2021	50
3.1	Entrance to the Ntarama Church Genocide Memorial	65
3.2	Skulls of genocide victims on display at the Ntarama Church Genocide Memorial	65
4.1	Statue of Robert E. Lee being removed in New Orleans on May 17, 2017	83
4.2	"Slave Auctions" marker, erected outside Charleston's Old Exchange Building, 2016	88
4.3	Memorial to the 1811 Slave Revolt at the Whitney Plantation Museum	92
5.1	Protester Toyin Agbetu disrupts a service to mark the bicentenary of the 1807 act to abolish the slave trade, attended by Britain's Queen Elizabeth II, at Westminster Abbey	109
5.2	Empty pedestal of the statue of Edward Colston in Bristol, the day after protesters felled the statue and rolled it into the harbor. The ground is covered with Black Lives Matter placards	112
6.1	The fallen Christopher Columbus statue (originally dedicated in 1931) outside the Minnesota State Capitol after a group led by American Indian Movement members tore it down in St. Paul, Minnesota, on June 10, 2020	129
6.2	Chali'Naru Dones, an Indigenous activist and member of the Taino tribe, delivered a speech during Boston's 2020 Indigenous Peoples' Day march on top of the pedestal that once held a Christopher Columbus statue in the North End	131

xvi *Illustrations*

6.3	Crowds gathered on Cole's Hill, under the Massasoit statue, to mark the 52nd Annual National Day of Mourning, in Plymouth, MA, November 25, 2021	148
7.1	Tuscaloosa County, Alabama, historical marker	165
8.1	View of the destruction of Greenwood, Tulsa, once a hub for Black opportunity and prosperity	176
8.2	Black woman gazing at the destruction inflicted on Greenwood, Tulsa, by the perpetrators of the Tulsa Race Massacre	177
8.3	Arrested Black residents of Greenwood, Tulsa, being marched to makeshift detention facility	182
9.1	What the National Pulse Memorial will look like during the day	200
9.2	Orlando Health Survivors Walk design	201
10.1	Zakes Mda, The Man in a Green Blanket #1, oil on canvas painting, 2015	224
10.2	Zakes Mda, The Man in a Green Blanket #3, oil on canvas painting, 2016	225
10.3	Zakes Mda, The Man in a Green Blanket #4, oil on canvas painting, 2016	226
12.1	*Siluetazo II*. 2004. ESMA, Buenos Aires	254
12.2	Baudizzone-Lestard-and-Varas Studio and the associated architects Claudio Ferrari and Daniel Becker. *Monumento a las Víctimas del Terrorism de Estado* (*Monument to the Victims of State Terrorism*), Parque de la memoria, Buenos Aires, Argentina, 2006	257
12.3	Barrios por Memoria y Justicia. *Baldosas* (*Sidewalk Tiles*), n.d., Buenos Aires, Argentina	260
13.1	Wounded Vietnam Veteran commences antiwar march at Concord's Minute Man statue	274
13.2	Members of VVAW-NE perform a mock search-and-destroy mission on the Boston Common, April 14, 1971	276

Acknowledgments

I want to thank Eve Setch of Routledge for inviting me to prepare this volume. I am grateful to Louis Hutchins. When we were in the National Park Service, he and I imagined a different book but with similar themes and concerns. My interactions with public history graduate students at Northeastern University were stimulating, interesting, and truly helpful in refining my thinking about the contours of this book. And I am deeply grateful to my wife Betty Munson who assisted me in many ways with the manuscript preparation.

Introduction

Martin Henry Blatt

The memory of my uncle Henry Freund impacted me profoundly, propelling me to a lifelong commitment to social justice through the telling of history in public contexts. He died aboard an American troop transport sunk by a mine; his ship was carrying reinforcements to the Battle of the Bulge. As a young boy, I had nightmares of drowning on board with Henry or watching him die and being powerless to help. Heidelberg, Germany, was my mother Molly's home and Henry was her brother. Her family was prosperous upper middle-class Jews. She managed to flee in the summer of 1938; Henry and my grandmother Clara departed in January 1940. The Nazis imprisoned my grandfather Adolf in Dachau for a month in the fall of 1938 and took him to the prison camp Gurs in fall, 1940, where he died of dysentery. They murdered many in my family.

The spirit of Henry Freund influenced me during my participation in the March Against Death, a 1969 protest against the Vietnam War in Washington, DC. Each participant carried the name of a dead American soldier around their neck on cardboard and carried a candle in a silent march from Arlington National Cemetery to the Capitol Building, where the placard with the name was laid to rest in a mock coffin. The name of the soldier I carried was Benjamin Kissling of Texas. I imagined a conversation which seemed and felt real. The participants were my uncle Henry, Kissling, and myself, and our focus was on the lunacy of war and the need to struggle against war and for social justice. The experience and lessons from that march remain with me to this day.

In the fall of 2001, my mother Molly and I traveled to Heidelberg. The city had invited the "former Jewish citizens of Heidelberg," those Jews who fled the Nazi regime between 1938 and 1945, to visit for a week-long, all-expenses-paid program with a companion of their choice. Scheduled at five-year intervals, the first gathering had been in 1996. In 2011, I attended another program; this time with my younger daughter. Such gatherings were not peculiar to Heidelberg. German cities and towns have been organizing programs for former Jewish citizens for decades. Such events function both as an apology and as a demonstration of the strength of Germany's contemporary democracy. Heidelberg and many other German communities no longer organize these events as the great majority of Jews with lived experience of the Nazis have passed away.[1]

DOI: 10.4324/9781003217848-1

2 Martin Henry Blatt

Throughout my professional career as a public historian, the relationship of violence to public memory has been a central recurring theme. When I worked at Lowell National Historical Park in the early 1990s, I tried, with mixed success, to get the park to foreground the issue of slavery. It had seemed clear to me then, and still does, that the labor of enslaved Africans in the South to produce the raw material cotton was crucial to the success of Lowell and the industrial North. I urged this interconnection be highlighted in tours, exhibits, and programming; this issue remains problematic in some ways still today at the park.[2] After moving to Boston National Historical Park, I was a key organizer of the 1997 centennial celebration of the Augustus Saint-Gaudens memorial to Robert Gould Shaw and the 54th Massachusetts Regiment. One of the greatest pieces of public art in the United States, this memorial celebrates the white commander and the first Black regiment comprised of primarily free Blacks in the Union army. The regiment, which suffered great losses in an unsuccessful effort to capture Fort Wagner in South Carolina, paved the way for the significant increase of Black troops which was critical in leading to the defeat of the Confederacy. With our centennial program, which featured the largest gathering ever of Black Civil War reenactors, a public outdoor ceremony, and a symposium, we sought to reframe the memorial so that attention would be focused on the Black troops and not narrowly on their white commanding officer.[3]

In 2003, I joined with my National Park Service (NPS) colleague Louis Hutchins to begin planning the first traveling exhibit on the history of the Soviet Gulag in the United States. This project grew out of a working relationship the NPS had initiated with the International Historic Site Museums of Conscience. We brought together a unique collaboration to produce the exhibit. Partners included the NPS, the Gulag Museum of Perm Russia; the International Memorial Society; and Amnesty International. The exhibit, "GULAG: Soviet Forced Labor Camps and the Struggle for Freedom," told a sharply critical story of the Gulag without allowing the traditional American Cold War anti-Communist narrative to predominate. The traveling exhibit was displayed in a variety of NPS sites, including Ellis Island and Martin Luther King, Jr. National Historic Site. The NPS also sent a team of curators to Perm to work with the museum on a variety of public history issues.[4] In 2014, with Putin controlling Russia and a change in the governor of the Perm region, our collaborators at the Gulag Museum were removed. The museum was repurposed; no longer is it a historic site devoted to the actual history of the Gulag but in a bizarre, sick twist, it now presents a narrative that represents the Gulag as a vital component of the Soviet victory in World War II. Further, in late 2021, Russia's Supreme Court, doing Putin's bidding, ordered the closure of the International Memorial Society.

Boston National Historical Park marked the 150th anniversary of the Emancipation Proclamation in 2013 with a series of programs. Most notable was "Roots of Liberty: The Haitian Revolution and the American Civil War," organized by the National Park Service along with Central Square Theater, the Museum of African American History [Boston], Harvard University, and others. This historical pageant focused on the significant impact of the Haitian Revolution on Black and white abolitionists and Black Union troops as well as the fear the revolution sparked among white slave owners in the South. The performance attracted a capacity crowd of 1,700 to Tremont Temple, the site where the Proclamation was first read in Boston in 1863. The pageant featured a large, diverse cast of actors and actresses, dancers, music, a choir, and an enormous puppet figure of the iconic Haitian leader Touissant L'Ouverture. The Haitian American writer Edwidge Danticat authored parts of the script and the actor Danny Glover portrayed Touissant.[5]

A few years later in 2015, I retired from the National Park Service in order to become professor of the practice and director of the public history program at Northeastern University. I focused a significant part of my work on my ongoing commitment to the exploration of the relationship between violence and public memory. I worked with my students to develop a module on Malcolm X and his participation on the debate team at Norfolk Prison for the national traveling exhibit, "States of Incarceration," organized by the Humanities Action Lab. My courses included public history of slavery; public history of incarceration; history and memory of King Philip's War; and violence and public memory. On the basis of the latter course, Routledge approached me to produce a book and this volume is the result.

★★★★

With the focus of this volume on violence and public memory, it is important to provide some basic definitions of terms for an overview. I approach violence in this volume in a capacious manner. Governments ranging from authoritarian regimes like Nazi Germany in the Holocaust to autocracies like fascist Argentina to democracies like the United States in Vietnam have perpetrated vast death and destruction. Settler colonial societies, including South Africa and Israel, have displaced Indigenous populations. Slave owners brutalized and dehumanized the enslaved in many ways. The legacies of slavery have included virulent racism which is a pernicious form of violence. Whites in the Jim Crow South in the United States enforced segregation and strict racial hierarchy by many means with the most horrible being lynching. Homophobic and racial hatred inspired the mass murder attack on the Pulse Nightclub in Orlando, Florida. Kenneth Foote, writing about sites of violence and tragedy in the United States, has identified four useful categories that fall along a continuum: "sanctification, designation, rectification, and obliteration. All four outcomes can result in major modifications of the landscape, but of very different sorts."[6]

There is the violence of murder, displacement, humiliation, or lynching, and then there is another kind of violence which constitutes a second wave or stage. The perpetrators of violence and subsequent generations seek to celebrate their legacies and to distort, lie, or obliterate the historical truth of what happened to their victims. Bryan Stevenson worked for years to free Blacks from the death sentence in the American South who were wrongly convicted of murder. It became clear to him that in order to truly understand the racism of the justice

4   *Martin Henry Blatt*

system, it was essential to comprehend the history of slavery, racism, Jim Crow violence, convict labor, and mass incarceration. Stevenson and his organization, Equal Justice Initiative, made this concrete through their establishment of a museum and national lynching memorial in Montgomery, Alabama.[7] British colonists and later American citizens dispossessed Indigenous Americans. Subsequently, they continued their violence by portraying Indians as largely disappeared and actively sought to eradicate their cultural identities through forcing Indigenous children to leave their homes and attend boarding schools where they were compelled to cut their hair, dress in American attire, and repudiate their native languages.[8] Zionist settlers and subsequently Israeli citizens dispossessed large numbers of Palestinians and then literally erased them from historical maps. Whites in the American South may have lost the Civil War but largely won the peace with their assertion of the Lost Cause argument. According to David Blight, the Lost Cause promoted the notion of an Old South rooted in the "chivalry and romance of antebellum plantation life." This totally false but wildly popular picture included Black "servants," and a "happy, loyal slave culture, remembered as a source of laughter, music, and contentment." Blight relates that the Civil War according to the Lost Cause became "essentially a conflict between white men; both sides fought well, Americans against Americans, and there was glory enough to go around. Celebrating the soldiers' experience buttressed the nonideological memory of the war." To most southerners, David Blight argues, the Lost Cause came to represent a "crucial double meaning: reunion and respect." And this Lost Cause ideology flourished and helped to nurture the terrible violence of the Jim Crow South.[9]

So we can define violence in multiple ways that play out over time. It is interesting to examine the image on the cover of this book which portrays a toppled statue of Christopher Columbus in Minnesota. Also, in Chapter 5 of this volume, we see the pedestal of a statue of a slave trader in Bristol, Great Britain, that was forcibly removed by protesters. Protesters attacked both statues in reaction to the police murder of George Floyd. Are these legitimate forms of dissenting action or are they acts of vandalism for which the perpetrators should be punished? Does removal of such statues constitute a bold effort to reframe what constitutes history or a forceful, crude action to remove history from public view? I would argue that these actions are appropriate steps by protesters seeking to redefine history in the public domain which is always a contested space. In her important study, *Memorial Mania*, Erika Doss relates that in 1946, Allied forces in Germany issued Directive No. 30, "The Liquidation of German Military and Nazi Memorials and Museums," and ordered that they be "completed destroyed and liquidated" within 18 months. She reports that in 2003, US soldiers in Iraq "pulled down multiple monuments to Saddam Hussein." And yet, she asks us to consider the contradiction that the United States on its own soil "allows – or more accurately ignores – memorials to the defeated states and underlying white supremacist politics of the secessionist Southern Confederacy." It is hypocritical to argue that only official military organizations can properly tamper with public memory but unofficial players have no right to do so.[10] The BBC reported on January 6, 2022, that the "Bristol Four" was acquitted on charges of criminal damage after tearing down the statue of slave trader Edward Colston. Historian David Olusoga, who supported the defendants and provided expert testimony on slavery at the trial, told the BBC:

> An English jury . . . has come to the conclusion that the real offence was that a statue to a mass murderer was able to stand for 125 years, not that that statue was toppled in the summer of 2020.

He argued:

> That is enormously significant and we are on this very long and difficult journey in this country of acknowledging all of our history, the bad as well as the good and I think this is a landmark in that difficult, tortuous journey.[11]

Let me turn now to a definition of public memory. This memory consists of tangible expressions of history – preservation and/or marking of historic sites, museum exhibitions, memorials, documentary films, and more. One of the leading scholars who have addressed public memory is historian Edward Linenthal. He has identified the crucial, "inevitable" tension that exists between a commemorative voice and a historical one which addresses nuance and complication. The commemorative voice, Linenthal argues, completely triumphed over the historical approach in the Enola Gay exhibit at the Smithsonian National Air and Space Museum in the 1990s. This had disastrous consequences at the time with the triumphalist, celebratory exhibit marking the dropping of the atomic bomb on Hiroshima and the exhibit's impact reverberates to this day. There is still a way that the resolution of this exhibit can chill contemporary efforts to tell critical narratives. At the time, historian Alfred Young argued that museum curators deserved the same protections of academic freedom afforded to scholars with tenure. Many argued, including Democrats and Republicans in Congress, that an exhibit should be objective and only convey facts, not opinions. Of course, just as there is no objectivity in scholarly publications, the same can be said for history exhibits. Linenthal cites museum critic Barbara Kirshenblatt-Gimblett who argues that every exhibit takes a position, takes a "point of view." Exhibits, she argues, are "full of points of view, full of messages – full of interpretation."[12]

As I am writing this introduction, the best contemporary exploration of violence and public memory is Raoul Peck's searing, challenging, multi-part documentary, "Exterminate All the Brutes." Peck, who created the outstanding film, "I Am Not Your Negro," centered around James Baldwin and an examination of racism in the United States, produced the four-part "Exterminate All the Brutes" in 2021 for HBO. Peck took the series name from Sven Lundqvist's book by the same name, a phrase he took from Joseph Conrad's

6 *Martin Henry Blatt*

novella, *Heart of Darkness*.[13] The Haitian Peck skillfully interweaves his own life narrative, which includes living in Haiti, the Democratic Republic of Congo, Europe, and the United States, into the larger framework of the documentary. Through a combination of documentary and dramatization techniques, Peck's series provides an unrelenting, necessary, indeed welcome, examination of colonization, genocides, imperialism, and white supremacy. Besides Lundqvist, Peck relies substantially on two other historians, Roxanne Dunbar-Ortiz and Michel-Rolph Trouillot.[14]

The study of memory is currently a vast territory. Several scholarly journals either focus on this field or feature it regularly. These include the *Journal of Memory Studies, History and Memory – Studies in the Representation of the Past, The Public Historian, International Public History*, the *Journal of American History*, the *American Historical Review*, and others. Some of these journals have devoted special sections to violence and public memory.[15] Many scholars have organized memory-related seminars and conference sessions and entire gatherings focused on an inquiry into the meaning and nature of memory.

Two important recent books examine how the memory of slavery has changed in the United States and how many challenges remain. Clint Smith provides a provocative, wide-ranging series of case studies of how slavery is remembered or misremembered, mostly in the South but he also includes New York City. He declares: "The history of slavery is the history of the United States. It was not peripheral to our founding; it was central to it. This history is in our soil, it is in our policies, and it must, too, be in our memories."[16] Not a native German, Susan Neiman relates in her book that one of the first words she added to her German vocabulary when she moved to Germany was *Vergangenheitsaufarbeitung*, which she translates as "working-off-the past." The contrast between how Germany works off the past of the Holocaust versus how the United States works off the past of slavery is the central focus of her book. Of course, in both countries, the present tense is appropriate. Neither nation will ever "complete" this process. That is neither desirable nor possible. Neiman concludes that America has failed to face its past while "German efforts to confront its own crimes have made it a better country."[17]

Several recent edited collections have explored such topics as global viewpoints on genocide; sites of traumatic memory; violence and memory in a digital context; and contested commemoration. Editors Ajlina Karamehic-Muratovic and Laura Kromjak relate that the focus of their volume is an interdisciplinary inquiry into what they characterize as the science of remembrance and forgiveness in global episodes of genocide and mass violence.[18] The editors of the volume addressing sites of traumatic memory assert that trauma results "when violence cannot be accommodated, happens suddenly, and is re-experienced in unexpected and uncontrolled ways." The memorials discussed in their book refer to places "dedicated to the commemoration of traumatic memories." Memorials, they argue, aim to "recognize the human right to memories which are often denied to persecuted people" and they serve to symbolically compensate victims and survivors.[19] Focusing on the digital treatment of violence and remembrance, editors Eve Monique Zucker and David Simon make an interesting case for "memorialization unmoored" with the proliferation of digital memory projects. They observe two linked phenomena – "an expansion of non-state memorialization efforts" and "a turn to memorialization in the digital realm." The essays they have curated focus on four areas – more traditional forms of digital media; social media; online databases and archives; and the employment of artificial intelligence. Regarding the latter, they pose the important ethical question of whether hologrammatic depictions of Holocaust survivors are "richer versions of single dimensional testimony or dehumanizing technological displays."[20] Melissa Bender and Klara Stephanie Szlezak have compiled an eclectic collection of essays that explore contested commemoration in US history. The central questions that underlie the writings they have assembled include "Who has the right to interpret and memorialize particular historical events? What is at stake for various constituencies in acts of commemoration?"[21]

★★★★

This edited volume assesses the relationship between violence and public memory in the twentieth and twentieth-first centuries by examining this interconnection in case studies from the United States, Germany, Rwanda, Great Britain, South Africa, Israel/Palestine, and Argentina. Besides a wide geographic range, the book also covers many types of memorialization – museums, historic sites, memorials, public art, and popular culture. The collection should find wide use among professors teaching in the fields of public history, public humanities, museum studies, and the examination of memory. It should also be of interest to anyone teaching about the Black Lives Matter (BLM) uprising worldwide in the aftermath of the police murder of George Floyd in Minneapolis in 2020 as some authors consider how Floyd's murder prompted reconsideration of public memorials. A point of emphasis in this collection is how memory of violence might advance ethical concerns and the promotion of social justice.

Those responsible for the violence addressed in these essays are quite varied. The political ideologies and governmental structures range from apartheid to fascism to homophobia and from democracies to military dictatorships. Racism and state terrorism play central roles in many of the case studies.

Every nation has painful, brutal chapters in its past. Across the world there are historic sites, memorials, and museums that mark places of significant violence and human rights abuses. Of course, much of this history is deliberately overlooked, distorted, or twisted to serve the interests of those in power. Some organizations and advocates specifically work not only to preserve the memory of past abuses but also to provide a sacred place of remembrance and to frame their examination of the past in a manner that confronts the ongoing, continuing legacy of the violent past. Many societies would rather preserve sites that serve to venerate and glorify the past by celebrating triumphs of war, technological advances, royalty, or great statesmen. It is a difficult choice to honestly

8   Martin Henry Blatt

examine the sites and history of repression. In many cases, the preservation of these sites and this memory are highly controversial. I believe that the measure of the integrity of a nation or culture is the degree to which there is an open, wide-ranging, and unflinching examination of the violent past and its meanings for contemporary society.

I have organized this volume into five thematic sections – genocide; slavery; racial and sexual hatred in the United States; apartheid; and fascism and war. Each section includes multiple chapters tied to the specific theme. The history and memory struggles that are addressed here are quite varied and profound. However, humanity has such a deep history of violence and efforts to recall or suppress memory of this violence that this collection can only be indicative and not comprehensive in its coverage. I have sought to include multiple references in this introduction to point readers to further areas to explore and each contributor has extensive references which can lead to further considerations of the chapter discussions.

Part I focuses on genocide. Nations and organizations have perpetrated genocide for centuries. However, genocide only became a formal category of human violence in the aftermath of World War II. Legal scholar Raphael Lemkin defined the term initially in 1944 as any attempt to physically or culturally annihilate an ethnic, national, religious, or political group. The 1948 United Nations Convention on the Prevention and Punishment of the Crime of Genocide more narrowly defined it as "acts committed with intent to destroy, in whole or in part, a national, ethnical, racial or religious group, as such."[22]

In Chapter 1, Elke Gryglewski and Katrin Unger, staff members of a Nazi concentration camp memorial, examine how Germany has dealt with its Holocaust past and the challenges that that experience poses for the future work of public historians in Germany. In particular, they argue that there were many problematic aspects of the response following the fall of Nazism and that this is part of the overall history that needs to be not only understood but also confronted. Part of their approach is to contrast developments in the Federal Republic versus the German Democratic Republic. In discussing how many former Nazis received lenient treatment, they critique a public history approach that can overly focus on victims while not subjecting perpetrators to significant, critical assessment. Gryglewski and Unger believe that the task of confronting the past has not been completed but rather is an ongoing process. This process, they contend, requires Germany's very diverse society to continuously prove that it is seriously and sustainably committed to confronting the consequences of systematic and industrialized mass murder and has not lapsed into superficial, ritualized gestures of remembrance.

In Chapter 2, Barry Trachtenberg discusses the shifting status of the Nazi Holocaust in American public memory and identifies three overlapping phases. During World War II and immediately after, commemorations and investigations of Nazi mass murder were largely a private matter among Jews. A second phase developed in the mid-1960s when Jews were more secure in their place within American society. As Holocaust awareness grew in the United States

Introduction 9

and elsewhere, it took on increasing importance in shaping the self-perception of American Jews. Trachtenberg marks a third phase starting in the 1990s as Holocaust memory moved to the center of American public memory with the establishment of the United States Holocaust Memorial Museum and the release of Steven Spielberg's film, *Schindler's List*. He concludes by speculating about the emergence of a fourth phase which features the Holocaust being applied to a broader range of social and humanitarian issues, both within and outside the American Jewish community.

Timothy Longman in Chapter 3 focuses on the political manipulation of the public memory of the genocide of the Tutsis in Rwanda. In 1994, a government-orchestrated campaign of violence targeted the Tutsi ethnic minority with devastating results. The military victory of the Tutsi rebel group, the Rwandan Patriotic Front (RPF), in 1994 ended the violence, and the RPF has dominated Rwandan politics since then. They have carefully shaped public memory of the 1994 violence by espousing a particular narrative that treats the genocide as the culmination of Rwanda's colonial and post-colonial history and that rationalizes the continuation of political power by the RPF. For the most part, Longman argues, the international community has bought into this narrative and used it to justify their strong support for the RPF. Yet, he contends, the government narrative is undermined by the lived experience of Rwandans, many of whom view the RPF as an authoritarian party that benefits an ethnic and national minority.

Part II deals with slavery. Renee C. Romano, in Chapter 4, examines the evolution and challenge of representing the violence of slavery in the United States in public history. Drawing on a variety of sources, she explores both the current state of the public history of slavery in the United States and the challenges of telling the truth about slavery and its legacies. In doing so, she joins the conversation as to why recent racial violence has sparked change in the way public history sites deal with slavery. To adequately answer that question, Romano relates the need to contextualize debates about slavery within a politics of historical justice that predates 2015, the year when a white supremacist murdered several Blacks in a church in Charleston, South Carolina. She also explores the contemporary political movement through the lens of historical justice. Romano argues that current interventions fall into three categories: battles to dismantle pro-slavery narratives and monuments; efforts to recuperate and mark erased or obliterated sites of slavery; and, what she terms the most challenging of all, imaginative work to construct and communicate new narratives of American history that acknowledge the centrality of slavery and its legacies to the American story.

In Chapter 5, Jessica Moody addresses the issue of remembering enslavement in Britain. Britain played a major role in the transatlantic trade of enslaved Africans until two acts in the early nineteenth century brought a faltering legal end. The public memory of this past has been highly contested in the 1990s; in 2007 at the time of the Bicentenary of the British Slave Trade Act; and in 2020, when Black Lives Matter protesters pulled down the statue of British

10   *Martin Henry Blatt*

slave merchant Edward Colston. Moody argues that until the later twentieth century, British public memory of this history did not focus on the scale and economy of slavery or its brutality and violence. During the nineteenth century and until close to the millennium, official public memory rather sought to celebrate its own – largely parliamentary – history of abolition. Britain's celebration of mainly white abolition heroes served to obscure the longer, violent history of enslavement and its legacies. Moody relates that this shifted in the 1980s onward with Black political protests, demographic change, and a shifting historiographical framework. By the end of the twentieth century, Britain's public memory of slavery had much more of a focus on issues including slave resistance, the experiences of the enslaved, and the brutal history of transatlantic enslavement. Moody's chapter considers broad patterns of public memory and forgetting as well as critical moments in the history of Britain's memory of transatlantic enslavement including the tensions around the public discourse in 2020 and 2021 following the police murder of George Floyd in the United States.

Part III is an examination of racial and sexual hatred in the United States. In Chapter 6, Maria John examines Native American history in the public sphere. Specifically, she is interested in the summer of 2020 in the aftermath of the police killing of George Floyd. She asks if this summer ushered in a new era of public history with regard to Native Americans or if moments like this have happened previously. She explores how museums, popular culture, monuments, and other forms of public memorialization and education in the United States have long misrepresented Native American history. To put this into context, she engages the works of Indigenous studies scholars to present a theoretical framework of "narrative erasure," the basis for violent structures of "elimination" that persist in settler colonial societies into the twenty-first century. John considers how Native forms of public memory, commemoration, and activism provide historical counternarratives to the dominant American public history narratives based on American exceptionalism and Indigenous erasure. She contextualizes these efforts in the framework of what Indigenous studies theorist Gerald Vizenour terms "survivance." John makes the case that recent uprisings against Columbus are not new but rather the continuation of a long history of Indigenous people challenging harmful, dominant public narratives. John argues that central to the work of Indigenous resistance is an insistence that settler society must confront the ways in which the violence of colonial history is essentially woven into the nation's past and present.

Karlos K. Hill and Karen Murphy in Chapter 7 discuss what they term creating the conditions for repair with an examination of the representation and memorialization of lynching. They introduce their chapter with a discussion of Claudia Rankine's alteration of the infamous 1930 Marion, Indiana, double lynching photo with the removal of the victims. In doing so, she sought to refocus attention away from those murdered and onto the white spectators. They note that the NAACP, without altering images, recontextualized these photos by focusing the photographic narrative on the violence of the mob. The

Introduction 11

co-authors call for a victim-centered public memory of lynching and racial violence and assert that there has been no justice for Black victims of white lynch mob violence. Hill and Murphy pay close and critical attention to the book and exhibition, *Without Sanctuary: Lynching Photography in America*, addressing the various ways that the exhibit has been displayed. They note that one of the more important impacts of the exhibition was that attention it generated led to the US Senate apology to the victims of lynching in 2005. In early 2022, the Senate finally passed an anti-lynching law, the Emmett Till Anti-Lynching Act. The co-authors discuss at length the efforts of Bryan Stevenson and the Equal Justice Initiative (EJI) in Montgomery, Alabama, to address the place of lynching in America's violent, racist history. EJI's publication of the report, *Lynching in America*, led to their creation of the National Memorial for Peace and Justice.

In Chapter 8, Caleb Gayle poses the question of what is owed in his examination of the issue of reparations. He centers his discussion on the Tulsa, Oklahoma, Race Massacre of 1921 and its aftermath. He draws on a wide variety of sources to explore the current state of memories of racial violence and how those relate to the failure of reparation policies in the United States. Gayle also examines German reparation policies for Holocaust survivors, reparations for Japanese Americans resulting from their imprisonment during World War II, and the attempts by Evanston, Illinois, to implement reparations for Blacks at a local level. Gayle discusses how reparation efforts in his hometown of Tulsa have to date failed to be implemented. What is owed, Gayle asserts, must be answered not only with a specific accounting for damages but also with a reckoning with the impacts of racial violence over centuries. For Gayle, most significantly, his chapter explores the changes in public memory possible only through a thorough and difficult – in terms of feasibility and emotional and psychological strain – reparative reexamination of the history that constructed this current moment.

Lisa Arellano, in Chapter 9, writes about remembering the mass shooting at the Pulse Nightclub in Orlando, Florida, in 2016. The perpetrator terrorized the club patrons for three hours until police shot and killed him. The incident left 50 people dead (49 victims plus the shooter) and another 53 injured. Arellano recounts that almost immediately the onePULSE Foundation was established by the club owner for the purpose of building a memorial to honor the event's victims and survivors, first responders, and the larger community impacted by the event. She discusses how examining the violence is complicated by different points of emphasis, including was this a terrorist act; the club was a focal point of the LGBTQ community; most of the victims were Latinx; and the phenomenon of mass shootings. Arellano identifies the extensive planning efforts for the memorial at the site and the resulting design that was commissioned, which will include the original nightclub building. She relates how the memorial planners seek to embed it within the surrounding area. The onePULSE project is the nationally designated, primary site of Pulse memory work. Arellano argues that it is achieving the nearly impossible task of creating a memorial experience that honors the event. Still, she advises, it

12   *Martin Henry Blatt*

is important for us to continue to pay attention to smaller, even temporary, memory projects.

Part IV focuses on apartheid in South Africa and Palestine/Israel. Apartheid, the Afrikaner word for separateness, was the "term for the legal and political system of racial segregation which whites imposed on blacks in South Africa."[23] Apartheid is defined as a crime against humanity by the United Nations' 1973 International Convention on the Suppression and Punishment of the Crime of Apartheid and by the 2002 Rome Statute of the International Criminal Court. Several human rights organizations have characterized Israeli policies as apartheid in nature. Amnesty International released a detailed report discussing what it terms Israel's decades-old system of apartheid which treats Palestinians as an "inferior non-Jewish racial group." Israel's leading human rights organization, B'Tselem, published a report titled "A Regime of Jewish Supremacy From the Jordan River to the Mediterranean Sea: This is Apartheid." This was followed by Human Rights Watch, which released a report arguing that Israel pursues a policy of ethnic supremacy that favors Israeli Jews over Palestinians in both Israel and the occupied territories.[24] There are several who have termed such critiques as antisemitic, but it is inaccurate to equate hatred of Jews with criticism of racist Israeli policies.[25] Indeed, one could make a plausible, strong argument that an end to the apartheid practices of Israel could be the best way to ensure the long-term security of Israeli Jews. Further, Judaism has never been the equivalent of Zionism. Also, Jews today, wherever they may live, have widely divergent views on Israeli policies.

In Chapter 10, co-authors Leah Nasson, Sihle-isipho Nontshokweni, and Dylan Wray address police brutality during the apartheid regime in South Africa and the echoes of police violence subsequent to the fall of apartheid. They then examine how police violence has been remembered and how their victims have been memorialized. Their chapter is a cautionary tale that even with the fall of the brutal apartheid regime, South Africans must contend with repressive measures and strive for continuing vigilance in the struggle for memory. They detail the brutality inflicted on freedom fighters against apartheid in the John Vorster Square police station and efforts at remembrance and commemoration. The station was renamed Johannesburg Central Police Station but the only physical marker to the dark apartheid history there is a memorial sculpture, a large imposing rock, which, with its plaque missing, does not serve to differentiate the building from others. The co-authors provide the history of the Marikana Massacre of 2013 when many striking miners were murdered and discuss efforts to commemorate the memory of the miners versus official actions to suppress the truth. They conclude with the powerful series of paintings depicting the nobility and strength of the striking miners by the notable South African artist Zakes Mda. By focusing on both apartheid and post-apartheid police violence and efforts to call out the police violence and to commemorate their victims, they provide us with important case studies of how dominant power shapes the memorialization of traumatic events.

In Chapter 11, Eitan Bronstein Aparicio and Eleonore Merza Bronstein facetiously title their chapter – the land of milk and honey, a popular name for

Israel calling forth visions of Israelis making the desert bloom and then add in parentheses – (and Palestinians). The focus of their chapter is their map, "Colonialism in Destru(A)ction," an attempt to expose the actual dimensions of the Israeli settler colonial enterprise. The map displays all the localities that they have been able to identify which were destroyed during Israeli colonial history from the first Zionist migration to Palestine to the present and they even attempt to project destructions into the future. The principal color of the map is red which indicates for the most part more than 600 Palestinian localities destroyed during the Nakba (Arabic for catastrophe) when 750,000 Palestinians were expelled in 1948. The color-coded map can be accessed on their website and in the ebook version of this book. The co-authors describe a map which is complex, thorough, and revelatory. They introduce us to the organization Zochrot, established in 2001 by Aparicio, which works to educate Israelis about the Nakba. The co-authors view the map as a tool for those who embrace the goal of bringing an end to the oppressive Zionist political regime. They hope that the map will serve as a means to help promote social justice in Palestine/Israel.

The focus of Part V is fascism and war. In Chapter 12, Marisa Lerer addresses public commemorations of Argentina's histories of violence. She explores the legacy of state-sponsored violence focusing on Argentina's 1976–1983 military dictatorship and the memorials dedicated to the estimated 30,000 victims of the dictatorship, often referred to as "the disappeared." These memorials encompass a wide range of physical forms – former clandestine centers for detention, murder, and extermination; cultural centers; monuments; public sculptures; and sidewalk tiles. Lerer demonstrates that the emergence of memorials to the victims of state-sponsored terrorism grew out of the grassroots organizing of human rights and neighborhood organizations. These memorials function both as public commemorative spaces and as places where families can mourn "the disappeared," as often they do not have the bodies of their loved ones. Lerer maintains that the development of commemorative spaces is part of a territorial struggle by human rights organizations to insert the history of the dictatorship into the fabric of the urban landscape.

In Chapter 13, Elise Lemire relates the central role that the organization Vietnam Veterans Against the War (VVAW) played in attempting to get the American public to acknowledge that the Vietnam War was an American crime against both the American citizenry and the people of Southeast Asia. She does so by presenting a close examination of the 1971 VVAW protest in Massachusetts which reversed the ride of Paul Revere made famous by Henry Wadsworth Longfellow's mythic poem. She examines how their actions exposed multiple myths about war promulgated at the memorialized Revolutionary War Massachusetts sites in Concord and Lexington. Lemire laments that the success of VVAW was relatively short lived. The federal government successfully countered the VVAW narrative, first with the Prisoners of War/Missing in Action (POW/MIA) campaign, and later with a return to traditional war memorialization practices. She critiques the addition of a militaristic memorial to three infantrymen soon after the dedication of the Vietnam Veterans

14 *Martin Henry Blatt*

Memorial in Washington, DC, which itself did not celebrate war. Lemire concludes by criticizing the triumphalist World War II memorial, also located in Washington, DC.

Notes

1 For descriptions of my two visits, see Martin Henry Blatt, "Holocaust Remembrance and Heidelberg," *The Public Historian*, Vol. 24, No. 4 (Fall 2002), pp. 81–96, and Martin Henry Blatt, "Holocaust Memory and Germany," *The Public Historian*, Vol. 34, No. 4 (2012), pp. 53–66.

2 See David Roediger and Martin Henry Blatt, eds., *The Meaning of Slavery in the North* (New York: Garland Publishing, 1998). I describe some of my efforts in the preface to the book.

3 See Martin Henry Blatt, Thomas Brown, and Donald Yacovone, eds., *Hope & Glory – Essays on the Legacy of the 54th Massachusetts Regiment* (Amherst, MA: University of Massachusetts Press, 2001); Martin Henry Blatt, "Hope and Glory: Shaw/54th Monument Centennial," *The Broadside – Boston National Historical Park*, No. 3 (1997), pp. 1, 5–7; Martin Henry Blatt, "Hope and Glory: The Centennial Celebration of the Monument to Robert Gould Shaw and the 54th Massachusetts Regiment," *CRM – Cultural Resource Management*, Vol. 21, No. 11 (1998), pp. 25–27.

4 See Louis Hutchins and Gay Vietzke, "Dialogue Between Continents: Civic Engagement and the Gulag Museum at Perm-36," *George Wright Forum*, Vol. 19, No. 4 (2002), pp. 65–74; Louis Hutchins, "What Does the Soviet Gulag Have to Do With the National Park Service?," in David Harmon, ed., *People, Places, and Parks: Proceedings of the 2005 George Wright Society Conference on Parks, Protected Areas, and Cultural Sites* (Hancock, MI: The George Wright Society, 2006), pp. 119–122. http://www.georgewright.org/0519hutchins.pdf; Martin Henry Blatt, "Remembering Repression: The Gulag as a National Park Service Exhibit," *Perspectives on History*, November 1, 2008, https://www.historians.org/research-and-publications/perspectives-on-history/november-2008/remembering-repression-the-gulag-as-an-nps-exhibit; For an online version of the traveling exhibit, see https://gulaghistory.org. For details on the International Historic Site Museums of Conscience and the Humanities Action Lab referenced two paragraphs later, see Liz Sevcenko, *Public History for a Post-Truth Era: Fighting Denial Through Memory Movements* (London: Routledge, 2022).

5 Martin Henry Blatt, "Reflections on Roots of Liberty: The Haitian Revolution and the American Civil War," *History@Work, the National Council on Public History blog*, August 29, 2013, https://ncph.org/history-at-work/reflections-on-roots-of-liberty/

6 Kenneth E. Foote, *Shadowed Ground – America's Landscapes of Violence and Tragedy*, revised and updated (Austin, TX: University of Texas Press, 2003), p. 7.

7 See Bryan Stevenson, *Just Mercy: A Story of Justice and Redemption* (New York: Spiegel & Grau, 2014).

8 See Roxanne Dunbar-Ortiz and Dina Gilio-Whitaker, *"All the Real Indians Died Off" and 20 Other Myths About Native Americans* (Boston, MA: Beacon Press, 2016).

9 David Blight, " 'For Something Beyond the Battlefield': Frederick Douglass and the Struggle for the Memory of the Civil War," in David Blight, ed., *Beyond the Battlefield: Race, Memory, and the American Civil War* (Amherst, MA: University of Massachusetts Press, 2002), pp. 103–104.

10 Erika Doss, *Memorial Mania – Public Feeling in America* (Chicago, IL: University of Chicago Press, 2010), pp. 9–10.

11 www.bbc.com/news/uk-england-bristol-59892211. For details on Olusoga, see Desiree Ibekwe, "Wanting Britain to Face Its Past. All of It," *New York Times*, February

Introduction 15

8, 2022, https://www.nytimes.com/2022/02/07/arts/television/david-olusoga-black-history.html

12 Edward Linenthal, "Anatomy of a Controversy," in Edward Linenthal and Tom Engelhardt, eds., *History Wars – The Enola Gay and Other Battles for the American Past* (New York: Metropolitan Books, 1995), pp. 9 and 26. Linenthal has written several outstanding contributions to the consideration of violence and public memory, including *Sacred Ground – Americans and Their Battlefields* (Chicago, IL: University of Illinois Press, 1993); *Preserving Memory – The Struggle to Create America's Holocaust Museum* (New York: Penguin, 1995); *The Unfinished Bombing – Oklahoma City in American Memory* (New York: Oxford University Press, 2001).

13 Sven Lundqvist, *"Exterminate All the Brutes": One Man's Odyssey Into the Heart of Darkness and the Origins of European Genocide* (New York: The New Press, 2007), first published in English, 1992.

14 Roxanne Dunbar-Ortiz, *An Indigenous People's History of the United States* (Boston, MA: Beacon Press, 2014); Michel-Rolph Trouillot, *Silencing the Past: Power and the Production of History* (Boston, MA: Beacon Press, 1995).

15 For example, "Universities Studying Slavery Roundtable," *The Public Historian*, Vol. 42, No. 4 (2020), with foreword by Tiya Miles and essays by Chana Kai Lee, Hilary Green, Rhondda Robinson Thomas, and Leslie M. Harris, pp. 9–62; Heather Goodall, Judith Keene, and Peter Read, guest editors, "Where Are the Bodies? A Transnational Examination of State Violence and Its Consequences," *The Public Historian*, Vol. 32, No. 1 (2010), with introduction by Judith Keene and essays by Beth Gibbings, Marivic Wyndham and Peter Read, Adrian Vickers, Judith Keene, Michael Pickering, and Richard Wright, pp. 7–107; "Sites of Conscience: Opening Historic Sites for Civic Dialogue," *The Public Historian*, Vol. 30, No. 1 (2008) with foreword by Liz Sevcenko and Maggie Russell-Ciardi and essays by (Madikida, Segal, and van den Berg co authored one essay. Baiesi, Gigli, Monicelli, and Perllizzoli co authored one essay) Churchill Madikida, Lauren Segal, Clive Van den Berg, Nadia Baiesi, Marzia Gigli, Elena Monicelli, Roberta Pellizzoli, Maggie Russell-Ciardi, Valmont Layne, Maria Laura Guembe, and Jan Munk, pp. 9–79; Greg Grandin and Thomas Miller Klubock, eds., "Truth Commissions: State Terror, History, and Memory," *Radical History Review*, Vol. 7, No. 97 (2007), with essays by (Loveman and Lira co authored one essay Grandin and Klubock co authored one essay) Alejandro Castillejo-Cuellar, Brian Loveman, Elizabeth Lira, Elizabeth Oglesby, Greg Grandin, Thomas Miller Klubock, Sally Avery Bermanzohn, Paul Ortiz, John J. Fitzgerald, Felipe Aguero, and Charles F. Walker, pp. 1–142.

16 Clint Smith, *How the Word Is Passed – A Reckoning With the History of Slavery Across America* (New York: Little, Brown and Company, 2021), p. 289.

17 Susan Neiman, *Learning From the Germans – Race and the Memory of Evil* (New York: Farrar, Straus, and Giroux, 2019), pp. 7–8 and 374.

18 Ajlina Karamehic-Muratovic and Laura Kromjak, eds., "Introduction," in *Remembrance and Forgiveness – Global and Interdisciplinary Perspectives on Genocide and Mass Violence* (London: Routledge, 2021).

19 Amy Hubbell, Natsuko Akagawa, Sol Rojas-Lizana, and Annie Pohlman, eds., *Places of Traumatic Memory – A Global Context* (London: Palgrave Macmillan, 2020), pp. 1–11.

20 Eve Monique Zucker and David Simon, eds., *Mass Violence and Memory in the Digital Age – Memorialization Unmoored* (London: Palgrave Macmillan, 2020), pp. 1–12.

21 Melissa Bender and Klara Stephanie Szlezak, eds., *Contested Commemoration in U.S. History – Diverging Public Interpretations* (London: Routledge, 2020), p. 8.

22 Benjamin Madley, *An American Genocide – The United States and the California Indian Catastrophe, 1846–1873* (New Haven, CT: Yale University Press, 2016), p. 4. See also, Philippe Sands, *East West Street – On the Origins of "Genocide" and "Crimes against Humanity"* (New York: Knopf, 2016).

16   *Martin Henry Blatt*

23 Phillip Wilkin, "Apartheid," in Peter Stearns, ed., *Encyclopedia of Social History* (New York: Garland Publishing, 1994), p. 44.
24 Omar Barghouti and Stefanie Fox, "Amnesty's Echo – Amnesty International's Report Confirming Israel as an Apartheid State Could Be a Turning Point – But It's Up to Us," *The Nation*, March 7–14, 2002, p. 6; Patrick Kingsley, "Rights Group Accuses Israel of Conducting Apartheid State," *New York Times*, April 28, 2021, p. A12.
25 See Peter Beinart, "Has the Fight Against Antisemitism Lost Its Way?," *New York Times*, Sunday Opinion, August 28, 2022, https://www.nytimes.com/2022/08/26/opinion/antisemitism-israel-uae-saudi.html

Part I

Genocide

1 A Model Way of Coming to Terms With the Past?

On the Relevance and Future Tasks of Historical–Political Education in (German) Memorial Sites

Elke Gryglewski and Katrin Unger

An attempt to examine and evaluate how Germany dealt with the country's past after 1945 can take place from two possible perspectives. First, there is an external perspective, based on one's own or others' experience of violent, post-dictatorial pasts. For obvious reasons, this approach will tend to draw a positive conclusion. For example, colleagues from South America, where places of remembrance and support for remembrance work on the military dictatorships of the 1970s still depend heavily on the respective governments, view the German culture of remembrance as exemplary. The same applies to representatives of civil society in Spain who remain committed to addressing the impact of Spanish fascism.

The fact that memorial work in Germany – for the time being and at least at the large, internationally known historical sites – is institutionally funded, that small memorial sites and memorial initiatives receive financial support through project funding and, with the exception of the right-wing AfD party, there is a general political commitment to remembrance policy are, from their point of view, evidence of this function as a role model.

It is this comparative perspective that leads Susan Neiman to the conclusion that one can "learn from the Germans." In her 2020 publication, the scholar compares how the Germans confronted Nazism with how Americans deal with their violent past of slavery and racist treatment of the Black population.[1] Neiman analyzes the development from the period immediately after the war to the present – prior to the COVID-19 pandemic; she looks at how the past was handled in West and East Germany and pinpoints deficits and lines of continuity. Her overall conclusion is positive: in short, she states that the Germans achieved a "transformation of their self-image from heroes to victims to perpetrators" and were thus "historically unique."[2]

Perspectives like Susan Neiman's are important; they are valid and serve as a corrective to overly negative or critical assessments of the culture of remembrance in Germany, because in terms of the arguments mentioned earlier, a lot has been achieved. However, it is important to remember that this viewpoint is based on the current status. The present reality is one with many working memorial sites, documentation centers, remembrance initiatives, and forms of

DOI: 10.4324/9781003217848-3

20   *Elke Gryglewski and Katrin Unger*

memorials, especially in Berlin. Against the backdrop of this wide range of activities, it seems difficult to imagine that things were once different.

There is, however, a second perspective. This one is grounded in the belief that the task of confronting the past has not been completed but is an ongoing process. This process requires Germany's – very diverse – society to evolve constantly and repeatedly prove that it is seriously and sustainably committed to confronting the consequences of systematic and industrialized mass murder and has not lapsed into superficial, ritualized gestures of remembrance.

To develop and continue learning, it is important to take a deeper look at the deficits in particular in order to avoid repeating specific mistakes that were made in the early phases after the war or reproducing their consequences. In other words, the focus here is on the perspective that views the period after Nazism as a part of the overall history we need to confront and understand, as this gives us the tools to learn from the past and orientation to the present.

As staff members of a Nazi memorial site, this perspective is important to us, as it can help to provide answers to issues that affect society today, for instance, why phenomena and attitudes that underpin the hatred of certain groups and the relativization and falsification of history have re-emerged on such a massive scale in German society in recent years.

In the following, our aim is to take selected aspects to illustrate our critical and reflective stance, as a comprehensive description would go well beyond the scope of this article. In doing so, we will be comparing the history of memorials in Germany to general social discourse and the treatment of the perpetrators – three aspects that are intertwined and very much mutually dependent. To illuminate these aspects, we will also be touching very briefly on other thematic issues, such as criminal prosecution or the role of the Allies in the early post-war years. In many cases, though, we will limit ourselves to proposing further reading for those interested in delving deeper.

Today's culture of remembrance is strongly dominated by the West German approach; however, it is often said that the German Democratic Republic's approach was more productive or better, and so in the historical analysis up to 1989 we will also be looking at how the GDR dealt with the country's past.

Whose Achievement Are the Places of Remembrance?

We should start by remembering that our present memorials were the result of many years of hard work and that the path there was strewn with obstacles until they became the places they are now.

As in Bergen-Belsen, in many places it was the survivors, organized individually or in associations, who set up the first small memorial signs and collective memorials shortly after liberation. Their motivation was the urge to remember relatives, friends, and camp inmates who were murdered or who died as a result of the appalling conditions.[3] In Bergen-Belsen, the existence on site of the camp for displaced persons until 1950 allowed the survivors' associations to exert pressure on the British and German authorities. As a result, an official memorial was erected in 1952 in a ceremony attended by the first federal president, Theodor Heuss. Elsewhere, however, the early signs of remembrance were soon forgotten. In Dachau, for example, the remaining prisoner barracks were used to house displaced persons from the former eastern territories of the German Reich. Survivors who visited the place where they had experienced such great suffering some ten years later were shocked to discover that the concentration camp history was in danger of being forgotten and overshadowed by its subsequent use, which even included a brothel in one of the barracks. They founded the Comité International de Dachau, raised their voices, and fought for the preservation and dignified treatment of the historical site. This took ten years to achieve[4] and in 1965, the Dachau Memorial was finally opened.

Figure 1.1 The first monuments in Bergen-Belsen were initiated and inaugurated by survivors – years before official commemoration signs were established by German authorities. On the first anniversary of the liberation, April 15, 1946, the first stone monument commemorating the Jewish victims was inaugurated by survivors living in the Displaced Persons camp nearby.

Source: Credit – Imperial War Museums

22   *Elke Gryglewski and Katrin Unger*

However, the establishment of memorial sites did not mean that a deep and lasting debate about the history of these historical places actually took place. Apart from the grounds and the design of the historical exhibitions, the sites were largely left to themselves, dependent on publicly funded landscape maintenance and spontaneous civil society initiatives. This observation can be documented by the organizational affiliation of the sites and the staff hired for the memorials. The Dachau memorial, for example, belonged to the Bayerische Verwaltung der staatlichen Schlösser, Gärten und Seen (Bavarian Administration of State-Owned Palaces, Gardens, and Lakes), which until well into the 1990s largely worked to keep the exterior of the site in an immaculate condition, and for decades had to get by with a staff of one director plus secretary, one archive employee and security personnel for the exhibition. The situation was similar in Bergen-Belsen: until the 1980s, there was only one caretaker who was responsible for opening and locking up the exhibition room and making sure that there were no disturbances.

As a result of the generational change in the Federal Republic and the willingness of the so-called 1968 generation to confront Nazism, largely driven by public prosecutor Fritz Bauer and his determination to hold the Auschwitz trial, as well as the many "grassroots initiatives" set up to research local and regional historical traces, in the 1970s and even more so in the 1980s, civic initiatives started focusing on the historical sites. Often this took place in the face of opposition from most of the regional population. In many cases, though, these activities were supported by regional political committees and their scope and the resources that were provided to examine the history in more detail or to offer guided tours for visitors grew steadily. It was not until the fall of the Wall in 1989 and the question of how to deal with memorials that had a dual past (their use as special camps by the Soviet military administration and the human rights violations committed in this period were never addressed in the GDR's memorial narrative) that the federal government set up an Enquete Commission. Ultimately, this commission presented a memorial concept that defined precise criteria required for memorials to receive institutional funding[5] and looked at how project-specific funding could be provided.

With minor variations, this development applies to most historical sites where Nazi crimes were carried out – sites that are also cemeteries and are referred to as victims' sites. For so-called perpetrator sites, that is, historical sites where the perspective of the perpetrators dominated, a far more complex story applies. This can be summed up with the example of the House of the Wannsee Conference memorial and educational site. In this villa, on January 20, 1942, 15 high-ranking representatives of the SS and the ministerial bureaucracy discussed the systematic murder of 11 million Jews in Europe. The building, which symbolizes the involvement of the state administration in the crimes, was used for decades as a school camp for a district in West Berlin. As early as the 1960s, survivor and scholar Joseph Wulf called for a "Documentation Centre for the Study of National Socialism and its Aftermath" to be opened in the historic building – a proposal that was rejected by all political parties in the

A Model Way of Coming to Terms With the Past?   23

city in view of the then still far-reaching personnel overlaps with Nazi society. After the final failure of his initiative, Joseph Wulf committed suicide.[6] The Memorial and Educational Site House of the Wannsee Conference opened its doors to the public only in 1992.

It took just as long before memorials and documentation centers such as the Topography of Terror Foundation, founded in 1992 on the grounds of the former office of the Geheime Staatspolizei (Secret State Police), the Reichsführung SS (Reich Leadership SS), and the Reichssicherheitshauptamt (Reich Security Main Office) on Prinz-Albrecht-Strasse in Berlin, or the Villa ten Hompel History Site, at the headquarters of the Münster Ordnungspolizei (Order Police), could be established as memorials to the victims of the crimes of the police and administration.

It is clear that society as a whole and policymakers found it much more difficult to set up memorials in places where the issue of culpability and involvement in the crimes inevitably arose.

The present German memorial landscape includes institutions that were not founded in historical sites, but which enjoyed strong political support. These sites are intended as manifestations of the political commitment to the culture of remembrance. One of these is the Memorial to the Murdered Jews of Europe, commonly known as the Holocaust Memorial, which was inaugurated in 2005 and which is often seen as one of the indicators of the overall success of the critical review of the past. As with all memorials, the initial impetus came from civic society. However, the decision of Helmut Kohl's government to erect a central memorial in the heart of Berlin was driven by a twofold motivation. After the Neue Wache[7] had been redesigned as the National Memorial to the Victims of War and Tyranny and was regularly visited by state guests, there was justified criticism that the inscription inappropriately equated perpetrators and victims. The timing of the political decision to build the memorial is also relevant. It was made shortly after the so-called Wende, when the Wall fell, at a time when several neighboring European countries were looking at the prospect of a reunified Germany with considerable concern. In 1966, the publicist Francois Mauriac said, "I love Germany so much that I am glad there are two of them," a sentiment that was frequently quoted at the time.[8]

The installation of a gigantic concrete memorial in the center of the capital, and the unequivocal statement it made that history should never be forgotten, could be seen as a ticket for admission as an equal partner to the European community. Memorial staff from all memorials which until then always had been established as authentic places were critical of the decision because they believed that in Germany – the country where these crimes were committed – remembrance work should take place more meaningfully at the actual historical sites, where the range and the scope of the crimes committed could be clearly illustrated. This approach was rejected by wide parts of society, and the memorial is now an important part of the remembrance landscape. Nevertheless, there remains a dilemma concerning policymakers' decisions to choose to build large, highly symbolic, new places of remembrance that consume considerable

24   *Elke Gryglewski and Katrin Unger*

investment funds, as these pose a threat to the already precarious financial situation of the country's remembrance landscape, especially for medium-sized and small memorials/historic sites.[9]

The GDR set up memorials very early on, which is not surprising given the government's self-image as the direct continuation of anti-fascist resistance. In the East, the process differed significantly from the development in the West: from the beginning it was the state leadership of the GDR who decided which content was to be presented and the order in which historical sites were to be established as national memorials. It can be argued that the Sachsenhausen concentration camp, for example, was far more important than Buchenwald concentration camp.[10] However, because the political leader Ernst Thälmann, who played a pivotal role in the government's self-concept, had been murdered in Buchenwald, the site was stylized as the place of ultimate anti-fascist resistance, and an imposing memorial was erected there as early as the 1950s. The design of the memorial resembled a sacred path along which visitors walked from the "darkness of history to the creation of the anti-fascist state" to arrive at the memorial for the fighters.[11] In the layout of the historical site itself, emphasis was placed on the aspects that corresponded to the political narrative, while other historical facts were ignored or omitted. The fact that the Communist prisoners overpowered the remaining SS guards with concealed weapons when they realized that the US army was approaching was transformed into a narrative of self-liberation. The story of the Jewish prisoners in the so-called Small Camp was ignored and featured neither in the displays nor in the archaeology of the site.[12] Above all, however, the history of Soviet Special Camp No. 2 was completely neglected. The design of other national memorials and memorial sites in the former concentration camps such as Sachsenhausen or Ravensbrück, which were set up later, also corresponded to the state's chosen narrative of remembrance. The exhibitions barely dealt with the specific history of each place but followed the script of delivering an overview of Nazi crimes, focusing on the victim groups of German Communists and Soviet prisoners. Every year, thousands of young people and adults, for example, members of the National People's Army, were brought to these places to take an oath of allegiance to the state.

Discourses of Remembrance in the West, the East and the Federal Republic, and How the Issue of the Perpetrators Was Addressed

The development of the memorial landscape reflects society's discourse about the past, especially in the Federal Republic. After the war, only a small minority were prepared to focus their thoughts and actions on the crimes which their own society had committed and for which it was jointly responsible. Far more prominent was the narrative of German suffering: the nights of bombing and the famine during the war, flight, and expulsion from their original homelands, including Silesia, Pomerania, Transylvania, and East Prussia. There was no de facto understanding of cause and effect, and since the perspectives of perpetrators, "fellow travelers" (*Mitläufer*) and predominantly silent bystanders were represented in society, while the survivors of German persecution and murderous programs made up an infinitesimally small minority, mostly spread throughout Europe and the world, defensive mechanisms and denial swiftly took hold. The population was also preoccupied with the very practical issues of returning to a "normal" life, such as finding housing or work, which was an understandable justification for avoiding having to deal with the past.

Although the Allies wanted to promote a new attitude in society and used various measures and educational programs[13] to achieve this, the majority adhered to the self-image of Germans as the victims and presented this with considerable assertiveness. There is no one single cause for this behavior, but one aspect seems particularly significant. The awareness of culpability and the grave nature of the crimes committed are always associated with the prosecution of crimes, and so the prosecution of Nazi perpetrators played an important role here. The Nuremberg Trials and the 12 subsequent tribunals up to 1949 were essentially directed against high war criminals or high-profile representatives of the Nazi regime. These trials laid important foundations for criminal prosecution,[14] but at the same time, through the group of defendants, they also gave the population as a whole, which had actively participated or at best silently looked the other way, the opportunity to distance itself from "those up there" as visible perpetrators who could also be held responsible for its own suffering.

This very swift assignment of blame and responsibility to the top of the regime paired with a defensive attitude could also be observed in another context.

Immediately after liberation, there were waves of arrests in all occupation zones, sending many members of the National Socialist German Workers' Party (NSDAP) or, in short, Nazi Party, and other Nazi organizations to internment camps. In 1946, the so-called denazification began in all occupation zones as an element of the planned cleansing and democratization of post-war Germany. This process and its implementation differed greatly from one occupying power to the next, despite commonly agreed categories for determining involvement in crimes.[15] In general, in the Western zones, there was a high level of public approval as long as it was a matter of punishing "those up there." In 1947, first the United States and then the other occupation zones introduced a questionnaire in which all adults had to give information about which organizations they had been active during the Nazi regime and in what capacity. Very quickly, the approval rate for denazification dropped to just under 18%.[16] And so it is not surprising that in the Western occupation zones – even if denazification differed in the details of implementation, for example, the Americans passed stricter judgment than the British – the overall result tended to exculpation. Those whose pasts were being examined could produce a range of exonerating references, so-called *Persilscheine*, aimed at proving that they had always been against the regime and, wherever possible, had treated those who were persecuted with kindness, if not even actively supported them.

26 *Elke Gryglewski and Katrin Unger*

Unaware of the social structures in Germany, the Allies for their part were often overwhelmed with the proceedings and soon staffed the commissions and trial chambers with Germans, who often classified their own compatriots as unencumbered and acquitted them. With the rapid emergence of the Cold War and the realization that a strong West Germany was needed at the heart of Europe to counter the Communists, the Western occupying powers faced new challenges and as a result accepted the increasing integration of even high-ranking former Nazis. Also missing at this early stage were important insights into the structure of the Nazi regime and its crime complexes, as well as an understanding of "complicity" in crimes, so that perpetrators who would have been brought to justice today, or still are being prosecuted, were at the time able to return to their everyday lives without sanctions. Wilhelm Stuckart, who had participated in the Wannsee Conference as a representative of the Reich Ministry of the Interior and had been involved in drafting the Nuremberg Race Laws as early as 1935, was classified as a "fellow traveler" in denazification proceedings in 1950 and was fined 500 deutsche mark (DM). One could, however, say that fate ruled otherwise, as he died in a car accident in 1953. His story illustrates the extent to which those highly involved in Nazi crimes could be integrated into post-war society with virtual impunity.

Personnel continuity was particularly high in the civil service, the police, and the judiciary.

In the first two decades, important trials against different groups of perpetrators, conducted by the occupying powers and, from 1950 onward, also by the Federal Public Prosecutor's Offices, took place, which we lack the space to discuss in detail here. In view of the process described earlier, the social and legal self-image of innocence and non-responsibility had become so embedded in society that agreements regarding convicted individuals, supposedly based on academic exculpatory expert opinions, resulted in acquittals, or suspended sentences as part of the daily routine. Most people were convinced that it was wrong to look back at the past, and that one should look forward to the future only. While people learned to avoid talking about the Nazi past in the public sphere, these conversations shifted to the regulars' tables at the pubs, where the good old days were blatantly celebrated.[17]

The fact that the few survivors – and there were some in Germany – were not only denied space but also denied the right to express their own needs can be seen in various examples not only from the immediate post-war years but also from later decades.

On January 7, 1951, thousands of residents of Landsberg demonstrated for the release of high-ranking Nazi war criminals convicted in the Nuremberg trials. They demanded that the Allies suspend the death sentences of 28 convicts, including Otto Ohlendorf, former commander of one of the Einsatzgruppen who had systematically shot and killed massive numbers of Jews in the Soviet Union during the war. The demonstrators appealed to Christian charity but chased away a small group of surviving displaced persons who were housed in camps not far from Landsberg and were protesting the calls for amnesty. The

A Model Way of Coming to Terms With the Past?   27

demonstrators were violent, and there were shouts of "Jews out" and "Why don't you go to Palestine?"[18]

Marianne Stern, née Winter, who was the only member of her family to survive deportation to the Riga ghetto and the shooting in the Rumbula forest, returned to her hometown of Hemmerden after the war. She campaigned for the restitution of the possessions stolen from her family, and as a consequence until well into the 1950s, her family — and especially her son at school — was ostracized, subjected to antisemitic insults, and physically attacked.[19]

Even in the 1980s, by which time a far-reaching change in the culture of remembrance had taken place in the Federal Republic and thousands of commemorative events were held to mark the 40th anniversary of the November pogrom often referred to as Kristallnacht, a lack of empathy toward relatives of those murdered is documented. For example, Hans Rosenthal, host of a popular entertainment show on public television, whose brother had been killed in the Holocaust, asked to postpone the broadcast of the program scheduled on November 9, 1978. His request was refused and so he hosted the show wearing a somber black suit. He explicitly pointed out at the end, deviating from the usual procedure, that this had been the program "Dalli Dalli on the 9th of November 1978," without commenting on the historical reference in any detail (Dalli Dalli was the name of Rosenthal's television program and November 9, 1938, marked the start of Kristallnacht).[20]

At the same time — and this is the remarkable thing — the discourse of remembrance with all its elements (exhibitions, commemorations, speeches, etc.) focused mainly on the victims and often particularly on the Jewish victims. Speaking about the victims and their suffering did not compel anyone to deal with the question of culpability. Critics speak of a "victim-centred culture of remembrance," the over-identification with the persecuted, which stands in the way of a lasting reflection and engagement with the issue.[21] This phenomenon can be observed repeatedly among visitors to memorial sites: there is great empathy and openness as long as the debate is about the victims, but any discussion of culpability and responsibility is resoundingly rejected.

The issue of culpability and the associated discourse of remembrance in the GDR is also very complex. The process of transformation in the Soviet occupation zone was in many respects fundamentally different from that in the Western zones; this is because of the different political systems of the occupying powers and the dominant political self-image of the later GDR as an "anti-fascist state."[22] Rooted in this self-image, the denazification panels were initially more rigorous and consistent; the committees were often staffed with people who had been persecuted, including social democrats and Communists who had returned from exile. Here too, however, pragmatic decisions increasingly played a role as a reaction to the intensifying Cold War and to consolidate the country's own image.

In the GDR, attempts were made to avoid employing former members of the NSDAP, especially in professions that could exert ideological influence, such as education, to the point that the state hired teachers who had not yet

28 *Elke Gryglewski and Katrin Unger*

completed their training. Decisions like these and the projected image as an anti-fascist state, which were emphasized with grand public gestures, like the erection of the large memorial next to the former Buchenwald concentration camp, encouraged emigrants, such as the writer Anna Seghers, to consciously choose to live in the GDR rather than the Federal Republic.

At the same time, denazification in the Soviet zone also served as an excuse and a weapon to purge political rivals and individuals with other political beliefs, so that even innocent people such as social democrats who had been deported to concentration camps during Nazism were now imprisoned in Soviet special camps.

During numerous trials,[23] not all of which were conducted according to the principles of the rule of law, alleged and actually incriminated Nazi perpetrators were sentenced, and denazification was declared officially completed earlier in the East than in the West. Even though there were far fewer high-ranking representatives of the Nazi regime living in the territory of the later GDR, they inevitably existed. However, in order to signal the greatest possible approval of the state and the party and uphold the idea that the East was far superior to the West when it came to dealing with the crimes of the past, "former and ordinary members of the Hitler Party were given the opportunity to cooperate and start a new life" and perpetrators of higher ranks were also integrated into society by performing various "atonement services."[24] The Staatssicherheit (State Security), the secret service of the GDR, in many cases leveraged the incriminated past of Nazi perpetrators by using it to exert pressure on the perpetrators themselves and against the Federal Republic: they were given the choice of working as informal collaborators or having their function under the Nazis revealed and being punished. The wealth of evidence collected during meticulous research was also used in a campaign against the Federal Republic, which the GDR sought to portray as a state that did not hold its Nazi functionaries accountable.[25]

Regardless of the fact that there were prosecution offices in both German states that initiated trials against Nazi perpetrators out of a deep conviction and carried them out with dedication, the system's deficits can be illustrated succinctly using the example of the criminal prosecution of two members of the Wehrmacht (the German army) who were involved in the gas van murders during the so-called partisan warfare in the Soviet Union.[26] Heinz Riedel (born in 1914) lived in the Federal Republic and was brought to trial in 1974.[27] He claimed that gassing was "a more humane way of killing" than shooting and had the defense submit a corresponding expert opinion[28] in order to plead manslaughter rather than murder.[29] Riedel was successful with this reasoning and was acquitted by the court.[30] In the opinion of the Kiel Regional Court, the gassing of people by engine exhaust fumes did not fulfill the definition of murder as the crime allegedly lacked cruelty.[31] The court received numerous letters of approval from the public, while the press reacted with indifference, incomprehension, or outrage.[32]

Hugo Paland (born in 1915) lived in the GDR. As early as the 1950s, the state security received a tip that he had been involved in Nazi crimes in the context of so-called partisan warfare.[33] Instead of investigating further to punish the crimes, they used the tips to put pressure on Paland and enlist him as an informal collaborator (IM).[34] For more than two decades, Paland worked for the state security and, in a cynical twist,[35] was given the code name I.M. Gas due to his job in gas cleaning in a chemical combine. It was only through a request for legal assistance from the Federal Republic to the USSR that his name resurfaced in further investigations. When the last statute of limitations debate on murder as a criminal offence took place in the Federal Republic at the end of the 1970s, the State Security decided, at the suggestion of the General Prosecutor's Office of the GDR, to stage a trial for publicity as proof that it had prosecuted Nazi crimes more consistently than the Federal Republic.[36] Paland was sentenced to life imprisonment in 1978 and died in prison.[37]

With its state doctrine and policy of being the successors of the anti-fascist resistance fighters, the GDR gave its citizens, in a different way than in the Federal Republic, the ideological basis on which to avoid having to confront their own guilt, and responsibility during the Nazi era. They belonged per se to the "good guys" who had nothing to do with the crimes committed in the past. Two examples show that a comparable narrative could emerge alongside or under the state narrative.

For example, the academic Lutz Niethammer conducted a series of important oral history projects in the Federal Republic of Germany from 1980 onward in order to gauge attitudes to Nazism among the general population.[38] After the fall of the Wall, he devoted himself to comparable questions in the field and in the context of the former GDR, and found very similar strategies of denial and defense.[39]

The second example is an individual one. Shortly after the fall of Communism, there was a political scandal in the Brandenburg state parliament when it became known that Gustav Just of the Social Democratic Party (SPD), president of the Landtag for many years and himself imprisoned in Bautzen prison in the GDR, had been involved in the shooting of Jews in Ukraine during the World War II, just resigned from office but spoke at length about the facts of the case, arguing that he had been treated unjustly and pleaded superior orders.[40]

Individuals living in the GDR who had been persecuted under the Nazis were not necessarily marginalized in the same way as in the Federal Republic, provided they belonged to the *right group* of victims who conformed to the narrative or defined themselves primarily by their political stance and not by their religion.[41] Although there were initially good relations between the SED (the ruling party of East Germany until 1989) and the representatives of Jewish communities in the GDR, the ideology of the anti-imperialist, and later also anti-Zionist state had an increasing influence on the treatment of Jewish survivors.

Despite this description, which admittedly focuses on the deficits, there was of course also a generational change in the GDR and among the descendants of the perpetrators there were many who not only internalized the discourse around "anti-fascism" but took it very seriously.[42]

30 *Elke Gryglewski and Katrin Unger*

This very condensed description perhaps illustrates the complexity of confronting the past in Germany. There are plenty of gray areas; there are not only successful approaches but also many things that have been implemented badly or only partly and fail to achieve a balanced, sustainable confrontation, or where the crimes committed and the underlying responsibility for these are not even remotely taken into account.

The consequences of this inadequate confrontation, the lack of criminal prosecution, and the resulting narrative remain visible to this day. As this has an impact on the work of the Nazi memorial sites, for example, through the visitors' own mental images and attempts to understand what happened – which visitors invariably have when they visit a site – it is essential that we, as the staff of the memorial site of a former prisoner of war and concentration camp, engage with them.

Legends, Narratives of Exoneration, and Traditional Ideologies

If we take the preceding description as a basis for examining phenomena and events observed today and in the recent past, it shows that they are not remarkable, but actually part of a very logical pattern. In both German states, for example, the myth of superior orders was explicitly and implicitly established along with the legend of the "clean Wehrmacht." In 1995 and 2001, the Hamburg Institute for Social research presented public exhibitions in several cities about the crimes committed by the Wehrmacht, triggering widespread protests and clashes. Thousands took to the streets under the slogan "Grandpa was not a Nazi" and a noteworthy, recorded debate took place in the Bundestag. After these debates, many accepted that the Wehrmacht had in fact participated in crimes committed in the countries occupied by the Germans in Europe, as well as in connection with the establishment of the many prisoner-of-war camps in the German Reich. These facts were considered to be sufficiently proven and entered the remembrance narrative as a consensus. But just how much a political or evidence-based narrative can differ from the hard-held beliefs of certain parts of society was shown again in 2020. In collaboration with the twin town of Bergen, the Bergen-Belsen memorial planned to issue a statement on September 1, the day on which Germany invaded Poland; this statement also addressed the responsibility of the Wehrmacht for the war crimes committed in this context. Individual town councilors demanded that the wording of the statement be modified so that the Wehrmacht as a whole would no longer be named as complicit in the crimes committed.[43] Only when the memorial threatened to withdraw the statement completely was it agreed that the statement would be published in its original version. However, private individuals filed charges against the then director of the memorial for "defamation of the Wehrmacht," but they were not brought to court – the proceedings were discontinued.

The idea of superior command as focused on the Wehrmacht – and the underlying excuse that anyone refusing to follow orders and participate in the crimes would have been "summarily executed" – deeply shaped the self-image and perception of an entire people that supposedly had no alternatives to their actions.

Another conscious or unconscious exoneration strategy that can be observed is the phenomenon of "Hitlerisation"[44] that was identified by Meik Zülsdorf-Kersting in 2007. "Hitler murdered the Jews," "Hitler built the concentration camps," and "Hitler invaded Poland": these phrases are constantly articulated by young people and adults at educational events in memorial sites. This narrative/discourse was established during the first decades after the war and continues to be transmitted from generation to generation. The staff of the educational department at Bergen-Belsen tries to counter this discourse by drawing the attention to the various examples where the society and different groups of professions supported actively the policies of persecution. This attribution corresponds to a disassociation from all obviously "evil" perpetrators and crimes, ranging from the murdering police task forces in Eastern Europe, the guards in the concentration and death camps to the bureaucrats complicit in ordering the crimes, like Adolf Eichmann, who as an employee of Department IV B 4 in the Reichsicherheitshauptamt organized the systematic deportations of Jews.

This also explains the results of recent studies, which find that there is still a partly divided attitude toward culpability and perpetrators under Nazism. Although there is a willingness to deal with perpetrators and crimes, this is not transferred to one's own family history. Instead, what remains dominant and very much in focus in the narratives of individual families are the purported acts of resistance by family members.[45] If all these perceptions would be based on real or true stories, the national socialist regime could never have been as stable as it was.

This failure to come to terms with what is also one's own complicity is usually accompanied by a lack of self-critical engagement with ideological traditions, as can be observed in the widespread revisionist and antisemitic slogans observed in the last two years at demonstrations across Germany in protests against the government's pandemic laws and regulations. This should not really come as a surprise: in the long periods of prevalent social silence and denial, no attempt was made to tackle the phenomena of discrimination against specific groups, especially antisemitism, antigypsyism, and racism, all of which had their origins well before Nazism and yet became firmly anchored in social consciousness during the Nazi regime.

Conclusion

If, as many claim to believe, we truly want to learn sustainably from the Nazi past and its aftermath, it is crucial that we subject this period to rigorous and critical analysis. We must define how we propose to confront this enduringly virulent ideology and its impact, and how we can avoid perpetuating the mistakes of the (post-war) past. For example, we must be willing to embrace and understand how the descendants of survivors view the memorial sites – and avoid marginalizing them, as noted earlier. We must view these historical sites as "places for all"; they must be places that deal with history from multiple

32 *Elke Gryglewski and Katrin Unger*

perspectives, which address the issue of culpability, analyze the perspective of those affected and the perpetrators, and also include the perspective of spectators and those who offered resistance.

History does not repeat itself. However, there are structures that are inherent in social interaction and which can unfold their potent negative impact at the heart of society. The perennial questions of when and how complicity and culpability begin in situations of marginalization, discrimination, or persecution are just as pertinent as understanding what constitutes and drives moral courage and scope for resistance, two aspects that have gained fresh relevance in recent times.

Notes

1 Susan Neiman, *Learning From the Germans. Confronting Race and the Memory of Evil* (London: Penguin Books, 2020).
2 Susan Neiman, "Von den Deutschen lernen?," *Aus Politik und Zeitgeschichte* (Geschichte und Erinnerung), Vol. 71, No. 40–41 (2021), p. S. 11.
3 Bergen-Belsen, "Stiftung niedersächsische Gedenkstätten," in Bergen-Belsen, ed., *Geschichte der Gedenkstätte. History of the Memorial* (Lohheide: Bergen Belsen Memorial Site, n.d.), p. 5.
4 Cornelia Siebeck, "50 Jahre 'arbeitende' NS-Gedenkstätten in der Bundesrepublik. Vom gegenkulturellen Projekt zur staatlichen Gedenkstättenkonzeption – und wie weiter?," in Elke Gryglewski et al., eds., *Gedenkstättenpädagogik. Kontext, Theorie und Praxis der Bildungsarbeit zu NS-Verbrechen* (Berlin: Metropol Verlag, 2015), p. 19 and Harold Marcuse, *Legacies of Dachau – The Uses and Abuses of a Concentration Camp, 1933–2001* (New York: Cambridge University Press, 2001).
5 This process is described in detail and with a list of memorials by Cornelia Siebeck, op. cit., pp. 19–44.
6 Cf. Gerd Kühling, *Erinnerung an nationalsozialistische Verbrechen in Berlin – Verfolgte des Dritten Reiches und geschichtspolitisches Engagement im Kalten Krieg 1945–1979* (Berlin: Metropol Verlag, 2016).
7 The Neue Wache (New Guardhouse) served throughout different historical periods as a monument and memorial site, being rebuilt/modified for each specific purpose. It was dedicated to the remembrance of the wars of liberation (until 1918), the fighters of World War I (1931–1945), and the victims of fascism and militarism (GDR, 1950–1989). After reunification, Kathe Kollwitz's sculpture, Pieta, was installed there and the monument dedicated to all victims of war and dictatorship.
8 Even though France, for example, officially supported reunification, there were understandable reservations in view of the long and complex Franco-German history. Luca Bonsignore, *Mitterand und die Wiedervereinigung 1989/90*, www.grin.com/document/16553 [Accessed March 15, 2022].
9 The latest example of such a place was the Bundestag resolution for a documentation centre called "The Second World War and German Occupation in Europe" on December 9, 2020.
10 With its architecture and camp order, Sachsenhausen was the prototype of the concentration camp system for the Nazis. To underpin this, the "Inspektion der Konzentrationslager" (Inspectorate of the Concentration Camps) was established in the immediate vicinity of the concentration camp.
11 Versteinerte Zeugen. Das Buchenwalder Mahnmal von 1958, hg. im Auftrag der Stiftung Gedenkstätten Buchenwald und Dora und dem Kuratorium Schloß Ettersberg/Weimar e.V., 2 Bde., Spröda 1997. Also at www.buchenwald.de [Accessed March 15, 2022].

A Model Way of Coming to Terms With the Past? 33

12 The remains of the foundations of this camp, which could have been used to address the catastrophic conditions in which this group of prisoners was housed, were not uncovered until the memorial was redesigned after the fall of the Berlin Wall, https://rotespuren.at/blog/2019/05/20/das-kleine-lager-in-buchenwald/.

13 This is one of the topics that cannot be discussed in depth here. However, examples include the "Law for Liberation from National Socialism and Militarism" of the American occupying power of March 5, 1946, its re-education approach, the Reconstruction Programme of the British or the "mission civilisatrice" of the French occupying power.

14 Since the crimes could not be assigned to a specific country and differed significantly in procedure and extent from earlier war crimes, special categories of crime had been introduced. The basis for the punishment of participation in the persecution and murder of the Jews of Europe was in particular the offence of "crimes against humanity."

15 Thus, the following categories applied: (1) main culprits, (2) incriminated/guilty, (3) lesser culprits, (4) fellow travellers, and (5) exonerated.

16 Wolf Kaiser, Graphic developed for seminars dealing with the Aftermath of National Socialism at the House of the Wannsee Conference Memorial and Educational Site.

17 For example, members of the Lübeck police battalion 307, which was responsible for at least 10,000 shootings and the deportation of over 63,000 Jews, celebrated cheerful "comradeship evenings" after 1945. A photo can be found in Wolf Kaiser, Thomas Köhler, and Elke Gryglewski, 'Nicht durch formale Schranken gehemmt.' Die Deutsche Polizei im Nationalsozialismus (Bonn: Materialien für Unterricht und außerschulische Bildung, Bundeszentrale für politische Bildung, 2012), p. 27. https://nam12.safelinks.protection.outlook.com/?url=https%3A%2F%2Fwww.bpb.de%2Fsystem%2Ffiles%2Fdokument_pdf%2FNS-Polizei.pdf&data=05%7C01%7Cm.blatt%40northeastern.edu%7Cc23be16f1f2c4b892 6e008db18184d68%7Ca8eec281aaa34daeac9b9a398b9215e7%7C0%7C0%7C638130265 488804532%7CUnknown%7CTWFpbGZsb3d8eyJWIjoiMC4wLjAwMDAiLCJQIjoiV 2luMzIiLCJBTiI6Ik1haWwiLCJXVCI6Mn0%3D%7C3000%7C%7C%7C&sdata=qNc ZdDXP0ZXWexYhco2Wv4lVrcZXoTOOrv1eP%2BSQ5NI%3D&reserved=0

18 www.dw.com/de/deutschland-1951-solidarität-mit-massenmördern/a-56136280 [Accessed March 16, 2022] or the exhibition at Flossenburg Concentration Camp Memorial "Was bleibt."

19 The story of Marianne Winter is impressively presented with sources in the documentary "Mariannes Heimkehr – Die Jüdin, der Beamte und das Dorf," produced by Westdeutscher Rundfunk in 2003.

20 This sequence is shown particularly impressively in the 2018 documentary film "Kulenkampffs Schuhe" by Regina Schilling.

21 See also Ulrike Jureit and Christian Schneider, Gefühlte Opfer. Illusionen der Vergangenheitsbewältigung (Stuttgart: Klett Cotta Verlag, 2010).

22 Thus, denazification here took place in the context of "Communist reconstruction," which, in addition to personnel checks, also provided for far-reaching economic and land reforms, for example.

23 The "Waldheim Trials" in particular, in which over 3,000 people were sentenced, are criticized today for lacking proper legal procedure.

24 Jürgen Danyel, "Die SED und die 'Kleinen PGs'". Zur politischen Integration ehemaliger NSDAP-Mitglieder in der SBZ/DDR," in Annette Leo and Peter Reif-Spirek, eds., Helden, Täter, und Verräter (Berlin: Studien zum Antifaschismus, 1999), pp. 177–196.

25 Henry Leide, Auschwitz und Staatssicherheit. Strafverfolgung, Propaganda und Geheimhaltung in der DDR (Berlin: German Federal Archives, 2021).

26 On Riedel and Paland, cf. Oliver von Wrochem, "Zwei späte Prozesse gegen Wehrmachtsangehörige in beiden deutschen Staaten," in Zeitschrift für Geschichtswissenschaft, 52nd year, Vol. 6 (Berlin: Metropol Verlag, 2004), pp. 528–544.

27 The files of the Kiel Regional Court, 2 Ks 2/74 are now in the Schleswig-Holstein State Archives (LASH), Dept. 352/3, Nos. 16681–16703.

34 *Elke Gryglewski and Katrin Unger*

28 Minutes of the public session of the Kiel jury court of April 23, 1974, quoted from Wrochem, "Prozesse," p. 537; expert witness was the forensic physician Prof. Dr. Emanuel Steigleder, at the time Dean of the Medical Faculty of Kiel University.

29 At that time, the statute of limitations had already expired for manslaughter, but not for murder.

30 The verdict is published in Justiz und NS-Verbrechen, *Sammlung deutscher Strafurteile wegen nationalsozialistischer Tötungsverbrechen 1945–1999* (eds. Christiaan F. Rüter et al.), vol. 39: Die vom 05.06.1973 bis zum 26.07.1974 ergangenen Strafurteile, Lfd. No. 795–813 (Amsterdam: DeGruyter, 2008), Lfd. No. 812.

31 On April 15, 1975, the Federal Supreme Court rejected the prosecution's appeal and thus confirmed the judgement of the Regional Court, cf. LASH, Dept. 352/3, No. 16689, pp. 1748–1752.

32 Cf., Wrochem, "Prozesse," p. 538.

33 Ibid., p. 539.

34 Somebody working voluntarily or due to pressure for the Ministry of State Security (Secret Service) without a regular salary and formal contract.

35 "Auskunftsbericht über den IMS 'Gas', Reg.-Nr.: Halle 4787/60 der Objektdienststelle Buna v. 30.4.1977," in *Bundesarchiv, Stasiunterlagenarchiv, Zentraler Untersuchungsvorgang (ZUV), 57: Herbert Hugo Paland, File 12* (Berlin: German Federal Archives, n.d.), pp. 105–113.

36 Ibid., pp. 539–540 and note by the General Prosecutor's Office of the GDR, Public Prosecutor Horst Busse, *Vorschlag zur Veröffentlichung des Prozesses gegen Paland wegen Verbrechen gegen die Menschlichkeit*, date illegible (Berlin: Bundesarchiv, April 1978), DP 3, 212–300/77, pp. 73–74.

37 The judgement of the Berlin Municipal Court, 101a BS 42/78 of August 14, 1978 is published in: Christiaan F. Rüter et al., eds., *DDR-Justiz und NS-Verbrechen, vol. 1. proceedings no. 1001–1030 of the years 1975–1990* (Amsterdam: DeGruyter, 2002), no. 1018.

38 Lutz Niethammer, ed., *"Die Jahre weiß man nicht, wo man die heute hinsetzen soll." Faschismuserfahrungen im Ruhrgebiet* and *"Hinterher merkt man, daß es richtig war, daß es schiefgegangen ist." Nachkriegs-erfahrungen im Ruhrgebiet* (both Berlin/Bonn: JHW Dietz Verlag, 1983).

39 See, among others, Lutz Niethammer, ed., *Der "gesäuberte" Antifaschismus. Die SED und die roten Kapos von Buchenwald* (Berlin: Dokumente, 1995), p. 199.

40 For example, Taz dated March 10, 1992.

41 Overall, many more Jewish survivors helped shape politics and social discourse in the GDR than in the Federal Republic. Cf. www.bpb.de/themen/deutschlandarchiv/324697/juedische-ueberlebende-ns-taeter-und-antisemitismus-in-der-ddr/ [Accessed March 20, 2022]. It is interesting to note that they were not perceived as Jews. We only found out which of the politicians mentioned were Jews through the article published by the Federal Agency for Civic Education.

42 After the so-called Wende, the fall of the wall between East and West Germany, and the reunification of the two countries, for example, there were very many teachers who, out of deep conviction, visited memorials in the former West Germany with their school classes, in addition to the familiar national memorials and remembrance sites in the GDR in order to continue to actively promote remembrance or "learning from history."

43 The original text read "During the Second World War, the SS and Wehrmacht committed unimaginable crimes on our doorstep." Some representatives of the city council wanted to change the text to "Parts of the Wehrmacht."

44 Cf. Meik Zülsdorf-Kersting, *Sechzig Jahre danach: Jugendliche und Holocaust. Eine Studie zur geschichtskulturellen Sozialisation* (Münster: LIT Verlag, 2007).

45 Memo Studie III (2020) by the Foundation Remembrance, *Responsibility and Future and the Institute for Interdisciplinary Research on Conflict and Violence*, www.stiftung-evz.de/was-wir-foerdern/handlungsfelder-cluster/bilden-fuer-lebendiges-erinnern/memo-studie/#c1146 [Accessed March 20, 2020].

2 The Holocaust in American Public Memory*

Barry Trachtenberg

On June 18, 2019, the United States Representative Alexandria Ocasio-Cortez (D-NY) referred to federal detention centers along the US southern border as "concentration camps." She was protesting the Trump administration's practice of detaining refugees and migrants in overcrowded conditions that lacked basic medical care and hygiene, separating families and children from one another, and preventing the arrivals from receiving adequate legal counsel. In defense of her choice of words, Ocasio-Cortez insisted that she was not engaging in "hyperbole" but was drawing upon the conclusions of scholars of concentration camps and the Nazi Holocaust who had been cited in a recent article in *Esquire* magazine making the claim.[1]

Immediately, Rep. Ocasio-Cortez drew sharp rebukes from defenders of Trump's refugee policy for allegedly comparing it to the Nazi Holocaust. As the *New York Times* and many other outlets reported, Ocasio-Cortez was accused of demeaning the memory of Jews and of equating President Trump to Adolf Hitler. The backlash against Ocasio-Cortez also included several major Jewish organizations and a number of Holocaust memorial sites, including Israel's Yad Vashem. Some critics went so far as to accuse Ocasio-Cortez of antisemitism by diminishing Jewish suffering in the Holocaust. Ocasio-Cortez defended her comments by stating, "I don't use those words lightly. I don't use those words to just throw bombs. I use that word because that is what an administration that creates concentration camps is. A presidency that creates concentration camps is fascist."

Most prominent among her detractors was the US Holocaust Memorial Museum (USHMM), which issued a statement the following week that stated in part:

> The United States Holocaust Memorial Museum unequivocally rejects efforts to create analogies between the Holocaust and other events, whether historical or contemporary. That position has repeatedly and unambiguously been made clear in the Museum's official statement on the matter – a statement that is reiterated and reaffirmed now.[2]

That the USHMM weighed in on the controversy came as vindication to many of Ocasio-Cortez's critics on account of the museum's presumed moral

DOI: 10.4324/9781003217848-4

36 Barry Trachtenberg

authority. It also came as a surprise to many scholars of genocide and the Holocaust, who noted that – as a governmental institution – the USHMM typically refrains from commenting on contemporary political affairs, as well as the fact that the term "concentration camp" has been used historically to describe a broad range of detention sites, not restricted to the Holocaust.[3] Others saw the statement as a preemptive measure on behalf of the museum's leaders to shield it from being attacked by the president and his supporters for *not* responding, a reflection of the fact that many such public institutions felt particularly vulnerable to governmental interference during the Trump administration. Regardless of the motivation for the museum's statement, its insistence that the Holocaust is a historically unique event against which nothing must be compared came in for a particular condemnation.[4] A letter of protest was signed by nearly 600 scholars, many of whom work in the fields of Holocaust Studies, Genocide Studies, and Jewish Studies, including many with direct ties to the museum as members of the USHMM's Academic Committee, as seminar instructors, fellowship recipients, and researchers. The letter repudiated the USHMM's refusal to allow comparisons between aspects of the Nazi Holocaust and other historical events, stating in part that

> Scholars in the Humanities and Social Sciences rely on careful and responsible analysis, contextualization, comparison and argumentation to answer questions about the past and the present. By "unequivocally rejecting efforts to create analogies between the Holocaust and other events, whether historical or contemporary," the United States Holocaust Memorial Museum is taking a radical position that is far removed from mainstream scholarship on the Holocaust and genocide. And it makes learning from the past almost impossible.
>
> The Museum's decision to completely reject drawing any possible analogies to the Holocaust, or to the events leading up to it, is fundamentally ahistorical. It has the potential to inflict severe damage on the Museum's ability to continue its role as a credible, leading global institution dedicated to Holocaust memory, Holocaust education, and research in the field of Holocaust and genocide studies. The very core of Holocaust education is to alert the public to dangerous developments that facilitate human rights violations and pain and suffering; pointing to similarities across time and space is essential for this task.[5]

In protesting the USHMM's statement, the signatories to the letter were decrying the museum's efforts to curb political and academic speech. They were also asserting the fact that for many scholars, they are in fact motivated to study the Holocaust precisely out of a commitment to defend universal human rights and to end preventable suffering in the present day, a task that regularly necessitates historical comparisons.

Occurring on the heels of nearly two-and-a-half years of escalating levels of racist and antisemitic rhetoric and violence that followed (and in some instances was instigated by) Trump's election, the controversy over Ocasio-Cortez's use of the term "concentration camp" suggests that a new stage is emerging in the complicated symbolic role of the Holocaust in the United States. In contrast to the past several decades, during which the Holocaust was widely considered to be a unique and sacrosanct historical event that should only be referenced by political leaders and public intellectuals on behalf of interests that were perceived to be particularly "Jewish" – such as in demonstrating one's opposition to antisemitism or in defense of the US government's support for the State of Israel – the Holocaust is increasingly being invoked by elected officials, scholars, and some sectors of the Jewish community toward a much broader range of interests. In particular, during the Trump administration, it was no longer uncommon to hear politicians, opinion makers, and activists reference the Holocaust in support of the Black Lives Matter movement, in defense of refugees, immigrants, and undocumented persons, and in opposition to travel bans that targeted residents of several Muslim-majority countries. At a time when "strong-man governments" that resembled mid-twentieth-century dictatorships were once again on the rise in many parts of the world, the specter of Nazism, the Holocaust, and totalitarianism was increasingly raised to examine and combat these regimes. In particular after the August 2017 "Unite the Right!" rally in Charlottesville, Virginia, in which white supremacists carried Nazi and Confederate flags and one counterprotester was murdered with several injured, many activists, scholars, and political commentators confronted the intersection between antisemitism in the United States and other expressions of racial, religious, and ethnic hatred, leading to further comparisons with Nazism and the Holocaust.

This essay traces the history of the shifting status of the Nazi Holocaust in US public memory. With reference to developments in public memorials, popular culture, political debates, and Holocaust scholarship, it shows that this relationship can be understood as having moved through three overlapping phases. It further argues that all phases of the relationship between the United States and the Holocaust are intimately tied to the changing racial and social status of Jews in America, particularly those of Ashkenazi ancestry (Jews who trace their heritage back to Northern, Central, and Eastern Europe). As it demonstrates, in the first of these phases, occurring during the war and in its immediate aftermath, commemorations and investigations of the Nazi mass murder of Europeans were predominately a private matter among Jews, which happened while the community as a whole was working to secure its position within the majority-white society. In these early years, Jewish communal groups and scholars were often focused on documenting the destruction and mourning the murdered, while also advocating on behalf of imperiled Jewish communities in Europe either as refugees or, after the war, on behalf of survivors. In a second phase that began to emerge by the middle of the 1960s, Jews grew increasingly secure in their position within American society. As awareness of the Holocaust grew among the broader American public (and around the globe), it also took on an increasingly significant role in shaping American

38 Barry Trachtenberg

Jews' self-perception.[6] In these years of the modern civil rights movement and the emergence of hyphenated ethnic American identities, preserving and commemorating the memory of the Holocaust's victims became increasingly central to many Jews' sense of themselves *as* Jews, and often fueled political and social campaigns in support of Israel and on behalf of Soviet Jewry. In a third phase that emerged by the early 1990s, Holocaust commemoration moved to the very center of American public memory, most notably with the establishment of the USHMM on the National Mall and the release of Steven Spielberg's blockbuster film *Schindler's List*. In spite of this widespread recognition of the Holocaust, however, its public expressions were regularly restricted to themes of Jewish suffering, heroism, and self-determination. The essay concludes by raising the possibility that a fourth phase is emerging, as exemplified by – but by no means limited to – the controversy over Rep. Ocasio-Cortez's comments, in which the Holocaust is being applied to a broader range of social and humanitarian issues, in academic scholarship and social protest movements, and within and outside of the American Jewish community.

Setting the Stage: Pre-war American Responses to Nazism

American Jews responded to Hitler's 1933 rise to power in Germany with shock and alarm. Calls for protests and boycotts of German goods were immediate and widespread. The Jewish press was filled with stories of Nazi atrocities against German Jews and with letters from readers demanding that the United States respond forcefully and decisively to come to their protection. Having assumed the presidency on March 4 of that year, Franklin D. Roosevelt quickly became the focus of Jewish political activism, having won an overwhelming majority of Jewish votes in the November election that swept him to victory. On March 10, an anti-Nazi rally organized by the American Jewish Congress in Madison Square Garden called for a bold American response and included issuing condemnations of the Nazi leader and insisting upon relaxing existing immigrations laws and policies that prevented many from finding refuge in the country. Over the next several years, as the situation in Germany grew more dire and increasing numbers of Jews sought to emigrate, organizations such as the American Jewish Committee, the American Jewish Congress, the Jewish Labor Committee, the Hebrew Immigrant Aid Society, and the National Coordinating Committee for Aid to Refugees and Emigrants were either formed or expanded their mission to respond to the growing crisis.

American Jews' ability to influence US actions was, however, limited. At about 4.5 million in number (approximately 3.5% of the total population) in the early 1930s, a majority of whom were either immigrants or the children of immigrants, Jews were relatively powerless outside of the few urban centers in which they were concentrated and they had few other political options available to them other than to support the Democratic Party. Instead, they largely put their faith in Roosevelt to constrain Hitler and pinned much of their hopes

Figure 2.1 Anti-Nazis hold demonstration, March 15, 1937
Source: Credit – Library of Congress

that forceful action would be forthcoming. Over the course of his presidency, Jewish Americans overwhelmingly supported Roosevelt, voting for him with wide majority of over 80% in each of his four elections.

However, the American response to Nazism was muted during the 1930s, in particular during the president's first term in office. As the scholars Richard Breitman and Allan J. Lichtman have shown, in this period, which corresponded with the increased persecution of German Jews (but long before the war and the Holocaust began), Roosevelt was focused almost exclusively on pressing his domestic agenda, in particular, his New Deal legislation.[7] The country was still in the midst of a severe economic Depression, and rebuilding the economy was the government's top priority. At the same time, the country's moral authority to condemn Nazism was sharply limited by its own structural racism. Jim Crow still reigned supreme in the American South, and racial violence, prejudice, and discrimination against African Americans and other people of color were either legal or widely tolerated throughout the entire country. As James Q. Whitman has shown, Nazi legal theorists even looked to American racial policies – in particular to its citizenship and anti-miscegenation laws – as potential models upon which to construct the 1935

40 *Barry Trachtenberg*

Nuremberg laws that stripped German Jews of their full citizenship.[8] Given that Roosevelt's governing coalition depended on the support of white Southern Democrats, he made little effort to ameliorate the oppressive treatment of Black Americans in the first years of his presidency and expended little energy countering German anti-Jewish activity.

Complicating the situation further was the fact that American Jews – the majority of whom themselves or their immediate ancestors had arrived in the United States from Eastern Europe – were themselves subject to frequent antisemitic discrimination and prejudice, often on the basis of perceived religious and racial differences. Nearly two million Jews had arrived in the United States in the last decades of the nineteenth and early decades of the twentieth centuries as part of a decades-long migration of nearly 25 million people largely coming from Eastern and Southern Europe as well as from Latin America and Asia. Arriving in a country with a preexisting color division that separated African Americans from the majority-white society, these immigrants, in the words of the scholar David R. Roediger, lay "in-between." They were clearly not Black but their status as "white" remained an open question and could not be taken for granted.[9] In response, many among these groups adopted strategies to assimilate into white America in order to avoid the consequences of being perceived as non-white, which included discrimination in housing, employment, education, and social institutions. This ambiguous racial status was compounded by the fact that Jews, unlike most other migrants from Europe, were not Christians, and thus had to contend not only with perceived racial differences but also with religious discrimination and intolerance.[10]

The presence of so many immigrants of indeterminate racial status arriving in the country in a relatively short period prompted new racial anxieties among many white Americans. These anxieties both drove and received support from the scientific field of eugenics, which warned against the dangers of racial degeneration. To curb the flow of these new arrivals, in the early 1920s Congress enacted a set of immigration laws with the goal of "restoring" the racial composition of the country to its previous levels of Northern European hegemony. The new laws set in place a quota system that heavily favored the entry of people from Northern European countries and placed severe limits on arrivals from the rest of Europe and many other parts of the world. After the Depression struck in 1929, President Hoover placed further restrictions on immigrants, insisting that they be able to prove that they were not likely to become a public charge. This "LPC Proviso," as it became known, along with strict enforcement of immigration laws by embassy and consular officials, led the number of new arrivals to drop precipitously, at times to only approximately 10% of the legally mandated quotas.[11]

With the absence of a clear refugee policy to support them, most of those fleeing Nazi-occupied Europe in the 1930s and early 1940s were forced to enter the country through these preexisting immigration laws. As a result, many German Jews were unable to find sanctuary in the United States. While it would have taken an Act of Congress to overturn the quota system, Roosevelt largely kept the Hoover-era isolationist policies in place and refused to take independent steps until a series of crises in 1938 prompted him to shift his stance regarding the Nazi threat. In March of that year, Germany seized Austria and subjected Austrian Jews to horrific violence and public humiliation; in September, it seized parts of Czechoslovakia and caused tens of thousands of Jews to flee; in November, Germany unleashed what became known as *Kristallnacht*, in which Jews across Germany were beaten, had their property destroyed, and were arrested. Many were murdered or died as a result of their ill-treatment. In response, Roosevelt took unilateral action to combine the German and Austrian quotas and directed that all available spaces be filled. With the start of war in September 1939, however, the strict policies were once again enforced in the name of state security, a decision strongly supported by the growing militancy of isolationists and antisemites who sought to keep the United States out of the war entirely. Brief exceptions were made in the late summer of 1940 following the German invasion of Western Europe. By the time that the United States entered the war, the country had a decidedly mixed record regarding its assistance to those fleeing Nazism. It had allowed in more refugees from Germany than any other country (approximately 125,000, most of whom were Jewish), and yet it had the capacity to have done much more, even under its existing legislation. By the end of 1941, approximately 60,000 visas for emigrating Germans had been left unissued.[12]

War Years and Aftermath

During the first years of America's involvement in the war, the government remained almost singularly focused on state security and military operations. Consequently, the waiting list for Germans seeking to enter the United States was canceled (by late 1941 it had grown to over 11 years long under the quota system), and the administration and military remained unresponsive (and in some instances even hostile) to appeals by refugee advocacy groups to intervene on behalf of European Jews. Reports of Jewish ghettos, mass killings, and even death camps began to make their way to the United States – some arriving as early as the summer of 1942 – yet did not initially change US policy, which was focused on defeating Hitler. And yet, by the time it entered the war, there was little that the United States could have done directly to stop the murder of European Jews. The invasion of mainland Italy only began in the summer of 1943 and the invasion of Nazi-controlled Western Europe began in the summer of 1944. Both operations, selected on account of military strategy and coordinated with the Soviet Union, placed the Western Allied forces far from the killing centers in the east. Roosevelt was limited to issuing threats to punish German leaders for crimes against civilian populations. However, in early 1944, as historian Rebecca Erbelding has shown, the United States shifted course, and with the creation of the War Refugee Board (WRB) began actively aiding European Jews, transferring much-needed resources to various rescue and relief organizations, as well as facilitating the escape of Jews fleeing Romania and the

42   *Barry Trachtenberg*

Balkans.[13] Among other activities, the WRB publicized Nazi atrocities against Jews and pressed the President to provide sanctuary to refugees, leading to the resettlement in the United States of nearly 1,000 refugees from Allied-occupied parts of Italy in the summer of 1944. Private initiatives – often coordinated with the WRB – went even further, including those by the American Jewish Joint Distribution Committee and the American Friends Service Committee, which assisted tens of thousands of refugees and even some Jews imprisoned in the Warsaw Ghetto, altogether spending more than $50 million toward relief and rescue programs.

Long before the Holocaust got its name, the first wartime commemorations and public events on behalf of endangered Jews occurred amid a deeply inhospitable climate for refugee advocacy and at a time when Jews' social standing and political clout in the United States was insufficient to make the case for greater intervention. Often led by Rabbi Stephen Wise, who was the head of the American Jewish Congress and the most visible spokesperson for American Jews, public events tended to be restricted to demonstration of support for the war effort, in which over half a million Jews (of an estimated overall population of just under 4.7 million) served. However, some Jewish groups and leaders criticized Wise's approach as too conciliatory and inadequate. In response, organizations such as the American Jewish Committee and the Jewish Labor Committee held their own large protest rallies. The Jewish Revisionist Zionist leader Hillel Kook, working under the pseudonym "Peter Bergson," who was often at odds with other Jewish groups, staged grand pageants, organized a march of orthodox rabbis on Washington, and took out hundreds of newspaper ads with the goal of prompting stronger action by the government.[14]

After the war, American Jewry was forced to confront the reality that one-third of global Jewry had been destroyed. The wellspring of American Jewry – Yiddish-speaking Jews from Eastern Europe – had been almost completely destroyed. For more recent migrants in particular, the loss was deeply personal: the murdered included family members, friends, colleagues, and *landslayt* (Yiddish: people from one's hometown or region). In addition, the United States was now home to the largest population of Jews anywhere in the world and had to assume new responsibilities of leadership for charting a path into the future.

American Jews thus found themselves in a paradoxical situation. On the one hand, the Holocaust was the most extreme example of Jewish vulnerability and it reinforced widespread perceptions of Jews as a marginalized group who were exceptionally hated in the world. On the other hand, Jews in America had made it through the Holocaust physically unscathed. They were safe in a country that had helped to defeat fascism and that promoted democracy, political and religious freedom, and economic opportunity, even in spite of the presence of persistent antisemitism. By the end of the war, America could even count itself among the liberators of the camps.

In the two decades that followed the end of the war, American Jews carefully navigated this tension. They were aware of the precarity of their status by virtue of being Jewish in a majority-white Christian country. At the same time, they were also enthusiastic participants in and beneficiaries of the expanded economic opportunities that were made available for white Americans, including those who had at one time fallen "in-between" the races. They made use of the GI Bill and new federal housing loans – regularly denied to African Americans – which helped to facilitate their movement into the middle class and into the newly built suburbs.[15] With varying degrees of force, they pushed against quotas and restrictive covenants that denied them access to white institutions and communities. At the same time as they were enjoying the new prosperity, they were renegotiating their own position within American society. Through a series of initiatives reflecting a widespread desire to carve out a space for themselves as Jews who were compatible with perceived American expectations, Jewish communal organizations promoted Jewish Christian dialogues, "modernized" many of their religious and communal institutions, and, through the popular media, sought to "reintroduce" themselves to their Christian neighbors. Jews' compatibility with the white majority society was a matter not only of practices and conversations within the Jewish community but also of public debate, as testified to by award-winning films such as *Gentleman's Agreement* and *Crossfire* (both 1947) and by a slew of books, journalistic projects, public polling, and lectures.[16]

Commemorating the murder of European Jewry was in this period largely – although not exclusively – a Jewish affair. The first journalistic accounts to report the genocide, the first efforts to publicly mourn, and the first historical studies to chronicle the destruction of European Jewry were generated primarily by Jews and from within Jewish communal institutions such as the Jewish press, synagogues and Jewish community organizations, and by Jewish scholars and scholarly institutions. As historian Hasia R. Diner and others have demonstrated, Jews in America memorialized the destruction of their co-religionists in a wide range of ways.[17] This included revising Jewish rituals and holidays to enshrine the memory of the dead, building physical memorials in Jewish spaces, such as synagogues, cemeteries, and Jewish community centers, and fundraising for Jewish communal support in memory of the catastrophe. Survivors and descendants of destroyed Jewish communities published what became known collectively in Yiddish as *Yizker-bikher*, memorial books to preserve the recollections of prior residents, lists of inhabitants, and communal records of individual towns. Many Jewish cultural and scholarly organizations, staffed in part by refugees or survivors, turned their focus over to the tasks of preserving the cultural legacy of European Jewry through the recovery of Jewish texts and artifacts that had been scattered across Europe, documenting the destruction itself, making a record of the world destroyed, and planning for a future in which American Jewry would take up the mantle of leadership.[18] For American Jews, Holocaust commemoration quickly became a widely shared obligation.

Exceptions to these private efforts were the very public campaigns on behalf of Jewish survivors, hundreds of thousands of whom were located in Displaced Person camps run by the Western Allies in former Axis countries. Unable or unwilling (for fear of violence) to return to the countries of their birth, many

44   Barry Trachtenberg

Jewish DPs, as they were known, were left languishing, often in deplorable conditions. Most countries were as uninterested in receiving DPs after the war as they had been in receiving refugees from Nazism. The United States still had no refugee policy, and DPs were forced to make their way through the quota system. Advocates on their behalf, who vigorously lobbied Congress and conducted repeated campaigns in the press, were constrained at times by the still precarious social position of American Jews. They sought, therefore, to portray the DPs in the most "American" light possible, including referring to them as "Delayed Pilgrims," stressing their compatibility with American values, and proclaiming their strong work ethic. After several years of contentious struggle against antisemitic opponents, shaped by Cold War sensibilities, Congress passed legislation that ultimately allowed for the admittance of a limited number of DPs. In all, approximately 140,000 survivors of the Holocaust entered the country between 1946 and 1954.[19]

While efforts within the Jewish community to contend with the Holocaust and aid its survivors were underway in the first two decades after the end of the war, awareness of the genocide was quickly growing more broadly. The Nuremberg Trials, conducted after the war, were closely followed by Americans who were brought – via regular newsreels and other reporting in the press – face to face with many of the architects of Nazism as well as with many Holocaust survivors, who told of their harrowing incarceration and the murder of their fellow prisoners. Similarly, the widely publicized 1961 trial in Jerusalem of Adolf Eichmann not only served to keep the Holocaust squarely in the public view but also refocused attention to Nazi crimes against Jews in particular. Published accounts of the Holocaust and of life in Nazi Germany by victims and survivors gave readers an intimate view both of the experiences of victims and of the mechanisms of destruction. These include the then widely read (and now largely forgotten) *Warsaw Ghetto: A Diary* by the survivor Mary Berg, who was imprisoned in the Warsaw Ghetto but released on account of her mother's US citizenship. Anne Frank's *Diary* became an international bestseller in print and then made its way to stage and screen, in forms thoroughly adapted to American sensibilities. Journalist William L. Shirer's *The Rise and Fall of the Third Reich* (1960), which won the National Book Award, was among the most-discussed books of its era. Bestselling novels and memoirs fed a growing appetite for literature about the Holocaust and included Elie Wiesel's *Night* (1961), Leon Uris's *Exodus* (1958), *Mila 18* (1961), and Jerzy Kosinski's *The Painted Bird* (1965). Many widely (and less widely) read and reviewed historical studies appeared over the course of this period, several of which were written by refugees and survivors of Nazism, including Eva Reichmann's *Hostages of Civilization: The Social Sources of National Socialist Anti-Semitism* (1951), Gerald Reitlinger's *The Final Solution* (1953), Leon Poliakov's *Harvest of Hate* (1954), Joseph Tenenbaum's *Race and Reich: The Story of an Epoch* (1956), and Philip Friedman's *Their Brothers' Keepers* (1957). The most influential and comprehensive study of this period was *The Destruction of the European Jews* (1961) by the political scientist Raul Hilberg, a work which drew upon German documents captured by the Allies to demonstrate that the murder of the Jews was a methodical campaign that intertwined with but was distinct from German war aims.[20] Filmmakers tended to be slower to depict Jewish suffering on screen, with a few exceptions such as the b-movie *None Shall Escape* (1944) and Orson Welles's *The Stranger* (1946). It was not until the 1959 release of *The Diary of Anne Frank*, Otto Preminger's *Exodus* (1960), and Stanley Kramer's *Judgment at Nuremberg* (1961) that the Holocaust hit the big screens to major audiences and experiences of European Jews began to be depicted by Hollywood.

Growing Holocaust Awareness: Mid-1960s, 1970s, 1980s

By the mid-1960s, American Jews could look back on their efforts to achieve the American Dream largely with satisfaction. By many standards, they had "made it" in America, having fulfilled many of the social and economic aspirations of pre-war American Jewry. They were comfortably middle class, well represented in the professions, and faced far fewer barriers in housing, education, and employment. Antisemitism remained a persistent concern, but attitudes toward Jews were improving and opportunities for advancement were expanding.[21]

However, at this very moment, a younger generation began reconsidering the choices and sacrifices that had been made on their behalf. Inspired by the civil rights movement at home and the anti-colonial movement abroad, they began to rethink both what it meant to be Jewish in America and the many decisions that had been made on their behalf to fit into American society. One significant manifestation of this reappraisal can be seen in the Jewish experience with civil rights activism and in radical protest movements. In the early 1960s, large numbers of Jews – primarily from the American north – were particularly active in civil rights activism in the south. By one estimate, close to two-thirds of the white northerners involved in Mississippi's 1964 Freedom Summer were Jewish.[22] Jews' involvement in civil rights work was informed not only by their commitment to fighting on behalf of equality, justice, and democracy – principles that had been so essential in their own struggle – but for many, it was also prompted by their growing understanding of the Holocaust and the previous generation's efforts to fight Nazism.

However, Jews' participation in civil rights work peaked in 1964. Changes within the movement led increasing numbers of Jews to look inward toward issues of particular concern to the Jewish community and less to the goal of African American equality. There were several reasons for this shift. Many African Americans, frustrated at the slow pace of social change, began to fight for deep structural changes in the foundations of American society in order to eliminate systematic racism, poverty, and injustice, repudiating the previously articulated goal of Black integration into the majority society. With the movement turning more toward the goals of Black Power and in cultivating ties with other colonized peoples, many Jews, who had materially benefitted from their inclusion within the majority-white society, found not only that there was less

46   Barry Trachtenberg

of a place for them to participate in the movement but that also they would have to confront the ways in which they too had benefitted from racial discrimination and prejudice at the expense of the very African Americans on whose behalf they had been working. As the historian Cheryl Lynn Greenberg argues, "Although Jews still expressed less racism than other whites, they nonetheless engaged in the same social segregation of blacks that white Christians had made a tradition."[23] While some progressive and liberal Jews took up this challenge and looked for ways to continue fighting for the goals of equality and freedom, many other Jews turned away, especially following, on the one hand, the legislative victories of the 1964 Civil Rights Act and the 1965 Voting Rights Act, and on the other, the emergence of a narrative of "Black antisemitism," which was more myth than reality but served to justify turning inward to focus on causes of particular concern to American Jews.

The experience with civil rights activism left a complicated legacy for American Jews and their memory of the Holocaust. On the one hand, many Jews reaffirmed their commitment to ending prejudice and fighting discrimination in a country that now – given the violence at home against African Americans and the war abroad against Vietnam – no longer seemed to be the standard bearer of democratic values. On the other hand, the emergence of the Black Power movement and other movements of ethnic pride that were demanding accountability for past injustices provided models for a newly assertive American Jewish identity to take shape. The 1967 war between Israel and its neighbors, in which Israel was widely seen at the time as the underdog but in which it emerged victorious and dramatically expanded the territory under its control, provided a cause around which American Jews of nearly all political persuasions would rally. At the time, many Jews expressed great relief that the possibility of another mass murder of Jews had been avoided. However, Israel's victory and conquest put them in conflict with many of their one-time allies in the civil rights movement who expressed solidarity with Palestinians who were now living under military occupation. The plight of Soviet Jewry and the 1973 Arab–Israeli war only served to reinforce a widespread belief in Jewish vulnerability and the need to prioritize organizing on behalf of Jewish self-interests.[24] Widespread resistance in the 1970s among Jews over issues such as affirmative action legislation, school desegregation initiatives, and other remedies to address historical injustices toward people of color demonstrate the shift occurring within the Jewish community.

As Jews in the later 1960s, the 1970s, and 1980s reconsidered what it meant to be Jewish and their place within American society, preserving the memory of the Holocaust and protecting the security of Israel became central (and often intertwined) components of a new Jewish identity. As Edward Shapiro writes, "For some American Jews, the Holocaust became central to their own image of themselves as Jews. With often only a tenuous relationship to Judaism, they clung to the Holocaust as the core element in their Jewish identity."[25] It was in this period that American Jews began commemorating the Holocaust in earnest, with expanded religious observances, through educational programs, and via rituals of public mourning. Although American Jews had begun laying physical memorials to Europe's murdered Jews as early as the late 1940s, the pace increased significantly. Engagement with the Holocaust also occurred through works of literature such as Saul Bellow's *Mr. Sammler's Planet* (1970), Leslie Epstein's *King of the Jews* (1979), Philip Roth's *The Ghost Writer* (1979), and Cynthia Ozick's "The Shawl" (1980). Elie Wiesel, who won the Nobel Peace Prize in 1986 (by which time his memoir *Night* had become for many akin to a sacred text), was widely revered in the Jewish community for his advocacy on behalf of survivors and his human rights work, and Simon Wiesenthal was widely lionized for his pursuit of Nazi criminals who were still at large.

This growing attention to the Holocaust made its mark on the broader public as well. Most influential in this regard was the airing of the 1978 miniseries *The Holocaust* which premiered on the NBC television network and had an estimated 120 million viewers in the United States alone. Weaving together a cast of over 150 characters and an intricate set of storylines that traced the histories of two German families – a Christian one who became Nazis and a Jewish one who became their victims – *The Holocaust* brought the suffering of European Jewry directly into the homes of American viewers. In spite of taking great liberties with the historical record as it was known at the time and notwithstanding a significant amount of criticism for its portrayal of the Holocaust by figures such as Elie Wiesel and others, the miniseries had a profound impact on how Americans – and eventually many viewers around the world – came to understand the Jewish experience. More than the story itself, the public debates and controversies around the miniseries resulted in many months of public debate and discussion and, perhaps more than any other single factor, helped to bring the term "Holocaust" into widespread use. By the late 1970s, "the Holocaust" was a household phrase, and referred, in the minds of most, exclusively to the murder of six million Jews by the Nazis during World War II and as a crime that was unique in all of human history.[26]

Throughout the 1980s, cultural productions continued to keep the topic of the Holocaust active. The nine-and-a-half hour documentary film *Shoah* by French director Claude Lanzmann was released in 1985 (shown on public television in 1987) and was widely regarded as a masterpiece for both its stark portrayal of the Holocaust and its filmmaking techniques, which focused on long and often intimate interviews with survivors, perpetrators, and bystanders. The graphic novel *Maus*, of which volume 1 appeared in 1986, won its creator Art Spiegelman the National Book Critics Circle Award for Biography that year (and the Pulitzer Prize upon the publication of volume 2). Political and legal controversies too kept the Holocaust in the news in this era, including President Ronald Reagan's May 1985 wreath-laying at a cemetery in Bitburg, Germany, where members of the Nazi S.S. were buried. Rather than cancel the event following protests, Reagan defended his decision by stating that members of the German military in World War II were "victims of Nazism, just as surely as the victims in the concentration camps." Related, one month later, Reagan signed a Congressional Joint Resolution designating June 12, 1985,

48   Barry Trachtenberg

"Anne Frank Day." Other events also contributed to keeping the Holocaust in the news, such as revelations that Austrian President Kurt Waldheim, who had served as the secretary general of the United Nations in the 1970s, had once been a member of a Nazi paramilitary organization, and had falsified his record. Also significant were highly publicized legal actions, such as against Swiss banks for withholding funds of Jews murdered in the Holocaust, and the repeated deportation trials of John Demjanjuk, who was charged with hiding his past as a guard in Nazi extermination camps.

In this period, a new narrative concerning the US involvement in the Holocaust began to take hold. If most American Jews in the 1930s and 1940s had looked to President Roosevelt and the US armed forces as the Jews' protector and liberator, by the late 1960s, this position was being reconsidered by a slate of historical studies that called this view sharply into question and which aligned with the larger reconsideration among many Jews of their relationship to their country. Works such as Arthur D. Morse's *While Six Million Died* (1967), David S. Wyman's *Paper Walls: America and the Refugee Crisis 1938–1941* (1968), and Saul S. Friedman's *No Haven for the Oppressed: United States Policy Toward Jewish Refugees 1938–1945* (1973) provided a new narrative of not merely American indifference to the plight of European Jewry under Nazism, but, as some among these scholars would claim, outright hostility toward them.[27] Over the 1970s and 1980s, this view would become dominant and eventually expanded into Jewish communal self-examinations as well. Figures such as Stephen Wise, who had once been lauded for his advocacy on behalf of Hitler's Jewish victims, were now regularly characterized as having been too concerned with maintaining his stature and access to Roosevelt to make demands upon him. The Jewish community was depicted as having been too fragmented and filled with infighting to have been able to mount an effective campaign on behalf of their European co-religionists. A 1984 report of the "American Jewish Commission on the Holocaust" and a 1985 study by Rabbi Haskel Lookstein, *Were We Our Brothers' Keepers?: The Public Response of American Jews to the Holocaust, 1938–1944*, declared what many were suspecting: the World War II generation of Jewish leaders and communal organizations failed to come to the aid of their co-religionists and bore a measure of responsibility for the Holocaust.[28]

An additional motivation for this narrative of America's failure to rescue European Jewry was concern over protecting US support for the State of Israel, as journalist Lawrence Zuckerman has argued.[29] In "FDR's Jewish Problem," Zuckerman makes the case that by blaming Roosevelt for not coming to the rescue of threatened Jews in World War II, supporters of Israel can effectively make the case for the United States to give uncritical support today for the Jewish state. If "betrayal happened before," the logic goes, "it can happen again."[30] As Zuckerman argues, "The stakes of this historical debate are high, because the myths that have been propagated about the actions of the United States during the Holocaust are being put to specific political uses today."

This new narrative of the US role in the Holocaust took firm hold by the late 1970s, in spite of some scholars' efforts to advance less strident conclusions.

It helped persuade Jimmy Carter in late 1978 to establish the President's Commission on the Holocaust, a group that was chaired by Elie Wiesel and which included more than 30 prominent figures, among them Holocaust survivors, religious leaders, politicians, scholars, and other public figures. In the Report issued the following year, the Commission articulated a set of principles for understanding the Holocaust as a historically unique crime of genocide, one that primarily targeted Jews, in which the United States largely failed to intervene, and which must be remembered. It also set forth a series of tasks for moving forward, including erecting a national memorial/museum, creating an educational foundation, and establishing a Committee on Conscience.[31]

Over the quarter century that covered the second half of the 1960s, 1970s, and 1980s, the Holocaust increasingly became part of the fabric of public life. If there had ever been a reluctance among Jews to speak too publicly about the Holocaust for fear of hindering their movement into the American mainstream, the situation had changed to such an extent that it was now assertions of Jewish victimhood and the corresponding goal of maintaining US support for Israel that became intimately tied to how American Jews saw themselves and their place in the United States.

The Holocaust at the Center of American Public Memory, 1990–2016

By the 1990s, the Holocaust had become fully a part of American memorial culture. At the onset of the decade, at least 17 states and the District of Columbia were homes to memorials and major Holocaust museums were soon to be inaugurated in Washington, DC, New York City, and Los Angeles.[32] In spite of the changing face of American Jewry – which was increasingly diverse religiously, denominationally, racially, economically, and politically – memorialization and commemoration of the Holocaust continued to gain momentum, a consequence in large part of the dedicated efforts of major Jewish organizations. Such momentum was not without its critics, however. In a long essay in the *New York Times*, Rabbi Arthur Hertzberg expressed his concerns over the practice of exercising Jewish communal power in order to mount public displays of victimhood:

> And so, in expiation of the sins of the fathers, whose quiet interventions in Washington did little good, this generation of American Jewish leaders is largely confrontationist with enemies and critics. Holocaust consciousness has created a sense of Jews in part of their souls as an embattled bastion in the very America of today that is free and open enough for Jews to enshrine their most painful memory in museums in very public places.[33]

The result of President Carter's Holocaust commission was the opening of the USHMM in 1993 on the National Mall in Washington, DC, which brought Holocaust commemoration to new heights of prominence. The USHMM

Figure 2.2 US Holocaust Memorial Museum, Washington, DC, 2021
Source: Credit – Reprinted with kind permission of David Enzel

quickly received an unprecedented number of visitors, far surpassing that of other museums and memorials in the country's capital. Just as quickly, it became recognized as the global authority on the Holocaust, on account of the prestige of its location, the quality and uniqueness of its exhibitions, the impressiveness of its overall design, and its promotion of research into Holocaust and genocide studies. In spite of a broad range of criticisms that were voiced at its opening and in the years immediately following – which included questions as to how the Holocaust itself would be defined (in terms of both its victims and its perpetrators) and as to why the murder of European Jewry should be memorialized in the US capital when Native American genocide and African American slavery were not at that time – it remains the premier institute for study of the Holocaust.[34]

The impact of the USHMM on subsequent Holocaust commemoration has been profound. In spite of the fact that the Holocaust did not physically occur in the United States and there are, therefore, no obvious physical sites for memorials, it is noteworthy that since the USHMM's opening, nearly every state in the country – and many major cities – hosts a memorial to the murdered Jews of Europe. Commemorations of International Holocaust Awareness Day (January 27), Yom ha-Shoah (27 Nissan according to the Hebrew calendar), and Kristallnacht (November 9–10) are commonplace, not only within the Jewish community but also widely in the larger public realm. In addition, the USHMM's founding set a standard for a new sort of national museum and helped to fuel momentum for completing the National Museum of the American Indian (opened in 2004) and the National Museum of African American History and Culture (2016).

Eight months after the opening of the USHMM, the film *Schindler's List* appeared in theaters and it too had an immediate and profound impact on how Americans – and eventually many parts of the world – understood the Holocaust. Steven Spielberg's epic work tells the story of Oskar Schindler (played by Liam Neeson), an ethnic German Czech, industrialist, and war profiteer during the war who came to sacrifice his fortune in order to save the lives of 1,100 Jews who worked in his factories as slave laborers.[35] In telling Schindler's story, Spielberg portrays the central figure in a deeply sympathetic light and whose financial downfall and moral uplift come as a result of witnessing firsthand the brutalization of the Jews in his care. Spielberg's film is deeply moving and often vividly depicts truly harrowing scenes, including the liquidation of the ghetto, the manifold efforts of Jews to save themselves and their loved ones from the impending slaughter, a prisoner selection, the collaboration of Jewish Police, and one in which a group of naked female prisoners are brought to showers, in which the viewers – and many of the prisoners themselves – are led to believe that they will be gassed, only to receive an actual shower. The film, which left many of its audience members in tears, was overwhelmingly hailed by critics and won major awards. Although film scholars, historians of the Holocaust, and feminist scholars have criticized *Schindler's List* on a range of issues, it remains the iconic film of the Holocaust.[36] As the USHMM did for museums and memorials, *Schindler's List* demonstrated the moral, pedagogical, and commercial potential of Holocaust movies, and prompted the production of many more in its wake. Moreover, visiting the USHMM and viewing it became acts of pilgrimage and obligation for many Americans, Jewish and non-Jewish, who believed that bearing witness to the Holocaust and perpetuating its memory might prevent such violent acts in the future.

These twin events of 1993 helped accelerate a dramatic rise of Holocaust awareness and memorialization and have woven the Holocaust into the fabric of everyday American life. Tens of thousands of nonfiction books for all ages of readers on Nazism and the Holocaust have been published since that time. The Holocaust is a regular subject of film, literature, music, art, and dance, as well as countless internet memes and videos. Holocaust Studies (sometimes paired with Genocide Studies or Jewish Studies) is a thriving academic subject that is now taught across the country and which has its own journals, professional associations, and pedagogy seminars. Holocaust education is a mandatory part of public school curricula in nearly three dozen states and the District of Columbia.[37]

Since the early 1990s, the Holocaust has been present at the very center – both physically and metaphorically – of American awareness and acceptance, in spite of the continuing presence of antisemitism and periodic attempts to deny or downplay the severity of the genocide. However, tensions and questions as

52 *Barry Trachtenberg*

to what is the purpose or consequence of these efforts to commemorate and teach the Holocaust have remained. While the Holocaust became accepted as the utmost expression of evil, it also had placed upon it – often by Jewish communal leaders and their allies – the expectation and even insistence that many of its central "truths" are inviolable and thus unchallengeable. Its invocation by political and public figures was often strictly governed so as to be restricted to what were perceived as particularly *Jewish* interests, in particular, combatting antisemitism and supporting the state of Israel against its critics. While Holocaust museums and institutions often engaged in genocide awareness, they also contributed to the Holocaust being considered the standard by which other genocides were "measured." Nazism became the greatest expression of evil and Jews as the symbol and embodiment of victims, a symbol that has been used to shield many Jewish organizations, as well as Israel, from criticism by elected officials and public intellectuals. Challenging or even complicating the narrative of the US "inaction" was often an invitation to widespread condemnation. Diverging from these tenets – at times even by scholars researching these topics – often came with professional consequences.

Conclusion – A New Phase?

While there have always been skeptics, critics, and even opponents of the "sacred" place that the Holocaust has held in the United States (both among Jews and non-Jews and in various locations along the political spectrum), among the many outcomes of Donald Trump's election to the presidency in November 2016 was a greater willingness among opponents of his policies to invoke the Holocaust in political debates. This may signal that the relationship between the United States and the Holocaust is beginning to undergo another shift in focus. The ease with which Trump employed racist, sexist, ableist, Islamophobic, and antisemitic rhetoric and his eagerness to enact policies against migrants and refugees immediately after assuming the presidency prompted many observers to wonder whether he was turning the country toward fascism or totalitarianism. His decision to enact the first of his "travel bans" on several Muslim-majority countries on International Holocaust Remembrance Day (January 27, 2017, a week after he assumed office) brought protesters to the streets, airports, and online. Many drew the comparison with the US anti-immigration policies of the 1930s that prevented Jews from escaping Nazi Europe. Trump's subsequent refusal to take seriously the spike in antisemitic acts that followed his election, his spokesperson's denial of the Nazis' use of gas, his show of support for the white nationalists who marched in the "Unite the Right" rally in Charlottesville, his regular depiction of the Jewish philanthropist George Soros as a bogeyman overseeing his opposition, and the blatant and generally un-repudiated antisemitism of many of his supporters prompted many American Jews and others to invoke the Holocaust as a warning of what could occur if such actions went unchecked.[38] The October 2018 shootings in Pittsburgh's Tree of Life – Or L'Simcha Synagogue by a gunman on account of its support of refugees and the presence of antisemitic and Nazi symbols during the January 6, 2021, insurrectionary attack on Congress gave further evidence for these fears.

As with Rep. Ocasio-Cortez's comments regarding American "concentration camps" and the protest against the USHMM's condemnation of them by scholars, it was increasingly common to see invocations of the Holocaust used in the protests against Trump's policies. It was present in the protests against police killings of African Americans by police officers. It was present when, in the summer of 2021, a new poll was released that found that not only did 25% of American Jews believe that Israel's treatment of Palestinians was comparable to apartheid, 20% found it a form of genocide, a comparison that would have been unthinkable in earlier years and which shocked many observers.[39]

Along with the growing willingness to draw broader comparisons to the Holocaust, recent years have also seen a historical reassessment of the role of the United States in the murder of European Jewry. In 2013, historians Richard Breitman and Allan J. Lichtman published *FDR and the Jews*, which demonstrated that President Roosevelt's stance toward American Jews and his response toward Nazism cannot be so easily summed up as either wholly "good" or "bad." Instead, they demonstrate that Roosevelt maintained a number of positions, including being dismissive of the perils of German Jewry, supportive of their efforts to escape to America, suspicious of the "threat" they might represent to American interests, and actively supporting efforts at aiding their survival. Following publication of that text, and the critical acclaim with which it was generally met (in spite of severe condemnation by scholars committed to preserving the earlier understanding), a number of new studies have appeared that challenged other aspects of the narrative of the US indifference or complicity with the Holocaust. Most notably, in 2018 the USHMM itself opened an exhibition titled "Americans and the Holocaust" that offers a critical reassessment of America's legacy, one which demonstrates the complexities of the historical record and depicts Roosevelt neither as European Jews' savior nor as complicit in their destruction. The exhibition shows why, in a country that was occupied by the economic Depression, riven by systematic racism, and constrained by isolationist principles, and then pulled into a war that most Americans initially did not want to fight, the goal of "saving Jews and others targeted for murder by the Nazi regime and its collaborators never became a priority."[40] The fact that such an exhibition – which does not attribute the US's lackluster response solely to the cause of antisemitism and therefore calls into question some of the core beliefs that led to the museum's founding – was mounted by the USHMM itself is perhaps the most dramatic sign of a shift in the relationship of the United States and the Holocaust.

Notes

* The ideas in this essay are adapted from Barry Trachtenberg, *The United States and the Nazi Holocaust: Race, Refuge, and Remembrance* (London: Bloomsbury, 2018), which contains more extensive citations than are provided in this essay. I am grateful to Marty

54 *Barry Trachtenberg*

Blatt for soliciting this contribution and for the opportunity to revisit and update the arguments in that book.

1 Sheryl Gay Stolberg, "Ocasio-Cortez Calls Migrant Detention Centers 'Concentration Camps,' Eliciting Backlash," *New York Times*, June 18, 2019, https://www.nytimes.com/search?query=Ocasio+Cortez+Calls+Migrant+Detention+Centers+%27Concentration+Camps%27 Also see Jack Holmes, "An Expert on Concentration Camps Says That's Exactly What the U.S. Is Running at the Border," *Esquire*, June 13, 2019, www.esquire.com/news-politics/a27813648/concentration-camps-southern-border-migrant-detention-facilities-trump [Accessed August 15, 2021].

2 United States Holocaust Memorial Museum, "Statement Regarding the Museum's Position on Holocaust Analogies," June 24, 2019, www.ushmm.org/information/press/press-releases/statement-regarding-the-museums-position-on-holocaust-analogies [Accessed August 15, 2021].

3 See, for example, Andrea Pitzer, *One Long Night: A Global History of Concentration Camps* (New York: Little, Brown and Company, 2017). It is also worth noting, as the scholar Aiko Herzig-Yoshinaga has shown, that the term "concentration camps" was in wide use by government officials to describe the "relocation centers" where people of Japanese ancestry residing in the United States were incarcerated during World War II. See Aiko Herzig-Yoshinaga, *Words Can Lie or Clarify: Terminology of the World War II Incarceration of Japanese Americas*, https://manzanarcommittee.files.wordpress.com/2010/03/wordscanlieorclarify-ahy.pdf [Accessed August 15, 2021].

4 See, for example, Timothy Snyder, "It Can Happen Here," *Slate*, July 12, 2019, https://slate.com/news-and-politics/2019/07/holocaust-museum-aoc-detention-centers-immigration.html [Accessed August 15, 2021].

5 Omer Bartov, Doris Bergen, Andrea Orzoff, Timothy Snyder, Anika Walke, et al., "An Open Letter to the Director of the US Holocaust Memorial Museum," *The New York Review of Books*, July 1, 2019, www.nybooks.com/daily/2019/07/01/an-open-letter-to-the-director-of-the-holocaust-memorial-museum/?fbclid=IwAR1AoKWPKzbxZfxd8ia48BuBjDfbyerfRizy7SZziGGWqnCShfUQ8LFZjyY. Note: I am a signatory to this letter.

6 For a global perspective on Holocaust representation, see Daniel H. Magilow and Lisa Silverman, *Holocaust Representations in History: An Introduction* (London: Bloomsbury, 2015).

7 Richard Breitman and Allan J. Lichtman, *FDR and the Jews* (Cambridge, MA: Belknap Press, 2013).

8 James Q. Whitman, *Hitler's American Model: The United States and the Making of Nazi Race Law* (Princeton, NJ: Princeton University Press, 2017).

9 David R. Roediger, *Working Toward Whiteness: How America's Immigrants Became White* (New York: Basic Books, 2005).

10 Eric L. Goldstein, *The Price of Whiteness: Jews, Race, and American Identity* (Princeton, NJ: Princeton University Press, 2006).

11 Breitman and Lichtman, p. 36.

12 United States Holocaust Memorial Museum, *How Many Refugees Came to the United States from 1933–1945?*, https://exhibitions.ushmm.org/americans-and-the-holocaust/how-many-refugees-came-to-the-united-states-from-1933-1945 [Accessed August 15, 2021].

13 Rebecca Erbelding, *Rescue Board: The Untold Story of America's Efforts to Save the Jews of Europe* (New York: Doubleday, 2018).

14 For an overview of American Jewish responses, see Gulie Ne'eman Arad, *America, Its Jews, and the Rise of Nazism* (Bloomington, IN: Indiana University Press, 2000). Also see Catherine Collomp, *Rescue, Relief, and Resistance: The Jewish Labor Committee's Anti-Nazi Operations, 1934–1945*, trans. by Susan Emanuel (Detroit, MI: Wayne State University Press, 2020).

15 Karen Brodkin, *How Jews Became White Folks and What That Says About Race in America* (New Brunswick, NJ: Rutgers University Press, 1998); and Ira Katznelson, *When*

Affirmative Action Was White: An Untold History of Racial Inequality in Twentieth-Century America (New York: W. W. Norton & Company, 2005).

16 Judith E. Doneson, *The Holocaust in American Film*, 2nd ed. (Syracuse, NY: Syracuse University Press, 2002); and Lawrence Baron, "The First Wave of American 'Holocaust' Films, 1945–1959," *The American Historical Review*, Vol. 115, No. 1 (2010), pp. 90–114.

17 Hasia R. Diner, *We Remember with Reverence and Love: American Jews and the Myth of Silence After the Holocaust, 1945–1962* (New York: New York University Press, 2009). Also see David Cesarani and Eric J. Sundquist, eds., *After the Holocaust: Challenging the Myth of Silence* (New York: Routledge, 2011); and Rachel Deblinger, "'In a World Still Trembling': American Jewish Philanthropy and the Shaping of Holocaust Survivor Narratives in Postwar America, 1945–1953" (PhD Dissertation, University of California, Los Angeles, 2014).

18 I write about this set of tasks in Chapter 3 of *The Holocaust & the Exile of Yiddish: A History of the Algemeyne Entsiklopedye* (New Brunswick, NJ: Rutgers University Press, 2022). Also see the essays in Eliyana R. Adler and Sheila E. Jelen, eds., *Reconstructing the Old Country: American Jewry in the Post-Holocaust Decades* (Detroit, MI: Wayne State University Press, 2017); and Markus Krah, *American Jewry and the Re-invention of the East European Jewish Past* (Berlin: De Gruyter Oldenbourg, 2018).

19 On the treatment of Jewish DPs in Europe and their reception in the United States, see Leonard Dinnerstein, *America and the Survivors of the Holocaust* (New York: Columbia University Press, 1982); Beth Cohen, *Case Closed: Holocaust Survivors in Postwar America* (New Brunswick, NJ: Rutgers University Press, 2007); and Rachel Deblinger's digital exhibition, *Memories/Motifs: Holocaust Survivor Narratives in Postwar America*, www.memoriesmotifs.com [Accessed August 15, 2021].

20 Raul Hilberg, *The Destruction of the European Jews* (Chicago, IL: Quadrangle Books, 1961).

21 See Samuel C. Heilman, *Portrait of American Jews: The Last Half of the 20th Century* (Seattle, WA: University of Washington Press, 1995).

22 Edward S. Shapiro, *A Time for Healing: American Jewry Since World War II* (Baltimore, MD: The Johns Hopkins University Press, 1992), p. 223.

23 Cheryl Greenberg, *Troubling the Waters: Black-Jewish Relations in the American Century* (Princeton, NJ: Princeton University Press, 2006), p. 209.

24 See Marc Dollinger, *Black Power, Jewish Politics: Reinventing the Alliance in the 1960s* (Waltham, MA: Brandeis University Press, 2018); Michael R. Fischbach, *Black Power and Palestine: Transnational Countries of Color* (Stanford, CA: Stanford University Press, 2018); and Michael R. Fischbach, *The Movement and the Middle East: How the Arab-Israeli Conflict Divided the American Left* (Stanford, CA: Stanford University Press, 2019).

25 Shapiro, p. 216.

26 See the discussion in Magilow and Silverman, pp. 103–110.

27 For an insightful review of this literature, see Rebecca L. Erbelding, "About Time: The History of the War Refugee Board" (PhD dissertation, George Mason University, 2015), pp. 4–17. Erbelding characterizes this historiographical debate as one between "moralists" and "contextualists."

28 Also see a rebuttal of this claim by Henry L. Feingold, "Was There Communal Failure? Some Thoughts on the American Jewish Response to the Holocaust," *American Jewish History*, Vol. 81 (1993), pp. 60–80.

29 Lawrence Zuckerman, "FDR's Jewish Problem: How Did a President Beloved by Jews Come to Be Regarded as an Anti-Semite Who Refused to Save Them from the Nazis?," *Nation*, July 17, 2013, pp. 29–32.

30 Ibid., p. 29.

31 President's Commission on the Holocaust, Elie Wiesel, Chairman, "Report to the President," September 27, 1979, www.ushmm.org/m/pdfs/20050707-presidents-commission-holocaust.pdf [Accessed August 15, 2021].

32 See Sybil Milton, "Selected List of Holocaust Memorial Sites," in Sybil Milton and Ira Nowinski, eds., *In Fitting Memory: The Art and Politics of Holocaust Memorials* (Detroit, MI: Wayne State University Press, 1991), pp. 317–335.

56   *Barry Trachtenberg*

33 Arthur Hertzberg, "A Lifelong Quarrel With God," *New York Times*, May 6, 1990.
34 See the discussions in Edward T. Linenthal, *Preserving Memory: The Struggle to Create America's Holocaust Museum*, 2nd ed. (New York: Columbia University Press, 2001).
35 *Schindler's List*, written by Steven Zaillian, directed by Steven Spielberg, featuring Liam Neeson, Ralph Fiennes, and Ben Kingsley, Universal, 1993.
36 For scholarly critiques of *Schindler's List*, see Yosefa Loshitzky, ed., *Spielberg's Holocaust: Critical Perspectives on Schindler's List* (Bloomington, IN: Indiana University Press, 1997). Also see the author, Auschwitz survivor and Nobel Laureate Imre Kertész's essay "Who Owns Auschwitz," *The Yale Journal of Criticism*, Vol. 14, No. 1 (Spring 2001), pp. 267–272, which takes Spielberg to task for a number of aspects of the film, including his attempt to make a "realistic" film about an event of which he can have no firsthand knowledge, and for making a film "that seek[s] to establish the Holocaust once and for all as something foreign to human nature; that seek[s] to drive the Holocaust out of the realm of human experience" (270).
37 Paul Warne Mathewson, "Mandatory Holocaust Education Legislation in the State of Illinois: A Historical Study" (PhD dissertation, University of Illinois at Urbana-Champaign, 2015), p. 3.
38 See, for example, Waitman Wade Beorn, "It's Not Wrong to Compare Trump's America to the Holocaust. Here's Why," *Washington Post*, July 16, 2018, https://www.washingtonpost.com/news/posteverything/wp/2018/07/16/its-not-wrong-to-compare-trumps-america-to-the-holocaust-heres-why/
39 Arno Rosenfeld, "What If a Quarter of Jews Really Do Think Israel Is a Genocidal, Apartheid State?," July 15, 2021, www.Forward.com [Accessed August 15, 2021].
40 "Americans and the Holocaust," curated by Daniel Greene, United States Holocaust Memorial Museum, 2018, www.ushmm.org/information/exhibitions/museum-exhibitions/americans-and-the-holocaust [Accessed August 15, 2021].

3 Memorializing Violence as a Political Tool

Public Memory and the Genocide of the Tutsi in Rwanda

Timothy Longman

As a small, land-locked country with few natural resources, the East African state of Rwanda long languished in international obscurity. Despite several waves of previous violence and a civil war that had been underway since 1990, Rwanda only came to the attention of the world in April 1994, when the assassination of longtime President Juvénal Habyarimana became the pretext for a massive campaign of violence. A small group of extremists from the majority Hutu ethnic group launched a systematic slaughter, first against perceived political opponents regardless of ethnicity, and then more specifically against members of the minority Tutsi ethnic group. An estimated 75–80% of Rwanda's Tutsi population lost their lives in just 100 days in the clearest case of genocide since the Holocaust.[1]

When the genocide began in April 1994, the Rwandan Patriotic Front (RPF), a rebel army comprised primarily of Tutsi refugees based in Uganda, relaunched their invasion of Rwanda, and by July, they had stopped the genocide and taken control of the country. Over the next several years, the RPF focused on rebuilding Rwanda's physical, social, and political infrastructure. They talked about reconciliation and formed a multi-ethnic coalition government, but the RPF also used considerable violence to establish their authority, both within Rwanda and in the wider Central African region. In 2000, the RPF gave up the pretense of shared power and took direct control, with RPF leader Paul Kagame assuming the presidency. Over the last two decades, Kagame and the RPF have governed Rwanda firmly, seeking to establish a developmental state with a strong focus on economic growth in a context where civil liberties are severely restricted. Despite the RPF's violent first years and strict authoritarian rule since, the international community has continued to provide strong support to the Rwandan government and broader Rwandan economy. According to the Organization for Economic Cooperation and Development, Rwandan received $1.3 billion in foreign assistance in 2019, including $184 million from the United States alone.[2] By some estimates, over half of the national budget is funded by international grants and loans.[3]

In this chapter, I explore how the RPF has manipulated memory of the genocide against the Tutsi to justify their policies to the international community. In my book, *Memory and Justice in Post-Genocide Rwanda*, I explain how the

DOI: 10.4324/9781003217848-5

58   *Timothy Longman*

regime has used commemorations, memorials, genocide trials, and numerous other programs to create a historical narrative that emphasizes the centrality of the genocide to Rwandan history while obscuring the RPF's own history of violence.[4] While in my book I focus on how the regime's collective memory project has been received by the Rwandan population, in this chapter, I analyze the impact of this narrative in international affairs. I argue that the RPF has effectively focused international attention on the genocide against the Tutsi to gain support while deflecting scrutiny of its own history of violence. By playing on guilt over the international community's failure to stop the genocide and conflating the genocide against the Tutsi with the Holocaust, the Rwandan government has won over powerful international allies in diplomatic, development, and humanitarian circles who have defended Rwanda against criticisms over its human rights record while ensuring that foreign assistance continues to flow into Rwanda. The strategic use of genocide memory has proven a highly effective tool to secure international support for the RPF's efforts to hold onto power.

The Political Uses of History in Rwanda

Over the past several decades, scholars have increasingly recognized the role that historical memory plays in shaping political realities. As numerous works have demonstrated, popular understandings of the past do not arise spontaneously but are crafted by social elites, governments, and the media.[5] Regimes in power, in collaboration with their key supporters, regularly manipulate history to gain popular compliance and justify their rule.[6] In Africa, both colonial and post-colonial governments have promoted selected and often falsified versions of the past that serve the interests of the state.[7] Regimes are particularly careful to control the memory of violent and traumatic events, like war, ethnic massacre, and genocide, because of the emotional weight people attach to these experiences and their potential to serve as a basis for challenging existing structures of power. As Pierre Nora has shown for French Republicanism, diverse sites of memory such as monuments, public holidays, museums, anthems, and flags are used to shape not only popular memory and identity but also political values,[8] and the memorialization of violence is the focus of a large portion of the tools used to shape public memory.

In Rwanda, regimes have used narratives of violence to shape social identities for well over a century. While in pre-colonial Rwanda, the three social groups – Hutu, Tutsi, and Twa – were not ethnic or racial groups in the modern sense, as they lived interspersed throughout the territory and shared a common language, the monarchy increasingly solidified and politicized group identity as it sought to consolidate rule.[9] Court histories simultaneously emphasized both the unity of the Rwandan people and the distinctions between the three groups, noting the superiority of the Tutsi who served as agents of the monarchy.[10] The distinction between the three groups was essential to German and Belgian colonial rule, as they concentrated power and opportunity in the hands of the Tutsi and required Hutu to labor and pay special taxes from which Tutsi were exempt. The system of indirect rule was based on a "mythico-history," developed in large part by Catholic missionaries and Rwandan priests, that traced Rwanda's three groups to distinct waves of migration and conquest and treated each as a part of a distinct racial group.[11] As Alison Des Forges wrote, "In a great and unsung collaborative enterprise over a period of decades, European and Rwandan intellectuals created a history that fit European assumptions and accorded with Tutsi interests."[12] This history justified Tutsi rule because of their supposed violent conquest.

When Hutu organized in the late 1950s and early 1960s to challenge Tutsi domination, they did not question the racialized history but instead used it to justify Hutu rising up to throw off supposed centuries of Tutsi oppression.[13] A 1959 *jacquerie* targeted Tutsi chiefs, burning homes and driving many elite Tutsi into exile, but over the next several years, the idea promoted by the new Hutu government that Tutsi were historic oppressors and that Rwanda was now a Hutu nation justified increasingly bloody attacks that left thousands of Tutsi dead and drove thousands more into exile.[14] The regime of President Grégoire Kayibanda established few concrete sites of memory – the Revolution of 1959 was commemorated annually as a holiday, and the deposition of the Tutsi king in 1961 was memorialized with a monument in Gitarama, the hometown of President Kayibanda. Nevertheless, memories of Tutsi repression of Hutu and the idea that the regime was carrying out the revolutionary empowerment of Hutu were central to official rhetoric, even after ethnic violence stopped in the late 1960s. Another wave of destabilizing anti-Tutsi attacks was one factor that inspired a 1973 military coup. After seizing power, military chief Juvénal Habyarimana promised to bring an end to Rwanda's ethnic conflict and instituted an ethnic quote to appease Hutu sentiments.[15]

For over a decade, the Habyarimana government eschewed the ethnic rhetoric favored by the first post-independence regime, focusing instead on economic development. Rwanda successfully attracted significant international assistance to fund projects like tea and pyrethrum plantations, allowing the economy to grow steadily. Yet ethnic tensions did not disappear. Habyarimana instituted an ethnic quota system that limited Tutsi enrollment in schools and other institutions to 10%, their share of the population, ostensibly to appease Hutu anger over continuing Tutsi economic and social dominance (the justification for the 1973 ethnic violence). But in practice, the quotas singled out Tutsi, with public institutions required to identify students or employees by ethnicity. Schools continued to teach the colonial-era history that mistakenly attributed Rwanda's ethnic difference to migration but with new discussions that portrayed the Tutsi as historic exploiters of Hutu. Tutsi who attended school in the 1970s and 1980s tell of being forced to stand up and identify themselves while teachers talked about how evil the Tutsi were.[16]

By the late 1980s, a sharp economic downturn and growing resentment of the one-party regime's authoritarian practices led to calls for reform. In 1990, international pressures combined with both an internal pro-democracy

60   *Timothy Longman*

movement and an RPF attack on Rwanda to push the government to accept political reforms, including allowing opposition political parties in 1991 and establishing a multi-party government in 1992. At the same time, Habyarimana and his backers sought to undermine these reforms and regain the support of the Hutu majority by promulgating an ideology that portrayed the Tutsi as the historic oppressors of the Hutu. The anti-Tutsi ideology claimed that Tutsi were outsiders who had conquered Rwanda several centuries earlier and then exploited the population for their own power and gain. The Hutu ethno-nationalists formed a right-wing political party, the Coalition for the Defense of the Republic (CDR), and organized youth from both the CDR and Habyarimana's party into militia groups charged with defending Rwanda from the RPF, whom they claimed sought to reimpose Tutsi control over the Hutu. The extremists used the ongoing violence of the RPF invasion to demonstrate the proof of the claims in their ideology that Tutsi were violent by nature. Periodic small-scale massacres of Tutsi and some moderate Hutu from 1990 to 1993 helped to polarize the population and set the groundwork for more widespread violence later.[17]

In August 1993, the Government of Rwanda signed the Arusha Peace Accord with the RPF that would end the civil war, allow the repatriation of Tutsi refugees, bring the RPF into government, and integrate RPF military personnel into the Rwandan army. Hutu extremists portrayed the accord as a sell-out to the RPF and used its unpopularity to feed anti-Tutsi sentiments and tarnish moderate opposition politicians as traitors to Hutu interests. Using tools like the new Radio Television des Milles Collines (RTLM) to disseminate their message, extremists portrayed Tutsi in Rwanda as allies of the RPF, and with a peace accord in place, many Tutsi did feel free to show public support for the RPF. When Burundi's first popularly elected Hutu president was assassinated in October 1993 by Tutsi troops, extremists used the event to reinforce claims that Tutsi have always oppressed Hutu and will never allow Hutu to succeed. While not all Hutu embraced this anti-Tutsi ideology, it nevertheless served to emphasize Rwanda's ethnic divisions and singled out Tutsi as a legitimate target for Hutu anger and violence. Few Rwandans questioned the false idea that Tutsi and Hutu had historically always been distinct and antagonistic groups.[18]

The campaign to use anti-Tutsi mobilization to consolidate the power of Hutu extremists culminated in an almost unthinkable wave of brutal violence in 1994. When President Habyarimana's plane was shot down on April 6, his death served as pretext for elite troops and militia groups to hunt down those perceived as regime opponents – journalists, human rights activists, moderate Hutu politicians, and prominent Tutsi. Minor instances of anti-Tutsi violence flared in some parts of the country, but for the first few days, violence was concentrated in the capital and was more political than ethnic in nature. In the struggle to succeed Habyarimana, however, extremists used the expansion of anti-Tutsi violence to push aside more moderate Hutu leaders and consolidate their hold on power. The extremists urged their supporters throughout the country to target Tutsi civilians in the name of "self-defense." As anti-Tutsi violence spread, the RPF relaunched its attack on the country, and the Hutu extremists used the renewed war once again to reinforce the idea that Tutsi were historic invaders of Rwanda. This time, the appeal to history was used to justify a final solution to the Tutsi "problem," by eliminating them once and for all from Rwandan territory.[19]

Rwanda's new government systematically spread genocide against the Tutsi throughout Rwanda. In Habyarmiana's home region in the north, local officials and their militia supporters willingly organized to murder their Tutsi neighbors. In regions in south and central Rwanda where support for the regime was weak, the government intervened to push compliance with the genocidal program, removing resistant officials and sending in presidential guards and other troops to initiate the killing. A similar mode of violence was used throughout the country. Officials first encouraged Tutsi to gather in central locations like churches and schools with promises of protection. Once most local Tutsi were gathered, soldiers or police shot into the crowd or threw grenades and militia groups then followed up, killing Tutsi men, women, and children with machetes, knives, and other weapons. The killing was such a difficult and brutal process that it often took several days. After the large-scale massacres were carried out by militia groups, local officials organized the entire community to participate in efforts to hunt down survivors with roadblocks and patrols. Hutu who resisted the genocide or sheltered Tutsi were fined, beaten, or killed, sending a message to everyone else that they should join in the genocide or step aside. By the time genocide ended in July 1994, the death squads had killed over 500,000 Tutsi and moderate Hutu.[20]

Initial scholarly analysis emphasized the significance of ideology in driving the genocide. The idea that Tutsi had a history of conquest and repression of Hutu was widely disseminated by government officials, RTLM, and other sources in an attempt to motivate people to hate Tutsi and participate in the killing.[21] Later research into the motivations of those who participated has questioned the primacy of hatred driven by ideology, arguing instead that participation was motivated by fear, social connections, and other factors.[22] But the ideology remained influential in a number of key ways. Despite its inaccuracy, almost no one in Rwanda challenged the narrative that treated Tutsi and Hutu as fully distinct ethnic groups, and the idea of ethnic differentiation was essential to identifying the target for violence. In my own research both prior to and immediately after the genocide, I found that the majority of the populations in communities that I studied in Central and Southern Rwanda were not moved by the ideology to hate Tutsi. They knew the official history of Tutsi migration, conquest, and oppression, but they also had lived in close proximity to Tutsi neighbors and many had Tutsi family members. Their own experience contradicted the idea that all Tutsi were by nature evil. But some local Hutu elites who found their power being challenged in the new democratic context of the early 1990s fully embraced the anti-Tutsi ideology, blaming Tutsi for what they saw as the country's poverty and insecurity. Some whose mixed ethnic background made them suspect also embraced the ideology to deflect attention from their

62 Timothy Longman

own questionable origins. While many of the foot soldiers of the genocide, the youths and poor farmers who were pushed to kill their neighbors, may not have been driven by hatred, the elite who organized the genocide often accepted the idea that Tutsi were foreign exploiters and acted out of hatred.[23]

The RPF and the Memorialization of the Genocide Against the Tutsi

The RPF was founded by refugees in Uganda who had been involved in the National Resistance Movement that brought Yoweri Museveni to power in 1986. While Tutsi refugees in Burundi and the Democratic Republic of Congo (DRC) were mostly integrated into existing communities, most Tutsi in Uganda lived in refugee camps, where they faced economic hardship and political harassment.[24] The Rwandan community in the camps cultivated a memory of Rwanda as a place whose harmony and promise were disturbed by colonialism. According to this account, Catholic missionaries invented the distinction between Hutu and Tutsi and then organized Hutu elite to rise up against the chiefs in 1959, while Belgian colonial authorities supported the Hutu rise to power in order to ensure their continued domination over Rwanda even after independence. This memory of Rwanda as a proverbial land of milk and honey together with anger at European responsibility for Tutsi persecution and exile drove refugees to join the RPF and has shaped RPF perceptions and actions ever since.[25]

The democracy movement and anti-government protests that emerged in Rwanda in early 1990 led the RPF to believe that the Habyarimana government was vulnerable to collapse. They invaded Rwanda on October 1, 1990, thinking that they could easily topple the regime, but their initial attack on northern Rwanda proved disastrous; the leader of the RPF, Fred Rwigyema, was killed on the second day of fighting, and Belgian, French, and Congolese troops arrived to bolster the regime in Kigali. Over the next several years, however, the RPF launched increasingly successful attacks on Rwanda, gradually occupying territory along Rwanda's border with Uganda. Tutsi from throughout the region came to join the RPF, including Tutsi who left Rwanda in reaction to the expanding anti-Tutsi rhetoric and violence. Between 1990 and 1993, a pattern emerged where RPF attacks were used by regime supporters to justify attacks on Tutsi within Rwanda, while those massacres of Tutsi civilians inspired additional attacks by the RPF. After a particularly brutal massacre of Tutsi civilians in northwest Rwanda in January 1993, the RPF launched a massive assault on Rwanda on February 7, 1993, occupying a large part of the country's north and displacing over one million people.[26]

After the Arusha Peace Accords were signed in August 1993, the United Nations established a mission for Rwanda to oversee the political transition, and a contingent of 500 RPF troops took up a position in Kigali. The party responsible for firing the missile that brought down Habyarimana's plane on April 6, 1994, remains a topic of intense debate. While initially, most observers believed Habyarimana's own troops shot down his plane as a pretext for launching the genocide, evidence over time has pointed increasingly to the RPF troops stationed in Kigali.[27] Since the president's assassination served as justification for Hutu extremists to launch their attacks, many scholars have considered the attribution of responsibility important to assigning blame for the genocide. According to this line of thinking, if the extremists themselves downed the plane, then their motives for violence were purely cynical. If on the other hand the RPF shot down the plane, it is argued, then their own actions helped drive the genocide, undermining their claims as heroes who stopped the genocide.[28] From my own perspective, the fixation on responsibility for the crash distracts from the fact that although the RPF's actions since 1990 had served as justification for anti-Tutsi violence, Hutu extremists alone bear the responsibility for the attacks that targeted not only those who could be viewed as potential combatants but also women, children, and the elderly. No matter who shot down the plane, the brutality of this genocide cannot be justified.

Hutu extremists launched their attack against moderate Hutu and Tutsi almost immediately after Habyarimana's death, and a day later, on April 8, 1994, the RPF renewed its assault on Rwanda. The RPF troops stationed in Kigali attacked government troops in what became a months-long siege of Kigali, while other RPF troops swiftly moved from their base in Northern Rwanda south and east to occupy the prefectures of Byumba and Kibungo and then moved west through the Bugesera region of Kigali-Rural toward Gitarama and Butare. The organizers of the genocide evoked the RPF's invasion, along with their purported assassination of President Habyarimana, to attract participants to their violent program. They appealed to the historical memory of Tutsi conquest and occupation to stoke fear in the population, using recent RPF violence as evidence of a Tutsi predilection for violence.[29]

While the genocide may have been a successful strategy for rallying support for the regime, it proved a terrible military strategy. The campaign against supposed internal enemies was so disruptive and diverted so many resources and military personnel away from defending the territory from the actual invading army that the RPF was able to occupy territory swiftly. Just a week after the conflict began, the government fled Kigali for the regional capital of Gitarama. The RPF occupied Byumba and Kibungo by the end of April, took Kigali-Rural in May, and drove the government from Gitarama to Gisenyi in June, before driving the genocidal regime entirely from the country in July. After capturing Kigali on July 4, the RPF declared victory only on July 18, 1994.[30]

As the RPF marched rapidly across Rwanda in April, they encountered the bodies of fellow Tutsi killed so recently that their killers had not had time to bury them before fleeing. In places occupied later by the RPF, bodies were not on display, but the rebels found numerous mass graves. Although it has gained little international attention, the RPF engaged in its own violence as it took over Rwanda. While this violence was not as systematic, extensive, or brutal as the genocide, the RPF nevertheless killed tens of thousands of civilians

64   *Timothy Longman*

between April and August 1994. In some communities, RPF troops opened fire on anyone they found, believing all remaining people to have participated in the genocide, even if most of the actual perpetrators had fled from Rwanda into Tanzania or the Democratic Republic of Congo. In many other cases, the RPF rounded up residents and either asked the crowd to identify those implicated in the genocide and took them away to be killed or simply pulled all of the young men aside and summarily executed them.[31]

After taking control of Rwanda, the RPF named a multi-party government loosely based on the model of the Arusha Accords. They named as prime minister a moderate Hutu from one of the parties that had opposed Habyarimana and as president a Hutu who had joined the RPF in exile. The RPF talked about reconciliation and national unity, which helped to attract considerable international assistance to the effort to rebuild the country. At the same time, the RPF retained actual control of the country and continued to use force to command the population. Numerous disappearances and summary executions continued. In March 1995, the most widely publicized act of RPF violence took place when efforts to shut down a camp of internally displaced people at Kibeho ended in the death of several thousand people. After a year in office, five of the Hutu members of the government, including the prime minister, quit in frustration over their lack of real power.[32]

The RPF maintained its pretense of shared power and national unity even as it continued to use extensive force. The genocide served as a centering idea for the regime's actions. The new government preserved a number of major massacre sites, including several churches, as memorials. The regime made clear a commitment to seeking accountability for genocide crimes, calling on the United Nations to create an international court for Rwanda[33] and beginning a process of prosecuting people inside Rwanda. Although most of the main perpetrators of the genocide fled as the RPF advanced, the government began a program in late 1994 of arresting thousands of suspects on genocide charges, often with almost no evidence. By the beginning of 1999, 126,000 people were in prison on genocide charges.[34] In 1996, citing security concerns posed by refugee camps just across the border where the remnants of the genocidal army and militias continued to operate, the RPF and its Ugandan allies organized an invasion of the DRC (then known as Zaire), forcibly closed the camps, hunted down and killed Rwandans who objected to returning to Rwanda, then advanced across the country and installed a sympathetic government in Kinshasa. The closure of the camps inadvertently drove Hutu rebels into Rwanda, leading to an insurgency and bloody repression in Rwanda's northwest in 1997.[35] When relations with the new Congolese government soured, the RPF and Uganda organized another invasion of the DRC in August 1998, justifying their actions this time as both a reaction to renewed Hutu security threats and an attempt to save Congolese Tutsi from violence. The Second Congo War fell into a stalemate that lasted for five years and left the DRC devastated, resulting in hundreds of thousands of deaths.[36] As I discuss in the next section, despite this extensive use of violence, the RPF has maintained widespread international support.

Memorializing Violence as a Political Tool   65

Figure 3.1 Entrance to the Ntarama Church Genocide Memorial
Source: Credit – Photo courtesy of Timothy Longman

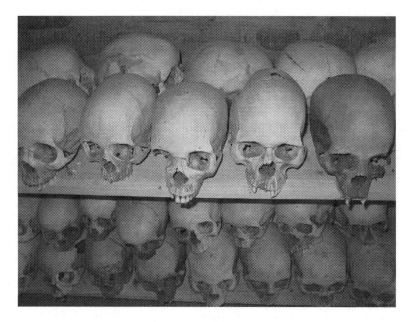

Figure 3.2 Skulls of genocide victims on display at the Ntarama Church Genocide Memorial
Source: Credit – Photo courtesy of Timothy Longman

66   Timothy Longman

In 2000, the RPF replaced the president, prime minister, and parliamentary speaker and took full, direct control of government. Paul Kagame, the RPF leader, defense minister, and vice-president who was long seen as the country's real power, became president and instituted a major shift in governance. He instituted an ambitious plan, *Vision 2020*, to transform Rwanda into a middle-income economy in 20 years. The plan to develop Rwanda into a high-tech information economy on the model of Singapore included a commitment to dealing with Rwanda's violent past and creating national unity as a basis for growth.[37]

To deal with the legacies of the 1994 genocide, the government implemented extensive programs for accountability, memorialization, and re-education. With more people in prison than the existing judicial system could process, the government created a new court system based loosely on a traditional dispute resolution system known as *gacaca* to prosecute all but the most serious genocide crimes. The new gacaca courts involved thousands of non-professional judges gathered in communities throughout the country to identify victims and judge the perpetrators of the genocide. Although the initial primary goal was to speed up the processing of prisoners, the government soon attached to gacaca many other goals associated with transitional justice, such as promoting reconciliation, creating a transcript of the past, helping survivors move on, and encouraging communities to discuss the past. National leaders likened gacaca to South Africa's Truth and Reconciliation Commission as a form of restorative justice. As numerous scholars have pointed out, however, despite their grassroots nature, the gacaca courts served the interests of the state in exerting control over the population. Between 2003 and 2012, over 1.8 million cases were tried, involving 1.1 million individuals accused, with a guilty rate of over 80%. Those found guilty faced a combination of prison time and forced public labor, much of which consisted of work camps used to build roads and sidewalks and gardens in Kigali. Gacaca courts were prohibited from talking about RPF violence, focusing exclusively on the genocide.[38]

The government initiated a wide range of programs alongside the legal proceedings to shape the national narrative of the past. The National Unity and Reconciliation Commission (NURC) and National Commission for Human Rights were charged with promoting unity and human rights within Rwanda, but much of their work focused on the genocide. A National Commission for the Fight Against Genocide was created a few years later to focus on identifying genocide ideology. Both the genocide commission and the human rights commission have focused mostly on targeting critics of the current regime, equating criticism of the current government with genocide denial. The NURC has had more extensive programs, including creating camps, known as *Ingando* (later developed into a program called *Itorero*), where returned Hutu refugees, released prisoners, university students, newly elected government officials, and others were taught the government's official interpretation of Rwandan history and pressured to support the government's program of national unity. The official history taught at both the Ingando and in civics classes in schools was based on a revised reading of the past, shaped by the political interests of the new rulers. The history emphasized the historic unity of the Rwandan people, the imposition of ethnic differences on Rwandans by colonial rulers, the tragedy and horror of the genocide, and the role of the RPF as the heroes who stopped the genocide and now are seeking to unify and develop Rwanda.[39]

Memorialization and commemoration have also been important parts of government programs to shape public memory. After the shift to direct RPF control in 2000, the national government centralized control over the mass graves and other memorials to the genocide that had existed in many communities since 1994. The government recognized six official national memorial sites, and local and regional governments authorized a small number of additional approved memorials, transferring remains of genocide victims from numerous smaller sites to the larger approved sites. A British NGO, Aegis Trust, worked with the government and official survivors' groups to build the Kigali Genocide Memorial, which opened in 2004 on the tenth anniversary of the genocide. Informed by modern museum practices, particularly Holocaust museums, the Kigali Genocide Memorial includes a historical narrative of Rwandan history, culminating in the genocide, several art installations, including an iconic room of victims' photos, and a mass grave in an open crypt.[40] Aegis Trust has also supported the government's efforts to create a national Genocide Archive of Rwanda that has collected testimonies of genocide survivors and gathered photographs, videos, and other documentation of the genocide and post-genocide reconciliation programs, both online and at the Kigali Genocide Memorial, representing an important international partnership to promote the RPF's official memory program.[41]

In addition to the memorials, the government has created several official commemorations that seek to shape public memory. July 5 is Liberation Day, commemorating the day the RPF took control of Kigali. February 1 is National Heroes' Day, which is "an annual event organized to pay tribute to the people who exemplified and defended the highest values of patriotism and sacrifice for the wellbeing of the country and its citizens."[42] This event focuses on Hutu who lost their lives protecting Tutsi or standing against the genocide, like Agathe Uwilingiyimana, the moderate prime minister who was killed on the first day of the genocide, and prominent historical figures (all of whom, it is worth noting, are Tutsi), like King Rudahigwa, the Rwandan king who reigned for much of the nineteenth century, and Fred Rwigyema, the RPF leader who died at the beginning of the civil war.[43]

The most important annual commemoration is Genocide Against the Tutsi Memorial Day, celebrated on April 7, the official holiday that kicks off Rwanda's Week of Mourning. Each year on April 7, a large national commemoration of the genocide is held, attended by most of Rwanda's government, international diplomats, and other important Rwandans and expatriates. In addition to the national commemoration, communities throughout Rwanda hold a commemoration either on April 7 or that week, and a range of other commemorative activities also happen during the Week of Mourning, like reburials

68   Timothy Longman

and dedications of memorials. While the local commemorations were initially sporadic and drew crowds of mostly community leaders and survivors, over time commemoration has become more regularized and universal. Every community in Rwanda now holds a genocide commemoration, and local officials take attendance to ensure that all community members participate. As one individual told me in a 2015 interview:

> The participation of the population is an obligation. Only, they don't say that it is an obligation. If you are absent, you could be considered as someone who rebels against the policies of the government. If you don't go, it's not that there are punishments laid out by the law. If you are sick and you decide not to go, you will not be well looked at by the authorities. If they find you busy playing music at home, or if you are in a bar having a glass to drink, that situation is not allowed. If you don't participate in the discussions organized during this national Week of Mourning, you are at risk of being punished, even if there's not a law.[44]

The obligatory participation in annual genocide commemorations suggests the degree to which the government of Rwanda uses a heavy hand in its efforts to shape public memory about the country's violent past. The activities of the various commissions, the gacaca and other trials, the Ingando re-education camps, memorials, and official commemorations all promote a narrative that portrays pre-colonial Rwanda as unified and peaceful, colonialism as having invented the Hutu–Tutsi divide, the genocide as the culmination of colonial-era divisions and ongoing international manipulations, and the RPF as a heroic movement that ended the genocide and seeks only the unity and development of the country. None of these sites of memory allows space for conversation about RPF violence; instead, they treat discussion of RPF abuses as genocide denial.[45]

The government's effort to retain tight control on public memory limits even the ability of Tutsi genocide survivors to narrate their own experiences. In the aftermath of the genocide, survivors formed numerous organizations around the country, and in 1998, a national umbrella group, Ibuka (which means remember in Kinyarwanda), formed to serve as a collective voice for survivors. In 1999, when the group began to criticize the government for failing sufficiently to support survivors, one founding leader of the group was assassinated, and several others fled the country. The government put in a member of the RPF central committee, who had been outside Rwanda in 1994, as leader, and since 2000, Ibuka has served more to defuse tensions between survivors and the government than to independently represent survivor interests. This corporatist role for Ibuka is evident in conflicts over genocide memorials, where survivors have objected to having the remains of their loved ones on public display. Ibuka, which has served as the voice of survivors in the memorialization process, has defended the interests of the state in displaying remains of genocide victims but tried to find a compromise, where bodies in several sites are buried in underground crypts that are nevertheless open for people to enter. In

Several sites, families that have been able to identify the specific remains of their loved ones have been able to put their cadavers in coffins within the crypts. Yet survivors are not allowed to bury their family members' remains elsewhere, as the government insists that the bodies of genocide victims be kept in official locations.[46]

The use of memorials and commemorations and other sites of memory as tools to promote the government's official interpretation of the past is well demonstrated. When I asked the National Director of Memorials why bodies were being displayed at memorial sites, despite objections from survivors and Rwandan traditions of burying bodies on their own land, he responded, "Rwanda does not have a tradition of genocide either!"[47] He went on to explain that the display of bodies at the memorials helps to demonstrate that genocide happened. Yet the evidence to prove this point is clearly manipulated, as many of the bodies now on display at memorial sites are not from those locations and may not all be genocide victims. The city government in Kigali has required that the remains of all genocide victims in Kigali be consolidated at the Kigali Genocide Memorial. According to the memorial's website, "more than 250,000 victims of the Genocide against the Tutsi have been buried at the memorial."[48] Yet since the population of Kigali at the last official census in 1991 was 237,782 and less than half of those were Tutsi,[49] all of the bodies buried at the memorial cannot possibly be victims of the genocide. The memorial is being used to make a political point, and anyone who chooses to challenge that message or the way that it is being expressed is denounced as denying the genocide. As if to emphasize the coercive nature of Rwanda's memory project, President Kagame has regularly used the annual genocide commemoration to give a harsh speech, in Kinyarwanda, denouncing critics of his government and calling for severe punishment for those who might challenge the official interpretation of the past and divide Rwanda.

Memorializing Rwanda's Genocide for the International Community

While the government of Rwanda's efforts to promote an official public memory about Rwanda's past seeks in part to transform Rwanda's population, influencing the international community is also a major focus. The genocide against the Tutsi did not immediately garner widespread international attention, despite its extraordinary extent and brutality. Rwanda's previous episodes of violence from 1959–1965 and its 1990–1993 civil war had drawn very limited international attention. For the general public, particularly in the United States, Rwanda was still best known in the years after the genocide as the place where Dian Fossey studied gorillas, a story made famous by the movie *Gorillas in the Mist*.[50] When I first gave talks about Rwanda just after the genocide, I inevitably got the question, "What about the gorillas?"

A concerted public relations effort by the RPF helped to create popular media interest that served to propel Rwanda into an international spotlight.

70   *Timothy Longman*

Johan Pottier shows how even before they took power, the RPF sought to shape international images of their movement and of Rwanda. Throughout the civil war, the RPF posted representatives in Washington, London, and Brussels, who cultivated ties with both diplomats and the media. As Kagame himself said, "We knew how the media works."[51] When the RPF took power, they very effectively promoted a sense of guilt in diplomatic circles for the failure of the world to intervene and in the international media for their failure to cover Rwanda. The RPF encouraged an exclusive focus on the genocide, presenting its own violence as morally justified and necessary to re-establish order after the ethnic slaughter. As Pottier explains, "Rwanda was now imagined as a place where every set-back could be explained exclusively in terms of international indifference."[52]

The RPF successfully courted international supporters to help shape the international narrative about the genocide and about the RPF. The non-governmental organization African Rights, led by Somali human rights researcher Rakiya Omaar, published a report on the genocide in 1995 that detailed the genocide throughout the country. As Rwandans told me at the time, Omar worked closely with officials in the RPF who supplied her with some of the research, which was of questionable validity.[53] The book, which entirely ignored RPF abuses, was highly influential in shaping discourse about the genocide. As Alison Des Forges, one of the most respected chroniclers of the genocide against the Tutsi, recounted to me, when she went to brief Clinton Administration officials about ongoing RPF violence in Rwanda in the late 1990s, Assistant Secretary of State for Africa Susan Rice waved a copy of African Rights' report and said, "You have to understand: There was a genocide here!"[54]

The RPF had a similar role in influencing Philip Gourevitch's book, *We Wish to Inform You That Tomorrow We Will Be Killed With Our Families.*[55] Gourevitch visited me at the Human Rights Watch office in Butare toward the end of the six months that he spent in Rwanda researching the book, and from my conversation with him, it became evident that the RPF had supported his work, including helping to provide translators. The book went on to become a bestseller and has been the entry point for many people to Rwanda. Like a number of others who have written on Rwanda, Gourevitch's approach to the genocide was shaped by ideas about the Holocaust, reflecting an effort by the RPF to link the two tragic events. While comparisons can be useful, the conflation of the Holocaust and the genocide against the Tutsi has distorted important differences, most importantly the fact that a largely Tutsi army was invading Rwanda as the genocide took place and then took control of the country at its conclusion.[56] A number of commercial films were released in the early 2000s that helped to draw considerable international attention to Rwanda, most notably *Hotel Rwanda.*[57] The films and books helped to reinforce in the international community the equation of Rwanda with genocide.

After the RPF took direct control of Rwanda in 2000, they became even more effective at shaping international understandings of Rwanda. Vision

2020's focus on developing Rwanda was appealing to many but so was its commitment to accountability and national unity. The RPF's visionary leadership and supposed magnanimous willingness to reconcile with the killers involved in the genocide were intentionally contrasted with the brutality of the genocide itself. Despite some criticism from human rights groups, the international community was largely supportive of gacaca. The official genocide memorial sites were developed in part to appeal to an international audience. In my research, I found that most of those who visited the sites were international travelers for whom a visit to genocide sites has become an obligatory part of any visit to Rwanda.[58] As one nun who had returned to Rwanda from the DRC after 1994 told me when I asked about the sites, "It helps to show those who said that there was no genocide what happened. It acts as a proof to the international community."[59]

The result of the RPF's effective shaping of international perceptions has been to deflect potential criticisms from their own actions and gain substantial international financial support. Focusing public memory on the genocide and diminishing the RPF's own violence as less widespread and less meaningful have protected the RPF from facing accountability for the violence it used to establish control over Rwanda and then repeatedly supporting intervention in the DRC. The RPF's repeated support for rebel groups in the DRC has created extraordinary insecurity in the region and arguably led to more deaths in Congo than in the 1994 genocide,[60] but the government has faced almost no consequences from the international community for its actions. Similarly, the government's very poor record on civil and political rights, which has included harassment and assassinations of opposition politicians, journalists, and civil society activists, has not led the international community to diminish its financial support for Rwanda's development programs. Instead, the regime has been quite effective at delegitimizing critics by accusing them of "genocide ideology." For example, when Paul Rusesabagina, the hero of the film *Hotel Rwanda*, began to use his fame as a platform to criticize the RPF's human rights abuses, the government and its supporters launched a campaign to deny his status as a hero. The campaign culminated in his kidnapping and extradition to Rwanda and a highly public trial in which he was found guilty of terrorism.[61] In my own work, I have repeatedly encountered development workers and government officials from Western countries who openly accept Rwanda's use of violence as necessary because of the history of genocide. While a few popular books have recently focused on the RPF's abuses,[62] they have not diverted international attention away from its focus on the genocide as the central event in Rwandan history that continues to justify RPF rule.

The Uses of Public Memory in Rwanda

In this chapter, I have argued that various governments in Rwanda have actively sought to shape public memory of Rwanda's past in order to justify their rule. During the colonial era, both the colonial administration and the Tutsi court

72 Timothy Longman

promoted the idea that the Tutsi were destined to rule, because they had conquered and subjugated the Hutu population. The post-independence Hutu governments justified their own rule by perpetuating the myth that the Tutsi had conquered and oppressed the Hutu. The manufactured memory of Tutsi violence, reinforced in the popular mind by the ongoing violence of the civil war between the RPF and the government, ultimately served to justify the genocide against the Tutsi.

Since taking power, the RPF has very effectively constructed public memory around the genocide while obscuring consideration of its own violence. The central memory of the genocide has been used to promote national unity within Rwanda and to justify the harsh tactics the RPF has used both domestically and in the region to maintain its control. The RPF has shaped public memory not only within Rwanda but even more effectively in the international community. By associating the genocide against the Tutsi with the Holocaust,[63] the RPF has successfully established its moral untouchability in the perception of many international observers. By portraying themselves as the good guys who stopped the genocide and playing on Western guilt for failing to act to stop the genocide, the RPF has been able to divert attention from its own extensive violence and attract substantial international financial support. Memory of the genocide remains central to the RPF's agenda, because it serves to justify almost any actions that the current regime might undertake.

Notes

1 The most extensive analysis of the genocide against the Tutsi in Rwanda is Alison Des Forges, *Leave None to Tell the Story: Genocide in Rwanda* (New York: Human Rights Watch and Paris: FIDH, 1999), for which I was a contributing author. See also Gerard Prunier, *The Rwanda Crisis*, 2nd ed. (New York: Columbia University Press, 1997), and André Guichaoua, *From War to Genocide: Criminal Politics in Rwanda, 1990–1994* (Madison, WI: University of Wisconsin Press, 2017).
2 OECD, *Geographical Distribution of Financial Flows to Developing Countries 2021: Disbursements, Commitments, Country Indicators* (Paris: OECD, 2021), p. 630, https:// read.oecd-ilibrary.org/development/geographical-distribution-of-financial-flows-to-developing-countries-2021_a50961e5-en-fr#page4.
3 David Himbara, "Kagame Regime Falsely Claimed That the 2019/20 Budget Proves Rwanda Is Achieving Financial Self-Reliance," *Medium.com*, June 15, 2019, https:// medium.com/@david.himbara_27884/kagame-regime-falsely-claimed-that-the-2019-20-budget-proves-rwanda-is-achieving-financial-bbc71b94ecc
4 Timothy Longman, *Memory and Justice in Post-Genocide Rwanda* (New York: Cambridge University Press, 2017).
5 See, for example, Benedict Anderson, *Imagined Communities: Reflections on the Origins and Spread of Nationalism* (London: Verso, 1999), on how elites crafted national identities through stories of shared origin.
6 Eric Hobsbawm and Terrence Rangers, eds., *The Invention of Tradition* (Cambridge: Cambridge University Press, 1992).
7 Terrence Ranger, "The Invention of Tradition in Colonial Africa," in Eric Hobsbawm and Terrence Rangers, eds., *The Invention of Africa* (Cambridge: Cambridge University Press, 1992), pp. 211–262; Leroy Vail, *The Creation of Tribalism in Africa* (Berkeley, CA: University of California Press, 1989).

Memorializing Violence as a Political Tool   73

8 Pierre Nora, ed., *Les Lieux de Mémoire* (Paris: Gallimard, 1984–1992).

9 Catharine Newbury, *The Cohesion of Oppression: Clientship and Ethnicity in Rwanda, 1860–1960* (New York: Columbia University Press, 1988); Jan Vansina, *Antecedents to Modern Rwanda: The Nyiginya Kingdom* (Madison, WI: University of Wisconsin Press, 2004).

10 The court histories were chronicled during the colonial era by Alexis Kagame, who recounted the division between Hutu, Tutsi, and Twa as part of Rwanda's foundation myths. See Alexis Kagame, *La Poésie Dynastique au Rwanda* (Brussels: Institute Royal du Congo Belge (IRCB), 1951).

11 Edith R. Sanders, "The Hamitic Hypothesis: Its Origin and Functions in Time Perspective," *Journal of African History*, Vol. 10, No. 4 (1969); Newbury, *The Cohesion of Oppression.* The term "mythico-history" is drawn from Liisa Malkki, *Purity and Exile: Violence, Memory and Cosmology among Hutu Refugees in Tanzania* (Chicago, IL: University of Chicago Press, 1995).

12 Alison Des Forges, "The Ideology of Genocide," *Issue: A Journal of Opinion*, Vol. 23, No. 2 (1995), pp. 44–47, citation pp. 44–45.

13 Ian Linden and Jane Linden, *Church and Revolution in Rwanda* (New York: Africana Publishing Company, 1977); René Lemarchand, *Rwanda and Burundi* (New York: Praeger Publishers, 1970).

14 Lemarchand, *Rwanda and Burundi.*

15 Filip Reyntjens, *Pouvoir et Droit au Rwanda: droit public et évolution politique, 1916–1973* (Tervuren: Musée Royale de l'Afrique Centrale, 1985).

16 On ethnic conflict in schools, see Elisabeth King, *From Classrooms to Conflict in Rwanda* (Cambridge: Cambridge University Press, 2013). On the Habyarimana regime more generally, see Marie-Eve Desrosiers, *Trajectories of Authoritarianism in Rwanda: Elusive Control before the Genocide* (New York: Cambridge University Press, 2023).

17 Des Forges, "The Ideology of Genocide," pp. 44–47; Des Forges, *Leave None to Tell the Story*, pp. 65–95; Prunier, *The Rwanda Crisis*, pp. 127–191; Jean-Paul Kimonyo, *Rwanda's Popular Genocide: A Perfect Storm* (Boulder, CO: Lynne Rienner Press, 2016), pp. 45–78.

18 Mahmood Mamdani, *When Victims Become Killers: Colonialism, Nativism, and the Genocide in Rwanda* (Princeton, NJ: Princeton University Press, 2001), studies how Hutu leaders exploited a sense of historic victimization among Hutu to justify violence against Tutsi.

19 André Guichaoua, *From War to Genocide in Rwanda* (Madison, WI: University of Wisconsin Press, 2015).

20 Des Forges, *Leave None to Tell the Story*, pp. 180–691.

21 Jean-Pierre Chrétien, ed., *Rwanda: Les Medias du Génocide* (Paris: Karthala, 1995); Des Forges, *Leave None to Tell the Story*, pp. 65–95.

22 Scott Straus, *The Order of Genocide: Race, Power, and War in Rwanda* (Ithaca, NY: Cornell University Press, 2006); Lee Ann Fujii, *Killing Neighbors: Webs of Violence in Rwanda* (Ithaca, NY: Cornell University Press, 2011).

23 I discuss popular attitudes in the build up to the genocide in Timothy Longman, *Christianity and Genocide in Rwanda* (New York: Cambridge University Press, 2009).

24 Michaela Wrong, *Do Not Disturb: The Story of a Political Murder and an African Regime Gone Bad* (New York: Public Affairs, 2021).

25 Malkki, *Purity and Exile*, demonstrates how among Burundian Hutu refugees, those in camps similarly maintained a strong mythico-history of their homeland while for those integrated into communities, memories of Burundi were less salient.

26 Prunier, *The Rwanda Crisis*, pp. 93–120; Wrong, *Do Not Disturb*, pp. 177–232.

27 Filip Reyntjens, *Rwanda, trois jour qui ont fait basculer l'histoire* (Paris: Harmattan, 1995).

28 Luc Reydams, "Politics or Pragmatism? The International Criminal Tribunal for Rwanda and the Burying of the Investigation Into the Assassination of President Juvénal Habyarimana," *Human Rights Quarterly*, Vol. 40, No. 4 (2018), pp. 989–1013; Henry Gombya, "Did RPF Kill Habyarimana?," *New African*, No. 386 (2000), p. 11.

74   Timothy Longman

29 Kimonyo, *Rwanda's Popular Genocide*; Mamdani, *When Victims Become Killers*.
30 Prunier, *The Rwanda Crisis*, pp. 268–335.
31 Des Forges, *Leave None to Tell the Story*, pp. 692–735; Prunier, *The Rwanda Crisis*, Chapter 10.
32 Judi Rever, *In Praise of Blood: The Crimes of the Rwandan Patriotic Front* (Toronto: Random House Canada, 2018); Anjan Sundaram, *Bad News: Last Journalists in a Dictatorship* (New York: Doubleday, 2016); Wrong, *Do Not Disturb*.
33 Although Rwanda called on the UN to create a court to prosecute the organizers of the genocide, Rwanda ultimately cast the sole vote against the resolution creating the International Criminal Tribunal for Rwanda, objecting to its lack of structural independence from the International Criminal Tribunal for the former Yugoslavia, its location outside Rwanda, and the failure to include the death penalty as a possible punishment. See Victor Peskin, *International Justice in Rwanda and the Balkans: Virtual Trials and the Struggle for State Cooperation* (Cambridge: Cambridge University Press, 2008).
34 Human Rights Watch, "Rwanda," *World Report 1999*.
35 Ibid.
36 Timothy Longman, "The Complex Reasons for Rwanda's Engagement in Congo," in John F. Clark, ed., *The Continental Stakes in the Congo War* (New York: Palgrave, 2002), pp. 129–144.
37 Jean-Paul Kimonyo, *Transforming Rwanda: Challenges on the Road to Reconstruction* (Boulder, CO: Lynne Rienner, 2019), pp. 203–230; An Ansoms and Donatella Rostagno, "Rwanda's Vision 2020 Halfway Through: What the Eye Does Not See," *Review of African Political Economy*, Vol. 39, No. 133 (2012), pp. 427–450.
38 Anuradha Chakravarty, *Investing in Authoritarian Rule: Punishment and Patronage in Rwanda's Gacaca Courts for Genocide Crimes* (New York: Cambridge University Press, 2016); Bert Ingelaere, *Inside Rwanda's Gacaca Courts: Seeking Justice After Genocide. Critical Human Rights* (Madison, WI: University of Wisconsin Press, 2016); Longman, *Memory and Justice in Post-Genocide Rwanda*, pp. 91–134.
39 Andrea Purdekova, *Making Ubumwe: Power, State and Camps in Rwanda's Unity-Building Project* (Studies in Forced Migration), Vol. 34 (New York: Berghahn Books, 2015); Susan Thomson, *Whispering Truth to Power: Everyday Resistance to Reconciliation in Post-Genocide Rwanda* (Madison, WI: University of Wisconsin Press, 2013).
40 Longman, *Memory and Justice in Post-Genocide Rwanda*.
41 Caroline Williamson Sinalo, *Rwanda Africa Genocide: Gender Identity and Post-Traumatic Growth* (Cambridge: Cambridge University Press, 2018).
42 Edwin Ashimwe, "Rwandan Heroes Celebrated Virtually," *The New Times*, February 1, 2021, https://www.newtimes.co.rw/article/183686/News/video-rwandan-heroes-celebrated-virtually Interestingly, the description quoted here in Rwanda's leading pro-government paper is a word for word copy of the Ugandan government's official description of Uganda's Heroes' Day. See Government of Uganda, *Press Statement for Heroes Day 2019*, June 9, 2019, www.gcic.go.ug/press-statement-for-heroes-day-celebrations-2019/.
43 Ashimwe, "Rwandan Heroes Celebrated Virtually."
44 Interview in Western Province, May 10, 2015. Quoted in Longman, *Memory and Justice in Post-Genocide Rwanda*, p. 264.
45 In Longman, *Memory and Justice in Post-Genocide Rwanda*, pp. 65–90, 135–186, I discuss in greater depth the coercive nature of the official memory project in post-genocide Rwanda.
46 Ibid.
47 Interview in Kigali, June 2003.
48 Kigali Genocide Memorial, https://kgm.rw/memorial/burial-place-gardens/.
49 Service National de Récensement, *Récensement général de la population et de l'habitat au 15 Août 1991* (Kigali: Government of Rwanda, 1991), p. 11.
50 *Gorillas in the Mist*, directed by Michael Apted, 1988.

Memorializing Violence as a Political Tool   75

51 Johann Pottier, *Re-Imagining Rwanda: Conflict, Survival and Disinformation in the Late Twentieth Century* (Cambridge: Cambridge University Press, 2002), quotation p. 90.
52 Ibid, p. 81.
53 Rakiya Omaar, *Rwanda: Death, Despair and Defiance* (London: African Rights, 1995). In a controversial article, Luc Reydams accuses Omaar of pro-RPF bias that influenced the narrative in *Death, Despair and Defiance*. Luc Reydams, "NGO Justice: African Rights as Pseudo-Protector of the Rwandan Genocide," *Human Rights Quarterly*, Vol. 38, No. 3 (2016), pp. 547–588.
54 Personal communication, 1999.
55 Philip Gourevitch, *We Wish to Inform You That Tomorrow We Will Be Killed with Our Families* (New York: Picador, 1998).
56 On differences between the Holocaust and the Rwandan genocide, see René Lemarchand, "Disconnecting the Threads: Rwanda and the Holocaust Reconsidered," *Journal of Genocide Research*, Vol. 4, No. 4 (2002), pp. 499–518.
57 *Hotel Rwanda*, directed by Terry George, 2004. Also see *Shooting Dogs*, directed by Michael Caton-Jones, 2005, and *Sometimes in April*, directed by Raoul Peck, 2005.
58 Longman, *Memory and Justice in Post-Genocide Rwanda*, pp. 65–90. See also, Annette Becker, "Dark Tourism: The 'Heritagization' of Sites of Suffering, with an Emphasis on Memorials to the Genocide Perpetrated against the Tutsi of Rwanda," *International Review of the Red Cross*, Vol. 101, No. 910 (2019), pp. 317–331.
59 Interview in Butare, June 10, 2002, in French. All translations from French to English by the author.
60 Benjamin Coghlan, Richard J. Brennan, Pascal Ngoy, David Dofara, Brad Otto, Mark Clements, and Tony Stewart, "Mortality in the Democratic Republic of Congo: A Nationwide Survey," *The Lancet*, Vol. 367, No. 9504 (2006), pp. 44–51, contends that the second Congo war led to 3.9 million deaths, most not directly from combat but from malnutrition and lack of access to healthcare.
61 "Hotel Rwanda Hero Paul Rusesabagina Convicted on Terrorism Charges," *BBC News*, September 20, 2021, www.bbc.com/news/world-africa-58624691.
62 Wrong, *Do Not Disturb*; Rever, *In Praise of Blood*; Sundaram, *Bad News*.
63 The Rwandan government has strengthened its ties with Israel, reinforcing the linkages between the Holocaust and Rwanda's 1994 genocide. Rina Bassist, "Israel, Rwanda Build Ties on Shared Experience of Genocide," *AL-Monitor*, April 7, 2014, https://www.al-monitor.com/originals/2014/04/israel-rwanda-bilateral-relations-holocaust-genocide.html

Part II
Slavery

4 From Rumblings to Roar

Racial Violence, Historical Justice, and the Changing Public History of Slavery in the United States

Renee C. Romano

In 2017, after years of student and community protest, Yale University finally renamed Calhoun College, one of its then 12 residential colleges. Opened in 1933, Calhoun College was named in honor of Yale graduate John C. Calhoun, a man who had served as US senator, as Secretary of State, and as vice president under both John Quincy Adams and Andrew Jackson. The South Carolinian also emphatically defended slavery in the 1830s and 1840s, making the case that slavery was a "positive good" that benefitted both slaveowners and the enslaved.

Students had been protesting against the college's name since at least the early 1990s, when a group of Calhoun residents demanded that the college remove a stained glass window showing an enslaved man kneeling at Calhoun's feet. But a chain of events starting in 2014 – the police murder of unarmed Black teenager Michael Brown, the 2015 massacre of nine people at a prayer meeting at the African Methodist Episcopal Church in Charleston, and the emergence of the Black Lives Matter movement to protest the seemingly daily killings of Black Americans by the police – gave new urgency and momentum to the struggle at Yale.[1] After 2015, the discussions over Calhoun "turned to urgent pleas," the *Washington Post* reported. As the *New York Times* described it, in the wake of the church massacre in Calhoun's native South Carolina, "the rumblings at Yale demanding removal became a roar."[2]

Yale is not the only site where "rumblings" to rethink American public history and memory of slavery have become a roar as a result of the charged politics around contemporary racial violence. Since 2015, activists, local, and state governments have taken down more than 200 monuments to the Confederacy. Plantation tourist sites that have long promoted a mythic nostalgic portrait of a romanticized Old South have faced new pressures to publicly acknowledge their histories of slavery. Historians, curators, and educators who gathered at James Madison's Montpelier for the 2019 National Summit on Teaching Slavery insisted that public history sites must do more to promote an understanding of slavery and its legacies in order to counter contemporary racial violence. When Americans failed to "tell the truth about race and slavery," they argued, it was "experienced tragically violently, and fatally in Ferguson, Charlottesville, Charleston, and places in between." The gift shop at George Washington's

DOI: 10.4324/9781003217848-7

80   *Renee C. Romano*

Mount Vernon even stopped selling souvenir magnets of Washington's dentures – dentures that had been made from the teeth of his enslaved workers – after scholar Ana Lucia Araujo wrote about the macabre souvenir on Twitter in 2020.[3]

This chapter draws on media reports, marketing material, web sources, and recent scholarship to explore both the current state of the public history of slavery in the United States and the challenges of telling the truth about slavery and its legacies.[4] It seeks to add to an ongoing conversation by focusing on the question of *why* recent racial violence has triggered such momentum to change the way public history sites deal with slavery. That question, I contend, demands that we contextualize debates about slavery within a politics of historical justice that emerged long before 2015. It also explores the changes in public history inspired by the current political movement through the lens of historical justice. While this brief chapter can discuss only a small sample of the ongoing work, it argues that current interventions fall into one of three categories: battles to dismantle pro-slavery narratives and monuments; efforts to recuperate and mark erased or obliterated sites of slavery; and most challenging of all, imaginative work to construct and communicate new narratives of US history that acknowledge the centrality of slavery and its legacies to the American story. These three core projects – delegitimizing historical narratives and symbols that feed division and support violence; honoring and marking the perspective and lived experience of victims of injustice; and crafting new ways of understanding the past that offer clarity about its relationship to the present – represent the key interventions that advocates of historical repair believe are necessary to confront social divisions and build a more equitable future.

Exploring contemporary debates about slavery and public history within the broader frame of historical justice helps us better understand the energy and urgency of the current moment. It also helps explain why public history sites have been called on not just to participate but to be leaders, in the fight for social justice.

The Politics of Historical Justice: A Longer View

Public history representations of slavery began to change well before the killing of Michael Brown or the massacre at the AME Emanuel Church. In the 1970s, Black nationalists who saw Black history as a way to build pride and group identity began building small museums that included material on the Middle Passage and slave revolts. The first Underground Railroad Reenactment, conceived by Black nationalist Kamau Kambui as a way to build character and instill racial pride among Black urban youths, was held in Minnesota in 1987.[5] By the 1970s and 1980s, pressure from the Black community and the rise of social history with its emphasis on the stories of non-elites, led at least some white-dominated social history institutions to begin paying more attention to the issue of slavery. Colonial Williamsburg, which had long ignored the topic of slavery even though half of that city's colonial population had been enslaved, developed its first interpretive programs on slavery in 1979 and launched its "Other Half Tour" in 1991. Over the course of the 1990s and 2000s, other "mainstream" public history institutions also began to take steps to incorporate the history of slavery into their presentations.[6]

But recent demands on institutions like colleges and museums to reckon more deeply with the history of slavery also reflect the influence of the historical justice movement. That movement originated in the wake of World War II when the United States pressured Germany to hold officials accountable for the Holocaust and to pay restitution to victims of the genocide. Germany soon took up the cause on its own, in part to restore its political and moral legitimacy in the post-war era. Historical justice efforts spread and gained popularity in the post-Cold War era as authoritarian regimes collapsed and new governments insisted on reckoning with the crimes of past regimes. The growing recognition of group rights has also led to more demands by survivors of injustice and their descendants for redress for past persecution. By the 2000s, calls for historical redress had spread around the globe and had given rise to new kinds of institutions, such as truth commissions, international tribunals, and memorial museums.[7]

While the United States has not been at the forefront of these efforts, the impact of the historical justice movement has been felt here too. In 1988, the US government paid historic reparations to Japanese Americans who had been interned during World War II. Activists across the country have launched projects seeking redress for some of the most egregious examples of racial violence in US history, resulting in everything from state commissions investigating racial massacres in Tulsa, Oklahoma, and Rosewood, Florida to new trials to hold men accountable for decades-old murders of civil rights protestors. In North Carolina, local activists inspired by South Africa created the Greensboro Truth and Reconciliation Commission in 2005 to investigate the 1979 killings of five civil rights and labor activists. There have also been insistent calls for reparations for slavery. H.R. 40, a bill calling for a congressional commission to investigate reparations for slavery, has been introduced in Congress every year since 1989.[8]

Proponents of historical justice insist that histories of oppression continue to shape the present and events since 2014 have seemed to confirm their most basic argument: that societies will only be able to build more equitable futures if they come to terms with the past. Contemporary police brutality, the resurgence of overt white nationalism, and the resistance to the seemingly straightforward statement that "Black Lives Matter" expose as fantasy any claims that the United States is a post-racial nation that has atoned for its past by passing civil rights legislation or electing a Black president.[9] In response, an increasing number of scholars, activists, and public figures have turned to the language of historical justice to explain the urgent need for action in the present. "Only by coming to terms with history can we free ourselves to create a more just world," Harvard University President Drew Gilpin Faust told the audience at a 2017 symposium exploring the historic connections between slavery and

82 *Renee C. Romano*

universities. Bryan Stevenson, the founder of the Equal Justice Initiative, draws a direct line between the unaddressed legacies of slavery and contemporary racial violence. As he sees it, the ideology of racial difference that resulted from slavery "got Michael Brown killed, got Eric Garner killed and got Tamir Rice killed, . . . [and] led to the executions in Charleston." Historians of slavery Daina Raima Berry and Jennifer Morgan agree that the legacies of slavery play out in racial violence in the present day. The "unprosecuted deaths of Trayvon Martin, Michael Brown, Eric Garner and countless others," they argue, makes clear that Americans have "failed to grapple with our past." The Southern Poverty Law Center points to this connection between past and present to explain the importance of improving how schools teach slavery. Getting this history right, they argue, "is a moral necessity if we are to move the country forward toward healing slavery's persistent wounds."[10]

But it is the nation's public history sites that have been pressed to bear the primary burden in this public reckoning with slavery. Public history, John Oldfield notes in a recent study of Britain, can offer a kind of symbolic reparations that are easier to achieve than other forms of historical justice, like monetary reparations or truth commissions. "In the absence of more radical gestures," these symbolic forms of redress, "have taken on added significance," he suggests.[11] Public history representations have the capacity to reach a wider audience of diverse backgrounds and ages than schools do. The emphasis on public history sites also reflects a growing recognition that their representations of slavery have long done more to buttress white supremacy than to further the cause of racial justice. Public history, in short, has a responsibility to undo the damage caused by past representations and to develop new practices that help undo slavery's legacies, and contemporary racial violence has motivated activists and public history professionals alike to take up this work.

Dismantling

On June 27, 2015, 30-year-old Bree Newsome made history when she scaled a flagpole outside the South Carolina State House and removed the Confederate Flag flying there. Describing the Confederate flag as a symbol of "racial intimidation and fear," Newsome was galvanized into action by the shooting of nine parishioners at Charleston's AME church, which had taken place only 10 days earlier. As Newsome explained, "This [massacre] was not a page in a textbook I was reading nor an inscription on a monument I was visiting. This was now. This was real. This was – this is – still happening."[12]

For years, African Americans had been arguing that Confederate flags were hateful symbols of white supremacy that should be removed from public grounds. The NAACP had, in fact, been boycotting South Carolina since 1999 in protest of the state's prominent display of the flag outside the state house. But pictures showing shooter Dylann Roof posing with the Confederate flag generated broader support for confronting the American memorial landscape.[13] On July 9, just 3 weeks after the AME Church shooting, South Carolina's

Republican Governor Nikki Haley signed legislation removing the flag from the state house grounds.

The historical justice movement has brought new attention to the ways in which the commemorative landscape can impede a process of historical reckoning and reconciliation. Monuments offer a particularly powerful way for a group to legitimize their version of history and to express their dominance over others. Monuments seek to "fix" interpretations of the past, to define which histories are worth remembering, and to organize public space to convey lessons about how to act and who is welcome. Moreover, as history "written in stone," they also have a permanence that most other forms of commemoration lack.[14] All of this makes addressing the burden of history on the landscape a necessary aspect of historical justice, especially in a place like the United States where memorials have long served to construct and communicate white supremacy.[15]

The hundreds of Confederate symbols that still mark America's twenty-first-century landscape reflect the success of what might be considered one of the first major public history projects in the nation.[16] Many were erected by the United Daughters of the Confederacy, a women's organization created in 1894 with the goal of shaping how Americans understood the Civil War. The UDC sought to legitimize and popularize the "Lost Cause" narrative, a mythic retelling of the Civil War that portrayed the southern cause as moral and honorable and insisted that the war was about states' rights, not slavery. To that end, they

Figure 4.1 Statue of Robert E. Lee being removed in New Orleans on May 17, 2017
Source: Credit – Abdazizar, Wikimedia Commons, CC BY-SA 4

84   *Renee C. Romano*

lobbied to shape the curriculum of southern schools, wrote their own history textbooks, and funded the placement of hundreds of monuments to Confederate soldiers and leaders.[17] These monuments sought not only to promote a white southern historical narrative but also to degrade and marginalize Blacks in public space. Most were constructed between 1890 and 1920, the same period that witnessed the rise of lynching and the imposition of segregation in the South. State and local governments erected others during the civil rights movement as a way to intimidate Black southerners and to express resistance to their protests against the status quo.[18]

Events since 2014 have intensified calls on authorities to dismantle this pro-slavery landscape. Between 2015 and 2019, the Southern Poverty Law Center documented the removal of 58 Confederate monuments and another 56 Confederate symbols. The horrific killing of George Floyd in May 2020 – where a crowd watched helplessly as a police officer callously kneeled on his neck for nine long minutes while his fellow officers protected him – led to a surge of demands for further removals of Confederate monuments and other symbols associated with white supremacy. To many people, Floyd's murder, coming after years of Black Lives Matter protests against police brutality and systemic racism, was conclusive evidence of the continued legacies of slavery. Books and articles quickly appeared that drew a direct line from slavery to George Floyd. Activists around the country made the case that municipal police forces had evolved from slave catchers and insisted that defunding and abolition of the police was the only way to truly dismantle the legacies of slavery. When a local organization launched a petition to knock down the old slave market building in what had been George Floyd's hometown of Fayetteville, North Carolina, they quickly garnered 125,000 signatures.[19] Angry protestors across the country took action by demanding the removal of Confederate monuments or by taking them down themselves when authorities failed to act. Within six months of Floyd's murder, an additional 64 Confederate monuments and 38 symbols of the Confederacy had been removed or renamed.[20]

Yet the history embedded in the landscape remains a pressing public issue for those working for racial justice. Over 1,700 Confederate symbols still mark the public landscape, including 725 monuments. Seven states have passed laws making them harder to remove, either by prohibiting the removal of historical memorials without state approval or by making it illegal to take down any war memorials. Opponents have turned to violence and intimidation to try to prevent removals. When the massacre at Emanuel AME Church convinced New Orleans's mayor that his city's four Confederate monuments must come down, he struggled to find a company willing to do the work. Eventually, the city had to hire a private security firm to protect the contractors and the workers took the precaution of wearing bulletproof vests and face masks to hide their identity.[21]

Confederate statues, moreover, are only one of the many manifestations of white supremacy in America's public landscape. Take 'Em Down NOLA, a grassroots organization dedicated to removing racist symbols from the public landscape in New Orleans, describes the four Confederate statues the city removed as "measly crumbs." They want to see "ALL symbols to white toxicity" dismantled. The group explains the urgency of this project using the language of historical justice. "In this moment of global reconciliation with age old truths around systemic racism," the city must "finally begin the real work of reckoning with the WHOLE truth of white supremacy in New Orleans." This work, they charge, is a "necessary step in the direction of racial and economic justice" in the city.[22]

Reckoning with the "WHOLE" truth of white supremacy has also led to new scrutiny of the nation's many plantation tourist sites. Plantations offer an easy target for critics of America's public history landscape, as most have long functioned more as monuments to enslavers than to the enslaved. A 2002 study of 122 plantation museums found that only 3.3% had made any meaningful effort to incorporate the history of slavery and the experience of the enslaved into their interpretations. Over 80% of the museums either "symbolically annihilated" their history of slavery or trivialized it with tours that portrayed enslavers as benevolent and enslaved people as well-treated, loyal, and happy. Most of these sites, the authors argued, actively worked as "agents of social injustice."[23]

Many plantation museums continue to minimize, erase, or distort the history of slavery. At Cannonball House in Georgia, a small Confederate Museum is housed in a former slave cabin, which the website refers to as a "quaint little room."[24] The Historic Mansfield Plantation, which describes itself as "South Carolina's authentic plantation bed and breakfast destination," urges visitors to "[C]ome experience true 18th century luxury and relaxation," while barely mentioning the hundreds of people who were enslaved there.[25] Some sites have even turned slave quarters into suites where visitors can spend a cozy night. At Virginia's Caledonia Farm 1812 Bed and Breakfast, the "kitchen dependency," which once housed six enslaved people, is now touted as a romantic honeymoon suite. As the director of the National Black Tourism Network charges, turning slave quarters into luxury accommodations is "TRULY whitewashing slavery."[26]

But just as in the case of Confederate monuments, the political and racial environment since 2015 has led to growing criticism and scrutiny of plantations that continue to celebrate white enslavers.[27] Numerous plantations have become the targets of protestors. In Virginia, "We profit off slavery" was painted on the entry pillars of Virginia's Tuckahoe plantation. In North Carolina, someone spray-painted a big red "X" through a historical marker for Orton Plantation. In Florida, "BLM" was painted on the sign of the Plantation Supper Club.[28] Perhaps that's why Rosedown Plantation, Louisiana's most visited historical site, finally took down signage in 2019 that claimed that the 850 people who had been enslaved there were "well taken care of and happy," lived in "prettily built and very comfortable cabins," and had "a natural musical instinct."[29]

These critiques seem to finally be having some impact on the bottom line of these tourist sites, especially in their role as rental venues for celebrations. Several major wedding planning sites announced in December 2019 that they

86   *Renee C. Romano*

would no longer promote plantations as potential wedding venues. The *New York Times* had beaten them to the punch, announcing just a few months earlier that they would not cover the weddings of couples being married on plantations. Celebrity couple Ryan Reynolds and Blake Lively, who were married in 2012 at South Carolina's Boone Plantation, have since apologized for doing so. "What we saw at the time was a wedding venue on Pinterest," Reynolds explains. "What we saw after was a place built upon devastating tragedy." McLeod Plantation, which was one of the South Carolina plantations Dylann Roof visited before his 2015 massacre, announced in 2019 that it would no longer host weddings.[30]

While plantation museums offer an easy target for critics, the political climate has also led to calls to discontinue another, very different artifact of America's public history of slavery: Underground Railroad Reenactments, or UGRRs. UGRRs use live reenactments to teach participants about both the history of the Underground Railroad and the visceral experience of being enslaved. Typically, a small group is told that they are fugitive slaves who are trying to escape to freedom; they must work together to evade slave catchers, while following the guidance of costumed interpreters who help them on their way. While UGRRs initially emerged from Black Nationalist politics in the late 1980s, schools, churches, YMCAs, and museums soon embraced the practice and began staging their own reenactments with the goal of teaching participants about slavery through an immersive, tactile experience.[31]

But in recent years, this popular public history practice has come under intensifying criticism on a number of fronts. For one thing, UGRRs contribute to the outsized attention that the story of escapees has assumed in America's narratives of slavery. The story of the Underground Railroad is popular in part because it can shore up comforting histories of both Black resistance and white saviors. With its emphasis on a fierce Harriet Tubman and the countless white conductors who hid runaways in secret rooms or safe houses, the narrative has the potential to both obscure the brutality of slavery and exaggerate the possibility of escape.[32] UGRRs have also been criticized for trivializing slavery. How, critics have asked, can any reenactment convey the brutality of slavery or truly communicate what it felt like to be enslaved? Children, the ACLU charged in a 2016 letter asking the national YMCA to end its longstanding UGRR programs, might leave these reenactments with "the misperception that slavery was comparable to an overnight camp adventure." Critics also fear that Black children could be humiliated and traumatized by these reenactments. YMCA permanently halted its UGRRs in 2016. The Southern Poverty Law Center has gone further by calling on schools to discontinue *all* simulations of slavery, arguing that they aren't an effective teaching tool, that they risk trivializing the subject, and that they are hurtful to students of color.[33]

UGRRs may well become a casualty of the Black Lives Matter era. Both their out-of-proportion emphasis on runaways and their claim that a two-hour reenactment can be a meaningful way to understand the horrors of slavery seem naïve in the face of contemporary racial violence and calls to recognize the continued legacies of slavery. The fact that they too, along with Confederate monuments and plantation museums, have faced heightened scrutiny and intensified protests in recent years points to the extent and breadth of the pressure on public history to interrogate, discontinue, and dismantle historical representations that either uphold white supremacy or downplay the brutality of slavery. But that work represents only a first step in a meaningful reckoning with America's history of slavery. Repairing this past also requires recuperating and honoring sites of slavery throughout the country.

Recuperating

In 1989, Nobel Prize-winning novelist Toni Morrison explained that she was driven to write *Beloved*, her novel about the traumatic legacies of slavery because of the nearly total absence of the history of slavery on the American memorial landscape.

> There is no place you or I can go, to think about or not think about, to summon the presences of, or recollect the absences of slaves. There is no suitable memorial, or plaque, or wreath, or wall, or park, or skyscraper lobby. There's no 300-foot tower, there's no small bench by the road.[34]

Her lament eventually gave rise to a project to install benches with memorial plaques at sites of significant events, individuals, and locations in the history of the African Diaspora. In 2006, the first bench was placed at South Carolina's Sullivan Island, a major point of entry for enslaved Africans.[35]

The "Bench by the Side of Road" represents an early rumbling of a second project that has gained momentum since 2015: the efforts to recuperate and mark America's often hidden histories of slavery. Violent events that a society deems important to remember, geographer Kenneth Foote argues in his book *Shadowed Ground* are either "sanctified" by being turned into permanent memorials or "designated" with a marker so at least the event will not be forgotten. But sites of violence that deeply divide society or that are seen as insignificant are reused without being marked or even obliterated so as to completely erase all evidence of the past.[36] The violence of slavery, as Morrison recognized, has largely been erased from America's landscape, with auction and jail sites unmarked and old cabins reused or left to decay.

From the perspective of historical justice, marking sites associated with a violent past brings the past into conversation with the present, offers a space for reflection and mourning, and signals a society's commitment to prevent similar injustices in the future. For Bryan Stevenson of the Equal Justice Initiative, marking sites of slavery is a crucial step for encouraging conversations about the legacies of slavery that "we all need to have." In 2013, the EJI dedicated three historical markers at different sites associated with the domestic slave trade in Montgomery, Alabama, a city that in 1861 had more slave depots than churches or schools. Stevenson drew inspiration for the project from the

Figure 4.2 "Slave Auctions" marker, erected outside Charleston's Old Exchange Building, 2016

Source: Credit – Warren LeMay, Wikimedia Commons, CC0

Stolpersteine or "stumbling stones" project in Europe, where over 1,200 commemorative brass plaques have been installed in front of the former homes of Holocaust victims. Walking around Berlin, Stevenson saw the plaques as constant "reminders of the people's commitment not to repeat the Holocaust."[37]

The markers in Montgomery are especially notable because the history of the domestic slave trade in particular has been aggressively obliterated from the American landscape, despite the fact that 1.2 million enslaved people were sold in the United States between 1760 and 1860.[38] Historian Anne Bailey, who has embarked on an ambitious project to compile a list of every site of a slave auction in the United States, has found that only a tiny number of the whole have been marked or preserved in any way. America, Bailey concludes, "has yet to adequately memorialize slavery."[39]

Yet here too things have begun to change in the last five years. The Middle Passage Ceremonies and Port Markers Project, a nonprofit that launched in 2011 with the goal of recognizing and honoring the enslaved by placing markers in every one of the 52 ports of entry in the United States, has erected 26 markers to date, the vast majority since 2015.[40] Charleston erected a marker focused on the history of its slave markets in 2016. Even New Orleans, a city that has crafted a tourist image as a site for jazz and wild parties, has finally begun to respond to longtime demands by historians and Black activists to recognize the vital contributions that enslaved people made to its economic growth and development. In 2018, New Orleans erected markers in six locations with ties to the slave trade and launched a free interactive app that offers audio tours of the sites and first-person accounts of individuals who were bought and sold there.[41]

The last decade has given rise to other efforts to map, uncover, and preserve the hidden and unmarked material culture of slavery as well. In 2012, preservationist Jobie Hill launched the "Saving Slave Houses" project. She records the coordinates where dwellings stood or still stand, makes sketches of site plans, takes pictures, and enters them into a public database. The project also seeks to interpret these houses by bringing together oral histories, public records, plantation records, and physical evidence to reveal the plantation landscape through the eyes of the enslaved. She argues that the stories these houses tell "have the capacity to facilitate our nation's efforts to collectively move forward from the legacy of slavery."[42] Historic preservationist Joseph McGill launched a similar campaign in 2010. The "Slave Dwelling Protect" seeks to heighten awareness of the still extant built environment of slavery. McGill sleeps in former slave dwellings around the country, often with large groups in tow. At every stop, McGill gives lectures with the goal of sharing a perspective on the past that has not been well preserved in our material culture. His passion has taken him to 14 states to date, which serves as a potent reminder of the extent and reach of slavery.[43]

This preservation work recognizes the importance of place in connecting people to the past and offering communal sites for remembrance and learning. But it also reminds us that preserving the material culture of slavery is important for constructing new historical narratives. Indeed, the Slave Dwelling Project defines its ultimate objective as "Changing the narrative, one slave dwelling at a time."[44] Designating sites of slavery, in short, is an important aspect of the third public history project that recent events have made more urgent: that of finding ways to construct new narratives about slavery that both honor the

90   *Renee C. Romano*

experience of the enslaved and complicate simplistic founding stories about freedom and liberty.

Constructing New Narratives

In August 2019, the media giant, the *New York Times*, launched an ambitious project to reframe how Americans understood their own history. Instead of using 1776 (the date when the colonies declared independence from Britain) as the starting date for the nation's history, the 1619 Project boldly argued for starting our national story with 1619, the year when enslaved Africans were first brought to North America. Everything that made America exceptional – its wealth, its power, its electoral system, and even its position as an example of freedom in the world – grew from slavery "and the anti-black racism it required," the project asserted. Using 1619 as our national birth year "requires us to place the consequences of slavery and the contributions of black Americans at the very center of the story we tell ourselves about who we are as a country."[45]

Political conservatives quickly attacked the project and its goal of making slavery central to an understanding of American history. Donald Trump so reviled the project that he created the 1776 Commission to promote "patriotic education" in schools and at National Park Service sites. The report that commission produced calls for teaching "inspiring and ennobling" histories and argues that America should be celebrated for leading the world in abolishing slavery. "The seeds of the death of slavery" were planted at the very founding of the nation, the report insists. While the commission and its report have been shelved since Trump left office, its argument reflects what is a longstanding conservative fear that characterizing American history as a story of oppression will lead to disunity and a loss of national identity.[46]

The debate over the 1619 project represents just one more chapter in America's long history of wars. In public schools, in textbooks, and in state teaching standards, ideological battles have raged over whether historical education should emphasize America's commitment to ideals of freedom and liberty, and tell its story as one of continual progress toward realizing the founding ideals, or whether any honest history must acknowledge that the United States was built on the backs of enslaved labor and stolen land and that racism and white supremacy have fundamentally shaped American society.[47] Advocates of historical justice argue that contradictory and competing historical narratives are common in societies that have failed to reckon with their histories of injustice. Perpetrators or beneficiaries of historical injustice typically embrace historical interpretations that minimize or negate histories of violence and that deny any kind of systemic wrongdoing. Such narratives subject victims of historical injustice to what one scholar has termed "epistemic impeachment" by denying the reality of their shared memory and lived experience.[48] For advocates of historical justice, achieving a more equitable future depends on discrediting historical narratives that deny atrocities and crafting new narratives that recognize the experience of victims of injustice.[49]

But complicating or contradicting the view of the United States as a land of freedom and liberty is challenging, and even more so for public institutions than for a private media company like the *New York Times*. In 2006, novelist and artist Barbara Chase-Ribaud offered a scathing critique of America's public history sites, charging that they erased or distorted the history of slavery because they felt compelled to protect "the founding public history of a nation that is supposed to be the innovator and exporter of the principle of the inestimable value of Liberty." In a 2014 report, Tracing History, an organization created in 2009 to spread awareness about slavery in the North, pointed to this same contradiction between America's foundational myths and the truth that slavery "was a cornerstone of the nation's economy and society" as a key reason why public history sites have failed so badly at educating the American public about slavery.[50]

But new public history sites are finding ways to craft new narratives that at least complicate celebratory foundational narratives. The National Museum of African American History and Culture in Washington, DC, which opened in 2015, provides one roadmap for how to do so. Its massive exhibit on slavery begins in Africa and goes through the Civil War and Reconstruction. The exhibit conveys the extent and brutality of the international slave trade with walls etched with information about every recorded slave voyage. Visitors are taken through the horrors of the Middle Passage and shown objects that communicate the violence of slavery, such as shackles, cages, and neck locks. But they also encounter objects that speak to the ways in which enslaved people resisted dehumanization and created their own cultures and communities. Most powerfully, the museum argues that both slavery and freedom are "shared American stories" and insists that American freedom has been fought for most fiercely by those who have been denied it. A statue of Thomas Jefferson standing in front of a wall listing the names of the people he owned under the words, "All Men Are Created Equal," serves as a powerful critique of the limitations of Jefferson's conception of freedom and as a symbolic expression of the literal ways that enslaved people built the nation.[51]

Plantations that are now museums or tourist destinations that have moved beyond ignoring slavery completely have struggled with how to incorporate the story of slavery into their overall interpretations. The solution for many has been to create separate tours that focus on the history of slavery while changing little about the main house or garden tours.[52] But the current racial climate has begun to push some of these sites to take more radical steps to transform their interpretations. Tours at Owens-Thomas House in Savannah, Georgia (rechristened the Owens-Thomas House and Slave Quarters in 2019), paid little attention to the lives of the 15 enslaved people who lived at the house before 2015. But in the past five years, interpreters have begun emphasizing that the wealth and power of those who owned the Big House were enabled by enslaving other human beings. They have changed their language by striving "to use words that are empathetic to those whose history has been marginalized," replacing "master" with the term "enslaver," referring to "escapees" rather than "runaways," and rechristening plantations as "slave labor camps."[53]

This work has not been easy and remains woefully incomplete. In her 2021 book, *Slavery in the Age of Memory*, Ana Lucia Araujo argues that most plantation sites still aren't doing enough to tell stories of enslaved individuals or to focus on the world that they made for themselves.[54] A recent study of plantation museums found that even those that incorporate slavery into the interpretation of their sites do not necessarily encourage visitors to feel the same kind of emotional connection to the enslaved as they do to the white enslavers, which the authors described as a form of "affective inequality."[55] Magnolia Plantations and Gardens in South Carolina embarked on a project in 2008 to save their remaining slave cabins and now runs a 45-minute Slavery to Freedom Tour, but their main webpage shows only pictures of flowers and its beautiful grounds. Virginia's Berkeley Plantation briefly put a "Black Lives Matter" statement on their landing page in the aftermath of George Floyd's murder, but within six months it had been relegated to the one small section of the website that discusses the enslaved population at Berkeley. The main page still invites visitors to "step back in time to a bygone era and experience a genteel 18th century lifestyle."[56]

To be fair, plantation museums face a handicap in their efforts to center the experience of the enslaved or to reckon with the violence of the institution

Figure 4.3 Memorial to the 1811 Slave Revolt at the Whitney Plantation Museum

Source: Credit – Cupreous, Wikimedia Commons, CC BY-SA 4.0

since neither the architecture nor the physical environment of plantations easily conveys slavery's brutality. Matthew Paul Smith has pointed to the challenges posed by what is the troubling contrast between the beauty of many plantations and their history as sites of violence and trauma. Visitors who come to plantations expecting to see something like *Gone with the Wind* and instead find tours that emphasize the brutality of slavery face a form of cognitive dissonance that visitors to Auschwitz do not.[57] As Lauren Northup, director of museums at the Historic Charleston Foundation and a tour guide at Charleston's Nathaniel Russell House, explains, when guests talk about the beauty of the mansion, she has to remind them that the house was designed to keep in and supervise enslaved people: "It was a prison. That is what I'm trying to make people understand – you are in a beautiful prison."[58] It is hard to communicate a history that highlights violence and oppression when the built environment, in historian Tiya Miles' words, "aggrandizes white mastery."[59]

But the challenges of communicating the horrors of slavery at sites associated with beauty and grandeur are not insurmountable. The Whitney Plantation Museum in Louisiana, which opened in December 2014, has sought to upend the tropes of typical plantation sites by focusing its interpretations on the lives and experiences of the Black people who were enslaved there.[60] In many ways, the Whitney has embraced the form and goal of the memorial museum. Memorial museums, like truth commissions, are an institutional manifestation of the politics of historical justice. They aim to preserve a record of past injustice and to instrumentalize that history to heal communities, promote reconciliation, and prevent future atrocities. Sites like the Auschwitz-Birkenau Memorial and Museum in Poland or the Kigali Genocide Memorial Center in Rwanda seek not just to educate their visitors but to transform them by connecting them to the past in a visceral, emotional way.[61]

The Whitney, which was created by wealthy white trial lawyer John Cummings, seeks to transform visitors by emphasizing the brutality and horrors of slavery. Tours there start at a church that was built by freed people after Emancipation, move on to slave cabins and a slave jail, and end at the big house, which is explored from the perspective of the enslaved. Interpreters draw on WPA Slave Narratives to tell stories of the enslaved in their own words.[62] The museum has three memorial walls which list the names of different groups of enslaved people from Louisiana. There are statues of enslaved children in tattered clothing and a memorial to enslaved children who died before reaching adulthood. The last thing visitors see as they leave the site is a memorial to men beheaded after an 1811 slave revolt – 60 ceramic heads set on rods. The Whitney embodies the belief that memorial museums can lead to transformational change that will encourage anti-racist action. "When you leave here," Cummings insists, "you are not going to be the same person who came in."[63] The experience at the Whitney suggests that plantations must be willing to completely reinterpret their sites if they seek to fundamentally transform the historical narrative they communicate.

94   *Renee C. Romano*

The Legacy Museum in Montgomery, Alabama, located on a site where enslaved people were warehoused, also aims to transform its visitors through an encounter with a painful past. Opened by the Equal Justice Initiative in April 2018, the Legacy Museum links contemporary mass incarceration to the unaddressed ideologies of white supremacy and Black inferiority that developed as a result of slavery. While only a small part of the exhibit deals with slavery directly, its representations are emotionally powerful. Visitors encounter a series of slave pens where they see representations of enslaved people telling their own stories. In one pen, two small children cry out and weep for their mother. Exhibits quickly move on to the lost promise of Reconstruction, the rise of convict leasing in the South, and the growth of the carceral state in the last part of the twentieth century. The Legacy Museum explicitly rejects the idea that the United States has made continual progress toward racial justice since Emancipation. It highlights instead how unaddressed legacies of past violence manifest in racial injustice in the present.

While these new memorial museums to slavery have earned praise, their efforts to upend traditional narratives about slavery have also been unsettling to some visitors. Many white visitors arrive woefully unprepared for a nuanced conversation about slavery or to hear a perspective that challenges a celebratory view of American history. They may contest not only the interpretation they encounter but also the basic facts that they are presented with.[64] As one white visitor to the Whitney complained, she hadn't come "to hear a lecture on how white people treated slaves." She wanted to "see some real plantations that are so much more enjoyable to tour." For this visitor, the *real* plantations were those that romanticized the old South.[65] Sites that emphasize the brutality of slavery or that try to challenge the deeply held assumptions of white visitors also run the risk of traumatizing Black visitors. While memory institutions created by African Americans often pair histories of persecution with stories of progress and community resiliency, the sites that most reflect the zeitgeist of the current political moment, like the Whitney Plantation or the Legacy Museum, see forcing a recognition of slavery as a precondition of historical justice. Their depictions of slavery thus highlight its brutality and violence rather than the resiliency or community building of those who were enslaved. Perhaps that helps explain why a 2016 South Carolina tourism report found that African American visitors were *less* interested in visiting sites like slave cabins and plantations than non–Black visitors were.[66]

While new museums and revised interpretations have begun the very difficult work of constructing new narratives that can foster a shared understanding of slavery and its legacies, this is certainly the most challenging of all three of the public history interventions that this chapter has considered. So few Americans learn any kind of meaningful history of slavery in school that public history sites can't easily build on preexisting knowledge. Effectively communicating a different history of slavery, moreover, depends in part on the success of the projects in dismantling America's old pro–slavery landscape and of recuperating sites associated with enslavement as a way to anchor and illuminate a better understanding of slavery's place in the national story.

Conclusion

Just months before Michael Brown's murder in 2014, a special issue of *The Public Historian* outlined "the continuing need" for public history sites "to deploy history inventively to unsettle, challenge, and provoke attentiveness and understanding of slavery and its legacies."[67] In the years since, artists, educators, public historians, and community organizations have responded to this call. Spurred by the recognition that contemporary violence reflects the continuing legacies of slavery, they have worked to deconstruct pro-slavery representations on the landscape and in historic sites, to preserve and recuperate physical sites of slavery, and to craft new historical narratives that connect the past and the present.

Advocates of historical justice believe that, as Birmingham civil rights leader Fred Shuttlesworth has argued, "If you don't tell it like it was, it can never be as it ought to be."[68] In the last decades, and especially in the past five years, the field of public history has made impressive strides in telling the story of slavery "like it was." But whether promoting a reckoning with the history of slavery – one that confronts its violence and brutality, its importance to the growth of the American nation, and its legacies in the present day – will help make the United States "as it ought to be" remains an open question. The ongoing work by public historians to interpret slavery more honestly and to create a landscape that honors those who were enslaved rather than their enslavers is in itself an important form of redress: it marks an effort to undo and repair the damage done by earlier representations that erased, distorted, or even celebrated slavery. But can these representations – this form of "symbolic reparations" – contribute to other forms of systemic change? Can they, as Lawrence Aje argued recently about Charleston's decision to erect a statue of Denmark Vesey, planner of a foiled 1822 slave revolt, "be the driving wedge" to pave the way for other forms of compensation?[69]

Public history matters because it can shape how people understand the world and their place in it. It offers a space for people to continue to learn, to encounter new ideas, and to cultivate a sense of empathy and a common humanity with people in different circumstances than themselves. The history written on the landscape helps make clear what a community or society value and who is considered worthy of remembrance. So the fact that visitors to port cities may now encounter a marker reminding them of the Middle Passage, that efforts are being made to value slave cabins as much as plantation mansions, and that new museum exhibits are communicating the experience of the enslaved in powerful and visceral ways has the potential to change how at least some Americans understand the nation's history and the way that history continues to shape contemporary society.

But that project will not be easy. Just browse through the January 2020 issue of *The Smithsonian*, the magazine run by one of America's premier public

96 *Renee C. Romano*

history institutions. Several pages feature a photo essay about performance artist Dread Scott's 2019 reenactment of the 1811 Slave Revolt. The pictures show costumed reenactors marching down highways once dotted with sugar plantations and now lined by refineries and poor Black neighborhoods. Reenactors are shown dancing in Congo Square in New Orleans, celebrating Black resistance and resiliency even though the actual uprising never made it that far.[70] But one only has to turn the page to find a very different version of America's slave past: an ad for a replica of a 1925 coin commemorating Stone Mountain, the largest existing Confederate Monument. The coin shows Jefferson Davis and Robert E. Lee on horseback, with the text celebrating "the valor of the soldier of the South." "Before they were carved in stone," the copy explains, "*they were struck in SILVER.*"[71] Actual statues of Davis and Lee may be falling around the country, but the ideology that animated them will be much more difficult to remove.

Notes

1 Karen Marks, "Students Rename Calhoun," *Down Magazine*, May 3, 2016, https://downatyale.com/students-rename-wrongmoveyale-college/.
2 Monica Wang and Susan Svrluga, "Yale Renames Calhoun College Because of Historical Ties to White Supremacy and Slavery," *Washington Post*, February 12, 2017, https://www.washingtonpost.com/news/grade-point/wp/2017/02/11/yale-renames-calhoun-college-because-of-historic-ties-to-white-supremacy-and-slavery/ Andy Newman and Vivian Wang, "Calhoun Who? Yale Drops Name of Slavery Advocate for Computer Pioneer," *New York Times*, September 3, 2017, https://www.nytimes.com/2017/09/03/nyregion/yale-calhoun-college-grace-hopper.html
3 Southern Poverty Law Center, "Whose Heritage: Public Symbols of the Confederacy," *The Southern Poverty Law Center*, February 1, 2019, www.splcenter.org/20190201/whose-heritage-public-symbols-confederacy; https://en.wikipedia.org/wiki/List_of_monuments_and_memorials_removed_during_the_George_Floyd_protests; National Summit on Teaching Slavery, "Engaging Descendant Communities in the Interpretation of Slavery at Museums an Historic Sites," *History News: Magazine of the American Association for State and Local History*, Vol. 74, No. 1 (Winter 2019), pp. 17, 16; Natalie Delgadillo, "Mount Vernon Stop Selling Souvenir Washington Dentures Over Ties to Slavery," *dcist.com*, February 20, 2020, https://dcist.com/story/20/02/20/mount-vernon-stops-selling-souvenir-washington-dentures-over-ties-to-slavery/.
4 Two very recent books explore the impact of recent racial unrest on representations of slavery in the United States and internationally. Lawrence Aje and Nicolas Gachon, eds., *Traces and Memories of Slavery in the Atlantic World* (New York: Routledge, 2020) offers a variety of case studies on recent public history of memory. Ana Lucia Araujo's *Slavery in the Age of Memory* (London: Bloomsbury Academic, 2021) provides an overview of recent developments in the United States, Latin America, Africa, and Europe.
5 Andrea Burns, *From Storefront to Monument: Tracing the Public History of the Black Museum Movement* (Amherst, MA: University of Massachusetts Press, 2013); Julian Lucas, "Can Slavery Reenactments Set Us Free?," *The New Yorker*, February 17 and 24, 2020, https://www.newyorker.com/magazine/2020/02/17/can-slavery-reenactments-set-us-free
6 On Colonial Williamsburg, see Erin Krutko Devlin, "Colonial Williamsburg's Slave Auction Re-Enactment: Controversy, African American History and Public Memory" (Dissertations, Theses, and Masters Projects. Paper 1539626387, 2003) https://dx.doi.org/doi:10.21220/s2-q9gm-6032. On efforts to change other sites, see Joanne Melish, "Recovering (from) Slavery: Four Struggles to Tell the Truth," in James Oliver

Horton and Lois Horton, eds., *Slavery and Public History* (New York: New Press, 2006), pp. 103–133.

7   On the history and emergence of historical redress as a global phenomenon, see Elazar Barkan, *Guilt of Nations: Restitution and Negotiating Historical Injustices* (New York: W. W. Norton & Company, 2000); John Torpey, ed., *Politics and the Past: On Repairing Historical Injustices* (Lanham, MD: Rowman and Littlefield, 2003); Pierre Hazan, *Judging War, Judging History: Behind Truth and Reconciliation* (Stanford, CA: Stanford University Press, 2010); Ashraf Rushdy, *A Guilted Age: Apologies for the Past* (Philadelphia, PA: Temple University Press, 2015); and Katherine Sikkink, *The Justice Cascade: How Human Rights Prosecutions Are Changing World Politics* (New York: W. W. Norton & Company, 2012).

8   For a brief review of some of these efforts, see James Campbell, "Settling Accounts: An Americanist Perspective on Historical Reconciliation," *American Historical Review*, Vol. 114, No. 4 (October 2009), pp. 963–977. See also Renee C. Romano, *Racial Reckoning: Prosecuting America's Civil Rights Murders* (Cambridge, MA: Harvard University Press, 2014).

9   Anne Stefani describes many of the manifestations that I see as an impact of historical justice politics as arising from a new racial era in the twenty-first century that emphasizes the responsibility that whites bear for upholding structural racism and that focuses on the negative, rather than positive, aspects of US history. She argues this new focus on white responsibility stems from the need to of scholars and activists to demonstrate the persistence of systemic racism in the face of the claims of colorblindness. See Anne Stefani, "From White Guilt to White Responsibility: The Traces of Racial Oppression in the United States' Collective Memory," in Lawrence Aje and Nicolas Gachon, eds., *Traces and Memories of Slavery in the Atlantic World* (New York: Routledge, 2020), pp. 112–127.

10 Jennifer Schuessler, "Confronting Academia's Ties to Slavery," *New York Times*, March 5, 2017, https://www.nytimes.com/2017/03/05/arts/confronting-academias-ties-to-slavery.html "Bryan Stevenson on Charleston and Our Real Problem with Race," *The Marshall Project*, June 24, 2015, www.themarshallproject.org/2015/06/24/bryan-stevenson-on-charleston-and-our-real-problem-with-race; Daina Raimy Berry and Jennifer Morgan, "#Blacklivesmatter Till They Don't: Slavery's Lasting Legacy," *American Prospect*, December 5, 2014, https://prospect.org/justice/blacklivesmatter-till-don-t-slavery-s-lasting-legacy/; Southern Poverty Law Center, "Teaching Hard History: American Slavery," *The Southern Poverty Law Center*, January 31, 2018, p. 21, www.splcenter.org/20180131/teaching-hard-history.

11 John Richard Oldfield, "Repairing Historical Wrongs: Public History and Transatlantic Slavery," *Social and Legal Studies*, Vol. 21, No. 2 (2012), p. 244.

12 Abby Philip, "Why Bree Newsome Took Down the Confederate flag in S.C.: 'I Refuse to Be Ruled by Fear,'" *Washington Post*, June 29, 2015, www.washingtonpost.com/news/post-nation/wp/2015/06/29/why-bree-newsome-took-down-the-confederate-flag-in-s-c-i-refuse-to-be-ruled-by-fear/.

13 Neely Tucker and Peter Holley, "Dylann Roof's Eerie Tour of American Slavery at Its Beginning and End," *Washington Post*, July 1, 2015, https://www.washingtonpost.com/news/post-nation/wp/2015/07/01/dylann-roofs-eerie-tour-of-american-slavery-at-its-beginning-middle-and-end/

14 Sanford Levinson, *Written in Stone: Public Monuments in Changing Societies*, 20th Anniversary ed. (Durham, NC: Duke University Press, 2018) and Cheryl Jimenez Frei, "Towards Memory, Against Oblivion: A Comparative Perspective on Public Memory, Monuments, and Confronting a Painful Past in the United States," *The Public Historian*, Special Virtual Issue: Monuments, Memory, Politics, and Our Publics (September 2017).

15 For more see Kirk Savage, *Standing Soldiers, Kneeling Slaves: Race, War, and Monument in 19th Century America* (Princeton, NJ: Princeton University Press, 1998).

16 "Whose Heritage? A Report on Public Symbols of the Confederacy," Prepared by the Southern Poverty Law Center, February 1, 2019, www.splcenter.org/data-projects/whose-heritage.

98　*Renee C. Romano*

17 Karen Cox, *Dixie's Daughters: The United Daughters of the Confederacy and the Preservation of Confederate Culture* (Gainesville, FL: University Press of Florida, 2003).

18 Adam Domby, *The False Cause: Fraud, Fabrication, and White Supremacy in Confederate Memory* (Charlottesville, VA: University of Virginia Press, 2020); W. Fitzhugh Brundage, *The Southern Past: A Clash of Race and Memory* (Cambridge, MA: Belknap Press of Harvard University Press, 2005).

19 See, for example, D.B. Marquis, "The List: From Slavery to George Floyd – Systemic and Structural Racism in America," *The Newark Times*, July 8, 2020, http://thenewarktimes.com/the-list-from-slavery-to-george-floyd-systemic-and-structural-racism-in-america/; Petition at change.org, 2020, www.change.org/p/city-of-fayetteville-nc-knock-down-slave-market-house-in-center-of-downtown-fayetteville-nc.

20 Southern Poverty Law Center, "SPLC's Whose Heritage Reports Over 100 Confederate Symbols Removed Since George Floyd's Murder," *Southern Poverty Law Center*, October 14, 2020, www.splcenter.org/presscenter/splcs-whose-heritage-reports-over-100-confederate-symbols-removed-george-floyds-murder; https://en.wikipedia.org/wiki/List_of_monuments_and_memorials_removed_during_the_George_Floyd_protests.

21 Mitch Landrieu, "Truth: Remarks on the Removal of Confederate Monuments in New Orleans," May 19, 2017, reprinted in Landrieu, *In the Shadow of Statues: A White Southerner Confronts History* (London: Penguin Books, 2018).

22 See Aneil Kovvali, "Confederate Statute Removal," *Stanford Law Review Online*, Vol. 82 (2017), www.stanfordlawreview.org/online/confederate-statute-removal; Kaeli Subberwal, "Several States Have Erected Laws to Protect Confederate Monuments," *Huffington Post*, August 18, 2017, www.huffpost.com/entry/states-confederate-statue-laws_n_5996312be4b0e8cc855cb2ab. On the challenges encountered in New Orleans, see Landrieu, *In the Shadow of Statues*, pp. 188–196; Website of Take 'Em Down NOLA, http://takeemdownnola.org.

23 Jennifer L. Eichstedt and Stephen Small, *Representations of Slavery: Race and Ideology in Southern Plantation Museums* (Washington, DC: Smithsonian Institution, 2002), pp. 65, 270.

24 Eichstedt and Small, p. 98; Website of the Cannonball House, www.cannonballhouse.org/tour/ [Accessed January 16, 2021].

25 Website of the Mansfield Plantation, www.mansfieldplantation.com/index.html [Accessed January 15, 2021].

26 Allen G. Breed, "People Get Cozy in Slave Cabins," *Associated Press*, March 18, 2002, www.bnb1812.com/. https://web.archive.org/web/20210506122204/http://www.stratalum.org/cabinsrented.html

27 Andrea Gallo, "Louisiana's Plantations Are Reckoning With the Racist Past," *nola.com*, September 4, 2020, www.nola.com/news/article_937000dc-d5d0-11ea-b150-237b10ac5da1.html. Similar stories interrogating plantations have appeared in *nola.com*, the *New York Times*, the *Washington Post*, *The Nation*, and the *Tampa Bay Times*, among others.

28 www.wect.com/2020/07/01/orton-plantation-historical-marker-vandalized/; "Tuckahoe Plantation Vandalized," *Richmond Times Dispatch*, February 19, 2019, https://richmond.com/tuckahoe-plantation-vandalized/image_077c4129-4fc3-542b-9b5a-890f5a05bd1f.html; "Investigation into Plantation Graffiti Continues," *Lakeland Times*, July 24, 2020, https://www.facebook.com/LakelandTimes/posts/3128490477234602/

29 Mark Ballard, "At Louisiana-Owned Plantation, a Sign Saying Slaves Were 'Happy' and 'Taken Care of' Is No More," *The Advocate*, March 19, 2019, https://www.theadvocate.com/baton_rouge/news/politics/at-louisiana-owned-plantation-a-sign-saying-slaves-were-happy-and-taken-care-of-is/article_3f658e42-4a8c-11e9-940b-a3be59fc8a2e.html

30 Heather Murphy, "Pinterest and the Knot Pledge to Stop Promoting Plantation Weddings," *New York Times*, December 5, 2019, https://www.nytimes.com/2019/12/05/style/plantation-weddings-pinterest-knot-zola.html; "Ryan Reynolds and Blake Lively 'Deeply and Unreservedly Sorry' for Plantation Wedding," *CNN*, August 4, 2020, www.cnn.com/2020/08/04/entertainment/ryan-reynolds-blake-lively-plantation-wedding/index.html; Michael T. Luongo, "Despite Everything, People Still Have Weddings at 'Plantation' Sites," *New York Times*, October 20, 2020, https://www.nytimes.com/2020/10/17/style/despite-everything-people-still-have-weddings-at-plantation-sites.html

31 Lucas, "Can Slavery Reenactments Set Us Free?"; Drew Swanson, "In Living Color: Early 'Impressions' of Slavery and the Limits of Living History," *American Historical Review* (December 2019), pp. 1732–1733.

32 Henry Louis Gates, Jr., "Who Really Ran the Underground Railroad?," website for "The African Americans: Many Rivers to Cross," *PBS*, www.pbs.org/wnet/african-americans-many-rivers-to-cross/history/who-really-ran-the-underground-railroad/. The National Park Service has marked more than 600 sites in the Underground Railroad "Network to Freedom." "The National Underground Railroad Freedom Center," which opened in Cincinnati in 2004, was among the first museums in the United States focused on the history of slavery.

33 Elahe Izadi, "Slavery Reenactment for Kids Canceled by YMCA after Parent Calls It 'Racially Insensitive,'" *Washington Post*, February 23, 2016, https://www.washingtonpost.com/news/post-nation/wp/2016/02/23/ymca-cancels-kids-slavery-activity-after-parent-complains-of-racially-insensitive-experience/
Mark Fancher to Kevin Washington, President and CEO of the YMCA, February 4, 2016, www.aclumich.org/sites/default/files/ACLU_letter_to_YMCA_about_slave_reenactments.020416.pdf; Lucas, "Can Slavery Reenactments Set Us Free?"; SPLC, "Teaching Hard History," pp. 11, 17.

34 Toni Morrison, "Melcher Book Award Acceptance Speech," originally published in *UUWorld Magazine*, January–February 1989, republished in "A Bench by the Road," *UUWorld*, August 11, 2008, https://www.uuworld.org/articles/bench-road

35 Toni Morrison Society, *Bench by the Road Project*, www.tonimorrisonsociety.org/bench_placements.html.

36 Kenneth Foote, *Shadowed Ground: America's Landscapes of Violence and Tragedy*, Rev ed. (Austin, TX: University of Texas Press, 2003).

37 Kala Kachmar, "New Markers Document Ala. City's Role in the Domestic Slave Trade," *USA Today*, December 11, 2013, www.usatoday.com/story/news/nation/2013/12/11/slave-trade-historic-markers-alabama/3989611/; "Bryan Stevenson Urges America to Heal Racial Tension by Facing Its Mistakes," *Charlotte Observer*, February 21, 2016, www.charlotteobserver.com/news/local/article61649457.html; https://eji.org/news/eji-dedicates-markers-montgomery-alabama-slavery-in-america/; www.stolpersteine.eu/en/home/.

38 Stephanie Yuhl, "Hidden in Plain Sight: Centering the Domestic Slave Trade in American Public History," *Journal of Southern History*, Vol. 79, No. 3 (August 2013), p. 594.

39 Anne C. Bailey, "They Sold Human Beings Here," *New York Times*, February 12, 2020, https://www.nytimes.com/interactive/2020/02/12/magazine/1619-project-slave-auction-sites.html

40 "Website of the Middle Passage and Port Ceremonies Project," www.middlepassageproject.org [Accessed February 22, 2020].

41 Marc Parry, "How Should We Memorialize Slavery?" *Chronicle of Higher Education*, September 8, 2017, https://www.chronicle.com/article/how-should-we-memorialize-slavery/ Lynnell L. Thomas, "Neutral Ground or Battleground? Hidden History, Tourism, and Spatial (In)Justice in the New Orleans French Quarter," *Journal of African American History*, (Fall 2018), pp. 609–636; www.hiddenhistory.us/home; Erin M. Greenwald and Joshua D. Rothman, "New Orleans Should Acknowledge Its Lead Role in the Slave Trade,"

100   *Renee C. Romano*

      nola.com, February 20, 2016, www.nola.com/opinions/article_ed1a704f-e341-551b-8ac1-0f901984272e.html; https://gonola.com/things-to-do-in-new-orleans/gonola-find-new-orleans-slave-trade-marker-and-interactive-app.

42 Amy Crawford, "Still Standing," *Smithsonian*, January–February 2020, p. 19.

43 Jennifer Schuessler, "Confronting Slavery at Long Island's Oldest Estates," *New York Times*, August 12, 2015, https://www.nytimes.com/2015/08/14/arts/confronting-slavery-at-long-islands-oldest-estates.html

44 https://slavedwellingproject.org, accessed February 2, 2021.

45 Jake Silverstein, "Why We Published the 1619 Project," *New York Times*, December 12, 2020, www.nytimes.com/interactive/2019/12/20/magazine/1619-intro.html.

46 Remarks by Donald Trump at the White House Conference on American History, National Archives, Washington, DC, September 17, 2020, www.whitehouse.gov/briefings-statements/remarks-president-trump-white-house-conference-american-history/; The President's Advisory 1776 Commission, "The 1776 Report," January 2021.

47 For more on these history wars, see Gary Nash, Charlotte Crabtree, and Ross Dunn, *History on Trial: Culture Wars and the Teaching of the Past* (New York: Vintage Books, 2000); Edward Linenthal and Tom Engelhardt, *History Wars* (New York: Holt Paperbacks, 1996); Fritz Fischer, *The Memory Hole: The U.S. History Curriculum Under Siege* (Charlotte, NC: Information Age Publishing, 2014).

48 Margaret Urban Walker, "How Can Truth Telling Count as Reparations?," in Klaus Neumann and Janna Thompson, eds., *Historical Justice and Memory* (Madison, WI: University of Wisconsin Press, 2015), pp. 130–145.

49 Meaningful redress offers what philosopher Richard Vernon calls the "right to clarity" in that it enables present generations to live lives "unmystified by false accounts of how things came to be." Richard Vernon, *Why Historical Redress: Must We Pay for the Past* (London: Bloomsbury, 2012), p. 16.

50 Kristin L. Gallas and James DeWolf Perry, "Developing Comprehensive and Conscientious Interpretation of Slavery at Historic Sites and Museums," *History News*, Vol. 69, No. 2 (Spring 2014), p. 2.

51 The exhibit is not without its critics. Ana Lucia Araujo argues that the Jefferson exhibit reinforces the centrality of white enslavers and makes the enslaved invisible, while Vision Cunningham charges that the museum offers a simplistic progress narrative, with the horrors of slavery eventually giving way "to emancipation, hidden, from the beginning somewhere deep within the national heart." I would argue that with later exhibits that reference the Black Lives Matter movement and contemporary racial inequalities, the museum might be more fairly characterized as suggesting that achieving freedom is a constant struggle and an unfinished process. Ana Lucia Araujo, *Slavery in the Age of Memory* (London: Bloomsbury Academic, 2021), p. 62; Vinson Cunningham, "Making a Home for Black History," *The New Yorker*, August 22, 2016, https://www.newyorker.com/magazine/2016/08/29/analyzing-the-national-museum-of-african-american-history-and-culture

52 Eichstedt and Small, *Representations of Slavery*, pp. 170–202.

53 Tariro Mzezewa, "Enslaved People Lived Here. These Museums Want You to Know," *New York Times*, June 26, 2019, https://www.nytimes.com/2019/06/26/travel/house-tours-charleston-savannah.html

54 Araujo, *Slavery in the Age of Memory*, p. 41.

55 E. Arnold Modlin, Jr., Derek H. Alderman, and Glenn W. Gentry, "Tour Guides as Creators of Empathy: The Role of Affective Inequality in Marginalizing the Enslaved at Plantation House Museums," *Tourist Studies*, Vol. 11, No. 1 (April 1, 2011), pp. 3–19.

56 The statement, originally titled "Berkeley Plantation Believes that Black Lives Matter," was gone from the landing page by January 2021. It now appears on the page on "Berkeley's enslaved," one of five pages in the History section of the site and has been retitled, *A Message From the Jamieson Family*, www.berkeleyplantation.com/berkeley-s-enslaved.html [Accessed February 1, 2021].

From Rumblings to Roar 101

57 Matthew Paul Smith, "'Ridiculous Extremes': Historical Accuracy, *Gone With the Wind,* and the Role of Beauty in Plantation Tourism," *The Southern Quarterly*, Vol. 55, No. 2/3 (Winter and Spring 2018), pp. 171–190.

58 Tariro Mzezewa, "Enslaved People Lived Here," *New York Times,* June 26, 2019, https://www.nytimes.com/2019/06/26/travel/house-tours-charleston-savannah.html

59 Tiya Miles, "What Should We Do with Plantations?," *Boston Globe*, August 8, 2020, https://www.bostonglobe.com/2020/08/08/opinion/what-should-we-do-with-plantations/

60 The McLeod Plantation Historic Site in South Carolina has also transformed itself to focus on the experience of the enslaved and the history of their Gullah culture.

61 For more on memorial museums, see Paul Williams, *Memorial Museums: The Global Rush to Commemorate Atrocities* (Oxford: Berg Publishers, 2007) and Amy Sodaro, *Exhibiting Atrocity: Memorial Museums and the Politics of Past Violence* (New Brunswick, NJ: Rutgers University Press, 2018).

62 Mimi Reid, "New Orleans Lawyer Transforms Whitney Plantation Into Powerful Slavery Museum," *The New Orleans Advocate,* October 14, 2014, https://www.nola.com/news/new-orleans-lawyer-transforms-whitney-plantation-into-powerful-slavery-museum/article_268ecb52-18b1-5110-abfc-b94432aad8d5.html

63 David Amsden, "Building the First Slavery Museum in America," *New York Times Magazine*, February 26, 2015, https://www.nytimes.com/2015/03/01/magazine/building-the-first-slave-museum-in-america.html

64 See Amy M. Tyson and Azie Mira Dungey, "'Ask a Slave' and Interpreting Race on Public History's Front Line: Interview With Azie Mira Dungey," *The Public Historian*, Vol. 36, No. 1 (February 2014), pp. 36–60.

65 Gillian Brockell, "Some White People Don't Want to Hear About Slavery at Plantations Built by Slaves," *Washington Post*, August 8, 2019, https://www.washingtonpost.com/history/2019/08/08/some-white-people-dont-want-hear-about-slavery-plantations-built-by-slaves/

66 See Lawrence Aje, "Memorial Equality and Compensatory Public History in Charleston, South Carolina," in Lawrence Aje and Nicholsa Gachon, eds., *Traces and Memories of Slavery in the New Atlantic World* (New York: Routledge, 2020), p. 200.

67 Randolph Bergstrom, "Still Provoking: The Public History of Race and Slavery," *The Public Historian*, Vol. 36, No. 1 (February 2014), p. 8.

68 David Blight, "If You Don't Tell It Like It Was, It Can Never Be as It Ought to Be," *Slavery and Public History*, Vol. 33.

69 Lawrence Aje, "Memorial Equality and Compensatory Public History in Charleston, South Carolina," in Lawrence Aje and Nicolas Gachon, ed., *Traces and Memories of Slavery in the Atlantic World* (New York: Routledge, 2020), p. 203.

70 From the website www.slave-revolt.com [Accessed February 3, 2021].

71 Ted Scheinman, "'Freedom or Death!': Revisiting the 1811 Louisiana Slave Uprising," *Smithsonian Magazine*, January–February 2020, pp. 20–23; "Advertisement for Stone Mountain Silver Dollar," *Smithsonian Magazine*, January–February 2020, p. 25.

5 From a Culture of Abolition to a Culture War

Remembering Transatlantic Enslavement in Britain, 1807–2021

Jessica Moody

Introduction

By the end of the eighteenth century, Britain had come to dominate the European transatlantic trade in enslaved African people and had a large slave-based empire in the Caribbean until the late 1830s. The Abolition of the British Slave Trade Act (1807) and the Emancipation Acts of the 1830s brought a faltering legal end to the traffic of human beings and their enslavement in the British Empire. This was a history which saw the forced trafficking of estimated 12 million enslaved African people across the Atlantic Ocean, a history of physical and sexual violence, torture, and degradation. The public memory of this past has been a point of prominent public contestation, reaching a particularly heated discourse in the 1990s, around 2007 as the Bicentenary of the British Slave Trade Act, and in 2020, when Black Lives Matter protestors pulled down the statue of Bristol slave merchant Edward Colston. However, until the later twentieth century, what Britain publicly "remembered" about its own slaving history was not the centuries of master-minding systems of enslavement around the Atlantic world nor the violence of this system and the experiences of the enslaved, or even the impact of this history on the economics, culture, and politics of either mainland Britain or the broader empire. Across the nineteenth century and up until close to the millennium, official public memory in Britain instead worked hard to celebrate its own – largely parliamentary – history of *abolition*. Britain's continual celebration of (largely white) abolition heroes such as William Wilberforce, Thomas Clarkson, and Thomas Fowell Buxton has acted to obscure the longer, violent history of enslavement, and its legacies until Black political protest, demographic change, and a shifting historiographical picture disrupted this narrative from the 1980s onward. By the end of the twentieth century, Britain's public memory of enslavement had turned toward incorporating representations of slave resistance, the experiences of the enslaved, and the long brutal history of transatlantic enslavement more broadly. This chapter considers these broad patterns of public memory (and forgetting) as well as milestone moments in the history of Britain's memory of transatlantic enslavement including the more recent and tense "culture war" around this topic in public discourse in 2020 and 2021.

DOI: 10.4324/9781003217848-8

A Culture of Abolition

Since the passing of the Abolition of the British Slave Trade Act of 1807 and the Emancipation Acts of 1833 and 1834, what Britain has "remembered" publicly is not its long history of enslavement at all but the history of its *abolition*. This "culture of abolition" as John Oldfield has termed it has been constructed through a mythologizing celebration of the predominantly white male figures of the abolition movement such as William Wilberforce and the "Clapham sect" through memorials and monuments, ceremonies, and rituals around anniversaries (especially 1933 and 1934 as the centenary of the Emancipation Act) and early museums such as Wilberforce House in Hull.[1] Even this narrative of abolition has been a mythologized version of the truth. Until the latter part of the twentieth century, the more prominent and authorized narrative of abolition continued to be one of parliamentary organizing by Members of Parliament (MPs) and petitioners with little recognition for the more popular forms of protest such as the Lancashire cotton workers' support for Lincoln's embargo on slave-produced cotton during the American Civil War, the work and campaigning of Black abolitionists in Britain such as Olaudah Equiano and Ignatius Sancho, or even the role of resistance and revolt of enslaved populations in the fight for freedom.[2]

The pro-slavery lobby had of course worked hard to obscure the full violence of slavery, to downplay the horrors and trauma of enslaved African people as part of their campaigns to prolong systems of enslavement or, after emancipation, to rework the public memory of their familial narratives in more positive ways.[3] However, it was not the euphemistically termed "West India Interest" (the slave traders, slave owners, and the pro-slavery lobby) who won the debate over the "slavery question." In significant ways, Britain's "culture of abolition" was initiated and sustained by the abolitionists themselves – the histories they wrote, the artifacts they created and curated, the narratives that they wove, and the gendered and racialized ideas they helped to construct and solidify through the imagery of their campaigns. Thomas Clarkson's 1808 history of the abolition movement quickly became the authoritative account of the movement itself and acted to reframe its historical narrative from a national perspective. It was remembering abolition in lieu of remembering slavery – the longer history of which was actively sidelined in public discourse – that allowed for the construction of national narratives which pivoted around liberal ideas of freedom and the emerging re-branded Victorian "antislavery empire."[4] The "usable past" of slavery, abolition, and emancipation was drawn upon in justifications of greater imperial expansion into Africa, and it was Britain's imperative to free the world through the expanse of empire which drew on a re-imagined "heritage" of emancipation.[5] Material culture, which formed a central part of the success of the abolition campaigns of the late eighteenth and early nineteenth centuries, came to form an important part of this broader "culture of abolition" through the display and reproduction of materials in contexts across the nineteenth, twentieth, and twenty-first centuries, and especially within museums.

104 *Jessica Moody*

Many museums in Britain hold artifacts of the abolition campaigns such as reticule bags, sugar boycott bowls, and other domestic items associated with the 1820s antislavery societies. Two of the most well-known items of antislavery material culture displayed and reproduced, especially within museological contexts, are the *Am I Not A Man and a Brother?* Wedgwood medallion of 1787 and the Brookes Slave ship design. Both images and associated artifacts present stereotyped, passive African figures. The Wedgwood medallion depicts a semi-nude African man, in chains, pleading for his freedom. The Brookes designs have rows and rows of identical black bodies lining the outline of a slave ship. Neither artifact speaks to the violence of enslavement nor to the active role enslaved African people took in the dismantling of these systems and yet both have become synonymous with the history and memory of slavery in Britain.[6]

The imagery created and promoted by the antislavery movements of the eighteenth and nineteenth centuries presented largely passive, nude, or semi-nude Black figures in need of white saviors. Such imagery drew on contemporary cultural contexts of sentimentality and often performative emotional morality.[7] Further, this sentimentality was also distinctly voyeuristic and disturbed by other cultural developments at this time, the rise of abolitionism and abolitionist imagery coinciding with the introduction of growing pornographic industry as Marcus Wood has argued.[8] The violence of slavery therefore, much like the bare-breasted hanging and tortured female body in William Blake's *Flagellation of a Female Samboe Slave*, was a violence twisted to align with contemporary tastes through the machine of abolitionist propaganda. It was these images which remained part of the cultural memory of slavery and abolition in Britain, in their display and repetition and in the ongoing celebration of abolition as a facet of national identity across the nineteenth and twentieth centuries.

Maritimization and Distance

While Britain's public memory of slavery has been dominated and framed by narratives celebrating abolition, it has also been displaced through processes of "maritimization" and geographical distancing. John Beech, writing in the early 2000s, initially argued that Britain had "maritimized" its history of slavery. This was achieved, he suggested, largely through the location of heritage sites associated with this history, restricted as they were at the time to Britain's former slave-port cities – London, Liverpool, Bristol, and Hull. The narrative framing of this past was often further restricted to maritime contexts, such as the positioning of Liverpool's *Transatlantic Slavery Gallery* within the basement of the Merseyside Maritime Museum.[9] This maritimization, however, had a longer genesis and was also achieved by Britain framing its history of slavery predominantly as the history of its slave *trade* in public memory discourse. This narrative placed overwhelming focus on the buying and selling of human beings on the West African coast and their transportation in the Middle Passage – as a history therefore largely about the movement of ships across the Atlantic

Ocean. Beech considered such transport-based framing as both "insensitive and misleading," that it would be "hard to imagine that any German recognition of the Holocaust would be placed in a railway museum simply on the basis that trains were used to transport victims to the concentration camps."[10] Similarly, Marcus Wood has argued that the Middle Passage became the central place for the expression of trauma within literature and visual culture, a phenomenon also seen within museums, where the center point in exhibition narratives is often some form of visual representation or physical reconstruction of the Middle Passage.[11] In many ways, this maritime-themed framing aligns with broader narratives of national identity in Britain which emerged particularly strongly from the eighteenth century onward; Britannia ruling the waves, her ships, and navigation as symbols of empire and growing imperial might which played out in art, literature, statues, and monuments to naval heroes and battles. This romanticization of maritime history is something museums have long played an important role within and the initial incorporation of the story of slavery in such contexts therefore inflected the public memory of enslavement through similar lenses.[12] However, at times the very maritimization of this history in Britain has led to counter-memories which place the human reality of this past squarely on British soil, such as the stories of slave sales in Liverpool which congregate at points along the historic river Mersey's edge.[13]

The history of the whole slavery business, moreover, is one which Britain had largely distanced itself from through a geographical displacement, framed as a history which happened elsewhere, in Africa or America. The plantations which fed into Britain's growing and industrializing economy at "home" were positioned some many thousands of miles away in the British Caribbean. While it has been harder to ignore the history of the slave trade in British port cities with their maritime-themed identity narratives and overt celebration of ships and seabound trade, the broader impact of the wealth and capital coming to mainland Britain from the Caribbean could more easily be marginalized in national frameworks. Eric Williams drew connections between slavery, industry, and capitalism in the 1940s and yet the more common public narrative of the Industrial Revolution continued to be much more parochial and inward looking in Britain across much of the twentieth century.[14] While at the time, much of the history of enslavement, especially experiences of Black people in the Caribbean were largely "out of sight and out of mind" as James Walvin suggested, so too were the ongoing impacts of their unpaid labor on mainland Britain, on industry, banking, wealth and produce both in growing urban and rural locations, on art and culture, investment, and so on.[15] More recent historiographical interventions have acted to displace this geographical distancing. The Legacies of British Slave Ownership project, directed by historians at University College London, analyzed the records of the compensation paid to slave owners in 1833 and 1834 who were being compensated for their loss of "property" following the Emancipation Acts which began to outlaw slavery in the British Empire (though a system of "apprenticeship" followed before full freedom was granted to the enslaved).[16] The huge sum of £20,000 was paid

106 *Jessica Moody*

to slave owners up and down the country, not just in the slave-port cities of Liverpool, London, and Bristol but in more rural locations and to women as well as men. A larger proportion of the British middle classes had investments in human property than had been thought, and the picture painted by this research showed a much broader involvement in slavery by the British populace than the maritimized and distanced public memory narratives had presented previously. This research has acted to draw focus away from the coastal peripheries to where this capital had an impact both in the metropole and elsewhere in the empire, in other imperial projects, and in industry, infrastructure, arts, and culture.

Black Resistance and the Turn to Memory in the Late Twentieth Century

It was not until the end of the twentieth century that the focus shifted from remembering abolition to remembering enslavement and the enslaved. This change was driven in part by demographic changes including growing multicultural urban areas and active anti-racist Black politics alongside historiographical shifts and reassessments of national narratives through the rise of social history, "history from below," and a general critique of the "white-washed" histories of empire. As a result, new public history initiatives emerged in the 1990s, though still largely within port cities. Resistance to institutionalized racism, especially that experienced by people of African descent by police forces and state institutions, through protest and the inner-city riots of the 1980s which took place in Bristol, Birmingham, Manchester, Leeds, Liverpool, and London accelerated work in this area. The Merseyside Maritime Museum's 1994 exhibition *Transatlantic Slavery: Against Human Dignity*, the first permanent museum exhibition of this subject in Britain without Wilberforce in the title, was spurred on in part because of criticisms made in the official report into these riots in Liverpool. The report, ominously titled *Loosen the Shackles*, criticized the museum for its lack of information on Liverpool's role in the transatlantic slave trade, describing the small panel text which had been in place as reading like "a lawyer's pleas for mitigation" in its justifying tone.[17] In Bristol where the first of the riots had started following a police raid on a café in St. Paul's in 1980, much controversy surrounded the International Festival of the Sea in 1996 which critics felt largely sidelined the history of the transatlantic slave trade in its public narratives and celebrated John Cabot's 1497 voyage without discussing New World colonialism or subsequent native genocides.[18] A small exhibition was hosted at the eighteenth-century Georgian House, a site which had also attracted criticism for its silence on the subject of slavery having once been the home of the slave-owning Pinney family but whose public narratives largely celebrated John Pinney's achievements or the house's fine Georgian architecture and design.[19] The largest exhibition in Bristol at this time was *A Respectable Trade? Bristol and Transatlantic Slavery* exhibition at Bristol Museum and Art Gallery which opened in March 1999, later moving to the Bristol Industrial

Museum. After the closure of this museum in 2006, a small corner of the city's social history museum, MSHED, was dedicated to the topic and remains. In London, the National Maritime Museum in Greenwich also opened an exhibition titled *Trade and Empire* in 1999 which included material on slavery and which attracted some heated responses from members of the public.[20]

A host of other public history and public memory initiatives and activities were held across the 1990s and early 2000s in what Elizabeth Kowaleski-Wallace has called a "millennial reckoning" because of its timing with the new millennium and against the social backdrop of racial tensions.[21] As well as the exhibitions and events put on by local and national museum bodies, walks and trails were created in Bristol and Liverpool and leaflets, books and other materials were produced by city councils, schools, and Black history organizations.[22] In 1999, Liverpool City Council staged an official apology for the city's role in the transatlantic slave trade and the city began marking Slavery Remembrance Day on August 23 that year (the date marking the start of the Haitian Revolution in 1791) which included a traditional African libation ceremony and has since grown to include an annual lecture, a Walk of Remembrance from the city center (since 2011) and a host of surrounding events.[23] Also in 1999 Bristol City Council named a newly constructed bridge across the floating harbor "Pero's Bridge" after an enslaved African man who had lived in Bristol and was owned by the Pinney family. Much of the tone and objectives of this memory work at this time centered around the need for racial healing in the aftermath of the riots and resistance of the 1980s and a tense racial politics in many British cities. These memorial interventions took place concurrently with the publication of significant and publicly debated race relations reports such as the Macpherson Report into the murder of Black Londoner Stephen Lawrence and the subsequent mishandling of the case by the Metropolitan Police (concluding that this was the product of institutionalized racism) and the Parekh Report into "multi-ethnic Britain" which considered the racial dynamics and experiences of British society and identity in the late 1990s.[24] The level of memory work undertaken in the 1990s, much of it temporary but with notable permanent additions to the memorial landscape, especially in Liverpool, would not be matched until a major round-number anniversary brought debates around race, history, and memory to a head again in 2007.

2007: The Bicentenary of the Abolition of the British Slave Trade

In 2007, 200 years after the passing of the Abolition of the Slave Trade Act of 1807, a year of national commemorations took place which brought a greater level of public focus to Britain's role in transatlantic enslavement and abolition than at any other point in time thus far.[25] Endorsed by the New Labour Government whose organizing committee was convened by William Prescott, Deputy Prime Minister and MP for Hull (William Wilberforce's hometown), small and large organizations took advantage of the £16 million made available

108   *Jessica Moody*

through the Heritage Lottery Fund's "Grants for All" program and state bodies such as the Department for Culture, Media and Sport (DCMS), and the Department for Education and Skills.[26] The availability of this funding and the national programming framework meant that a greater diversity of organizations and people were involved in the public history of enslavement than had ever been the case. A number of large public historical institutions also created new permanent exhibitions including the major redesign of Wilberforce House Museum in Hull, a new permanent gallery at the National Maritime Museum in Greenwich, the "London, Sugar Slavery" gallery in the Museum of London Docklands in London, and the opening of the International Slavery Museum in Liverpool. No longer confined simply to the port cities, projects took place around the country in community centers, museums, archives, libraries, theaters, and many other locations. The scale of national commemorative focus in 2007 was unprecedented, and no other European countries marked similar anniversaries of abolition and emancipation on the scale Britain did. While this renewed attention was welcomed by many, including many historians, for shining a light on a history not otherwise discussed in any great depth beyond the port cities of Hull, Bristol, and Liverpool, there were a number of criticisms leveled at the Bicentenary. These included the overwhelming focus given over, yet again, to celebrating the role of abolitionists in place of a more honest confrontation of the violence and trauma of the history of enslavement and its broader ramifications; the erroneous conflation of the abolition of the slave trade with the abolition of slavery itself, which would remain legal in the British Empire into the 1830s; and a host of debates around the ethics of representation.

Through a focus on the British parliamentary abolition campaign, the redeployment of eighteenth- and nineteenth-century abolitionist imagery – much of which was racist, passive, and demeaning – the full horror of the experiences of the enslaved were largely subdued and sanitized in much of the official discourse of the anniversary year, especially from Government. The narrative of abolition had expanded to include women (usually Hannah More, 1745–1833) and Black abolitionists (usually Olaudah Equiano, 1745–1797), and there was a notable theme of enslaved resistance running throughout the museum displays in particular.[27] However, the tone of abolitionist celebration and perceived white self-congratulation was one that attracted criticism, especially from Black activists who termed the year a "Wilberfest."[28] In a moment described as the "only real moment of catharsis" by David Spence (Director of Museum of London, Docklands), Toyin Agbetu, Black British Pan-African activist and founding member of Ligali, protested by interrupting the official Westminster Abbey commemorative ceremony attended by the Prime Minister Tony Blair and the Queen among a congregation of other high-profile figures.[29] Agbetu's protest criticized the tone of the commemorative year and called for an official apology for Britain's role in the slave trade.

Museums were a major focus of activity during the bicentenary, hosting both temporary and permanent exhibitions, events, and becoming organizing

From a Culture of Abolition to a Culture War 109

Figure 5.1 Protester Toyin Agbetu disrupts a service to mark the bicentenary of the 1807 act to abolish the slave trade, attended by Britain's Queen Elizabeth II, at Westminster Abbey

Source: Credit – PA images/Alamy stock photo

110　*Jessica Moody*

hubs for broader public history initiatives. However, as the *1807 Commemorated* project at the University of York revealed, this was an "anxious and ambiguous" time, and museums became embroiled in debates over not just the history of slavery and abolition, but questions over the ethics of representation, the role of museums in society and their place in solidifying or challenging established identity narratives.[30] The *1807 Commemorated* project analyzed responses to the Bicentenary at over 200 museums through large-scale, semi-structured, qualitative interviews with visitors, alongside exhibition analysis, interviews with museum professionals, and analysis of political discourse.[31] Many of these museum exhibitions around the country sought connections to this history in local settings, researching local industries which were connected with the trade, local abolitionists, and the Black presence. There was a concerted attempt to try and weave the narrative of transatlantic slavery into broader economic narratives including the impact on the Industrial Revolution, which has long been a topic of academic interest for economic historians.[32] In community consultation, museum professionals found that there was a complex relationship expressed toward the representation of enslavement from Britain's African-descendant community, where there was a sense of wanting the full story to be told and also foreground the rich diversity of African diasporic culture.[33] Further, many groups were skeptical that such institutions, many having long been active in constructing and maintaining the culture of abolition that had obscured the full history of slavery, would now be able to fully both represent the truth of this past and engage with pressing present-day legacies around race and racism in British society.[34]

It was museums more than any other organization which grappled with difficult questions over the ethics of representing violence, derogatory racialized imagery, and trauma. The display and interpretation of the imagery of enslavement (including that produced by the abolition campaigns of the late eighteenth and early nineteenth centuries in visual, textual, and tangible objects), or what Geoffrey Cubitt has termed "atrocity materials" caused a mixture of anxiety and concern for museum professionals and a range of responses from museum visitors.[35] In Cubitt's analysis of 2007 exhibitions, including interviews with curators and visitors to museums, there was a discernible tension felt between depicting the "full horror" of the experience of enslavement – the violence, torture, and restraint – especially that experienced during the Middle Passage, and a desire not to impose too much distress on visitors, especially visitors of African descent and children.[36] These concerns echoed those of the previous decade. There was a tension between the need for "truth-telling," deemed necessary to counter an otherwise sanitized public memory, and a desire not to encourage a form of voyeuristic fascination with the abuse of Black bodies. This was a fascination which had long been a feature of Britain's historic and memorial culture of abolition.[37] There were also concerns over the familiarity of some of the "atrocity materials" on display – the chains and whips which had become clichés of the public memory of enslavement and had perhaps lost their power or ability to shock, especially when used, as they were in one exhibition in 2007, as bordering around interpretation boards, appearing more as decoration and marketing techniques than representations of a brutally violent system.[38]

The Bicentenary might not have had the revolutionary revision of public memory that some sections of British society may have wanted. However, it did have meaningful impacts on broader trends and assessments of the place of the history of enslavement in narratives of British history in ways that for some were more disturbing than reassuring. The availability of public funding and the consensus gained from a national program of events meant museums, archives, and other public bodies were conducting often new and ground-breaking research into the presence, lives, and experiences of not only local abolitionists but also enslaved people and people of African descent who lived in their areas.[39] Moreover, other connections were made to local industries, institutions, and cultures which were connected to systems of enslavement in varying ways such as cotton manufactures, steel and metal works, potteries, and financial institutions. The public marking and subsequent public debate over how Britain should remember slavery during the 2007 Bicentenary commemoration marked the first real large-scale public "history war" Britain had seen in relation to its history of Empire. 2007 called into question issues of national identity, previous efforts to sanitize, obscure, and "forget" slavery and celebrate abolition, and broader societal issues over whose voices were heard in this process and who was represented by and within this history in levels of public debate which would not be matched until 2020.

Black Lives Matter: 2020, "Culture Wars" and Decolonizing Public Memory

The Black Lives Matter (BLM) protests of the summer of 2020 in Britain, part of a broader global response to the killing by police of George Floyd in Minneapolis on May 25, 2020, drew focus to a multitude of issues around institutionalized racism and police violence, alongside bringing a renewed and urgent attention to the public memorialization of slavery and empire. Protesters focused on the public celebration of slave traders and slave owners in statues, naming of streets and buildings, and monuments to colonialism and imperialism. On June 7, 2020, BLM protesters pulled down the statue of seventeenth-century slave merchant Edward Colston (1636–1721) which had stood in the center of Bristol since 1895. The statue was rolled into Bristol harbor from Pero's bridge, a bridge commemoratively named after an enslaved African man. The statue, having been retrieved and conserved, was transferred into the care of Bristol Museum which opened an exhibition about the statue and its contested history within the broader context of Bristol's history of enslavement on the one-year anniversary of the statue having been pulled down. The action in 2020 marked the first time a statue of an enslaver had been removed in Britain. Although no other statue was torn down in as dramatic a fashion as Colston's, other statues were targeted including that of plantation owner Robert Milligan

Figure 5.2 Empty pedestal of the statue of Edward Colston in Bristol, the day after protesters felled the statue and rolled it into the harbor. The ground is covered with Black Lives Matter placards

Source: Credit – Photo with the kind permission of Caitlin Hobbs

which was removed by city authorities from West India docks in London on June 9. There is, however, a longer history of protest and challenge around Britain's public celebration of enslavers – a number of public debates have taken

From a Culture of Abolition to a Culture War   113

place around the streets named after slave traders in Liverpool and the statue of Edward Colston has long had its critics including through targeted campaigns, vandalism, and challenges since at least the 1990s. Like the monuments to the Confederacy in America, many such memorials and statues to slave owners were erected in the late nineteenth and early twentieth centuries, at a time of high imperial expansion of the British Empire and as part of a broader Victorian memory cult intent on creating paternalistic heroes of empire often to quell working-class unrest.[40]

What followed after the dramatic events of June 7 constituted a burgeoning, and at times artificially engineered and overtly politicized, "culture war" over race, class, identity, and history. There had not been a public debate of this scale over Britain's memory of enslavement since 2007 – which, as I have argued elsewhere, constituted Britain's first real foray into publicly fought history and culture wars, the kind seen more clearly in America over topics such as the display of the Enola Gay and public debates over the extent of frontier massacres and the stolen generations in Australia.[41] However, the emotion and drama of the 2020 culture wars, which the right-wing press, and Conservative MPs stoked particularly strongly, clearly overtook the tenor of the discussion seen in 2007.

The debates of 2020–2021 did not just concern the public memorialization of figures associated with transatlantic enslavement but included tensions over Britain's even less well-grounded and underdeveloped public memory of empire more broadly. Britain's "imperial nostalgia" has long clouded any meaningful and honest engagement with its history of empire and colonialism.[42] This mythologizing of empire has shaped and been shaped by the memory of the world wars, World War II in particular, and has encouraged a perception of empire based largely on its own myths of a civilizing mission, the implementation of the democratic process, free trade, and infrastructural development (especially around the construction of railways as nothing but a positive good for less "developed" areas of the world).[43] This mythologizing has become louder and more urgently articulated since the stoking of racial and class-based tensions and anxieties around national identity and belonging and Britain's place in the world preceding and following the "Brexit" vote of 2016 in which the British people voted in favor of leaving the European Union by a narrow 51.9% margin. One of the imperial statues at the center of public debates in 2020 was the statue of Cecil Rhodes which stands above the entranceway to Oriel College at the University of Oxford. Debates around this statue and other commemorative naming of Rhodes at Oxford preceded the Black Lives Matter protests and were part of an Oxford response to the Rhodes Must Fall/Fees Must Fall campaign (hereafter RMFO) which started at the University of Cape Town, South Africa. Part of a broader student-led campaign to decolonize the curriculum and the university and to draw focus to experiences of racism on campus, RMFO had been calling for the removal of the statue of Rhodes since 2015.[44] Oriel College Governing Body initially voted in favor of exploring the statue's removal. However, following an independent commission set up after this vote, which also found

114   *Jessica Moody*

in favor of the statue's removal, the University suggested that removal would in fact be too expensive.[45]

Much of the early debate in 2020–2021 following the fall of Colston's statue focused on the argument that the removal of material culture was paramount to "erasing" or "rewriting" history.[46] The discourse of erasure over the following months argued that the removal of statues and re-naming of streets and buildings was akin to "sweeping historical mistakes under the carpet," of removing evidence and forgetting slave traders, of a misguided attempt at atonement for racism in America, of "rewriting history to accommodate political trends," of censorship, or even when commenters suggested it wasn't "erasing" history, it was nonetheless denying members of the public the opportunity to meet "their history face-to-face."[47] A counter-campaign group called *Save Our Statues* was established to help Boris Johnson, Priti Patel, and many Conservative MPs who had "promised they'd save our history from mob rule."[48] One of the group's actions in this regard was to try and stop visitors from booking in to see the exhibition and display of the Colston statue at the MSHED museum in Bristol by block booking for the free tickets.[49] Even some academic historians suggested that removing statues was erasing history, with Emeritus Professor of Medieval Theology and Intellectual History at the University of Cambridge stating that "it is important to learn from our history rather than simply erase it."[50]

Much of this discourse was coupled with a criticism of the apparently left-wing, "Marxist" academy, of students, academics, and broader work to decolonize university curricula and public spaces which was apparently a "movement in which predominantly white academics take a deeply unhistorical view of history, devoid of context, and seek to teach predominantly white students to feel ashamed of their country and its past," according to the *Telegraph* journalist Simon Heffer.[51] It was also an argument interweaved with concurrent obsessions on the right with so-called cancel-culture, no-platforming, and free speech, especially on social media and on university campuses, as if statues, like disgraced celebrities, were being "canceled" or it was an issue of freedom of speech that statues celebrating slave traders were no longer standing proud in city centers.[52] It was, more disconcertingly, a discourse which was also coupled with a distinct reactionary nationalism, that "[o]ur heritage, freedom and identity are now under greater threat than at any times since the Second World War"[53] and a language of violence, where critiques of the public memory of slavery and empire were discussed alongside flag-burning, de-facing the Cenotaph, and protestors described as a violent mob.[54] This was a discourse which played well into the populist Johnson government, where Prime Minister Boris Johnson could be cast as the heroic savior of the "nation's heritage," fighting against the culture war of the Left.[55] In response, Samuel Kasumu, Johnson's only Black advisor and former race relations advisor, stepped down over the government's role in these culture wars.[56] New, more stringent and centralized processes to "protect" all statues, monuments, and other public material culture, whether listed or not, were announced in January 2021, as part of the government's "retain and explain" policy.[57] This policy was also directed at museums and heritage organizations, stifling ongoing work around decolonization and representing a marked departure from Britain's "arms-length" relationship between government and cultural bodies.[58] The Culture Secretary, Oliver Dowden, also issued a letter (leaked to the press) which instructed publicly funded museums and institutions not to remove statues or other artifacts or otherwise "eras[e] these objects," or they would risk losing central financial support.[59] The letter also stated that as tax-payer-funded institutions, museums should act "impartially" and not be "motivated by activism or politics." In a particularly threatening tone, the Culture Secretary stressed how important this was "as we enter a challenging Comprehensive Spending Review, in which all government spending will rightly be scrutinised."[60] In a meeting held between the Culture Secretary and 25 heritage bodies, institutions were told to use their collections to provide a "more rounded view" of the history of the British Empire, by "neither air brushing the past nor denigrating our history."[61]

A number of historians challenged the idea that the removal of statues rewrites or erases history. Their challenge lay first in arguing that rewriting history is precisely what historians do – they research and reinterpret the past based on ever-changing and evolving information and re-interpretation.[62] Second, they argued that statues themselves are not history but rather memory. Public historian David Olusoga stated that far from being an attack on history, the toppling of Edward Colston's statue was itself history.[63] Further, he argued that

> [s]tatues aren't the mechanism by which we understand history. We learn history through museums, through books, through television programmes. Statues are about adoration, about saying that this man was a great man and he did great things. That is not true; he was a slave trader and a murderer.[64]

Arguably, the forced removal and protest around statues of slave traders and merchants in 2020–2021 in Britain led to a greater public awareness and engagement in the history of slavery and empire than these statues ever achieved as inanimate objects largely passed by in busy shopping areas of towns and cities.

By 2020–2021, the geography of this public debate and interventions in changing public memorialization was also no longer confined to the port cities and, while having a larger focus on England, ranged across Wales, Northern Ireland, and Scotland. An audit commissioned by Wales's first minister, Kark Drakeford, identified over 200 street names, statues, and buildings connected to slavery and colonialism.[65] The National Trust for Scotland carried out a review of its properties, reporting that 18 were connected to slavery and colonialism and announced a further £380,000 for a two-year research and public engagement project on the topic called Facing Our Past.[66] In Edinburgh, the statue of Robert Dundas had been graffitied during the BLM protests in 2020 drawing attention to his father Henry's role in delaying abolition, and Henry Dundas's

116 *Jessica Moody*

monument (the "Melville monument") is due to have a contextual plaque added acknowledging these and other aspects of Dundas's imperial career.[67] A number of different kinds of British institutions across the country came forward and highlighted their historical connections to enslavement such as the Bank of England and companies such as Lloyds of London and the brewery Greene King.[68] Guy's and St Thomas's hospitals in London announced that they would be removing statues of Robert Clayton and Thomas Guy who had connections to slavery through the Royal African Company and the South Sea Company, respectively.[69]

A greater connection began to be forged between histories of enslavement and more rural parts of Britain's heritage landscape. This included work by heritage bodies such as Historic England's work listing connections between villages where halls, churches, pubs, and industries connected such places to a broader slave economy.[70] The National Trust (a conservation charity and membership organization founded in 1895) had been working toward re-developing its public history of slavery and empire for some time, and especially since new exhibitions and public history projects drew attention to these connections in 2007. While most of the plans around re-interpretation and reframing public narratives at these sites considered the connections between residents and owners, some debates centered on artifacts owned by the Trust including an eighteenth-century statue of a Black man at Dunham Massey Hall in Greater Manchester which was removed because of its offensive aesthetic.[71] The National Trust's own research strategy had highlighted the year 2020 as time to focus public programming on "legacies of slavery" and the year 2022 to consider broader legacies of empire.[72] In 2020, these plans were both disrupted by the COVID-19 pandemic which led to widespread site closures and staff off work through the British government's furlough scheme, and concurrently accelerated plans in motion in response to the summer of protests. In September 2020, the Trust published a report on the connections between its properties, slavery, and colonialism.[73] The report argued that around one-third of its properties were connected in some way to historic slavery and/or colonialism, and that 90 of its properties were connected to histories of slavery and empire through slave trading, slave ownership and compensation, colonial expansion and administration, and cultural links to empire such as through writers including Rudyard Kipling.[74] The Trust received a notable public reaction, much of it supportive but alongside a sizeable hostile backlash with some of its own members threatening to cancel their memberships over the issue.[75] The British right-wing press was particularly outraged. The *Daily Mail* claimed that as "the single most important custodian of our national story," the National Trust was "wilfully misrepresenting Britain's history" in an act which was "the latest example of a pervasive culture of ignorant, nihilistic antipatriotism."[76] In particular, the perceived conflation of the histories of slavery and colonialism struck a nerve, with popular historian and Winston

Churchill biographer Andrew Roberts claiming that to do so was "mixing the two very separate things up."[77] The highlighting of Churchill's connections to empire in the report in particular raised criticism from a number of prominent figures including from government. Culture Secretary Oliver Dowden stated that the Trust should focus instead on "preserving and protecting our heritage for future generations" and that "Churchill is one of Britain's greatest heroes."[78] Conservative MP Guy Opperman similarly criticized the connections and suggested that the report would encourage further attacks on the statue of Churchill in Parliament Square which had been graffitied with the words "was a racist" in BLM protests earlier that year.[79] The National Trust received a greater degree of critical, angry, and otherwise emotional reaction to its report than any earlier work undertaken by similar organizations. The report was castigated in the right-leaning press for being "self-flagellation," "depthless virtue signaling," and "woke nonsense."[80] Several of the academics involved in the report and ongoing work with the National Trust on projects around slavery and colonialism were the subjects of targeted and often personal abuse by the press. Corinne Fowler, an academic at the University of Leicester and one of the co-editors of the report, who also led the *Colonial Countryside* project with school children and the Trust, suggested that the backlash was in part because of the largely rural location of these places. She wrote that "[t]he countryside has turned out to be a particularly sensitive topic" when it comes to histories of race, slavery, and empire.[81]

These "culture wars" were overtly political on a number of levels, not least for their political usefulness as a scapegoat and distraction from other pressing issues and political failings during a year marred by a mishandled public health crisis and ongoing fallout from Brexit but also as a ground for drumming up antagonism in the name of nationalism for political gain. As David Olusoga eloquently put it, the 2020–2021 "culture wars" created new enemies as Britain's exit from the European Union meant losing otherwise handy scapegoats in Brussels. Conservative politicians in Boris Johnson's populist government pitted racial and class identity groups against each other while presenting themselves as "the defenders of British institutions and the champions of British history."[82] What the debates revealed more broadly, however, was the dearth of a developed and honest public understanding of Britain's history of enslavement and its legacies, not only through its pervasive culture of abolitionism, maritimization, and distancing motifs seen for centuries previously but also through an underdeveloped understanding of the role of slave traders, slave merchants, and the involvement of others in the broader slave economy. Moreover, the lack of public awareness of the history of memory, the provenance of these largely nineteenth-century statues and monuments and cults of memorialization and the purpose of statutory skewed a public debate which some sections saw only as wanton vandalism of a proud "heritage" they'd been taught to accept and embrace as theirs.

118 *Jessica Moody*

Conclusion

Britain's public memory of enslavement has been dominated by its nineteenth-century "culture of abolition," but efforts have been made more recently to accommodate narratives of enslavement, slave resistance, and experiences of the enslaved around. However, the contested nature of this history and the pervasiveness of its mythologizing can clearly be seen in the "culture wars" of the twenty-first century. Changes in public memory have been instigated because of Black political protest and changing demographics, cultural changes around museums, heritage and historiography, new historical research, and unpredictable disruptions sparked by a national anniversary that proved commemoration can be both conservative in official tone and radical in local and grassroots implications and effects simultaneously. It is therefore fitting that the largest public debate, or "culture war," over Britain and slavery was sparked in 2020 by anti-racist protest and action through Black Lives Matter activists challenging racist societal structures which are themselves legacies of the history of enslavement.

Britain's dogged determination to celebrate abolition in official public memory has meant that the country has not faced many other facets of this past and its pressing present-day legacies. Where the violence of slavery is remembered, it is done so through the abolitionist gaze, consisting of propaganda which adhered to contemporary cultures of sentimentality, emotion, and white charitable ambition. Efforts to remember the experiences of the enslaved in the upsurge of public history in the 1990s focused on the trauma of the Middle Passage, but veered toward a voyeuristic engagement with Black pain, and raised difficult ethical questions about what appropriate representations of race and violence in the public museum space should look like. Historical research and public memory in the twenty-first century have tried to bring the history of enslavement "home," away from maritimized spaces of port cities at the peripheries of the country, back from the Atlantic Ocean or the Americas, and into rural spaces and industries and areas less readily connected to this past previously. This has caused a huge emotional reaction from those who connect rural heritage sites such as the British country house with a sense of national "heritage," featuring a racialized sense of class and belonging in the countryside which is so often seen to be a white space.

The culture wars of 2020–2021 drew stark attention to the inadequacies of public memory around histories of race, slavery, and empire in Britain. They showed the pervasive mythologies of these pasts as presented through education and politics for decades as histories of success and triumph, liberal ideals and morality, progress, and positive contributions to the world by the British Empire. The challenge to this general mythologizing of empire occurred at an uncertain time for Britain's sense of global standing. The country officially left the European Union on January 31, 2020, following the Brexit vote of 2016. There were also uncertainties about the future of the Union with ongoing calls for Scottish Independence and deep running tensions over the Irish border. Alongside this, tensions and uncertainties were further aggravated by the deep state of despair and anxiety shared by many during the COVID-19 pandemic. For Britain, it is both the dominance of its celebratory culture of abolition and the efforts of the slave owners which have shaped its public memory of enslavement. The planter class and their descendants in the nineteenth century reworked memories of enslavement to downplay, justify, and gloss and thereby cast familial legacies in better lights. This has meant that Britain has not honestly faced or understood its enslavers in history and memory nor the pervasive interconnectedness of the history of enslavement with a much broader swathe of British society. While the place of enslavers in public memory as philanthropic benefactors, progressive industrialists or patrons of the arts have long been challenged by groups and activists, the power of their public commemoration to shape their memory, to instill a sense of "heritage" which elevates, celebrates, and obscures their crimes through tangible statues, monuments, and commemorative naming needs to be better acknowledged and communicated. This has raised important questions and shifted a deeply held consensus around who is celebrated in public memory, why and with what effect.

Notes

1 John Oldfield, *'Chords of Freedom': Commemoration, Ritual and British Transatlantic Slavery* (Manchester: Manchester University Press, 2007).

2 On these topics, see Alan Rice, "The American Civil War and European Anti-Slavery," *Revealing Histories: Remembering Slavery*, http://revealinghistories.org.uk/the-american-civil-war-and-the-lancashire-cotton-famine.html [Accessed July 13, 2021]; R.J.M. Blackett, *Divided Hearts: Britain and the American Civil War* (Baton Rouge, LA: Louisiana State University Press, 2001); Ryan Hanley, *Beyond Slavery and Abolition: Black British Writing 1770–1830* (Cambridge: Cambridge University Press, 2018); David Richardson, "Shipboard Revolts, African Authority, and the Atlantic Slave Trade," *The William and Mary Quarterly*, Vol. 58, No. 1 (2001), pp. 69–92.

3 Catharine Hall, "Reconfiguring Race: The Stories the Slave Owners Told," in C. Hall, N. Draper, K. McClelland, K. Donington, and R. Lang, eds., *Legacies of British Slave-Ownership: Colonial Slavery and the Formation of Victorian Britain* (Cambridge: Cambridge University Press, 2014), pp. 163–202; Catharine Hall, "Whose Memories? Edward Long and the Work of Re-Remembering," in Katie Donington, Ryan Hanley, and Jessica Moody, eds., *Britain's History and Memory of Transatlantic Slavery: Local Nuances of a 'National Sin'* (Liverpool: Liverpool University Press, 2016), pp. 129–149.

4 Linda Colley, *Britons: Forging the Nation 1707–1837* (London: Pimlico, 1994); Richard Huzzey, *Freedom Burning: Anti-Slavery and Empire in Victorian Britain* (Ithaca, NY: Cornell University Press, 2012).

5 Huzzey, *Freedom Burning*; Oldfield, *'Chords of Freedom'*.

6 Marcus Wood, *The Horrible Gift of Freedom: Atlantic Slavery and the Representation of Emancipation* (Athens, GA: University of Georgia Press, 2010), Chapter 6; Mary Guyatt, "The Wedgwood Slave Medallion: Values in Eighteenth-Century Design," *Journal of Design History*, Vol. 13, No. 2 (2000); John Oldfield, *Popular Politics and Antislavery: The Mobilisation of Public Opinion against the Slave Trade 1787–1807* (Manchester: Manchester University Press, 1998).

120   *Jessica Moody*

7 Brycchan Carey, *British Abolitionism and the Rhetoric of Sensibility: Writing, Sentiment and Slavery, 1760–1807* (Basingstoke: Palgrave Macmillan, 2005).

8 Marcus Wood, *Slavery, Empathy, Pornography* (Oxford: Oxford University Press, 2002), p. 12.

9 John G. Beech, "The Marketing of Slavery Heritage in the United Kingdom," in G.M. Dann and A.V. Seaton, eds., *Slavery, Contested Heritage, and Thanatourism* (New York: Haworth Hospitality Press, 2001).

10 Beech, "The Marketing of Slavery Heritage," p. 103.

11 Wood, *Blind Memory*, p. 14. There was a tendency toward models and physical reconstructions of the lower decks of slave ships in the 1990s, whereas more recent museological representations have tended toward more abstract forms such as the International Slavery Museum's film. See Jessica Moody, *The Persistence of Memory* (Liverpool: Liverpool University Press, 2020), ch. 5; Ana Lucia Araujo, *Museums and Atlantic Slavery* (Abingdon: Routledge, 2021); Ana Lucia Araujo, *Slavery in the Age of Memory: Engaging the Past* (London: Bloomsbury, 2021).

12 See Ann Day and Ken Lunn, "British Maritime Heritage: Carried along by the Currents?," *International Journal of Heritage Studies*, Vol. 9, No. 4 (2003).

13 I discuss this in more detail in Jessica Moody, "Liverpool's Local Tints: Drowning Memory and 'Maritimizing' Slavery in a Seaport City," in Katie Donington, Ryan Hanley, and Jessica Moody, eds., *Britain's History and Memory of Transatlantic Slavery: Local Nuances of a 'National Sin'* (Liverpool: Liverpool University Press, 2016), pp. 150–171.

14 Eric Williams, *Capitalism and Slavery* (Chapel Hill, NC: University of North Carolina Press, 1944).

15 James Walvin, *Britain's Slave Empire* (Stroud: Tempus, 2000), pp. 8–9.

16 See *Centre for the Study of the Legacies of British Slavery*, www.ucl.ac.uk/lbs/ [Accessed July 13, 2021]; Catherine Hall, Nicholas Draper, Keith McClelland, Katie Donington, and Rachel Lang, *Legacies of British Slave-Ownership Colonial Slavery and the Formation of Victorian Britain* (Cambridge: Cambridge University Press, 2014); Nicholas Draper, *The Price of Emancipation: Slave-ownership, Compensation and British Society at the End of Slavery* (Cambridge: Cambridge University Press, 2013).

17 The panel text read: "The slave trade did make a significant contribution to Liverpool's prosperity. However, Liverpool's trading wealth was firmly established before it began to dominate the slave trade from the 1760s. Between 1783 and 1793, 878 Liverpool ships carried 303,737 slaves. Sailings to Africa represented only 10% of outward bound tonnage from Liverpool. On the other hand slaves produced the sugar and tobacco which were Liverpool's most important imports." Lord Gifford QC (chair), Wally Brown, and Ruth Bundey, *Loosen the Shackles: First Report of the Liverpool 8 Inquiry into Race Relations in Liverpool* (London: Karia Press, 1989), p. 26. See Moody, *The Persistence of Memory*, p. 86.

18 In 1497, Italian born explorer John Cabot led the earliest known European expedition to the North American coast since Norse voyages of the eleventh century. Cabot and his crew sailed from Bristol and landed somewhere around Newfoundland and is widely credited for initiating English transatlantic exploration. See Evan Jones and Margaret M. Condon, *Cabot and Bristol's Age of Discovery: The Bristol Discovery Voyages 1480–1508* (Bristol: University of Bristol Press, 2016); Elizabeth Kowaleski-Wallace, *The British Slave Trade and Public Memory* (New York: Columbia University Press, 2006), p. 25; Firstborn Studios, *Under the Bridge*, 2000, https://vimeo.com/11471392.

19 On John Pinney and Bristol's social history of enslavement more broadly see Madge Dresser, *Slavery Obscured: The Social History of the Slave Trade in Bristol* (Bristol: Redcliffe Press, 2007).

20 Douglas Hamilton, "Representing Slavery in British Museums: The Challenges of 2007," in John Oldfield and Kora Caplan, eds., *Imagining Transatlantic Slavery and Abolition* (Basingstoke: Palgrave Macmillan, 2021), pp. 127–144.

21 Kowaleski-Wallace, *The British Slave Trade and Public Memory*.

22 See Moody, *The Persistence of Memory*, Chapter 2.

From a Culture of Abolition to a Culture War   121

23 See Moody, *The Persistence of Memory*, Chapter 6.
24 William MacPherson, *The Stephen Lawrence Inquiry: Report of an Inquiry* by Sir William MacPherson of Cluny (February 1999), https://assets.publishing.service.gov.uk/government/uploads/system/uploads/attachment_data/file/277111/4262.pdf; Commission on the Future of Multi-Ethnic Britain, *The Future of Multi-Ethnic Britain: The Parekh Report* (London: Profile Books, 2000).
25 There is a large body of scholarship which has analyzed public history and commemorative work in this year. See, for example, the special issues of the following journals: *Museum & Society*, Vol. 8, No. 3 (2010); *History Workshop Journal*, Vol. 64, No. 1 (2007); *Slavery & Abolition*, Vol. 30, No. 2 (2009).
26 The Heritage Lottery Fund (HLF) is a key funder of public history and heritage projects and organizations in Britain.
27 See Geoff Cubitt, "Lines of Resistance: Evoking and Configuring the Theme of Resistance in Museum Displays in Britain around the Bicentenary of 1807," *Museum and Society*, Vol. 8, No. 3 (2010).
28 Used especially by Toyin Agbetu, activist and founder of the Pan-African organization Ligali.
29 Ligali are an African British organization who campaign for human rights and social justice. David Spence, "Making the London, Sugar and Slavery Gallery at the Museum of London Docklands," in Laurajane Smith, Geoffrey Cubitt, Kalliopi Fouseki, and Ross Wilson, eds., *Representing Enslavement and Abolition in Museums: Ambiguous Engagements* (Abingdon: Routledge Research in Museum Studies, 2011), p. 154.
30 Geoffrey Cubitt, Laurajane Smith, and Ross Wilson, "Introduction: Anxiety and Ambiguity in the Representation of Dissonant History," in Laurajane Smith, Geoffrey Cubitt, Kalliopi Fouseki, and Ross Wilson, eds., *Representing Enslavement and Abolition in Museums: Ambiguous Engagements* (Abingdon: Routledge Research in Museum Studies, 2011), pp. 1–2.
31 See https://archives.history.ac.uk/1807commemorated/index.html.
32 Eric Williams, *Capitalism and Slavery*.
33 Cubitt, Smith, and Wilson, 'Introduction,' p. 4.
34 Cubitt, Smith, and Wilson, 'Introduction,' p. 5.
35 Geoffrey Cubitt, "Atrocity Materials and the Representation of Transatlantic Slavery: Problems, Strategies and Reactions," in Laurajane Smith, Geoffrey Cubitt, Kalliopi Fouseki, and Ross Wilson, eds., *Representing Enslavement and Abolition in Museums: Ambiguous Engagements* (Abingdon: Routledge Research in Museum Studies, 2011), p. 229.
36 Cubitt, "Atrocity Materials," pp. 232–233.
37 See Zoe Norridge, "Finding a Home in Hackney? Reimagining Narratives of Slavery Through a Multicultural Community Museum Space," *African and Black Diaspora: An International Journal*, Vol. 2, No. 2 (2009).
38 For example as seen in the "Everywhere in Chains . . . ? Wales and Slavery" exhibition at the National Waterfront Museum, Swansea, though this was a motif seen at a number of museums. Cubitt, "Atrocity Materials," p. 242.
39 Caroline Bressey, "The Legacies of 2007: Remapping the Black Presence in Britain," *Geography Compass*, Vol. 3, No. 3 (2009).
40 Madge Dresser, "Colston Revisited," *History Workshop Online*, www.historyworkshop.org.uk/colston-revisited/; E.J. Hobsbawm and T. O Ranger, *The Invention of Tradition* (Cambridge: Cambridge University Press, 1983); James Watts, "The History Behind the Edward Colston Statue Pulled Down by Anti-Racism Protesters in Bristol," *The Conversation*, June 11, 2020, https://scroll.in/article/964230/the-history-behind-the-edward-colston-statue-pulled-down-by-anti-racism-protesters-in-bristol.
41 Jessica Moody, "History and Heritage," in Emma Waterton and Steve Watson, eds., *The Palgrave Handbook of Contemporary Heritage Research* (Basingstoke: Palgrave Macmillan, 2015), p. 121. On History and Culture Wars in America and Australia, see S. Dubin, *Displays of Power: Memory and Amnesia in the American Museum* (New York: New York

122 *Jessica Moody*

University Press, 1999); Anna Clark and Stuart Macintyre, *The History Wars* (Carlton: Melbourne University Press, 2003).

42 Bill Schwarz, *The White Man's World* (London: Oxford University Press, 2012); Robert Spencer, "The Politics of Imperial Nostalgia," in Graham Huggan and Ian Law, eds., *Racism Postcolonialism Europe* (Liverpool: Liverpool University Press, 2009); Astrid Rasch and Stuart Ward, eds., *Embers of Empire in Brexit Britain* (London: Bloomsbury, 2019).

43 Paul Gilroy, *Postcolonial Melancholia* (New York: Columbia University Press, 2005).

44 See Rhodes Must Fall, *Rhodes Must Fall: The Struggle to Decolonise the Racist Heart of Empire* (London: Zed Books, 2018).

45 Aamna Mohdin, Richard Adams, and Ben Quinn, "Oxford College Backs Removal of Cecil Rhodes Statue," *The Guardian,* June 17, 2020, https://www.theguardian.com/education/2020/jun/17/end-of-the-rhodes-cecil-oxford-college-ditches-controversial-statue [Accessed February 27, 2023]; Aamna Mohdin, "Cecil Rhodes Statue at Oxford College Should Go, Says Independent Report," *The Guardian*, May 19, 2021, https://www.theguardian.com/education/2021/may/19/cecil-rhodes-statue-at-oxford-college-should-go-says-independent-report [Accessed February 27, 2023]; Aamna Mohdin, "Oxford College Criticised for Refusal to Remove Cecil Rhodes Statue," *The Guardian*, May 20, 2021, https://www.theguardian.com/education/2021/may/20/cecil-rhodes-statue-will-not-be-removed-for-now-says-oxford-oriel-college [Accessed February 27, 2023].

46 William Hague, "Exposing Injustice, Not Destroying Statues, Brought the Ban on Slavery," *The Daily Telegraph,* June 8, 2020, https://www.telegraph.co.uk/news/2020/06/08/exposing-injustice-not-destroying-statues-brought-ban-slavery/ [Accessed February 27, 2023]; "[P]erhaps a Proliferation of Wilberforce Statues Would Now Be Appropriate to Explain to a New Generation Our Country's Role in This," *Liam Fox*, "All Lives Matter: There Is Too Much at Risk for Us to Let the 'Culture Warriors' Win," *The Telegraph*, June 14, 2020, https://www.telegraph.co.uk/politics/2020/06/14/lives-matter-much-risk-us-let-culture-warriors-win/?utm_content=telegraph&utm_medium=Social&utm_campaign=Echobox&utm_source=Twitter#Echobox=1592164250 [Accessed February 27, 2023]; "Let's Not Forget Britain Was the First Country to Abolish Slavery"; Carole Malone, "History Can Never Be Erased with Violence," *The Express*, June 13, 2020, https://www.express.co.uk/comment/expresscomment/1295315/black-lives-matter-protests-Edward-Colston-statue-Bristol [Accessed February 27, 2023].

47 Tom Harris, "These Protesters Are Deluded If They Think Toppling Statues Is a Victory for Their Cause," *The Telegraph*, June 9, 2020, https://www.telegraph.co.uk/news/2020/06/09/protesters-deluded-think-toppling-statues-victory-cause/ [Accessed February 27, 2023]; Simon Heffer, "Britain's Statues Must Not Fall – They're at the Heart of Our Cultural Heritage," *The Telegraph*, June 10, 2020, https://www.telegraph.co.uk/art/architecture/britains-statues-must-not-fall-heart-cultural-heritage/ [Accessed February 27, 2023]; "Must Britain Atone for the Death of George Floyd by Erasing Its Past?," *The Telegraph,* June 11, 2020, https://www.telegraph.co.uk/opinion/2020/06/11/must-britain-atone-death-george-floyd-erasing-past/ [Accessed February 27, 2023]; Andrea Hosso, "As the Soviets Found, Rewriting History to Suit an Agenda Is Doomed to Fail," *The Telegraph*, June 12, 2020, https://www.telegraph.co.uk/politics/2020/06/12/soviets-found-rewriting-history-suit-agenda-doomed-fail/ [Accessed February 27, 2023]; Daily Mail Reporter, "Protection for Our Statues," *Daily Mail*, January 18, 2021, p. 23; Emma Webb, "We Are Witnessing a Cultural Purge with an Unquenchable Appetite," *The Telegraph*, June 10, 2020, https://www.telegraph.co.uk/politics/2020/06/10/witnessing-cultural-purgewith-unquenchable-appetite/ [Accessed February 27, 2023].

48 "Action This Day," *Save Our Statues*, https://saveourstatues.org.uk.

49 Tristram Cork, "Pro-Colston Campaigners Try to Sabotage M-Shed Statue Exhibition," *Bristol Post,* June 6, 2021, https://www.bristolpost.co.uk/news/bristol-news/pro-colston-campaigners-try-sabotage-5496346 [Accessed February 27, 2023].

From a Culture of Abolition to a Culture War   123

50 Gill Evans, "We Must Challenge Those Who Would Topple Our Statues – Otherwise This Will Never End," *The Telegraph*, June 9, 2020, https://www.telegraph.co.uk/news/2020/06/09/must-challenge-would-topple-statues-otherwise-will-never-end/ [Accessed February 27, 2023].

51 Heffer, "Britain's Statues Must Not Fall." See also, Leo McKinstry, "We Cannot Let These Marxist Vandals Humiliate Us in Their Mindless Iconoclasm," *The Telegraph*, June 11, 2020, https://www.telegraph.co.uk/politics/2020/06/11/cannot-let-marxist-vandals-humiliate-us-mindless-iconoclasm/ [Accessed February 27, 2023].

52 Simon Heffer, "If Gladstone Can Be Cancelled, Nobody in Our History Is Safe," *The Telegraph*, March 14, 2021, https://www.telegraph.co.uk/news/2021/03/14/gladstone-can-cancelled-nobody-history-safe/ [Accessed February 27, 2023].

53 McKinstry, "We Cannot Let These Marxist Vandals Humiliate Us."

54 Webb, "We Are Witnessing a Cultural Purge"; "The Great Evil of Slavery is Being Used to Mount an Assault on Britain's Past, and Subvert the Sense of National Identity of Many People," Stephen Glover, "If the Left and Its BBC Cheerleaders Have Their Way, Britain will be Forced to Renounce Its Past. So Why is No One Fighting Back, Not Least Our Supposedly Tory Government?," *The Daily Mail*, June 11, 2020, https://www.dailymail.co.uk/debate/article-8408587/If-Left-way-forced-renounce-past-no-one-fighting-back.html [Accessed February 27, 2023].

55 David Maddox, "Boris Leads Armada to Save Our History," *Sunday Express*, October 18, 2020, p. 9.

56 Steven Swinford, "Ex-Race Adviser Takes Aim at Culture War," *The Times*, June 16, 2020, p. 15.

57 Ministry of Housing, Communities & Local Government, *Press Release: New Legal Protection for England's Heritage*, www.gov.uk/government/news/new-legal-protection-for-england-s-heritage.

58 "Museums Body Warns of Government 'Interference' in Contested Heritage," *BBC*, www.bbc.co.uk/news/entertainment-arts-56185566.

59 Edward Malnick, "Museums Told to Stop Pulling Down Statues or Risk Funding Cuts," *The Daily Telegraph*, September 26, 2020, https://www.telegraph.co.uk/news/2020/09/26/museums-told-stop-pulling-statues-risk-funding-cuts/#:~:text=Government%2Dfunded%20museums%20and%20galleries,the%20Culture%20Secretary%20has%20warned [Accessed February 27, 2023]; Nadeem Badshah, "Museums Warned Not to Drop Contentious Works," *The Times*, September 28, 2020, https://www.thetimes.co.uk/article/museums-warned-not-to-drop-contentious-works-2722gmv07 [Accessed February 27, 2023].

60 Malnick, "Museums Told to Stop Pulling Down Statues."

61 Harry Yorke, "Present a More Positive View of Our History, Museums Told," *The Sunday Telegraph*, February 21, 2021, p. 9.

62 Charlotte Lydia Riley, "Don't Worry About 'Rewriting History': It's Literally What We Historians Do," *The Guardian*, June 10, 2020, https://www.theguardian.com/commentisfree/2020/jun/10/rewriting-history-historians-statue-past [Accessed February 27, 2023].

63 David Olusoga, "The Toppling of Edward Colston's Statue Is Not an Attack on History. It Is History," *The Guardian*, June 8, 2020, https://www.theguardian.com/commentisfree/2020/jun/08/edward-colston-statue-history-slave-trader-bristol-protest [Accessed February 27, 2023].

64 Chris Baynes, "Edward Colston: The Other Controversial Statues in UK Which Have Faced Calls to Be Pulled Down," *The Independent*, June 8, 2020, https://www.independent.co.uk/news/uk/home-news/uk-statues-removed-down-colston-rhodes-baden-powell-racism-a9560736.html [Accessed February 27, 2023].

65 Task and Finish Group, *The Slave Trade and the British Empire: An Audit of Commemoration in Wales*, November 26, 2020, https://gov.wales/sites/default/files/publications/2020-11/the-slave-trade-and-the-british-empire-an-audit-of-commemoration-in-wales.pdf. Task and Finish Group comprised of Gaynor Legall (Chair), Dr Roiyah Saltus, Professor

124   *Jessica Moody*

Robert Moore, David Anderson, Dr Marian Gwyn, Naomi Alleyne, Professor Olivette Otele, Professor Chris Evans.

66 John Jeffay, "Trust Uncovers Slavery Links at 18 Properties," *The Times*, August 3, 2020, p. 6.

67 Kirsty Feerick, "Edinburgh Statue of Robert Dundas Latest to Be Targeted With Anti-Slavery Graffiti," *The Daily Record*, June 10, 2020, https://www.dailyrecord.co.uk/scotland-now/edinburgh-statue-robert-dundas-latest-22167600 [Accessed February 27, 2023]; Joseph Anderson, "Slavery Plaque Approved for Edinburgh's Henry Dundas Monument," *Edinburgh News*, March 17, 2021, https://www.edinburghnews.scotsman.com/news/politics/slavery-plaque-approved-for-edinburghs-henry-dundas-monument-3168888 [Accessed February 27, 2023].

68 Catherine Hall, "There Are British Businesses Built on Slavery. This Is How We Make Amends," *The Guardian*, June 23, 2020, https://www.theguardian.com/commentisfree/2020/jun/23/british-business-slave-trade-university-college-london-slave-owners [Accessed February 27, 2023].

69 April Roach, "Guy's and St Thomas's Hospital to Remove Two Statues Linked to the Slave Trade," *The Evening Standard*, June 11, 2020, https://www.standard.co.uk/news/london/guys-st-thomas-hospital-remove-statue-slave-trade-a4466846.html [Accessed February 27, 2023].

70 Craig Simpson, "Historic England Lists Villages' Ties to Slavery; Review by Heritage Body Aims to Appeal to 'New Priority Audiences' Such as Ethnic Minorities," *The Sunday Telegraph*, February 7, 2021, https://www.telegraph.co.uk/news/2021/02/06/historic-england-lists-villages-ties-slavery/ [Accessed February 27, 2023].

71 Nicholas Hellen, "Third of National Trust Properties Tainted by Slave Trade Money," *The Sunday Times*, June 14, 2020, https://www.thetimes.co.uk/article/third-of-national-trust-properties-tainted-by-slave-trade-money-p3rkbf70h [Accessed February 27, 2023].

72 The National Trust, *Research Strategy 2017–2021*, https://nt.global.ssl.fastly.net/documents/national-trust-research-strategy.pdf.

73 "It's not that we haven't explored this . . . What I would say is, this moment, the Black Lives Matter movement, has made us realise that we need to go much faster," John Orna-Orstein (Director of Culture and Engagement, National Trust) quoted in Caroline Davies, "National Trust Hastens Projects Exposing Links of Country Houses to Slavery," *The Guardian*, June 22, 2020, https://www.theguardian.com/uk-news/2020/jun/22/national-trust-hastens-projects-exposing-links-of-country-houses-to-slavery [Accessed February 27, 2023]; Sally-Anne Huxtable, Corinne Fowler, Christo Kefalas, and Emma Slocomb, eds., *Interim Report on the Connections between Colonialism and Properties Now in the Care of the National Trust, Including Links with Historic Slavery* (Swindon: The National Trust, 2020), www.nationaltrust.org.uk/features/addressing-the-histories-of-slavery-and-colonialism-at-the-national-trust.

74 Sarah Young, "National Trust Lists Churchill's Home Among 93 Properties With Links to Slavery and Colonialism," *The Independent*, September 22, 2020, https://www.independent.co.uk/life-style/national-trust-slavery-colonialism-links-list-properties-churchill-home-b526697.html [Accessed February 27, 2023].

75 Catherine Bennett, "With Its Slavery List, the National Trust Makes a Welcome Entry to the 21st Century," *The Observer*, September 27, 2020, https://www.theguardian.com/commentisfree/2020/sep/27/with-its-slavery-list-the-national-trust-makes-a-welcome-entry-to-the-21st-century [Accessed February 27, 2023]; Sarah Young, " 'Do Not Lecture Us': People Cancel National Trust Memberships in Anger After It Discusses Links to Slavery," *The Independent*, August 24, 2020, https://www.independent.co.uk/life-style/national-trust-slave-trade-colonialism-links-cancel-membership-twitter-a9685026.html [Accessed February 27, 2023]; "National Trust sparks woke row after tweeting about artefacts and buildings linked to slavery and the British Empire – as dozens vow to cancel membership over historical 'virtue signalling'," *Daily Mail*, August 24, 2020, https://www.dailymail.co.uk/news/article-8658855/National-Trust-sparks-row-tweeting-buildings-linked-slavery.html [Accessed February 27, 2023];

Simon Heffer, "The National Trust's Job Is to Conserve Our History – Not Vilify Its Heroes," *The Times*, September 22, 2020, https://www.telegraph.co.uk/books/news/national-trusts-job-conserve-history-not-vilify-heroes/ [Accessed February 27, 2023].

76 Dominic Sandbrook, "How Dare the National Trust Link Wordsworth to Slavery Because His Brother Sailed a Ship to China," *The Daily Mail*, September 23, 2020, https://www.dailymail.co.uk/news/article-8762205/DOMINIC-SANDBROOK-dare-National-Trust-link-Wordsworth-slavery.html [Accessed February 27, 2023].

77 Andrew Roberts, quoted in Christopher Hope, "National Trust 'Wrong to Target Churchill': Charity Under Fire for Criticising Former PM in Review of Links to British Slavery and Colonialism," *The Daily Telegraph*, September 23, 2020, p. 13; "But these days, with our cultural institutions awash in 'woke' hysteria, it is not done to point this out. Instead, slavery and empire must be conflated at every turn." Sandbrook, "How Dare the National Trust . . ."

78 Christopher Hope, "Culture Secretary: The National Trust Should 'Preserve' Our Heritage, Not Criticise Churchill," *The Telegraph*, September 22, 2020, https://www.telegraph.co.uk/politics/2020/09/22/culture-secretary-national-trust-should-preserve-heritage-not/ [Accessed February 27, 2023]. See also Craig Simpson, "Churchill's Home Included on National Trust BLM List of Shame," *The Telegraph*, September 22, 2020, https://www.telegraph.co.uk/news/2020/09/22/churchills-home-national-trusts-blm-list-shame/ [Accessed February 27, 2023].

79 Hope, "Culture Secretary: The National Trust Should 'Preserve' Our Heritage"; Peter Stanley, "Winston Churchill Statue Daubed with 'Was a Racist' Graffiti During Black Lives Matter Protests," *The Independent*, June 8, 2020, https://www.independent.co.uk/news/uk/home-news/winston-churchill-racist-graffiti-statue-blm-protest-westminster-a9553476.html [Accessed February 27, 2023].

80 *The Daily Telegraph* in particular produced many articles, opinion pieces, and printed numerous letters replicating such language. Benedict Spence, "National Trust's Self-Flagellation Over Slavery Links Is Depthless Virtue Signalling," *The Daily Telegraph*, September 25, 2020, https://www.telegraph.co.uk/news/2020/09/25/national-trusts-self-flagellation-slavery-links-depthless-virtue/ [Accessed February 27, 2023]; "The National Trust Needs to Drop Its Woke Nonsense," *The Daily Telegraph*, September 25, 2020, https://www.telegraph.co.uk/opinion/2020/09/25/national-trust-needs-drop-woke-nonsense/ [Accessed February 27, 2023].

81 Jamie Doward, "I've Been Unfairly Targeted, Says Academic at Heart of National Trust's 'Woke' Row," *The Observer*, December 20, 2020, https://www.theguardian.com/uk-news/2020/dec/20/ive-been-unfairly-targeted-says-academic-at-heart-of-national-trust-woke-row [Accessed February 27, 2023]. The *Colonial Countryside* project was also the target of abuse in the rightwing press and from Conservative politicians. Christopher Hope, "National Trust's Scheme Where Children Educated Workers on Colonial History Was Funded by Taxpayer," *The Daily Telegraph*, January 31, 2021, https://www.telegraph.co.uk/news/2021/01/31/national-trusts-scheme-children-educated-workers-colonial-history/ [Accessed February 27, 2023]. For more on the *Colonial Countryside* project, see www.nationaltrust.org.uk/features/colonial-countryside-project; Corinne Fowler, *Green Unpleasant Land: Creative Responses to Rural England's Colonial Connections* (Leeds: Peepal Tree Press, 2020).

82 David Olusoga, "'Cancel Culture' Is Not the Preserve of the Left. Just Ask Our Historians," *The Observer*, January 3, 2021, https://www.theguardian.com/commentisfree/2021/jan/03/cancel-culture-is-not-the-preserve-of-the-left-just-ask-our-historians [Accessed February 27, 2023].

Part III

Racial and Sexual Hatred in the United States

6 Myths, Mascots, Monuments, and Massacres

Rethinking Native American History in the Public Sphere

Maria John

Figure 6.1 The fallen Christopher Columbus statue (originally dedicated in 1931) outside the Minnesota State Capitol after a group led by American Indian Movement members tore it down in St. Paul, Minnesota, on June 10, 2020

Source: Credit – Original image by Tony Webster. Wikimedia Commons, CC BY-2.0

On a Wednesday afternoon in the middle of June 2020, just outside the State Capitol in St. Paul, Minnesota, a 10-foot bronze statue of Christopher Columbus came toppling down against a backdrop of singing and drumming. A group of protesters – led by members of the American Indian Movement (AIM) Twin Cities and local Native community residents – tied ropes to the statue's neck and wrenched it from its pedestal. As it lays face first on the concrete, demonstrators kicked the head of the statue and danced around it. Minnesota State Troopers, among the witnesses to this historic moment, looked on and notably did not intervene. This occurred approximately two weeks after and about 10 miles

DOI: 10.4324/9781003217848-10

130 *Maria John*

from where a Minneapolis police officer pinned his knee on George Floyd's neck for over nine minutes, ultimately murdering the 46-year-old Black man in an act of violence that would define the summer of 2020 around a single phrase: Black Lives Matter. The day before this Columbus statue fell in Minnesota, another was beheaded in Boston's North End, and yet another was tossed into a lake in a city park in Richmond, VA, where protesters had gathered for a demonstration in support of Indigenous peoples. A member of the Richmond Indigenous Society, which took part in the rally, was quoted in the *New York Times* the following day: "We stand in solidarity with black and brown communities that are tired of being murdered by an out-of-control, militarized and violent police force."[1] By the ensuing fall, showing no signs of abatement, the movement against Columbus resurfaced during Boston's first Indigenous People's Day march to follow George Floyd's murder. There, Chali'Naru Dones, an Indigenous activist and member of the Taino tribe, delivered a speech atop the pedestal that once held the Columbus statue in the North End. As her children were hoisted up to stand beside her, she called for solidarity in the struggle to remove the legacy of white supremacy from the land and honor Indigenous people everywhere. The crowd responded: "City by city, town by town, Christopher Columbus must come down."[2]

What has been happening to public history in the United States in the wake of a politically charged summer that many have likened to the historically significant summer of 1968? This chapter considers this question from a historical perspective. It asks, has 2020 ushered in a new era for American public history – is this, at last, a reckoning? Or have moments like this occurred before? I consider these questions as they relate to Native American history specifically. More particularly, this chapter examines the ways in which museums, popular culture, monuments, and other forms of public memorialization and education in the United States (what I cluster together as "the public sphere") have long (mis)represented Native American history. Until the later part of the twentieth century, many venues of public history and memory across the United States simply ignored, or else distorted and actively erased, Native American history (most still do). To account for this, this chapter begins by engaging the works of Indigenous studies scholars to present a theoretical framework of "narrative erasure" that explains these absences and distortions, not as benign omissions but as central features of the violent structures of "elimination" that persist in settler colonial societies into the twenty-first century.[3] By contrast, and underscoring the ways Indigenous peoples have long refused and resisted these forms of narrative erasure, this chapter closes by considering how Native peoples have long enacted their own forms of public history and memory. In the final section of this chapter, I focus on key examples of Native, community-based forms of public memory, commemoration, and activism that offer a set of historical counternarratives to the dominant US public history narratives rooted in notions of American exceptionalism and Indigenous erasure. I understand these efforts to foreground Indigenous perspectives in historical counternarratives as manifestations of what Indigenous studies theorist Gerald Vizenor

Myths, Mascots, Monuments, and Massacres 131

Figure 6.2 Chali'Naru Dones, an Indigenous activist and member of the Taino tribe, delivered a speech during Boston's 2020 Indigenous Peoples' Day march on top of the pedestal that once held a Christopher Columbus statue in the North End

Source: Credit – Image by oj_slaughter. October 14, 2020, Instagram

132 Maria John

(Anishinaabe) terms "survivance."[4] This chapter seeks to assert two final arguments: (1) it makes the case that the recent uprisings against Columbus are indeed not new, but the continuation of a long history of Indigenous people challenging dominant public and historical narratives that seek to erase them, their voices, histories, and communities; and (2) the chapter asserts that Indigenous peoples' critical public history counternarratives face mainstream resistance because they explicitly draw attention to continuing histories of violence in settler societies. That is, central to the ongoing political work of these forms of counter-memory is an insistence that settler peoples must "*rethink*, rather than merely reject," their colonial history.[5] This requires looking at violence squarely in the face and recognizing the ways in which it is woven into the very fabric of the nation's past and present.

Settler Colonial Myths

Within the scholarly research fields of settler colonial studies and Native American and Indigenous Studies (NAIS), critical conversations about settler colonial "myths" are germane to any understanding of US history and culture. In her field shaping 2010 book, *Firsting and Lasting: Writing Indians out of Existence in New England*, historian and NAIS scholar Jean M. O'Brien (White Earth Ojibwe) writes about the development of the "myth of Indian extinction" (sometimes referred to as the "myth of the vanishing Indian") in colonial New England.[6] Her meticulous historical research shows that a key site where this narrative of extinction was created and proliferated was in early local New England histories and commemorative celebrations. By looking at these (she analyzed some 600) early local histories and events, and by seeking to understand them as a key means through which colonial New Englanders constructed their developing sense of community and self-identity, O'Brien uncovers a process by which non-Indians in New England convinced themselves that Native people had become extinct even as they remained within the community at large – and indeed, do so to this day. She writes:

> The overwhelming message of these narratives was that local Indians had disappeared. These local stories were leashed to a larger national narrative of the "vanishing Indian" as a generalized trope and disseminated not just in the form of the written word but also in a rich ceremonial cycle of pageants, commemorations, monument building, and lecture hall performance. They both served as entertainment and they inscribed meanings in particular places. More specifically for my purposes, these scripts inculcated particular stories about the Indian past, present, and future into their audiences. The collective story these texts told insisted that non-Indians held exclusive sway over modernity, denied modernity to Indians, and in the process created a narrative of Indian extinction that has stubbornly remained in the consciousness and unconsciousness of Americans.[7]

Like O'Brien, the foundational work of historian and NAIS scholar Philip Deloria (Lakota) critiques similar processes of "myth-making" at the level of US culture from the revolutionary era through to the present. Deloria's much cited *Playing Indian* (1998) and *Indians in Unexpected Places* (2004) both advance an influential set of critiques that show how American culture has continually boxed Native peoples into a distinct set of stereotyped roles within US history and in the social imagination.[8] As Deloria writes, his work seeks to,

> smash apart the expectations that continue to linger in far too many American hearts and souls. Those expectations have concerned, among other things, Native technological incapacity, natural proclivities toward violence and warfare, a lack of social development, distance from both popular and aesthetic culture, and an inability to engage a modern capitalist market economy.[9]

In short, his work exposes how American Indians only ever show up in dominant US history and culture as warriors, noble savages, and certainly never as figures that might embody modernity. Writing for *The New Yorker* in 2019, Deloria applied his persuasive cultural and historical critiques much more directly to the harmful perpetuation of specific myths attached to the American holiday of Thanksgiving. He wrote:

> We falsely remember a Thanksgiving of intercultural harmony. Perhaps we should recall instead how English settlers cheated, abused, killed, and eventually drove Wampanoags into a conflict, known as King Philip's War, that exploded across the region in 1675 and 1676 and that was one of the most devastating wars in the history of North American settlement. . . . The Thanksgiving story buries the major cause of King Philip's War – the relentless seizure of Indian land. It also covers up the consequence. The war split Wampanoags, as well as every other Native group, and ended with indigenous resistance broken, and the colonists giving thanks. . . . During the next two centuries, New England Indians also suffered indentured servitude, convict labor, and debt peonage, which often resulted in the enslavement of the debtor's children. Thanksgiving's Pilgrim pageants suggest that good-hearted settlers arrived from pious, civilized England. We could remember it differently.[10]

In recent years, critiques of these persistent settler colonial tropes – harmonious settler-Native relations in early New England, and the myth of so-called Indian "extinction" that continues to permeate the present through the consistent denial of modern–day identities to Native peoples – are steadily entering public discourse, thanks to the popularization of books written for more general audiences, such as the highly popular 2016, '*All the Real Indians Died Off': And 20 Other Myths About Native Americans* by NAIS scholars Roxanne Dunbar-Ortiz

134   *Maria John*

and Dina Gilio-Whitaker. Summing up the devastating and long-lasting consequences of a dominant culture that has continually pigeon-holed Native peoples into these circumscribed cultural, historical, and political roles, these scholars write:

> On the whole, it can be said that the average US citizen's knowledge about American Indians is confined to a collection of well-worn myths and half-truths that have Native people either not existing at all or existing in a way that fails to live up to their expectations about who "real" Indians are. If Indians do exist, they are seen as mere shadows of their former selves, making counterfeit identity claims or performing fraudulent acts of Indianness that are no longer authentic or even relevant. Non-Natives thus position themselves, either wittingly or unwittingly, as being the true experts about Indians and their histories – and it happens at all levels of society, from the uneducated all the way up to those with advanced college degrees, and even in the halls of Congress. The result is the perpetual erasure of Indians from the US political and cultural landscape. In short, for five centuries Indians have been disappearing in the collective imagination. They are disappearing in plain sight.[11]

Two recent publications have aimed such critiques squarely at the enormous productive power of specific dominant US national narratives and the politics of American collective memory. In his *Settler Memory: The Disavowal of Indigeneity and the Politics of Race in the United States* (2021), political theorist and NAIS scholar Kevin Bruyneel argues that what he calls "the work of settler memory" is ubiquitous in the United States. Bruyneel describes this as "a process of remembering and disavowing Indigenous political agency, colonist dispossession, and violence towards Indigenous peoples."[12] And it is so common, he asserts, that we even find some of America's most critical thinkers failing to acknowledge (and thus they reproduce) the presence of settler colonial assumptions within their understandings of history and the politics of race in the United States.[13] For Bruyneel, the specific problem of America's collective memory in relation to the politics of race thus becomes a site through which to critique and intervene in processes, practices, frameworks, and narratives that actively disavow Indigenous political agency in both the past and the present. Drawing on the words of Indigenous scholar Lee Maracle, Bruyneel aims, then, to expose what he calls the "tricky" and "slippery" ways in which "the constitutive relationships of, in particular, white supremacy to colonialism, enslavement to dispossession, labor to land, Blackness to Indigeneity, and whiteness to settlerness are elided."[14] As a starting point, he therefore draws our attention to how the work of settler memory, or "settler memory at work" can be found almost everywhere in the United States. Specifically, in:

> place names (numerous states, cities, streets, and other topographical markers, including Wall Street, initially built as a wall to protect Dutch settlers

from Indigenous people); sports team names past and present (e.g. Washington Redsk★ins, Kansas City Chiefs); holidays and holiday rituals (e.g. Thanksgiving and Columbus Day); consumer products (e.g. Jeep Cherokee, Pontiac); literary film, and television stories (e.g. Pocahontas, The Last of the Mohicans, and the many cowboy-and-Indian-themed shows); U.S. military nomenclature (Blackhawk and Apache helicopters); and the myths and narratives (e.g. manifest destiny) that have a shaping force of the story of the nation that calls itself America.[15]

The productive power of specific US national narratives is perhaps tackled most squarely by Roxanne Dunbar-Ortiz, in her most recent publication, *Not a Nation of Immigrants: Settler Colonialism, White Supremacy, and a History of Erasure and Exclusion* (2021). In this prodigious work, Dunbar-Ortiz calls out the popular refrain that identifies the United States as a "nation of immigrants" for being "a mid-twentieth-century revisionist origin story."[16] She cites author Osha Gray Davidson, who has collected dozens of examples of how the phrase gets used, in order to point out that the notion of the United States as a nation of immigrants is typically used in contexts to "counter xenophobic fears."[17] Put another way, according to Dunbar-Ortiz, this phrase falls prey to Bruyneel's charge of "settler memory at work" since it actively works to erase the history and reality of the United States as a settler colonial society. In countless speeches by politicians and patriots, Dunbar-Ortiz points out how attractive the notion of being descended from immigrants is for contemporary Americans. As Presidential candidate Hilary Clinton once expressed in 2016, "We are a nation of immigrants, and I am proud of it."[18] Dunbar-Ortiz notes that this particular narrative emerged in the 1950s and reflected the US ruling-class response to the moral and political challenges of post-WWII anti-colonial national liberation movements and civil rights movements. Moreover, she underscores how a "nation of immigrants" narrative specifically erases the fact that the United States was founded as a settler state and spent the next 100 years at war against Native nations in conquering the continent. Rather than the conquering of the West being cast as a story of settlers violently displacing Native peoples from their homelands, Western expansion is taught, celebrated, and mythologized in popular culture as a fulfillment of the great American promise of manifest destiny; a nation of immigrants steadily and courageously forging the way for a new nation to live up to its promise.

If this overview of foundational and recent works in Native American and Indigenous Studies gives us an indication of just how central settler colonial myths are to any critical understanding of the US history as it is taught and understood at large, then the point I want to stress is that these critiques, collectively, advance a view of the US history that centers an enduring problem of Native erasure. What is especially important about the ways in which NAIS scholars understand this problem of erasure is that it is not cast as a matter of mere historical accident or habit, or of benign oversight or neglect. Neither is it a merely passive process of omission. Rather, scholars like O'Brien, Dunbar-Ortiz, Deloria, Bruyneel, and others are at pains to show how this

136   *Maria John*

centuries-long practice of erasure is in fact an active and unrelenting process, bound up with structures of violence and "elimination" that have been responsible for dispossessing Native peoples of their land since colonization began. In a much cited 2006 essay that has since become central to the field of settler colonial studies, Australian scholar Patrick Wolfe famously wrote about the very specific form of colonialism (settler colonialism) that has imposed itself on Indigenous peoples in what became the United States, as well as Australia, Canada, and New Zealand. In this essay, Wolfe explained that central to the very foundation of the project of settler colonialism are structures of what he calls "elimination."[19] Specifically, Wolfe theorized that a "logic of elimination" governs the ideologies, racial categories, policies, and actions of settler colonial societies across the stretch of their histories. He argued that the "genocidal logic" at work in historical policies of territorial appropriation, which aimed to dispossess and eradicate Indigenous people and to replace them with a settler population, could also be identified in more contemporary policies and practices such as child removal, residential schooling, blood quantum requirements for federal recognition of indigeneity, or simply the broader project of Indigenous assimilation writ large.[20] In these ways, he pointed out how structurally, settler colonial societies have depended on and are maintained by, institutions, policies, and ideologies that continually seek to "eliminate" Native people from the land. As he underscores, "the elimination of the Native" is necessary for the continuing viability, moral justification of, and presence of the settler colonial society on Indigenous land, which is why, as long as Native people remain present on the land, settler colonial societies will continually seek out their elimination: "the primary motive for elimination is not race (or religion, ethnicity, grade of civilization, etc.) but access to territory. Territoriality is settler colonialism's specific, irreducible element."[21] Wolfe is equally clear about the ways that forms of "elimination" can change over time:

> When invasion is recognized as a structure rather than an event, its history does not stop – or, more to the point, become relatively trivial – when it moves on from the era of frontier homicide. Rather, narrating that history involves charting the continuities, discontinuities, adjustments, and departures whereby a logic that initially informed frontier killing transmutes into different modalities, discourses and institutional formations as it undergirds the historical development and complexification of settler society.[22]

Collectively, what these scholars demonstrate is that the centrality of settler myths within commonplace understandings of US history is (or should be) of much concern for public historians in the United States. To take seriously the idea and the productive power of settler colonial myths and their capacity to not simply omit, but actively erase Indigenous presence, is therefore to assert that dominant narratives like those critiqued by Dunbar-Ortiz are distorting at best, violent at worst.[23] Because if there is one thing we might identify at the collective center of these scholarly critiques, it is that these settler colonial

Myths, Mascots, Monuments, and Massacres   137

myths commit a deep and ongoing act of erasure (or "elimination" in Wolfe's terms). What these dominant historical narratives and mythologies erase are, in essence, threefold: (1) the fact of Indigenous survival; (2) the significance of Indigenous historical and political agency in the United States – past and present; and (3) the extraordinary, and ongoing, forms of literal and structural violence that continue to uphold the United States on stolen land.

Mascots, Monuments, and Massacres

In this section of the chapter, I look at a few illustrative examples of public history and of history in the public sphere that perform "the work of settler memory" or which engage explicitly in the perpetuation of narratives that erase Native survival, presence, and/or historical agency or which actively erase the ongoing history of settler violence toward Native peoples.

In his powerful treatise on the workings of power in the making and recording of history, Haitian historian Michel-Rolph Trouillot demonstrates how power operates, often invisibly, at all stages in the making of history to silence certain voices. *Silencing the Past: Power and the Production of History* (1995) is by now a staple of public history scholarship and discourse, especially for those attempting to deal with so-called difficult histories. Thanks in part to the prominent (and arguably successful) example of how German public history and memory have countered the dangerous specter of Holocaust denialism, there is now an entire subfield within public history scholarship dedicated to the question of "difficult histories." Recent books and articles, such as Bain Attwood's "Difficult Histories: The Museum of New Zealand Te Papa Tongarewa and the Treaty of Waitangi Exhibit" (2013), Julia Rose's *Interpreting Difficult History at Museums and Historic Sites* (2016), and James Miles's "Scattered Memories of Difficult History and Museum Pedagogies of Disruption" (2021), demonstrate the ubiquity of this framework and language within public history scholarship and practice in the twenty-first century.[24] But in 1995, Trouillot's work arguably set something of an early foundation for these conversations. In the opening pages of *Silencing the Past*, Trouillot wrote:

> This book is about history and power. It deals with the many ways in which the production of historical narratives involves the uneven contribution of competing groups and individuals who have unequal access to the means for such production. The forces I will expose are less visible than gunfire, class property, or political crusades. I want to argue that they are no less powerful.[25]

Later, Trouillot explains where some of these sites of production are to be found:

> Most Europeans and North Americans learn their first history lessons through media that have not been subjected to the standards set by peer

138 *Maria John*

reviews, university presses, or doctoral committees. Long before average citizens read the historians who set the standards of the day for colleagues and students, they access history through celebrations, site and museum visits, movies, national holidays, and primary school books.[26]

These locales of "history-making" that Trouillot identifies are precisely the places I have in mind when I refer to the "public sphere." Notably, these sites of narrative production are also where Bruyneel tells us to find "settler memory at work" and where O'Brien, Deloria, Dunbar-Ortiz, and Gilio-Whitaker alert us to be aware of historical and ongoing processes of settler "myth-making."

To ground our understanding of how specific instances of Native cultural and historical representation within the public sphere actively erase or silence certain perspectives on the American past and present, I will now consider in brief what settler memorial "work" is done through the continued use of Native mascots within professional sports and by collegiate and high school teams; what narratives are perpetuated (and erased) by specific monuments and related celebrations; and what the absence of any significant attention to the sites of massacres (of Native peoples) has allowed this nation to erase from its history and collective memory.

Mascots

In the United States, the ubiquity of Native mascots in professional, collegiate, and high school sports teams is astounding when one considers the numbers. According to the *New York Times*, as recently as December 2020, approximately 1,900 public schools across the United States still used Native American nick-names or mascots for their sports teams.[27] In New England alone, according to the New England Anti-Mascot Coalition, a total of 46 high schools across Connecticut, Massachusetts, New Hampshire, Rhode Island, and Vermont still use "Indian" mascots in 2021.[28] From the Lowell High School "Red Raiders" to the Merrimack High School "Tomahawks" to the Tewksbury Memorial High School's "Redmen," all these team names carry in common a tradition of upholding the stereotype of the "warrior" or "savage" Indian figure. While there is some hope that the tide is finally turning – Rhonda Anderson, the Western Massachusetts Commissioner on Indian Affairs, noted in a recent interview that when she began her post in 2017, the numbers in Massachu-setts alone were in the forties, but that well over a dozen schools have dropped offensive names or logos in the past year – the fact that this fight has been ongoing since at least the 1960s shows how slow-moving change has been.[29]

What explains the reluctance to get rid of Native mascots in the United States, and what harms are these stereotyped images and representations doing? Decades of social science research have shown that Native American mascots have serious psychological, health, and social consequences for Native peo-ple.[30] As stereotypes, these mascots do not accurately represent Native peoples nor do they honor them. What they do, rather, is reinforce one-dimensional stereotypes that overshadow the contributions, perspectives, and struggles of past and contemporary Native American people. For many Native people, these racial stereotypes are therefore painful reminders of historical trauma and of the limited ways that others see them. Research shows that Native American youths are especially vulnerable to the dehumanizing effects of these mascots. Exposure to mascots has been shown to cause stress, negative feelings, lowered self-esteem, and less future aspiration among Native students. Studies have also shown that when non-Native people are exposed to Native American mascots, this triggers negative and stereotypical views of Native people. In short, these mascots normalize culturally insensitive behaviors and teach inaccurate understandings of Native people. To use the language of NAIS scholars Bruyneel, O'Brien, Deloria, and others, these mascots also engage directly in the "work" of myth-making, allowing for a sense that "Indians can never be modern."[31] These problems are of course compounded by limited media coverage, and insufficient curricula at all grade levels on the histories and contemporary lives of Native peoples (including colonial US policies of removal and extermination, and facts about contemporary Native tribal nations) that would give students a more accurate frame of reference with which to understand problems with these mascots and other Native American stereotypes.

The National Congress of American Indians (NCAI), the Country's Largest and Most Representative

Native American advocacy organization has been fighting to end Native mascots since the 1960s.

Currently, over 145 tribal nations, as well as government, education, professional, civil rights, and religious organizations across the United States have recognized the negative health impacts of Native American mascots and called for the elimination of these offensive symbols.[32] Yet, in spite of this long history of advocacy, and a very vocal consensus from tribal leadership that mascots are offensive and harmful to the majority of Native peoples, there is still a staunch debate in the public sphere about the legitimacy of the campaign to end mascots. What do this intransigence and the nature of the public debate over the mascot issue tell us? Bruyneel's framework of "settler memory at work" makes a crucial, nuanced distinction in the heated debates over Native mascots:

> One cannot grasp the team names and mascot issue adequately without attending to settler colonialism, past and present. However, what most political actors and observers see and discuss in this debate is not settler colonialism but rather race and racism, specifically through a liberal framework in which the focus is on redressing offensive representations and exclusions through greater inclusiveness into the society as it is presently constituted. To deem as racist names such as the Redsk★ins is not so much wrong as analytically incomplete and politically limited for grasping why these names and mascots get a "free pass" – why so many were created in

140   *Maria John*

the first place, persist, and are vehemently defended today by those who
seek to maintain the status quo.

The work of settler memory is one of the primary reasons why Indian-
themed sports team names and mascots persist as popular representations
into the twenty-first century. These names and mascots are mnemonic
devices, which tell us that Indigenous peoples are both everywhere in
symbolic form and absent as active, contemporary political subjects. The
disavowal thus also applies to settler colonial practices of dispossession, violence, and forced assimilation.[33]

If we take Bruyneel's point, then essentially we start to see how mascots that
perpetuate racist stereotypes of Native people simultaneously work to deny
their political presence and agency in the present, while also erasing the ongoing fact of settler colonial power structures that uphold the contemporary
United States. Bruyneel further clarifies that to fully address why mascots are
such an enduring problem, we must understand their historical and contemporary political function. To do this, he argues that we must put them into "historical and mnemonic perspective," that is, we must recognize them as part of
"a persistent, deeply rooted settler colonial logic and set of practices traceable
from the past to the present and thereby tying it to, rather than cleaving it off
from, the history and present of settler colonial governance."[34] This approach,
he asserts, puts the fact of ongoing settler colonialism at the very "center of this
debate such that it can facilitate racial critique that goes beyond the parameters
of racial liberalism."[35]

When we understand that mascots are much more than culturally offensive –
when we come to see how the myths and stereotypes they uphold are a continuation of, and constitutive of power relations in the present that maintain
white supremacy and deny Native people historical or political agency in the
present, nor even a basic level of humanity – it is hard to let the critique of
these symbols rest at the level of a charge against racism. (Though that matters
too!) Much more important, it would seem, is that by allowing mascots to
continue, we allow a centuries-long and ongoing process of Native "elimination" to continue. Mascots erase Native peoples in the present – either by perpetuating stereotypes that lock them in a grossly exaggerated colonial version
of their culture and identities or by actively denying the very real, very vocal
opposition of Native voices in the present, which are calling for the practice
to stop.

Monuments and Celebrations

To put the mascot issue in conversation with the problem of monuments and
related holidays or celebrations that uphold specific historical narratives is to
recognize a through line that centers the work (and problem) of settler memory. We can see the point quite clearly through a consideration of the "work"
monuments to Christopher Columbus do, and the historical narratives that are

upheld (but also erased) by the celebration of both Columbus Day and Thanksgiving. As ever, the significance of historical context matters. And once again, we can frame a critique of national holidays as an effort to track the work of settler memory.

Most people, if they recognize a problem with Columbus Day, are inclined to the argument that it is wrong to celebrate a historical figure whose actions led to the enslavement, displacement, and attempted genocide of Indigenous peoples.[36] In many ways, this position is much like the arguments we see in the debates over Confederate monuments and statues. (Essentially, the idea is, when we understand the historical circumstances under which such monuments were built and thereby recognize that their original purpose was to celebrate the so-called lost cause, this requires us to remove them from the landscape if we want to cease celebrating the ideals they represent.) Just as there has been a successful campaign in recent years to take down and otherwise condemn Confederate monuments on these grounds, statues of Columbus have steadily been folded into this public issue.

While these are obviously very powerful critiques, if we take the perspective that tries to identify the settler memory "at work" in the celebration of Columbus as a hero, we quickly see that this version of history erases two key historical facts: (1) the notion that Columbus "discovered" anything completely erases the fact of Indigenous presence on these lands for generations before colonizers ever showed up; and (2) as many people argue in the public debates over celebrating Columbus, to celebrate him as a historical hero is to present a one-dimensional and incomplete version of the man, who ought to be better known for the violence he perpetuated against Indigenous peoples. To celebrate him in this one-dimensional manner without acknowledging the atrocities he committed is therefore to erase that violence.

As historians remind us, though, it isn't just the myths perpetuated (or the violence erased) by monuments and national holidays that we should be attuned to; the origins of the national holidays themselves matter too.[37] This kind of historical context tells us a great deal about the original intention behind – and thus one might assume, the continuing meaning of – precisely what is being celebrated and intended for, when we uphold certain traditions (whether we realize it or not). In terms of both Columbus Day and Thanksgiving, we should understand that both national holidays were created – that is, recognized by the federal government as an official "day" on the national calendar – during circumstances in which the United States needed what Dunbar-Ortiz might describe as a salve or convenient revisionist narrative, precisely to "counter xenophobic fears" or tensions within the nation. In the case of Columbus Day, few people understand that President Franklin D. Roosevelt created the first federal observance of Columbus Day in 1937 – a time when, given the global rise of totalitarian regimes, the Italian American community faced forms of hostility, suspicion, and backlash in a domestic context of increasing anxiety over fascism. Similarly, in the case of Thanksgiving, it wasn't until October 3, 1863, at the height of the Civil War, that President Abraham Lincoln,

142   *Maria John*

in an effort to unite a broken nation, issued a Thanksgiving Day proclamation encouraging all Americans

> in every part of the United States, and also those who are at sea, and those who are sojourning in foreign lands, to set apart and observe the last Thursday of November next as a Day of Thanksgiving and Prayer to our beneficent Father who dwelleth in the heavens.[38]

Just as we might understand Roosevelt's efforts in establishing Columbus Day as an attempt to ease national tensions, Lincoln's efforts in establishing the Thanksgiving holiday can be understood as a similar effort, to forge ties of unity between North and South, via a romanticized shared past.

One critique we might pursue in light of how these national holidays were established then, is that in both cases, the unity and domestic stability of the nation were sought through the elevation of historical narratives that at once celebrated a one-sided, sanitized version of the past, while also inculcating traditions that silenced and erased the violence that accompanied such events for Native peoples. As Americans reached for the celebration of Columbus in the 1930s to dissipate hostility toward Italian Americans, and as divided Civil War era Americans reached for a distant Thanksgiving story that idealized a past in which their forebears struggled against a hostile landscape (into which Native peoples were often collapsed), the reality of settler colonial violence and the displacement of Native peoples was nowhere to be seen. Monuments to Columbus, and the celebration of Columbus Day and Thanksgiving thereby serve the national interest at the expense of Native people; they represent a metaphorical reprising of the violence of settlement and colonization.

Massacres

Another common instance of myth-making and erasure in the public sphere in which we can see settler memory at work concerns the complete absence, for the most part, of any attention to the many massacres of Indigenous peoples that took place across the history of colonial settlement and westward expansion, and that solidified the borders of the United States. Examples of settler violence in American history dating to the vicious Puritan assaults against the Pequot in the 1630s (incidents seldom spoken of in celebrations of the mythical first Thanksgiving) continue to be excluded from dominant narratives of American history, but for Native communities these massacres exist as a perpetual presence, operating as living memory and history as much as a site of enduring trauma.

Recently, these absences have started to be addressed. For example, for over a century, the history of the Sand Creek Massacre in Colorado – where at dawn on November 29, 1864, about 675 volunteer cavalrymen under the command of Col. John Chivington opened fire on a peaceful encampment of Cheyenne and Arapaho people – was ignored or mischaracterized. Even when a historic marker was installed at the site in 1950, it was called a "battleground" – a term many see as inaccurately implying a degree of nobility in combat to what was essentially a mass murder. Finally, in 1998, Congress directed the US Department of the Interior to begin work with the Cheyenne and Arapaho tribal governments to establish a Sand Creek Massacre National Historic Site as part of the National Park System. The site was dedicated in 2007. On December 3, 2014, then Governor John Hickenlooper officially apologized for the massacre to the Cheyenne and Arapaho people on behalf of the state. And on November 20, 2020, the Colorado state Capitol's Building Advisory Committee voted 7–2 to recommend placing a sculpture of a grieving Native American woman outside the Capitol as a memorial to the 1864 massacre. The sculpture replaces a statue of a Civil War soldier that was toppled by protesters earlier in the year – a monument that originally listed the Sand Creek Massacre as a battle.[39] In his award-winning 2013 book, *A Misplaced Massacre: Struggling over the Memory of Sand Creek*, historian Ari Kelman details how the Sand Creek Massacre site opened after a long and contentious planning process in which Native Americans, Colorado ranchers, scholars, Park Service employees, and politicians alternately argued and allied with one another around the question of whether the nation's crimes, as well as its achievements, should be memorialized.[40]

We have seen similar dynamics unfold in relation to the Great Swamp Massacre in the Northeast – a violent episode during the conflict known as King Philip's War. In December 1675, about 1,000 English colonists attacked a Narragansett stronghold, killing an estimated 650 Indian men, women, and children, and taking 300 more captives. The militia set the Narragansett fort on fire and killed men, women, and children as they ran from the flames. The attack was spurred by the belief that the tribe was harboring neighboring Wampanoag. A roadside memorial marker was placed near the presumed site of the massacre in 1906. The granite shaft mentions only the date, December 19, 1675, and labels the massacre, "The Great Swamp Fight." The small amount of descriptive text engraved on the marker states, "Three quarters of a mile to the southwest on an island in the Great Swamp the Narragansett Indians were decisively defeated by the united forces of the Massachusetts Bay, Connecticut, and Plymouth colonies."[41] We can note what the framing of a "fight" and a "defeat" achieve: this effectively works to justify the settler violence and reframe a massacre as a conflict of two military forces. In October 2021, the site of the Great Swamp Massacre was officially returned to the tribe in a land transfer that has been described as "monumental."[42]

Perhaps the most recent example of this sort concerns the uncovering of mass unmarked graves of hundreds of Indigenous children at the sites of boarding and residential schools in both the United States and Canada. Throughout the nineteenth and twentieth centuries, thousands of Native children in the United States and Canada were forced into assimilationist boarding schools that sought to strip them of their culture and heritage. Many died from disease, starvation, or physical abuse. Most were buried hastily, sometimes with two

144　*Maria John*

or three small bodies in a grave. Starting with the unearthing of grave sites in Canada in the early summer of 2021, as more and more of these stories have emerged in quick succession in the news media, they have been met with a mix of shock and despair by many mainstream audiences. However, to Native peoples, the uncovering of these gravesites has just been a public confirmation of histories they have always known. While Native peoples have mourned these violent histories without having the material evidence of bodies and bones to "prove" it, what the absence of any significant mainstream attention to these histories of violence in the boarding schools (nor to the histories of massacres like the Sand Creek Massacre or the Great Swamp Massacre) should tell us, is just how easy it has been for a nation to completely "forget" or rather, deny a history of attempted genocide that was committed at first in the openly violent context of colonial and frontier expansion, but which later shifted into what Patrick Wolfe has termed more "genteel" forms of violence.[43] As Bruyneel and others would have us understand, these processes of forgetting (or actively denying) settler violence are actually active processes of erasing violence from the American collective memory. With the recovery of remains of Native children at these boarding and residential schools, where there was an explicit effort by the United States and Canadian governments to shift strategy from the overtly violent frontier warfare of the nineteenth century, to efforts targeting the elimination and erasure of Native culture via forms of assimilation, we see the settler nations of Canada and the United States having to squarely face not only the violence of their past but also the explicit act of covering this up.

Rethinking Native American History in the Public Sphere

One of the essential questions this chapter set out to answer is to what extent recent events might suggest there has been some sort of reckoning within public history in America over the course of the last few years. Rather than seeking to answer this question by appraising the extent and significance of changes recently implemented or currently afoot, I am more interested in thinking about this question historically. Have we ever "been here" before?

At least with respect to Native American history, it seems the clear answer to this question is yes. Since at least the 1970s, Indigenous activists in the United States have been calling attention to the problems of representation related to mascots, the Hollywood portrayal of Native people, and the false mythologization of Thanksgiving. For generations, Native communities have also engaged in acts of community remembrance in an effort to uphold their own understanding of history. Therefore, essential to any understanding of Native American history in the public sphere must be a recognition that in spite of the unrelenting acts of settler myth-making, erasure, and the constant silencing of Native voices and perspectives that persist in dominant culture and society, Native communities have also consistently pushed back against these

Myths, Mascots, Monuments, and Massacres   145

dominant narratives and advanced their own forms of public memory, commemoration, and public history. To illustrate the different forms these counter-
memories and narratives can take, I discuss a few prominent examples later.
Essential in framing my discussion of these examples is an understanding of
Anishinaabe cultural theorist Gerald Vizenor's concept of "survivance," which
he describes in his book *Manifest Manners: Narratives on Postindian Survivance*,
as "an active sense of presence, the continuance of native stories, not a mere
reaction, or a survivable name."[44] While even by his own admission, Vizenor
asserts that "theories of survivance are elusive, obscure, and imprecise by definition," many have come to understand and use the notion of survivance to
describe a complex interplay of survival and resistance – an understanding of
Native survival that seeks to guard against a more passive rendering of Native
presence as merely remaining or enduring. Specifically applying the concept
of survivance to aesthetics and processes of narrative construction, Vizenor has
also written that Native survivance stories are "an active resistance and repu-
diation of dominance, obtrusive themes of tragedy, nihilism, and victimry."[45]
In the discussion that follows, I suggest that the historical counternarratives
put forward by ceremonial practices within Native communities to remember
the Sand Creek Massacre, the hanging of the Dakota 38, The National Day
of Mourning, and the Annual Deer Island Sacred Paddle and Run, exemplify
"survivance narratives" in Vizenor's terms. When we recognize these forms of
counter-memory in this light, it allows us to see that the alternative histories of
Westward expansion, King Phillip's War, and Thanksgiving that are advanced
by these forms of counter-memory challenge a notion of Native victimhood
and passivity in the past and present, and instead emphasize themes of Native
agency, resilience, and strength.

Remembering Sand Creek, the Dakota 38, and Native Histories in the Colonial Northeast

Arapaho and Cheyenne people participate in annual commemorative activities for the Sand Creek Massacre including ceremonial practices that occur
during community gatherings and involve travel to the Sand Creek Massacre
site. These assertions of communal memory and perseverance are reverently
observed each year in the days before the anniversary. From this sacred site
where the pain of ancestors is remembered, runners partake in the Sand Creek
Massacre Spiritual Healing Run. In this run, they retrace the route the murderous soldiers took in their return to Denver in possession of grisly trophies that
served as gruesome confirmation of their horrific deeds while also being used
in celebrations that treated them as returning heroes. According to Northern
Arapaho educator Gail Ridgley, this community event, which takes place at the
hallowed ground of Sand Creek, remains an essential act not only to "honor,
remember and memorialize" their ancestors but also to serve as a kind of "ceremonial for burial because there were no ceremonies performed for their dead

146   *Maria John*

at the time."[46] The prayers, honor songs, and stories that give substance to their presence at the site represent acts of sacred obligation ensuring that the memories of those who experienced the horror of that day shall never be forgotten. For Ryan Ortiz, another member of the Northern Arapaho Tribe and Sand Creek descendent, the ongoing commemoration of Sand Creek is of critical importance as it speaks to the distinctions between understanding and historical amnesia while observing, "if we lose these memories, those soldiers will have succeeded in what they set out to do that day when they murdered our people."[47] Eugene Blackbear Jr., a Southern Cheyenne Sundance leader and Sand Creek descendent, asserts that the continued commemoration of Sand Creek is as important as ever since, "Cheyenne people must always remember our relatives who lost their lives" there.[48] But, as Blackbear also notes, such acts of remembrance go beyond Cheyenne and Arapaho communities, as the "Spiritual Healing Run is a way that we forgive our oppressors and move forward with respect and honor!" The significance of the Healing Run as a space for healing is a point that Ortiz reiterates, "healing isn't just for us, it's for everyone."

We see similar goals of remembrance and healing expressed in relation to the memorialization of the "Dakota 38" – a form of shorthand that refers to the largest mass execution in US history, ordered by Abraham Lincoln on December 26, 1862. The Dakota 38 Memorial is a commemorative and restorative event that honors the memory of 38 Dakota men who were publicly executed in Mankato, Minnesota, in 1862. Each year, horse riders and distance runners gather to cover 330 miles from the Lower Brule Sioux Reservation in South Dakota to Mankato, Minnesota, and relay distance runners cover 90 miles from Fort Snelling, Minnesota, to Mankato, Minnesota, the site of the Dakota hangings that occurred in 1862. The Dakota 38 Memorial began in 2005, when Jim Miller of Porcupine, South Dakota, dreamed of riding on horseback across the South Dakota plains to a riverbank in Minnesota, where he saw his Dakota ancestors hung. He woke from sleep, inspired to gather horse riders for the 16-day reconciliation ride which has since come to be known as the Dakota 38 Memorial. In 2012, a film was created to document the first ride, and in an effort to spread the message and the counter-history embodied in the ride, it is now free to screen through the production company's website.[49] As the site explains,

> This film was created in line with Native healing practices. In honoring this ceremony, we are screening and distributing "Dakota 38" as a gift rather than for sale. This film was inspired by one individual's dream and is not promoting any organization or affiliated with any political or religious groups. It was simply created to encourage healing and reconciliation.[50]

In the Northeast, two annual events carry a similar set of goals as they commemorate an understanding of colonial history that challenges dominant representations and silences. Every October, descendants of the primarily Nipmuc and Massachusetts elders, women and children who were forcibly removed from their homes and put in chains to be taken by water to Deer Island for the duration of King Phillip's War, gather at two sites to begin the Annual Deer Island Sacred Paddle and Run. The sacred run starts around 5 am at the Falls in South Natick, where in 1675, 500 primarily Nipmuc ancestors were forcibly removed from their homes. The sacred paddle begins on Deer Island itself, where anywhere between one and three mishoonas (traditional dugout canoes) full of paddlers traverse Boston Harbor to travel up the Charles River toward Brighton in a symbolic return of the ancestors. Paddlers, runners, and other participants in the day's events gather for a closing ceremony at the Falls in South Natick, where a potluck feast and social provides the opportunity for participants to reflect on the day and the history it represents. Further south, in the town of Plymouth, Massachusetts, every November on Thanksgiving Day, crowds gather on Cole's Hill, which overlooks Plymouth Rock, to mark The National Day of Mourning. 2021 marked the 52nd anniversary of the event. An annual tradition since 1970, The National Day of Mourning is a solemn, spiritual, and highly political day. Many participants fast from sundown the day before through the afternoon of that day (and have a social after the event so that participants can break their fasts). The day consists of speeches from representatives of local Native organizations and communities in New England and beyond. An annual message from political prisoner Leonard Peltier is read every year. And afterward, participants embark on a march around the town, ending at Plymouth Rock where more speeches and music follow. As the organizers – The United American Indians of New England (UAINE) – explain, "we are mourning our ancestors and the genocide of our peoples and the theft of our lands. NDOM is a day when we mourn, but we also feel our strength in action."[51] In an unambiguous expression of what Vizenor terms "survivance," the always visible banner of the UAINE reads,

UNITED AMERICAN INDIANS OF NEW ENGLAND

We Are Not Vanishing.
We Are Not Conquered.
We Are As Strong As Ever.

The consistency of such acts of engaged community memory and the alternate forms of public memorialization they represent explicitly express an active Native presence and historical agency, while rejecting the incapacitating narratives of tragedy and victimry in an example of "survivance." Hence, such observances and practices form vital elements of healing against the

Figure 6.3 Crowds gathered on Cole's Hill, under the Massasoit statue, to mark the 52nd Annual National Day of Mourning, in Plymouth, MA, November 25, 2021. The orange banner visible in the midground of the image contains the message:

UNITED AMERICAN INDIANS OF NEW ENGLAND

We Are Not Vanishing.

We Are Not Conquered.

We Are As Strong As Ever.

Source: Credit – Photo courtesy of Maria John

weight of historical trauma, while being essential to more complete, critical, and inclusive understandings of American history. These are insights that many Americans well understand through generation-defining events like Pearl Harbor or 9/11, while, at the same time, cultivating a profoundly ironic sense of historical ignorance of the Sand Creek Massacre and similar atrocities perpetrated against Native peoples in the annals of American history, and in the stories and myths that shape the American consciousness and national identity. By engaging in such public forms of counter-memory, Native communities across the United States have long challenged the dominant settler myths that continually seek to erase them and deny their political voice in the present.

Rethinking Rather Than Merely Rejecting Colonial History

In a recent article for the *Washington Post*, Secretary of the Interior Deb Haaland (an enrolled member of the Laguna Pueblo and the first Native American to be a Cabinet secretary of an executive branch agency) wrote that

> [m]any Americans may be alarmed to learn that the United States also has a history of taking Native children from their families in an effort to eradicate our culture and erase us as a people. It is a history that we must learn from if our country is to heal from this tragic era.[52]

Her words echo the insistence of many Indigenous peoples, that if settlers want to truly deal with the "difficult histories" they do not want to inherit or reproduce, then settler peoples must rethink, rather than merely reject, their colonial history. Speaking of New Zealand's settler colonial history, the historian J.G.A. Pocock has cautioned:

> a historiography which undermines the traditional narratives that have been providing identity may carry the pseudo-radical implication that [a new] identity may be found simply in the rejection of the under-mined tradition.[53]

But most importantly, he suggests, "those who are forever emancipating themselves will never be free, and the perpetually reiterated rejection of imperial myths serves to perpetuate them."[54] If settlers are to rethink rather than merely reject their colonial history, then Indigenous Studies scholars and Native activists would agree that this means they must study it in all its complexity, but most especially, they must confront the continuing violence that pervades colonial structures that uphold the present.

Perhaps this is why Native counternarratives center not just on the themes of Native survivance but also on settler violence. In this, their narratives refuse the work of settler memory. They also refuse the simpler liberal project of merely "rejecting" dominant narratives and instead insist on an engagement with the political work (erasure) that has been perpetuated by these narratives. This requires looking at settler violence squarely in the face, and at how the ongoing structures of settler colonialism that continue to shape this nation implicate all of us in these historical injustices. No matter how we got here, if we live in the United States, we profit off the settler colonial project. This is essentially what Native American historical counter-memories are forcing us to see. However, the message of Native counter-memories and historical narratives is not predominantly one of attributing blame, but of healing – for Native people, for settler people, and for the nation. In Haaland's words,

> Though it is uncomfortable to learn that the country you love is capable of committing such acts, the first step to justice is acknowledging these painful truths and gaining a full understanding of their impacts so that we can unravel the threads of trauma and injustice that linger.[55]

150　*Maria John*

Notes

1 Johnny Diaz, "Christopher Columbus Statues in Boston, Minnesota and Virginia Are Damaged," *The New York Times*, June 10, 2020, https://www.nytimes.com/2020/06/10/us/christopher-columbus-statue-boston-richmond.html

2 David Detmold, "Indigenous Peoples' Day Now!," *changethemassflag.com*, October 10, 2020, https://changethemassflag.com/2020/10/12/indigenous-peoples-day-now/.

3 Patrick Wolfe, "Settler Colonialism and the Elimination of the Native," *Journal of Genocide Research*, Vol. 8, No. 4 (December 2006).

4 Gerald Vizenor, *Native Liberty: Natural Reason and Cultural Survivance* (Lincoln, NE: University of Nebraska Press, 2009), pp. 1–2.

5 The historian J.G.A. Pocock has cautioned: "A historiography which undermines the traditional narratives that have been 'providing identity may carry the pseudo-radical implication that [a new] identity may be found simply in the rejection of the undermined tradition." Most importantly, he suggests, "those who are forever emancipating themselves will never be free, and the perpetually reiterated rejection of imperial myths serves to perpetuate them." Pocock has argued that in order to deal with difficult histories, settler peoples must rethink, rather than merely reject, their colonial history. This means, in his terms, that they must study it in all its complexity. See J.G.A. Pocock, "The Antipodean Perception," in *The Discovery of Islands: Essays in British History* (Cambridge: Cambridge University Press, 2005), p. 9.

6 Jean M. O'Brien, *Firsting and Lasting: Writing Indians Out of Existence in New England* (Minneapolis, MN: University of Minnesota Press, 2010).

7 Ibid., p. xiii.

8 Philip Deloria, *Playing Indian* (New Haven, CT: Yale University Press, 1998); Philip Deloria, *Indians in Unexpected Places* (Lawrence, KS: University Press of Kansas, 2004).

9 Deloria, *Indians in Unexpected Places*, p. 230.

10 Philip Deloria, "The Invention of Thanksgiving: Massacres, Myths, and the Making of the Great November Holiday," *The New Yorker*, November 18, 2019, https://www.newyorker.com/magazine/2019/11/25/the-invention-of-thanksgiving

11 Roxanne Dunbar Ortiz and Dina Gilio-Whitaker, *'All the Real Indians Died Off': And 20 Other Myths About Native Americans* (Boston, MA: Beacon Press, 2016), p. 1.

12 Kevin Bruyneel, *Settler Memory: The Disavowal of Indigeneity and the Politics of Race in the United States* (Chapel Hill, NC: UNC Press, 2021), p. xv.

13 Ibid.

14 Ibid.

15 Ibid., p. xiii.

16 Roxanne Dunbar-Ortiz, *Not a Nation of Immigrants: Settler Colonialism, White Supremacy, and a History of Erasure and Exclusion* (Boston, MA: Beacon Press, 2021), p. xiii.

17 Ibid., p. xii.

18 Clinton, cited in Ibid., p. xiii.

19 Patrick Wolfe, "Settler Colonialism and the Elimination of the Native," *Journal of Genocide Research*, Vol. 8, No. 4 (December 2006).

20 Ibid., pp. 387–409.

21 Ibid., p. 388.

22 Ibid., p. 402.

23 I discuss how forms of omission can constitute a kind of violence in this article: Maria K. John, "The Violence of Abandonment: Urban Indigenous Health and the Settler Colonial Politics of Non-Recognition in the United States and Australia," *NAIS: Native American and Indigenous Studies*, Vol. 7, No. 1 (Spring 2020).

24 Bain Attwood, "Difficult Histories: The Museum of New Zealand Te Papa Tongarewa and the Treaty of Waitangi Exhibit," *The Public Historian*, Vol. 35, No. 3 (August 2013); Julia Rose, ed., *Interpreting Difficult History at Museums and Historic Sites* (Lanham, MD: Rowman & Littlefield Publishers, 2016), pp. 46–71; James Miles, "Scattered Memories

of Difficult History and Museum Pedagogies of Disruption," *Journal of Museum Education*, Vol. 46, No. 2 (2021), pp. 272–281.

25 Michel Rolph-Trouillot, *Silencing the Past: Power and the Production of History*, 20th Anniversary ed. (Boston, MA: Beacon Press, 2015), pp. 29–30.

26 Ibid.

27 David Waldstein, "For Opponents of Native American Nicknames, 2020 Has Brought Hope," *The New York Times*, December 18, 2020, https://www.nytimes.com/2020/12/18/sports/nicknames-mascots-native-americans.html?searchResultPosition=1

28 New England Anti-Mascot Coalition, "New England High Schools," October 2021, https://sanfacon.com/mascots/schools_NE.html.

29 Rhonda Anderson, cited in Rosemary Ford, "Bill Would Ban Native American Mascots in Massachusetts Public Schools," *Boston.com*, November 17, 2021, www.boston.com/news/local-news/2021/11/17/bill-to-ban-native-american-mascots-in-public-schools/.

30 For examples of this research, see: Laurel R. Davis-Delano, Joseph P. Gone, and Stephanie A. Fryberg, "The Psychosocial Effects of Native American Mascots: A Comprehensive Review of Empirical Research Findings," *Race Ethnicity and Education*, Vol. 23, No. 5 (2020), pp. 613–633; Melissa Burkley, Edward Burkley, Angela Andrade, and Angela C. Bell, "Symbols of Pride or Prejudice? Examining the Impact of Native American Sports Mascots on Stereotype Application," *The Journal of Social Psychology*, Vol. 157, No. 2 (2017), pp. 223–235.

31 This is the title of O'Brien's Introduction in *Firsting and Lasting*.

32 http://maindigenousagenda.org/native-mascots/.

33 Bruyneel, pp. 111–112.

34 Ibid., p. 125.

35 Ibid., p. 126.

36 The following piece demonstrates how this stance is often articulated: Sam Hitchmough, "Columbus Statues Are Coming Down – Why He Is So Offensive to Native Americans," October 12, 2020, https://ohiocapitaljournal.com/2020/10/12/columbus-statues-are-coming-down-why-he-is-so-offensive-to-native-americans/.

37 Karl Jacoby, "Which Thanksgiving?," *Los Angeles Times*, November 26, 2008, www.latimes.com/archives/la-xpm-2008-nov-26-oe-jacoby26-story.html.

38 Abraham Lincoln, *Transcript for President Abraham Lincoln's Thanksgiving Proclamation from October 3, 1863*, https://obamawhitehouse.archives.gov/sites/default/files/docs/transcript_for_abraham_lincoln_thanksgiving_proclamation_1863.pdf.

39 Scott Franz, "Colorado Lawmakers Poised to Replace Capitol's Civil War Monument With Sand Creek Massacre Memorial," *KUNC.org*, March 2, 2021, www.kunc.org/news/2021-03-02/colorado-lawmakers-poised-to-replace-capitols-civil-war-monument-with-sand-creek-massacre-memorial.

40 Ari Kelman, *A Misplaced Massacre: Struggling Over the Memory of Sand Creek* (Cambridge, MA: Harvard University Press, 2013).

41 An image of the marker can be seen here: https://en.wikipedia.org/wiki/Great_Swamp_Fight#/media/File:Great_Swamp_Fight_Roadside_Marker.jpg.

42 Alex Nunes, "Site of 'Great Swamp Massacre' Returned to Narragansett Indian Tribe," *The Publics Radio*, October 23, 2021, https://thepublicsradio.org/article/site-of-great-swamp-massacre-returned-to-narragansett-indian-tribe; For more about the Great Swamp Massacre and the significance of its history in the Northeast, see: Christine M. DeLucia, *Memory Lands: King Philip's War and the Place of Violence in the Northeast* (New Haven, CT: Yale University Press, 2018).

43 Patrick Wolfe, cited in, J. Kēhaulani Kauanui and Robert Warrior, eds., *Speaking of Indigenous Politics: Conversations with Activists, Scholars, and Tribal Leaders,* (Minneapolis, MN: University of Minnesota Press, 2018), p. 347.

44 Gerald Vizenor, *Manifest Manners: Narratives on Postindian Survivance* (Lincoln, NE: University of Nebraska Press, 1994), p. vii.

45 Gerald Vizenor, ed., *Survivance Narratives of Native Presence* (Lincoln, NE: University of Nebraska Press, 2008), p. 1.

46 Gail Ridgley, cited in Bill Stratton, "Honoring Memory of the Sand Creek Massacre in the Age of COVID," *History News Network*, December 5, 2021, https://historynewsnetwork.org/article/181905.

47 Ryan Ortiz, cited in Ibid.

48 Eugene Blackbear Jr., cited in Ibid.

49 Smoothfeather Films, "Dakota 38," www.smoothfeather.com/dakota38.

50 Ibid.

51 United American Indians of New England, "National Day of Mourning," November 25, 2021, www.uaine.org/.

52 Deb Haaland, "My Grandparents Were Stolen From Their Families as Children. We Must Learn about This History," *The Washington Post*, June 11, 2021, www.washingtonpost.com/opinions/2021/06/11/deb-haaland-indigenous-boarding-schools/.

53 J.G.A. Pocock, "The Antipodean Perception," in *The Discovery of Islands: Essays in British History* (Cambridge: Cambridge University Press, 2005), p. 9.

54 Ibid.

55 Haaland, "My Grandparents Were Stolen From Their Families as Children. We Must Learn About This History."

7 Creating the Conditions for Repair

Representation, Memorialization, and Commemoration

Karlos K. Hill and Karen Murphy

Introduction

Claudia Rankine's *Citizen: An American Lyric* (2014) is a haunting meditation on modern-day anti-Black violence and the history of lynching. In Part VI, she writes: "In the next frame the pickup truck is in motion. Its motion activates its darkness. The pickup truck is a condition of darkness in motion. It makes a dark subject. You mean a black subject. No, a black object."[1] Her book takes the reader on an emotional journey through contemporary discourses on racial violence, ranging from well-known instances such as Hurricane Katrina (2005) to the 2014 killing of 17-year-old Trayvon Martin, to lesser-known Black victims such as James Craig Anderson, who was killed by a group of teenage vigilantes in Jackson, Mississippi, in 2011. Of particular note, Rankine introduces her brief section on the Anderson murder with the infamous photograph of a 1930 double lynching in Marion, Indiana. Interestingly, however, she has altered the original photo by removing the victims (Thomas Shipp and Abram Smith) from the image. She did so, she said, because she wanted to refocus contemporary viewers' attention on the white spectators in this iconic photograph, one of whom, for instance, is defiantly pointing his finger at the two lynched men. For Rankine, removing the Black bodies from the photo strategically interrupts the intended white spectatorial gaze and thereby precludes contemporary audiences from re-creating it.

Without Shipp and Smith as the focal point, viewers of this photo are now forced to stare back at the white men, women, and children who are gazing at the lynched Black bodies while simultaneously looking out at us. Rankine's alteration of this historic photograph is a visual reminder that white supremacist narratives of lynching, and especially photos that glorify the violence of white lynch mobs, must be handled with great care and intentionality when we view and discuss them in contexts such as exhibitions, films, and presentations. For Rankine, contemporary viewers inadvertently participate in the continued objectification and dehumanization of Black lynching victims by looking at such photos in the very ways that the lynch mob intended. When the victims are not present in an image, the intended white gaze at a lynched Black body is temporarily disrupted which then creates space for intentional dialogue.

DOI: 10.4324/9781003217848-11

154 *Karlos K. Hill and Karen Murphy*

Taking our cues from Rankine's *Citizen*, we believe that altering lynching photos in this way can ironically help center the victims, survivors, and their descendants because it forces us to account for who these Black victims were, why they were removed in the first place, and, most importantly, what it might mean for a community of viewers to add them back into the photograph. In other words, viewers are forced into a moment of reckoning, positioned to think about why they are choosing to look at imagery of a lynching decades after it took place, as well as what it means for them to do so.

Removing Black victims from historical lynching photographs can be an important methodology for combatting the white supremacist gaze embedded within them. However, it is not the only means of centering public memory on the victims, survivors, and their descendants. Re-remembering the history of lynching in this way constitutes a transgressive act of public memory rooted in progressive Black anti-lynching politics of the early twentieth century. At the height of the anti-lynching movement in the United States, activists utilized photographs and postcards that had been created to glorify white lynch mobs to instead document the mobs' brutality and the danger that lynching posed to American democracy. Although they did not make any changes to the images themselves, the NAACP and other anti-lynching groups recontextualized these photos by focusing the photographic narrative on the violence perpetrated by the mob rather than the victim's alleged crimes. By the late 1920s, lynching imagery had been recontextualized in ways that highlighted white barbarity and helped to erode public support for lynching.

Building upon the efforts of the NAACP and other anti-lynching groups, Rankine's alteration of the Indiana lynching photograph suggests that not only do we need to approach such images with care and intentionality, but we must actively re-remember lynchings and lynch victims in ways that counter anti-Black justifications for the practice. By re-remembering, we mean adding, subtracting, or in some way modifying content from a historical document or narrative, with a goal to accomplish a particular objective or set of objectives in relation to remembering the past or a particular history.

In helping to make clear both the historical and the current-day stakes involved in viewing/exhibiting racist objects and images, Rankine's approach to re-remembering the 1930 Marion lynching can serve as a model not only for how we approach lynching photography but more broadly for how we can begin negotiating our country's public memory of lynching. By removing the lynched Black bodies from this image, Rankine reminds us that we do not have to accept the lynching archive as it is; we have the ability and even the responsibility to present it in ways that challenge the vision and goals connected to the very creation of lynching photos.

Rankine's controversial alteration of this historic photograph raises an additional question: What needs to be remembered or re-remembered about lynching in an intentional dialogue that seeks to honor the lives of the victims, survivors, and their descendants? How can lynching as a term or historical framework be constructed so as to center the vantage and experiences of

Creating the Conditions for Repair 155

victims, survivors, and descendants in the telling? In what follows, we will outline some key considerations that should define or help frame a victim-centered public memory of lynching and racial violence.

1) More than 5,000 documented lynchings of Black Americans occurred in the United States between 1880 and 1950. Black Americans have been the primary targets of lynch mob violence in the United States.

Racial violence has a long and circuitous history in the United States. While white Americans, Native Americans, and members of various immigrant communities have been subjected to lynching, most of the violence perpetrated by lynch mobs since the late 1880s has been directed at Black Americans. It is estimated that a Black person was lynched every 3 days during the 1890s, leading the American writer and satirist Mark Twain to lament in 1901 that the United States of America would ultimately be remembered as "the United States of Lyncherdom."

2) Between 1901 and 1950, when the majority of lynchings occurred in the United States, the US Congress debated more than 200 anti-lynching bills. Three anti-lynching bills were passed by the House of Representatives during those years, in 1922, 1935, and 1940, but the US Senate never took a vote on any of them.

There has been no justice for Black victims of white lynch mob violence. During the lynching era, white mobs not only lynched Black people in broad daylight but also encouraged other whites to participate as spectators. In many cases, white authorities, and particularly white law enforcement officers, did not interfere, or even took part in the violence and chaos. In 99% of the more than 5,000 documented lynchings of Black American men, women, and children between 1880 and 1950, no one was ever held accountable.

3) Local, state, and federal entities have refused to pay reparations to victims, survivors, and descendants of historical lynchings and anti-Black mob violence.

In 1892, the United States paid $25,000 in reparations to the Italian government for the lynching of 11 Italians in New Orleans in 1891. Despite this precedent, Congress ignored or blocked similar efforts to obtain restitution for Black lynch victims and their families. To date, the only Black Americans who have received reparations for historical racial violence from a governmental entity are the dozen or so survivors of the 1923 Rosewood (Florida) Massacre.[2]

4) Reckoning with the present-day legacies of slavery, lynching, and other forms of anti-Black violence is crucial. Doing it in a way that centers

156   Karlos K. Hill and Karen Murphy

victims, survivors, and descendants will be vital to the efficacy of any reparation program.

There should be no statute of limitations on matters of humanity and justice.
Even though many of the historical lynchings took place nearly 100 years ago,
the passage of time has not erased the crime or the debt owed to the victims
and their families and communities. The payment of reparations does not pre-
suppose atonement. Without it, however, repair cannot occur.

Representation, Memorialization, and Commemoration

The photograph that Claudia Rankine used in *Citizen* also appears in the book
Without Sanctuary: Lynching Photography in America (1999).[3] The 98 images in
the latter book were selected from a collection of 145 photographs of lynchings
amassed by James Allen, a white Southern American antiques collector. Many
were originally printed as postcards, which were a popular way to communicate and share photos in the early twentieth century. Allen's collection has also
been the focus of numerous public exhibitions at museums, historical sites, and
galleries, and individual images can be accessed online at withoutsanctuary.org.

In many ways, the uses of these photographs exemplify significant efforts to
create more widespread and nuanced understandings of lynching in the United
States, including the demythologization of racial violence and its disarticula-
tion from extremism by placing lynching more squarely within the context of
American history and of the everyday lives and cultural practices of American
institutions and some white Americans. The photographs have also been used,
as in Rankine's essay, to make contemporary connections to ongoing anti-
Black violence and the objectification of Black people by white people. These
images might be considered an element of the work of acknowledgment and
reckoning that Americans must do to create the conditions for repair. This is
one of several efforts that we will explore in the following pages. Additionally,
it is one that requires the active engagement of the viewer, reader, or exhibition
visitor, or the creative work of the writer, artist, poet, or historian.

The perpetrators of the depicted lynchings are not identified in *Without Sanctuary*, and we are told little about the victims save for their names, the locations
of their murders, and the dates. A reckoning with these images thus requires
the intentional engagement of our ethical, civic, and moral imaginations. Passive engagement might provoke pathos or anger, but perhaps little else. The
Equal Justice Initiative (EJI), on the other hand, takes a fundamentally different
approach, as we will discuss in more detail later. EJI as an organization seeks
to transform the American legal system, to realize *justice* as its foundation, and
the lynching memorials and monuments it has created represent critical acts of
laying that foundation, of showing that Americans cannot change the future if
they have not addressed the past. These, too, require intentional participation,
civic, ethical, and moral acts, but they reposition the viewer, visitor, and reader,
along with the victims of these horrific crimes, which are, necessarily, *speakable*.

The photographs in this collection have inspired reflection upon a range of questions in regard to human behavior. In addition to acts of murder – perpetration – the images highlight questions about complicity, rituals of pride, bystanding, conformity, and belonging on the part of white Americans, as well as what constitutes community, community membership, and participation. They further inspire questions about guilt, accountability, responsibility, and witnessing.

Without Sanctuary: The Early Exhibitions

One of the images in Allen's collection, a gelatin silver print measuring seven by ten inches, captures a gruesome scene from a stark winter's night. The dead bodies of two Black brothers, George and Ed Silsbee, hang from leafless trees. Standing between and around them are a group of unidentified white men. Most of the men are wearing suits, some are wearing hats, and some have their hands tucked into their pockets as if they are about to pontificate on an important issue or are thoughtfully reflecting upon something. The date is January 20, 1900; the place is Fort Scott, Kansas. The etching on the photograph reads "George and Ed SILSBEE HANGED by a MOB of CITIZENS IN FRONT OF JAIL." Ironically, the victims in this grotesque act of dehumanization and violence are named, while the perpetrators are reduced to an anonymous "mob." It is a compelling inversion. The act of naming is often part of the process of humanization, whereas presenting people only as members of a group is often a means of dehumanizing them.

In January 2000, a century after the Silsbees' murder, hundreds of New Yorkers visited the Roth Horowitz Gallery on the Upper East Side of Manhattan to view *Witness*, an exhibition of 60 of Allen's photographs, postcards, and artifacts of lynchings that took place across the United States between the 1880s and 1960. Visitors learned about the event from cable news, internet sources, radio, newspapers, and by word of mouth. The gallery, which normally hosted some 15 to 20 visitors at a time, now found itself managing hundreds of people as they waited patiently to enter the small space, which can hold only 25 people. The *New York Times* was among the newspapers that covered the exhibition.[4] In addition to interviewing some of the visitors, the *Times* talked to scholars and historians, asking for their views on both the implications of such a showing and its seeming popularity. Some people expressed hope that it might symbolize a willingness to face the past. Historians pointed to other events related to what appeared to be a growing reckoning, such as the critical attention being given to the Confederate flag flying over the South Carolina State Capitol, or the increasingly common knowledge of Thomas Jefferson's sexually intimate relationship with his slave Sally Hemings. Historian Eric Foner suggested that the interest in *Witness* "should serve as an argument for a museum devoted to slavery." Cultural historian Maurice Berger referred to the exhibition as "a zeitgeist moment in the culture." Others related it to contemporary examples of racial violence, including the 1998 murder of James Byrd, who

158   *Karlos K. Hill and Karen Murphy*

was dragged to his death by three white men in Jasper, Texas. The gruesome killing invoked explicit comparisons to the period of "Jim Crow" in the United States and was characterized by some as a lynching. Other historians called on by the *Times* to comment were less hopeful that the interest in *Witness* would translate into a meaningful willingness to contend with America's violent past and its legacies. Visitors kept coming nevertheless, and many of them made connections to other events and places, including Nazi Germany, as well as to their own lives and to ongoing racism and racist violence. Black visitors, in particular, drew connections to stories they had learned from family members. Importantly, the exhibition did not contextualize the photographs; they were displayed alone, against the bare walls of the gallery. The effect was simple and intimate, according to observers – an intimacy that was further magnified by the small size of the space.

Betsy Gotbaum, then executive director of the New York Historical Society (NYHS), was among those who attended *Witness*. Understanding its importance and believing that it deserved more visibility, historical context, and space, Gotbaum secured funding from Peter Norton and the Gilder Lehrman Foundation for an expanded version of the exhibition. Seven weeks later, it reopened as *Without Sanctuary: Lynching Photography in America* in the much larger and better-known NYHS, which sits on the edge of Central Park West at 77th Street. Karen Murphy, one of this chapter's authors, was directly involved with NYHS's programming at the time. She was also a member of the program staff of the New York City office of Facing History and Ourselves, an educational nonprofit organization. NYHS reached out to Murphy, who had partnered with the society on other teacher education workshops, and asked for her advice regarding the exhibition. Murphy, whose doctoral work and teaching focused on racial violence and the construction of American national identity, was among many experts who were consulted as NYHS planned. She contributed some ideas regarding the tone and tenor of the exhibition, the inclusion of materials on the anti-lynching movement, and the addition of public discussions, which she personally facilitated. There was such a demand for these discussions that she was later joined by her Facing History and Ourselves colleague Tracy Garrison-Feinberg.

In keeping with Facing History and Ourselves' practices, the purpose of the facilitated public discussions was not to offer a lecture but rather to provide visitors to the exhibition with the opportunity to reflect *in conversation* with each other. The hour-long sessions, which were free of charge, took place in a separate room and were open to anyone who visited the exhibition. The number of discussants varied, from ten to as many as 80. Ranging across racial, ethnic, and age groups (adolescents and older), the participants were mostly (roughly 60% or more) Black and brown Americans. As the exhibition became more widely known, people also came from outside of New York City, with some traveling by bus from Philadelphia and Washington, DC, to take part in the discussions.

Murphy has written and spoken about this experience, detailing particular dynamics that she observed over the course of the several months of the

Creating the Conditions for Repair   159

exhibition and the facilitated discussions. She reports that the conversations were thoughtful and searching. They also followed a pattern. The Black participants would usually say that they had some knowledge of the history of lynching, having learned either from family members or by researching the subject themselves, by taking African American history courses and/or looking for books and other materials on the subject. In contrast, most of the white participants admitted to knowing little about the history of lynching, and what they did know often conformed to the wider mythologies that surround lynching in the United States. For example, many believed that lynchings were relegated to the South; that they took place in secret; that they were perpetrated by extremists, particularly by groups such as the Ku Klux Klan, which they identified as made up of people who were outside the mainstream; and that lynching was something that took place in "the past" – a somewhat fuzzy period after slavery. Some also believed that lynching, though wrong, was used in response to a crime that had been committed. Despite the Black participants' greater familiarity with the subject, many of them were nonetheless shocked, albeit not surprised, by the images in the exhibition, and what those images revealed about the geographical range and public nature of lynching, as well as the involvement of photographers. The use of postcards also raised questions about the part played by the federal postal system, since postcards are by their nature visible. Viewers were invited to ask their own questions, to confront possibilities: Did these images move from hand to hand, from person to person, and through post offices on a regular basis? How many people would have seen such a postcard even if they had not sent one themselves? How much of a "secret" could lynching have been, given the public nature of postcards? How did something so public end up being hidden away in attics and memories, out of public view? And what does the role of the postal system in the dissemination of these images mean? The wider contexts of these lynchings also invited questions regarding the complicity of law enforcement, journalists, publishers, and others.

Without Sanctuary received widespread media attention and became part of conversations among museum curators and scholars. Following its run at the NYHS, it moved to the Andy Warhol Museum in Pittsburgh. The Warhol further expanded the exhibition, offering a robust range of complementary activities. Decisions about presentation and interpretation were made with the guidance of an advisory committee, which included the Greater Pittsburgh Chapter of the ACLU, the African American Chamber of Commerce, the Anti-Defamation League, the Pittsburgh Branch of the NAACP, the National Conference for Community and Justice, the Urban League of Pittsburgh, and the YWCA of Pittsburgh's Center for Race Relations. Outside evaluators were brought in to assess the process and the programming. Facing History and Ourselves also served in an advisory role and provided support for programming and facilitator training modeled on the NYHS public conversations. According to a case study on the project, "More than 31,000 people saw the exhibition and approximately 1,000 engaged in dialogues."[5] As at the NYHS, the success of the exhibition led the Warhol to extend it.

160   *Karlos K. Hill and Karen Murphy*

Without Sanctuary resulted in the highest attendance for any exhibition since the Museum opened in 1994, with one of the smallest marketing budgets. The rich dialogues, depth of audience response, and community engagement and support attest to the reach of the Project's impact. It also generated significant funding nationally and locally. This response, viewed in the context of the fact that the Project opened ten days after the World Trade Center attacks on September 11, 2001, demonstrates a collective community willingness to deal with and address challenging and painful subjects. Overall, the Project illustrated how difficult subject matter has the potential to be a galvanizing force for collaboration and dialogue within and across communities and organizations.[6]

For the most part, these institutions sought to create historical context for the images through a combination of public programming and materials within the exhibition itself. Visitors who chose to walk through and look only at the images were presented with the photographs and little accompanying text. They could not learn who the perpetrators were from merely looking at the images nor could they learn anything about the people in the surrounding crowds – whether we should imagine them as bystanders, because they were not actively involved in the killing; or collaborators, because of their presence and participation; or passive perpetrators, because they contributed to the event and the spectacle. Little information was also provided about the victims and their lives before they were so grotesquely murdered.

In historian Grace Elizabeth Hale's review of the exhibition, she takes on the absence of information regarding the perpetrators and the focus on Black people only as victims. She asks –

> Why do we learn the names of the dead in those images and not the names of the living?
>
> Why do we learn very little about the people who participated in the tortures, took the photographs, and sent the postcards? Why do we learn nothing about the people who saved the images down through the years and the people who sold them to James Allen, the antique and junk dealer who purchased the photographs in recent years and assembled this collection? Whose desk was it, after all, where Allen has claimed he located his first lynching photograph, an image of Leo Frank he bought for thirty dollars?[7]

Hale also points to the fact that the NAACP (National Association for the Advancement of Colored People) investigated many of these cases and that their reports are publicly available at the Library of Congress.

Moreover, she challenges us to consider the implications of Allen's choices. She writes:

> Without the information that the people who collected the photographs chose to ignore, viewers are left with an exhibit that is too close to the spectacle created by the lynchers themselves. "Without Sanctuary's" focus

Creating the Conditions for Repair   161

on blacks as victims rather than whites as murderers, torturers, or at best spectators – its refusal to ask the hard questions about race and violence in American history – produces an updated version of that old segregated story. Martin Luther King Jr., with his commitment to nonviolence and his vision of a common humanity, seems sadly as radical today as he did when he died. How much does our moral revulsion change the fact that these photographs still, as their creators and original purchasers intended, present victimization as the defining characteristic of blackness? A much more accurate exhibition, far closer to [anti-lynching crusader, Ida] Wells-Barnett's challenge to (white) America, would foreground violence as a defining characteristic of whiteness.[8]

Following the initial showings, *Without Sanctuary* began traveling throughout the United States, frequently setting attendance records at the exhibition sites. Its popularity reflects and has contributed to a growing interest in America's history of racial violence, as well as a fuller and more nuanced understanding of history itself. It also reflects work happening in other contexts, including within Holocaust and genocide studies, as well as the growth and diversification of ethnic studies and fields such as African American studies. More scholars, writers, artists, curators, and civil society leaders representing communities of color are now asking probing questions, excavating the past, and in some cases seeking accountability and justice. And there is a greater interest among the audience in learning about these histories, in engaging with the process of reckoning with the past, and in the possibilities of repair.

An Apology From the US Senate

One of the more important impacts of the exhibition and the public engagement it generated was that it led to an apology "to the victims of lynching" by the US Senate in 2005. The resulting resolution read in part:

> Whereas the crime of lynching succeeded slavery as the ultimate expression of racism in the United States following Reconstruction;
> Whereas lynching was a widely acknowledged practice in the United States until the middle of the 20th century; . . .
> Whereas protection against lynching was the minimum and most basic of Federal responsibilities, and the Senate considered but failed to enact anti-lynching legislation despite repeated requests by civil rights groups, Presidents, and the House of Representatives to do so;
> Whereas the recent publication of "Without Sanctuary: Lynching Photography in America" helped bring greater awareness and proper recognition of the victims of lynching;
> Whereas only by coming to terms with history can the United States effectively champion human rights abroad; and

162   *Karlos K. Hill and Karen Murphy*

> Whereas an apology offered in the spirit of true repentance moves the United States toward reconciliation and may become central to a new understanding, on which improved racial relations can be forged: Now, therefore, be it
>
> Resolved, That the Senate –
>
> (1) apologizes to the victims of lynching for the failure of the Senate to enact anti-lynching legislation;
>
> (2) expresses the deepest sympathies and most solemn regrets of the Senate to the descendants of victims of lynching, the ancestors of whom were deprived of life, human dignity, and the constitutional protections accorded all citizens of the United States; and
>
> (3) remembers the history of lynching, to ensure that these tragedies will be neither forgotten nor repeated.[9]

Unfortunately, this statement did not result in legislation or in governmental efforts to redress the past nor did it spur curricular recommendations or other forms of institutional acknowledgment. While it was significant, it was ultimately unsubstantial.

In many ways, the momentum that had seemed to be building dissipated. The Senate apology did not lead to specific interventions on the part of the federal government, and lynching did not become part of mainstream public consciousness. However, lynching was invoked again and again, particularly by Black Americans, in response to the murders of Black people by police officers. This connection became particularly pronounced following the murders of Trayvon Martin in 2012 and Michael Brown in 2014.

America's history of racial violence was also re-emerging in the public landscape through the efforts of the Equal Justice Initiative. EJI was founded in 1989 by Bryan Stevenson, a lawyer who has dedicated his life to transforming the criminal justice system. Stevenson, who was awarded the MacArthur Foundation's celebrated "Genius Grant" in 1995, gave a TED Talk in 2012 titled "We Need to Talk about an Injustice" that has, as of this writing, been viewed more than 7.5 million times. Stevenson builds a narrative in his talk that begins with his own story of growing up in a "traditional African American home." He draws a connection to his grandmother, whose parents were enslaved, and then moves to the US criminal justice system, to contemporary mass incarceration and the disproportionate percentage of Black and brown men among the prison population, and to US history, specifically slavery, Jim Crow, and the terror of racial violence, racism, and discrimination. He also argues that Americans need to take a lesson from countries such as Germany and South Africa that have made substantive efforts to acknowledge and redress their violent pasts, and that will mean learning, understanding, and talking about the United States' own history and its legacies. Stevenson's deeply personal presentation is a critical analysis of structural racism and violence, an indictment of the criminal justice system and the way that Americans deal with history that also allows

Creating the Conditions for Repair 163

people to imagine that they are part of the solution, a movement toward justice, dignity, compassion, and human rights. While many were already familiar with *Without Sanctuary* because of the exhibitions, the book, and the media attention, EJI's work shed light on lynching in America and the nation's history of racial violence in new ways, and that likely spurred renewed interest in the photographs, which have more recently been included in nonfiction books, articles, and textbooks.

Without Sanctuary and James Allen more specifically have also faced criticism. In a 2000 article for the *Los Angeles Times*, journalist J. R. Moehringer wrote that "[m]ost blacks thank [Allen] for his efforts, but many are troubled that he is earning money from his $60 book, which has sold 20,000 copies and briefly became a top seller on Amazon.com." Michael Eric Dyson, a well-known Black author and academic, reinforced this point: "To commercialize the suffering of black people is to do the ultimate disservice to black people. . . . To make coffee-table books out of that kind of pain is highly problematic." Moehringer also refers to criticism of Allen focused on his representation of himself as an "avenger." Julia Hotton, a Black museum professional and cultural historian in New York City, is quoted as saying, "He's not a saint. I know why he did it. He did it because he's a dealer. And that's all he has to say." Adds Moehringer:

> Hotton says older Blacks especially can't help feeling suspicious when they see Allen, and when they hear him. "If they hear a white man with a Southern accent is collecting these photos," she says, "they get a little skittish." On Internet bulletin boards, some blacks talk angrily about the fact that a white man is telling their story. One man says that white people exhibiting lynching photos is like Germans running a Holocaust museum. Others question the value of anyone, black or white, perpetuating such painful images. In the comment section of the online general-interest magazine Journal E, someone writes: "If Mr. Allen really wants to help African Americans, he could do much, much better than to pound fresh salt into old wounds."[10]

These responses illuminate some of the complexities of representation, particularly the representation of racial violence in the United States and its inextricable connection to identity. The discussions regarding who can represent whom and how, as well as the implications of financial profit, are reminiscent of debates in Germany around monuments and memorials. These public criticisms, the tensions and discussions involved, might be thought of as part of the "memory work" a society must do in order to contend with its violent past and its legacies.

Bryan Stevenson and the Equal Justice Initiative: Racial Terror and Trauma

In 2015, the Equal Justice Initiative released a report titled *Lynching in America: Confronting the Legacy of Racial Terror*. It received massive media attention, in large part because of Stevenson's public profile and impeccable reputation. Now in its third edition, this groundbreaking report framed the lynching of African Americans as terrorism, providing a vocabulary that has entered common use. EJI – and Stevenson individually, in interviews and op-eds – has reiterated the idea that "public conversations about racial history . . . are necessary to begin a process of truth and reconciliation in this country."[11] *Lynching in America* also connects lynching to EJI's primary mission:

> Most critically, lynching reinforced a narrative of racial inequality that has never been adequately addressed in America. The administration of criminal justice in particular is tangled with the history of lynching in profound and important ways that continue to contaminate the integrity and fairness of the justice system. . . . Mass incarceration, excessive penal punishment, disproportionate sentencing of racial minorities, and police abuse of people of color reveal problems in American society that were framed in the terror era.[12]

This connection provided the public with a way to understand lynching both as a past crime and as a living institutional legacy.

Conducted under the leadership of EJI's team of lawyers, the research for *Lynching in America* was rigorous, richly detailed, and contextualized. The report includes examples of resistance to lynching such as the public campaigns led by journalist Ida B. Wells, Frederick Douglass, W. E. B. Du Bois, and the NAACP. With these details, EJI offers more context for understanding resistance, and it amplifies the roles of Black scholars, public intellectuals, and Black-led institutions. It also makes the case for "Northern and federal complicity," as well as for accountability, acknowledgment, and commemoration both nationally and locally, particularly in the places where lynchings occurred. These investigatory efforts helped to lay the foundation for the EJI's National Memorial for Peace and Justice in Montgomery, Alabama. Work on the memorial began in 2010, five years prior to the release of the first edition of *Lynching in America*. The completed site opened in 2018.

> EJI partnered with artists like Kwame Akoto-Bamfo whose sculpture on slavery confronts visitors when they first enter the memorial. EJI then leads visitors on a journey from slavery, through lynching and racial terror, with text, narrative, and monuments to the lynching victims in America. In the center of the site, visitors will encounter a memorial square, built in collaboration with MASS Design Group. The memorial experience continues through the civil rights era made visible with a sculpture by Dana King dedicated to the women who sustained the Montgomery Bus Boycott. Finally, the memorial journey ends with contemporary issues of police violence and racially biased criminal justice expressed in a final work created by Hank Willis Thomas. The memorial displays writing from Toni Morrison and Elizabeth Alexander, words from Dr. Martin Luther King Jr., and a reflection space in honor of Ida B. Wells.

Creating the Conditions for Repair 165

Set on a six-acre site, the memorial uses sculpture, art, and design to contextualize racial terror. The site includes a memorial square with 800 six-foot monuments to symbolize thousands of racial terror lynching victims in the United States and the counties and states where this terrorism took place.

The memorial structure on the center of the site is constructed of over 800 corten steel monuments, one for each county in the United States where a racial terror lynching took place. The names of the lynching victims are engraved on the columns. The memorial is more than a static monument. It is EJI's hope that the National Memorial inspires communities across the nation to enter an era of truth-telling about racial injustice and their own local histories.[13]

Visitors to the EJI website have the opportunity to virtually visit the memorial, along with access to racial terror maps and survivor testimony.

EJI's efforts also push local communities to contend with their violent pasts through active commemorations, including the collection of soil from the sites of lynchings, the establishment of historical markers, and organizing commemorative events. Some of these historical markers include details about the victims and the lynchings, serving as both memorials and contributions to the historical record. They also invoke the language of racial terror.[14] And the 800

Figure 7.1 Tuscaloosa County, Alabama, historical marker
Source: Credit – Equal Justice Initiative

166   *Karlos K. Hill and Karen Murphy*

corten steel column monuments in the memorial provide a unique opportunity for historical engagement and civic action. Through the Community Remembrance Project, which has thus far included 250 communities across the South, people are able to participate in the work of acknowledgment and repair. EJI's vision is multifaceted, recognizing that community participation, truth, historical acknowledgment, commemoration, and dialogue are essential ingredients for repair. Moreover, EJI's work has brought the language of trauma in relationship to lynching and racial violence into more general use, reinforcing a need for public commemoration, conversation, institutional reforms, and redress. In the words of the report,

> Lynching – and other forms of racial terrorism – inflicted deep traumatic and psychological wounds on survivors, witnesses, family members, and the entire African American community. Whites who participated in or witnessed gruesome lynchings and socialized their children in this culture of violence also were psychologically damaged. And state officials' indifference to and complicity in lynchings created enduring national and institutional wounds that we have not yet confronted or begun to heal. Establishing monuments and memorials to commemorate lynching has the power to end the silence and inaction that have compounded this psychosocial trauma and to begin the process of recovery.[15]

Stevenson has said that EJI's focus was more on the communities in which lynchings took place and less on the violence suffered by victims. "I think for some people 'Without Sanctuary' created this optic that was shocking," he said,

> and we were less interested in shocking optics. . . . We really wanted to create a narrative that is in some ways even more shocking. That it wasn't the Klan. It was the teachers and the lawyers and the journalists and law enforcement officers cheering as a man was brutalized.

This distinction aside, both Without Sanctuary and EJI, shares an interest in not just adding to the historical record, but correcting it, addressing myths and misrepresentations, untruths, and omissions. Their work is also tied to advocacy: they seek change through public history education.[16]

A year after the memorial's opening, nearly half a million people had visited. Social media is filled with moving responses from visitors, many of whom were accompanied by family members. A wide range of media have covered the memorial and endorsed it as a must-visit site for all Americans. The decidedly mainstream and upmarket *Town and Country*, for example, headlined an article "Visiting the National Memorial for Peace and Justice Should Be a Requirement for Every White American."[17] *Time* declared the memorial one of the "world's greatest places" in 2018.[18] Some reviewers have adopted an architectural focus, praising Murphy and MASS Design Group as well as Stevenson for a vision that inspires reflection and elicits emotional, historical, and ethical connections. Others use words such as "pilgrimage" to describe their visits, suggesting a religious or spiritual journey. For some, the memorial brings to life a history that they were familiar with but had not yet acknowledged. For others, it is a powerful introduction to a history that is not sufficiently well known. For those outside Montgomery and neighboring areas, a visit to the memorial requires effort and intention; it is not a site that one would stumble upon or come across while visiting other national memorials. Stevenson's visibility – his memoir, the film version, media coverage, and the way that influential individuals, including scholars such as Eddie Glaude Jr., have incorporated their visits into their writing and speaking – means that the memorial has become part of public awareness even if people have yet to experience it themselves.

The Use of *Without Sanctuary* Photographs: Exploring Human Behavior

Like Claudia Rankine, Pulitzer Prize-winning author Isabel Wilkerson includes powerful references to *Without Sanctuary* photographs in her 2020 book *Caste: The Origins of Our Discontents*. Both authors focus on the white people in the images, inspiring profound questions about human behavior and decision-making, white culture and white supremacy in America, and the savagery that was considered an acceptable part of white middle-class respectability. *Caste* received glowing reviews and recommendations from a wide range of people, including Oprah Winfrey. Wilkerson's introduction of the caste system as a way of understanding and addressing America's identity-based divisions and hierarchy quickly caught on in popular culture, among policymakers, scholars, and other influential actors. She offered both a powerful analysis and a new language. Wilkerson opens the ninth chapter of her book, "The Evil of Silence," with an evocation of the crematoria at Auschwitz. She then moves to another scene, this one based on a photograph from *Without Sanctuary*. The image is chilling.

> The little girls appear to be in grade school, in light cotton dresses with a sailor's collar and their hair cut in precise pageboys just below their ears. In the picture the two younger girls seem to be fidgeting in shadow, close to the women in the group, who were perhaps their mothers or aunts. The girl you notice first, though, looks to be about ten years old, positioned at the front of the group of grown-ups and children, her eyes alert and riveted. A man is at her side, crisp in his tailored white pants, white shirt, and white Panama hat, as if headed to cocktail hour at a boating party, his arms folded, face at rest, unperturbed, vaguely bored.
>
> It is July 19, 1935. They are all standing at the base of a tree in the pine woods of Fort Lauderdale, Florida. Above them hangs the limp body of

Rubin Stacy, his overalls torn and bloodied, riddled with bullets, his hands cuffed in front of him, head snapped from the lynching rope, killed for frightening a white woman.

Wilkerson goes on to describe the girl in front looking up at the murdered Black man. She then describes another lynching, this one on a postcard.

> This was singularly American. "Even the Nazis did not stoop to selling souvenirs of Auschwitz," wrote *Time* magazine many years later. Lynching postcards were so common a form of communication in turn-of-the-twentieth-century America that lynching scenes "became a burgeoning subdepartment of the postcard industry. By 1908, the trade had grown so large, and the practice of sending postcards featuring the victims of mob murderers had become so repugnant, that the U.S. postmaster general banned the cards from the mails."

However, this did not deter Americans from the gruesome practice of murder and torture, or from photographing themselves with the human beings who were murdered. "From then on," writes Wilkerson, "they merely put the postcards in an envelope."[19]

Wilkerson puts lynching in conversation with another brutal history – that of Nazi Germany and the Holocaust – and she provides a frame focused on human behavior, specifically silence and complicity. She also leaves the reader asking what it means that these young girls were present at this murder, what it means that they were all dressed up, what they saw and imagined, and what the one little girl looking up at Rubin Stacy might have been thinking and feeling. What became of these little girls? What became of Stacy's family, who are not pictured? And how do we imagine the adults who brought their children to this murder, asked them to pose, and then took their picture – and distributed it, seemingly, with pride and the confidence that it was not only socially acceptable but socially significant? And what of the silence of the people involved – those who allowed the murder to take place, those who saw the photograph and did not report the perpetrators, those who passed these postcards through the mail, including the government employees who chose not to report the murders they were witnessing?

In the lynching photograph from *Without Sanctuary* that Rankine uses in *Citizen*, many of the white people in attendance are smiling, including a couple who look as though they are laughing – a man and a woman turning toward the camera, she with one arm reaching back and he with one reaching forward, as if they were holding hands on a date. Most of the men in the photo are wearing white button-up shirts and dark trousers; some are wearing white hats. The women are wearing dresses. It's nighttime and the darkness makes their white shirts glow. They are standing in front of and around a large tree. One man is pointing upward. In the original photograph, he is clearly pointing at two murdered human beings hanging from the tree. In the image as altered by Rankine,

Creating the Conditions for Repair 169

however, which appears on the page facing the last portion of the poem "February 26, 2012/In Memory of Trayvon Martin," the two Black victims have been erased. The reader's focus is thereby directed to the white people in the photograph, provoking questions about their presence: What are they doing? Why are they there? What does this photograph tell us about America, about what is acceptable in American life, about what is celebrated, about who is erased from our collective history and our moral and civic imaginations? The connection to Martin, who was killed by George Zimmerman, the neighborhood watch coordinator for his gated Florida community, also begs questions. Zimmerman's acquittal was the catalyst for the Black Lives Matter movement. Rankine places Martin's killing in a wider context of racial violence, injustice, and lack of redress and accountability. She spotlights white people's celebration of violence as she memorializes Martin, naming him and specifying the date of his killing.

Without Sanctuary has been invoked by other prominent scholars as well, and in popular media such as podcasts. The Reverend Doctor Serene Jones, president of Union Theological Seminary, has talked many times – and in a number of popular forums – about the impact that seeing one of the *Without Sanctuary* postcards had on her. A white woman who grew up in Oklahoma, Jones is perhaps the most well-known person to claim kinship with some of the white people represented in the *Without Sanctuary* photographs. One of the times she told this story was in 2019, on one of America's most popular podcasts, *On Being with Krista Tippett.* Jones describes the image and the impact, the moment of recognition when she realized that she was intimately connected to racial violence.[20] It is her story and America's story.

> But then it all sort of comes together, for me, in a very troubling story that I think is key to our nation, one that literally knocked the breath out of me. I still remember, to this day, when it hit me. I was in a classroom at Yale, leading a search committee – I was the chair – for a new position in African-American religious thought. And the person was giving the lecture; behind him were pictures from postcards of lynchings. And as I sat there looking at these postcards, suddenly, one dropped. And it was of a young woman, lynched from a bridge. You couldn't see in the frame her son who was next to her, who had also been lynched. And at the bottom it said, "Laura Nelson, 1911" – it's hard to even talk about – it said, "Okemah, Oklahoma." And my world just, inside me, imploded. There were maybe 300 people in the town in 1911, and two-thirds of them were my family.[21]

REV. JONES: So there was no way that my family did not know or, most likely, participate in –
TIPPETT: But it's not a story that had been passed down.
REV. JONES: And if they had not participated, they would've told the story.
TIPPETT: So there's that –
REV. JONES: So there's America. There is the whole of it.

Conclusion

Racial violence, particularly violence against Black people, remains a persistent part of American life. Lynching is sometimes invoked by activists, scholars, writers, and artists as a way to name that violence. It is a way of connecting the brutality of the past to the brutality of the present, the injustices of the past to the injustices of the present, and the terror of the past to the terror of the present. The word has been used as a way to highlight a type of violence that is extreme and common. Public representations of that violence in photographs, writing, museums, and memorials provide opportunities for re-remembering. But while they can provide the space, the re-presentation, the context, and the call to action, they cannot do the work of repair for us. Repair and reckoning require active engagement, curiosity, compassion, and courage. Re-remembering is an active process – a moral and ethical act.

Notes

1 Claudia Rankine, *Citizen: An American Lyric* (New York: Graywolf Press, 2014).
2 Robert Samuels, "After Reparations: How a Scholarship Helped – and Didn't Help – Descendants of Victims of the 1923 Rosewood Racial Massacre," *Washington Post*, April 3, 2020, www.washingtonpost.com/graphics/2020/national/rosewood-reparations/ [Accessed October 28, 2021].
3 James Allen, *Without Sanctuary: Lynching Photography in America* (Santa Fe, NM: Twin Palms Publishers, 2000).
4 Somini Sengupta, "Racist Hatred in America's Past Stirs Emotions at Exhibition," *New York Times*, January 24, 2000, p. B1.
5 Jessica Arcand, "Without Sanctuary Project Case Study: The Andy Warhol Museum, Pittsburgh, PA," *Animating Democracy*, http://animatingdemocracy.org/resource/ without-sanctuary-project-case-study-andy-warhol-museum-pittsburgh-pa.
6 Jessica Gogan, "The Warhol: Museum as Artist: Creative, Dialogic & Civic Practice," *Animating Democracy*, http://animatingdemocracy.org/sites/default/files/documents/ labs/andy_warhol_museum_case_study.pdf.
7 Grace Elizabeth Hale, review of "Without Sanctuary: Lynching Photography in America," *Journal of American History*, (December 2002), pp. 993–994.
8 Ibid.
9 S. Res. 39, 109th Cong., 1st sess., February 7, 2005, www.govinfo.gov/content/pkg/ BILLS-109sres39is/html/BILLS-109sres39is.htm.
10 J.R. Moehringer, "An Obsessive Quest to Make People See," *Los Angeles Times*, August 27, 2000, www.latimes.com/archives/la-xpm-2000-aug-27-mn-11152-story. html.
11 "EJI Report on Lynching in America Fuels National Conversation," *Equal Justice Initiative*, February 18, 2015, https://eji.org/news/eji-lynching-report-fuels-national-conversation/.
12 Equal Justice Initiative, *Lynching in America: Confronting the Legacy of Racial Terror*, 3rd ed., 2017, https://lynchinginamerica.eji.org/report/.
13 "The National Memorial for Peace and Justice," *Equal Justice Initiative*, https:// museumandmemorial.eji.org/memorial.
14 "Community Historical Marker Project," *Equal Justice Initiative*, https://eji.org/projects/ community-historical-marker-project/.
15 Equal Justice Initiative, *Lynching in America*, 3rd ed. See introduction to Section VI, Trauma and the Legacy of Lynching, https://eji.org/reports/lynching-in-america/

16 Brian Lyman, " 'Without Sanctuary' and How We Remember Lynching," *Montgomery Advertiser*, April 25, 2018, updated April 27, 2018, www.montgomeryadvertiser.com/story/news/2018/04/25/without-sanctuary-and-how-we-remember-lynching/499641002/.
17 Klara Glowczewska, "Visiting the National Memorial for Peace and Justice Should Be a Requirement for Every White American," *Town and Country*, June 9, 2020, www.townandcountrymag.com/leisure/travel-guide/a32770006/montgomery-legacy-museum-national-memorial-for-peace-and-justice/.
18 "World's Greatest Places 2018," *Time*, https://time.com/collection/worlds-greatest-places-2018/.
19 Isabel Wilkerson, *Caste: The Origins of Our Discontents* (New York: Random House, 2020), pp. 93–94.
20 Serene Jones, "Grace in a Fractured World," *On Being with Krista Tipett* (podcast), December 5, 2019, transcript by the On Being Project, last updated April 1, 2021, https://onbeing.org/programs/serene-jones-grace-in-a-fractured-world/#transcript.
21 According to US government records, the town of Okemah had a population of about 3,000 in 1907.

8 What Is Owed?

Reparations, an Indictment of Public Memory

Caleb Gayle

In 2003, I was starting my freshman year at the high school my Christian, conservative parents had selected where I attended as the sole Black male student. The school focused on telling history in ways that would help us "realize our Christian roots as a country" – that we would somehow realize the inherent destiny of America as a Christian nation. We would read erroneous, pseudo-historians like David Barton, founder of Wall Builders, a small for-profit distributor and developer of ahistorical curricular materials.[1]

Aside from trying to convince students of what we were told in our homes – that America was, in fact, a Christian nation – we were actively given a picture of an America that was continuously being improved – no setbacks, just progress. We would quickly glaze over slavery, but dwell on the redemptive nature of outlawing slavery. We would mention only briefly Jim Crow era policies, Black codes, and more, but then laud how it was only possible in America that we could pass the Civil Rights Bill, the Voting Rights Act, the Open House Act, and more.

The narrative of evergreen, linear progress of the United States of America was an inevitable steady state I had reached by the time I was sitting in those classes. Any notion that we had work yet to do or that those who founded or led this country should be subject to any measure of criticism appeared to not be an option for me. What is owed to the descendants of those who have been counted as less than human is a question that upends our narrative of continued progress. It shoots darts into the once seemingly impenetrable fabric of American exceptionalism. What is owed indicts our public memory not so much as too rosy, but rather as void of the historical richness that can help the United States and its citizens recast and expand their moral imagination to build a more inclusive future.

Reparation was not a topic worth considering in any real sense attending that school because it would admit that America had not reached its steady state. It would confirm that perhaps the persistence of Black life in America demands that our country not laud itself for correcting the problems it created. That instead, the memories of the harm done must be preserved to generate reparative solutions.

DOI: 10.4324/9781003217848-12

What Is Owed?   173

Answering "what is owed" provides the framework through which societies can more fully indict public memory. Responding to that question compels a more thorough view of history than our history classes may have ever demanded. And it is essentially this question that seems hardest to even get our political institutions and its leaders to acknowledge, let alone answer.

This essay draws on firsthand accounts, memoir, reporting, media reports, web sources, journalistic accounts, and recent scholarship to explore the current state of our memories, especially as those memories pertain to the pursuit of recovering that which was lost through the failed policy vehicle of reparations in the United States. In so doing, it will add to the growing canon of research, advocacy, and reporting which has excoriated the current state of public memory and memorialization. Through specific case studies – Germany and its reparations toward the survivors of and descendants of survivors and victims of the Holocaust, the cases of Japanese American reparations and Evanston's recent attempt at reparations, and through an ongoing, yet unsuccessful example in my hometown, Tulsa, site of the 1921 Tulsa Race Massacre – we will layer onto the public narrative an understanding about the political and policy precarity in advocating for reparations.

That question, "what is owed," I contend, demands that we contextualize debates about the advancement of marginalized communities within a politics of memory that emerged long before discussions of HR 40 which began in the 1980s through the work of Congressman John Conyers[2] but then the bill was reintroduced by Congresswoman Sheila Jackson Lee in January 2019.[3] What is owed demands a specific accounting for damages not just experienced in one moment, but experienced in an ongoing fashion for centuries – arguing that the pains and the effects of those harms are in no way static, but are rather ongoing.

To ground this arc of memory, both initial incidences of harm and their ongoing effects, it will be critical to examine the outcome of racial violence most saliently expressed. First, the story of the burning of Black Wall Street in 1921 will be examined, but more specifically its long-lasting effects. The examination of this true tale, its silencing, and the clamor to retell its story display the reparative elements included in a more comprehensive public memory. Second, the disruption of silence in other contexts will be explored to provide case studies of what repairing the past does to public memory. Last, this chapter unravels the go-forward implications of fully remembering and repair. Reparations are the table stakes for fulsome public memory.

Most importantly, this chapter explores the changes in public memory possible only through a thorough and, at times, difficult – both in terms of feasibility and emotional and psychological strain – reparative reexamination of the history that built this current moment. Actively in the United States, and even throughout the world, the attention of this current political moment has been fixated on attempting to reeducate ourselves on what American history means. Even more, the uptick in discussions about what children are taught

174 *Caleb Gayle*

in schools, what training programs on diversity, equity, and inclusion should include, and what language we should use collectively to describe ourselves and our counterparts all point toward a desperate need to identify more thoroughly what public memory can do. Exploring how communities now reckon with their past provides the blueprint for best practices as to how moral imagination can be expanded to include aspects of our public memory which have been intentionally and unintentionally obscured.

Present–Day Tulsa

Without comprehensive memory, current events live without context. The current predicaments which ensnare specific communities then become the fault of those communities and not the unfortunate outcome of discriminatory policies, exclusionary politics, and limited moral imagination.

At 11 am on May 17, 2021, hundreds of people from across the city of Tulsa gathered in North Tulsa to celebrate the opening of a grocery store. Oasis Fresh Market, a 16,245-square-feet grocery store, had been erected at the center of North Tulsa.[4] But grocery store openings do not usually prompt press, community residents, and chamber of commerce officials, from top brass to rank and file, to gather in exuberant celebration. However, for the residents of this part of town, a food desert, traveling miles for fresh groceries made the opening of a grocery store nearby local transit a cause for celebration.

Exuberance was evident on the faces of those in attendance that day. Nearly a year before the grocery store made its debut, Tulsa's mayor, GT Bynum, proclaimed the grocery store would be "the result of the relentless pursuit of bringing a grocery store to North Tulsa."[5] It was a badge of honor – of celebration. A symbol of what communities could do when they cohered around a strategy they would deem worthy of fighting for. But the truth is that the mere fact that the building of a grocery store for this area of town would signal triumph and would trigger celebration represents the limited depth of our public memory.

Public memory steeped in a full recounting of what has happened would first seek to tie the celebration with the pain that delayed the gratification in the first place. And in the city of Tulsa, the pain that delayed the gratification of fair access to healthier livelihood outcomes found its roots almost 100 years before, barely but a few miles from where the Oasis Fresh Market sits. Perhaps if the stories of what happened 100 years ago were told formally, our public memory would have been chastised and would have tempered the celebration of the building of one of the first fresh grocery stores in the area in almost 100 years.

The Memory of 1921 Tulsa

Tulsa was radically growing by 1921 – growing from a population of 18,000 in 1910 to 140,000 by 1930.[6] And its oil and gas roots attracted all sorts of people to work to support the oil and gas industry – leading to newcomers by the thousands. Though throughout the rest of the country, where growth and opportunity would pass over the Black communities in different towns, success and opportunity had reached Tulsa's Black community. Tulsa's growth was also bursting in its Black neighborhoods. Though you could find some Black people in different parts of the city, just north of the city's downtown quickly became known as Black Tulsa, Greenwood, Black, or Negro Wall Street[7] – a term given to several prosperous Black communities across America – and Little Africa. And even today, if you hear "North Tulsa," it's often synonymous with all these names. It is the home of the grocery store now celebrated.

Residents of this neighborhood, however, were not relegated to one grocery store. Rather, they were able to go to 191 stores, a library, and doctors' offices. They could shop at 38 grocery stores, fruit stands, vegetable stands, and meat markets, according to Scott Ellsworth, the author of *The Ground Breaking: An American City and Its Search for Justice*.[8] There were even two theaters. And in each of these places, they were more likely to see Black owners and operators than white ones.

Tulsa, and Oklahoma more generally, was becoming a hub for Black families who wanted to begin again. An article in the Black newspaper, the *Muskogee Comet*, from June 23, 1904, said of this area that it "may verily be called the Eden of the West for the colored people."[9] And it was considered the "Eden of the West for colored people" because the money these Black residents would earn or spend with their businesses or their jobs would cycle through the community many times before a white hand would touch it.[10] These residents, according to Ellsworth's book, could've bought "clothes at Black-owned stores, drop off their dry cleaning and laundry at Black-owned cleaners, and have their portraits taken in a Black-owned photography studio."[11]

But even as Tulsa was booming for Black families as well as white Tulsans, the city was growing more racist. The first law passed by this relatively new state in 1907, Senate Bill One, was a Jim Crow-type law that segregated Black folks from everybody else.[12] Tulsa's success had not skipped over Black Wall Street but neither did Tulsa's racial hate. In fact, it came to be targeted directly at Black Wall Street.

Destruction of a Memory

The May 31, 1921, edition of the *Tulsa Tribune*, now defunct, included this headline: "Nab Negro for Attacking Girl in Elevator."[13] According to the account that followed, "Dick Rowland, was arrested on South Greenwood this morning." Rowland was "charged with attempting to assault the 17-year-old white elevator girl in the Drexel building early yesterday."[14] Rowland, the article went on to say, had "attacked her, scratching her hands and face and tear[ing] her clothes."

After this story ran, it stopped being readily accessible. In fact, the microfilm copy of this account was found to have been ripped and removed from that part of that day's editorial page with other copies of this edition destroyed.[15] The only reason we know about this headline is because a graduate student found a tattered original of that day's paper and included it in their 1946 thesis.[16] Stories published by this local newspaper that stoked the ire of a white mob were almost ripped from any chance of memory.[17]

Rowland was being held on the top floor of the courthouse where a white mob formed outside. By 9 pm, this crowd grew to approximately 400. Twenty-five to 30 Black men, having heard about Rowland's imprisonment and worried about a potential lynching, made their way to the courthouse, with guns in hand. Many of them had served in World War I. Later that night, the white mob had swelled to nearly 2,000, and an additional 25 to 50 Black men had also come to the courthouse.[18] After it seemed as if both sides' concerns had been allayed, an unnamed white man aggressively confronted a Black man holding a military-issued gun and then tried to take it away. A shot was fired. Other shots, many shots, followed. An estimated 12 men were killed.

Over the next 14 hours, the cleavage between Black and white Tulsa split wider and more ruinously than ever before. By the end of those 14 hours, the 40-square blocks of Black businesses and homes had been burned to the ground.[19] Bombs, paid for by the proprietors of Sinclair Oil, had been dropped on this part of the city. The community was no more.[20] To this day, the estimated number of the dead stands at 300 though the actual amount still is unknown because many ended up, nameless, in potter's fields. Almost 4,000 were transported into internment camps and approximately 9,000 were left homeless.[21]

Figure 8.1 View of the destruction of Greenwood, Tulsa, once a hub for Black opportunity and prosperity

Source: Credit – Tulsa Historical Society & Museum

Figure 8.2 Black woman gazing at the destruction inflicted on Greenwood, Tulsa, by the perpetrators of the Tulsa Race Massacre

Source: Credit – Tulsa Historical Society & Museum

The city's white ruling class, however, knew that destruction of this part of the town would in no way lead to the destruction of the memory. That was a feat left yet to accomplish. Tulsa's white leaders did their best to make sure not to sacrifice the growth they were experiencing with an ever-growing influx of white coastal elites looking to make their fortune in this burgeoning town. So, they let few cries from their aggrieved Black residents reach the world.

The silence meant that investors and would-be recruits to this bustling town had nothing to worry about from any loud, meddlesome Black people, people whose rights to vote, obtain housing fairly, or even sit in the same train cars had not yet been secured and protected. And silence still persists today because Tulsa then, like now, is booming, attracting yet again coastal elites to make their homes in this midsized city.

Mayor TD Evans, two days after the burning had ended, told his city commission about the Black part of town, "Let us immediately get to the outside the fact that everything is quiet in our city, that this menace has been fully conquered, and that we are going on in a normal condition."[22]

Black Tulsa was sitting in ruins. And white Tulsa was left scrambling – trying to keep quiet the roar of its racism. Word had gotten out that Tulsa had a race problem. The Red Cross descended on the city to provide immediate medical care and rapid rehousing – in tents, not homes. The Universal Negro Improvement Association tried to send 50 Black nurses, and 100 tents from the National Guard were supposed to be sent to house Black bodies. But each was blocked by the then Governor of Oklahoma, James B.A. Robertson.

178   *Caleb Gayle*

The Red Cross was let in but, for the first week after the Massacre, was barred from feeding any Black person who wasn't deemed "ill." The city encamped nearly 4,000 Black Tulsans in internment camps. And when the *Chicago Tribune*, among many other outside groups, tried to send $1,000 to aid in recovery, they received word that "the citizens of Tulsa were to blame for the riot and that they themselves would bear the costs of restoration," according to local NAACP leader, Walter White.[23]

The president of the Tulsa Chamber of Commerce, Alva Niles, told the Executive Welfare Committee, which had no Black members,

> Leading business men are in hourly conference and a movement is now being organized, not only for the succor, protection and alleviation of the sufferings of the negroes, but to formulate a plan of reparation in order that homes may be re-built and families as nearly as possible rehabilitated.

In the rush of the moment, he promised that if the city could be depended on during the war effort of World War I, they certainly could be depended on to "make a proper restitution and to bring order out of chaos at the earliest possible moment."

One person attending that meeting was LJ Martin, who ran the Executive Welfare Committee. He told the reporters at the now-defunct *Independent* newspaper that Tulsa's only path of redemption from the shame the city was receiving across the country would only be achieved by being "plunged by complete restitution of the destroyed black belt." And he thought that the rest of the country should take note, saying that the "real citizenship of Tulsa weeps at this unspeakable crime and will make good the damage, so far as be done to the last penny." But the words restitution, reconstruction, and restoration were wielded without discussing what would be included. Even the Mayor, TD Evans, created a Reconstruction Committee without mandating what policies they would pursue or implement.

With these guarantees of Tulsa needing to repair the damage done, who would want to make a ruckus? The white leaders of Tulsa promised restitution. Then-Mayor TD Evans told the City Commission,

> It is in the judgement of many wise heads in Tulsa, based on a number of years that this uprising was inevitable . . . it was good generalship to let the destruction come to that section where the trouble was hatched up, put in motion and where it had its inception.[24]

For the Mayor, with the world hearing that restitution was being made – though it was not – the destruction of Black Wall Street meant there was an opportunity for business to boom even further in North Tulsa. In his words, "let the negro settlement be placed farther to the north and east" because "a large portion of this district is well suited for industrial purposes than for residences." The reality is that white Tulsans wanted the land on which Black Wall

Street stood for industrial development. Instead of spending the time rebuilding the Black community angry mobs sought to bring low, they rejected offers from the *Chicago Tribune* who offered to send money to help with the improvement of Black Tulsa. Instead of accepting it, Tulsa said no.

The empty promises were quiet threats. Not long after the destruction of Black Wall Street, Caleb Ridley, a Baptist minister, and National official within the Ku Klux Klan, whose members included Tate Brady (the once namesake of parts included in and abutting Black Wall Street), came to Tulsa with a congratulatory word to his audience at Tulsa Convention Hall. For Ridley, the terror some of his members generated "was the best thing to ever happen to Tulsa and that judging from the way strange Negroes were coming Tulsa we might have to do it all over again."

Less than three months after this terror, perhaps out of a note of accomplishment and admonishment to the Blacks who persisted in living in Tulsa to keep quiet, approximately 300 Tulsans were initiated as part of the Tulsa Klan. And they gathered in a building they called the "Be No Hall" to signify that there'd "Be No Nigger, Be No Jew, Be No Catholic, Be No Immigrant." They placed it such that its shadow would hover over Greenwood as families tried to rebuild.[25]

As time went on, the reneging on the promises of restitution became more blatant. A month after the Massacre, Alva Niles and the Chamber of Commerce pivoted to pushing for a railroad station terminal to be built where Black folks once lived. When the Chamber of Commerce was told that it would be nearly impossible for Black folks to rebuild there, its board appointed a special committee to investigate. After four days, they came back with the recommendation, "We therefore recommend that permission be granted by the city to the negroes to build on their own property as a solution of the problem facing the city at this time." The city's reconstruction committee rejected this out of hand.

Why?

The *Tulsa Tribune's* June 3rd story, *headlined* "Plan to Move Negroes into New District" explains why. This chapter suggests that

> the two races being divided by an industrial section will draw more distinctive lines between them and thereby eliminate the intermingling of lower elements of the two races, which in our opinion is the root of the evil which should not exist.[26]

In an effort to get the restitution the survivors of this massacre were promised, 193 lawsuits were filed against the city and insurance companies to make families whole again for damages totaling $1,470,711 ($21,264,591 in 2021).[27] It took until 1937 or 16 years for those cases to get a hearing, at which point Judge Bradford Williams summarily dismissed most of them.

180   *Caleb Gayle*

When the Red Cross recommended that the city allow Black residents to build even "temporary wooden houses on their lots," the city gave them permission but then rescinded that permission citing a contrived fire code stipulation. Black attorneys had to argue before the state's supreme court to get even the right to build homes on the lots they owned. They won, allowing them to rebuild Greenwood. But without the ability to earn money and the buildings they once treasured living in ruins, the victory seemed almost pyrrhic.

The goal of the city was clear – quell the hysteria it allowed to be visited upon Black Tulsa. Almost formulaically, this is how you keep a community silent. You demolish the town, then you formalize – if not institutionalize – the groups who did the demolishing, then you dare what's left of the Black community which had been demolished to get loud about their troubles by placing a tower to white supremacy, like the local KKK's "Be No Hall," over them.

Or, in other words, this is how public memory gets lost: you keep silent the stories that if told could compel the action to repair.

Another Round of Destruction

The destruction of the town's Black community decimated a community, but it also gave way to the chance of ultimate destruction. Some commented that Black Wall Street came back even stronger after the white mob torched so much of it. Just four years after the Massacre, Black Wall Street played host to the National Conference of the National Negro Business League, Booker T. Washington's organization, which was established "to promote the commercial and financial development of the Negro." According to Hannibal Johnson, the author of several books about Black Wall Street, "There [were] well over 200 documented black owned and operated businesses in the community. It was a thriving time in the Greenwood district in the 1940s." By the 1940s, there were many more stores, homes, and opportunities. After half a century of growth, destruction, and restoration, Greenwood was knocked down again – this time by public policy. From the 1950s through the early 1970s, urban renewal granted cities federal funding to plow under blighted areas – supposedly to clear a path for public-housing projects or other new buildings, though these projects displaced hundreds of thousands of people, predominantly people of color in low-income neighborhoods.

But the stumbling block for preserving the memories of this idiosyncratic neighborhood was fundamentally *the failure to preserve* this neighborhood. The Housing Act of 1949 represented perhaps one of the most ambitious housing plans in American history – doling out over 13.5 billion dollars over the course of nearly 30 years. Local, state, and regional governments, however, were given these funds with very little by way of restrictions. Local leaders who had the opportunity to clear slums, per the expectation of the Housing Act, were supposed to replace those slums with more low-income and affordable and public housing. But without much by the way of restrictions, guidelines, and guardrails, local leaders could pursue the development of more profitable, and thereby more tax-bearing opportunities, like parking lots, commercial real estate, and industrial development. As a result, this Black community in Tulsa, along with so many other Black communities, had the remnants of its success bulldozed and not redeveloped. All told, urban renewal granted cities federal funding to remove blighted areas – supposedly to clear a path for public-housing projects or other new buildings, though these projects displaced hundreds of thousands of people, predominantly people of color in low-income neighborhoods. Black businesses, schools, and family homes were destroyed and replaced with a highway that choked off the Greenwood community from the rest of the city but made it easier for mainly white families in the suburbs to commute to and from downtown Tulsa. Black residents made up 76% of the population loss in Greenwood and the surrounding areas by 1979.

This destruction did more than just level a community. It also destroyed the physical manifestation of where Black Wall Street once stood. Where homes once stood and theaters once hosted families and restaurants once welcomed plenty, silence now reigned.

For decades, schools did not integrate the history of Black Tulsa into classes. So, of course, reparations of any kind, let alone reparations for the community so devastated in my proverbial backyard, seemed improbable and unnecessary to many. My school never discussed it, like many other schools around the state and country. This lack of knowledge, which was induced by intentional silence, however, was disrupted.

Disrupting the Silence in Tulsa

> Tulsa's race relations are more ceremonial – liken to a bad marriage, with spouses living in the same quarters but housed in different rooms, each escaping one another by perpetuating a separateness of silence.
> – Former State Representative Don Ross, the Prologue of the Tulsa Race Riot Commission Report, February 28, 2001

With very little acknowledgment and recognition of the events of the Tulsa Race Massacre etched anywhere for people to learn, silence had taken hold. However, in the years leading up to the Massacre's eightieth anniversary – long before the Massacre was widely known – a Black Tulsan and state representative, Don Ross, set in motion the ways in which we would all come to learn about and commemorate this Massacre. And perhaps he set in even more motion the direct call for reparations, the biggest indictment of public memory.

In 1997, several Black elected officials in Oklahoma, under the leadership of Ross, passed a joint resolution to establish the 1921 Tulsa Race Riot Commission, which would later become known as the 1921 Tulsa Race Massacre Centennial Commission. By 2000, the governor, Frank Keating, signed the resolution into law. The main goal was to produce a final report about what happened to Black Wall Street. In the cover letter from the Commissioners to state and local Tulsa officials, the Commissioners wrote in 2001, "reparations

Figure 8.3 Arrested Black residents of Greenwood, Tulsa, being marched to makeshift detention facility

Source: Credit – Tulsa Historical Society & Museum

to the historic Greenwood community in real and tangible form would be good public policy and do much to repair the emotional and physical scars of this terrible incident in our shared past." They then went on to list specific actions which included, "direct payments to riot survivors and descendants; a scholarship fund available to students affected by the riot; establishment of an economic development enterprise zone in the historic Greenwood district; a memorial for the riot victims."

However, subsequent to the commission's report, not one dollar has been issued to the descendants of the survivors or victims of the Massacre. And though lawsuits have ensued both in 2003 and in 2020 and 2021 by descendants and survivors of the Massacre, not one provision of recompense has been made.

Disrupting the Silence in Other Contexts

The tragedies of the Tulsa Race Massacre are in conversation with several other tragedies for which the United States has had a poor record on repairing the racial violence it either inflicted or allowed to be visited upon people of color.

At a national level, Black political and activist leaders have been trying to get the United States to simply commit to *studying* the issue of reparations for Black Americans. In 2019, the US House of Representatives finally took up a resolution – initially proposed by former Congressman John Conyers in 1989 – to study reparations called House Resolution 40. When asked what he thought of the resolution, the then-Senate Majority Leader Mitch McConnell of Kentucky said, "I don't think reparations for something that happened 150 years ago for whom none of us currently living are responsible is a good idea." Arguing that the country should not even study reparations, McConnell added, "We've tried to deal with our original sin of slavery by fighting a civil war, by passing landmark civil rights legislation. We elected an African American president."

On the day of H.R. 40s hearing, Ta-Nehisi Coates, author of the seminal essay "Case for Reparations," testified before the committee, saying, "Many of us would love to be taxed for the things we are solely and individually responsible for. But we are American citizens, and thus bound to a collective enterprise that extends beyond our individual and personal reach."[28]

However, long before Coates' essay and Congressional testimony, several academics had called for reparations. For example, Carla D. Pratt, now Dean of the Washburn University School of Law, wrote about micro-targeting reparations toward the descendants of Black people once held as slaves of the Creek Nation as a means of repayment of the damage done by slavery.[29] Even more, the important article she wrote made the case that reparations extended beyond pecuniary compensation. It also included a focus on reclaiming history. Her purpose was leveraging reparations as a method by which to hold fast to memory as a motivator to maintain history.

William "Sandy" Darity has been a veritable economics luminary on, among many other things, the racial wealth gap. Without the explanatory features of history, he argues, the racial wealth gap can never be fully understood. Darity has spent much of his latter stage of his career unearthing how the racial wealth gap could be narrowed through reparations. As Darity put it in a Brookings report,

> The origins of this gulf in Black and White wealth stem from the immediate aftermath of slavery when a promise made to provide the formerly enslaved with 40 acres in land grants went unmet – while many white Americans were provided substantial "hand outs" (typically 160 acres) of land in the west.[30]

In his book, *From Here to Equality: Reparations for Black Americans in the Twenty-First Century*, Darity, like many other social scientists, points out that pains inflicted upon Black life in America did not stop with the lack of fulfillment of the promises in the aftermath of the Civil War.[31] Massacres, redlining, urban renewal, lack of full inclusion of Black people in benefits like the GI Bill, the growth of the prison industrial complex, and more all reflect the barriers to wealth generation for Black Americans. His work has demonstrated that "Public policy has created the Black – White gulf in wealth, and it will require public policy to eliminate it." Public policy that eliminates this gulf must remember

184   *Caleb Gayle*

the origins of that gulf to appropriately fix it. Without an understanding of where this gulf began, it is nearly impossible to understand what a total repair would cost. And because Darity recognizes the origin of the gulf between Black and white wealth as the scourge of slavery, his estimation to erase the gulf is far larger – totaling between 10 trillion and 12 trillion dollars. This direct transfer of wealth from the government to the people aggrieved as a means of recompense is, for Darity, the litmus test for assessing whether that attempt to deliver reparations has been successful. So, when examining Japanese American reparations, the experiment of reparations in Evanston, and Holocaust reparations, I will do so relative to the standard Darity establishes.

Japanese-American Reparations

A blind spot in my education was the unnecessary and racist fallout that targeted Japanese Americans following the start of World War II. In fact, in my small conservative, Christian school, the only critique of President Franklin Delano Roosevelt was his big government approach to solving economic crises which our right-leaning history teachers believed austerity measures would have solved. On February 19, 1942, President Roosevelt signed an executive order that authorized the evacuation of "all persons deemed a threat to national security from the West Coast to relocation centers further inland." Put another way, he focused the attention of the federal government on mitigating what he found to be a threat, an irrational notion spurred by preexisting racial prejudices against Japanese people. Over the course of the following six months, over 100,000 people of Japanese ancestry were moved to assembly units and they were evacuated to and confined in isolated, fenced, and guarded relocation centers, known as internment camps.

President Roosevelt justified this action based on the Japanese attack on Pearl Harbor on December 7, 1941, which triggered the United States to enter World War II.

In his book, *Redress: The Inside Story of the Successful Campaign for Japanese American Reparations*, survivor John Tateishi tells the reader not only how significant the trauma of that experience was on him and the thousands of other Americans of Japanese descent but also the tale of how Japanese Americans received reparations. Though wholly different, the throughline between the Tulsa Race Massacre and the internment of Japanese Americans was and is silence – in that, silence enabled the persistence of inaction and limited results.

There was, according to Tateishi, a generational split in the way that trauma was processed and justice was sought. The Nisei generation included people who were born between 1910 and 1930 to immigrant parents, and the Sansei represented people who were either held in internment camps at a very young age or born after the war. According to Tateishi, the Nisei held fast to traditional values that compelled them to bury the past – to subdue the memories and not lift up public memory which would raise the fundamental question: what is owed? For the Sansei, the internment was another, perhaps more specific form of racial oppression, one that could be quantified and qualified with those affected by it and those who inherited the racial trauma which came along with it. The lifting up of the narrative and not putting the past behind them led to answer specifically what is owed. And consequently the redress campaign was launched, but it was not, like the case of the Black Tulsans, a legal case that was initiated. Rather than litigating this matter in courts, the Japanese American movement became organized around getting the recognition for what happened and then pushing legislatively for actions to be taken to pay those affected what they were owed. Tateishi and his wife created the Japanese American Citizens' League. Perhaps as a symbol of success, reparations of some kind did happen. In 1988, President Ronald Reagan signed the Civil Liberties Act, which not only issued a formal apology to Japanese Americans and specifically the survivors of those internment camps but also paid $20,000 to each survivor.

Whether this amount, $20,000 to each survivor, is commensurate to the degree of pain and ongoing trauma experienced by Japanese Americans is still a matter of divergence. In a *Washington Post* story, reporter Tracey Jan chronicled the stories of a Japanese American family. One of the family members, Ginny Yamamoto Syphax, conveyed that the government payout would not be "enough for what Japanese American families lost."[32] But Yamamoto Syphax continues,

> I don't think you can put a dollar amount on it. It's not just financial loss. It's also emotional loss. You're being uprooted from a place that, for my grandparents, was the land of opportunity. You come and work your tail off, and then to lose that sense of security of having a home – suddenly it's all gone.[33]

This is where public memory of the trauma inflicted surpasses the financial compensation for the trauma. Public memory allows us to consider not just what financial considerations must be made. Public memory also enables an evolving set of conversations about who we are as a country and what is the basis for our deeply racist past. So, from Darity's perspective, the payment to Japanese Americans might be a signal of success or he might view it as too limited. But in the grander project of public memory, the payment – no matter how small or large – is one critical step in the direction of righting grievous wrongs.

Evanston

Perhaps one of the most recent examples of how a city, not too dissimilar from Tulsa, has grappled with answering how what is owed indicts public memory is Evanston, Illinois. In March 2021, Evanston became the very first city in the United States to issue reparations. But its version of reparations is quite different from the Japanese American experience. The City Council of Evanston, 8 to 1,

186   *Caleb Gayle*

voted to approve Resolution 58-R-19, "Commitment to End Structural Racism and Achieve Racial Equity."[34] With $10 million, the city created the structure to distribute $25,000 in housing grants to a very targeted group of Black people in Evanston.

The champion of this effort, Robin Rue Simmons, a city councilor herself, made it clear that, "It is the start." But this start did what places like the city of Tulsa have never done. "It is the reckoning."[35] And that is particularly the aim of reparations: to reckon with the impacts of past injustices on contemporary life.

In 2019, the city council put the structure of this effort together. They created a reparation fund that they thought would be financed by a combination of private donations and tax revenue leveraging sales from marijuana. But it became clear that the city believed that it could not offer money directly to the citizens as payments. So, the reparations came in the form of grants. Perhaps what mattered far more is that like the case of Tulsa and like the Japanese American reparations for internment, the advocacy of reparations was tied to direct inflictions of racial discrimination and the social and economic pain that persisted as a result. In the case of Evanston, the housing grants are limited to particular Evanston residents. And these residents must demonstrate that they themselves or their ancestors were subject to the harm of redlining[36] or other discriminatory housing practices and policies that limited the neighborhoods where Black people could access and live. To be deemed eligible, applicants would need to demonstrate that they are descendants of people who were residents of the town between 1919 and 1969 or they must be able to prove that they were subject to housing discrimination after 1969.

No direct payments were made. One thing that the Evanston case and many other similar attempts around the country demonstrate are limits we place on living out an expanded moral imagination through policy. Darity argues that policy is the instrument which has inflicted much of the harm. And, as such, it should be policy that is the instrument of repair. But if policy is the instrument of repair, the viability of reparations becomes wholly and completely subject to the whims of our politics. Every policy measure – no matter how perceptively just the cause – is subject in our democracy, to a host of political factors. It is and will remain politics – the political attitudes and leanings of voters, politicians who answer to those constituents, political messaging, and more – as the Rubicon which must be crossed for reparations to be implemented.

Repairing the Past Is Continuous

At perhaps the height of the COVID-19 pandemic, a headline grabbed the attention of the television broadcast of *60 Minutes*. "Germany to give $662 million to Holocaust survivors struggling during the coronavirus pandemic." Gideon Taylor, the president of the Conference on Jewish Material Claims Against Germany, stated, "We must meet the challenges of the increasing needs of survivors as they age, coupled with the new and urgent necessities caused by the global pandemic. It will *always remain our moral imperative to keep fighting for every survivor.*" Though the limits of success and legitimate critiques abound with the cases of Tulsa or Evanston, those critiques do not apply nearly to the same extent in the case of reparations for Holocaust survivors. The dispensation of reparations, unlike what Darity advocates, or what has been attempted in Tulsa, Evanston and for Japanese Americans, is not static. In the case of the Holocaust, the solidification and depth of public memory have enabled a more dynamic approach to reparations that are not time-bound. Rather, the ongoing and lingering effects are accounted for in the way in which reparations are allocated even today. That is why Germany just recently committed $662 million to Holocaust survivors – because as Gideon Taylor said, "it will always remain our moral imperative to keep fighting for every survivor." This contrasts drastically with the way we deal with past atrocities in the United States where the brutality of the past has lingering effects. It interrupts the ability of our collective memory to leave out what happened. If atrocities are statically held as moments frozen in time, our memories have little import for our current moments. In the case of the Holocaust, public memory not only extends the consideration of these atrocities but also doubles down on our responsibility to correct for the pain caused.

In German-occupied Europe, six million Jews were systematically murdered through various forms of persecution, execution, labor in concentration camps, gas chambers, death marches, pogroms, and more. Jews were the target of state-sponsored and coordinated extermination. The depths, however, of repairing the damage done have come with an explicit determination to make abundantly clear the facts that comprise the history of this gruesome moment in history.

Unlike the United States, the repairing was not restricted to limited financial recompense. Reparations launched from a platform of jurisprudence and due process, even if it began in military tribunals held by the Allied Forces. From 1945 to 1946, 22 political and military leaders were brought before military tribunals which were convened by international bodies. These were known as the first set of Nuremberg trials. The second phase of Nuremberg Trials brought another 185 cases. The German government established a government entity to continue the prosecution of those who committed these genocidal acts.

Financially, the reparations reaffirm and cement the public memory that Germany was at fault for the devastation it visited upon the survivors and victims of the Holocaust. The level of German financial reparations has been substantial. In 1951, Konrad Adenauer, then chancellor of West Germany, publicly confirmed his and his country's intention to pay for the "moral and material indemnity" for the "unspeakable crimes . . . committed in the name of the German people"[37] during World War II. By the next year, West Germany signed an agreement[38] directly with the nation of Israel and the very group Gideon Taylor now runs, the Conference on Jewish Material Claims Against Germany. For the following two decades and longer, Germany went even further promising to other countries and non-Jewish survivors and victims and

188   *Caleb Gayle*

their families' reparations. During this over two-decade period, approximately $91.9 billion were distributed.

In the case of Tulsa, no political and military or police leaders have been brought to trial – even though the Oklahoma Military Commission, the National Guard, the Mayor, and many in the Tulsa Police Department allowed, and, in some cases, enabled the massacre to take place. Attempts to bring these individuals to trial have, in every case, been dismissed. The Chamber of Commerce in Tulsa who promised restitution of some sort in 1921 has never repaid. Not even those buried in potters' fields have been given a proper burial. The case of reparations for Holocaust survivors demonstrates exactly what Tulsa should aspire to: an ongoing account of the pain caused and the resolutions that can be made. Memory is not static. And repairing painful memories is a commitment to be fulfilled in an ongoing fashion. There can be no end point to memory, accountability, and responsibility.

But regarding the money, as Ta-Nehisi Coates put it in his essay "Case for Reparations," "reparations could not make up for the murder perpetrated by the Nazis." The same could be said of Tulsa, Evanston, Japanese Americans, and more. Coates continued, "But they did launch Germany's reckoning with itself, and perhaps provided a road map for how a great civilization might make itself worthy of the name." This is what is at stake and this is what public memory generates. It generates the platform from which to launch a road map for how to create a great civilization – one that accommodates the full humanity of all people. And we cannot begin to accommodate the full humanity of all people if we do not consider, appreciate, and repair all parts of various histories.

Public Memory as Context and Pathway

It takes very little reading and analysis to realize that the gulfs between certain groups in the United States appear entrenched and wide and intractable. The gaps that exist between Black and white America illustrate inequity and inequality most saliently. In 2016, a study by the Brookings Institution found that the net worth of a typical white family was $171,000, compared to $17,150 for a Black family.[39] Though median unemployment in "major metropolitan areas was between 3 and 10 percent," some majority-Black neighborhoods had median unemployment as high as nearly 30%.[40] And in less extreme situations, the median unemployment of majority-Black neighborhoods was still almost 10% higher than majority-white areas. To illustrate this more intimately, the Greenwood neighborhood where Black Wall Street once stood tall sits in what is now called "North Tulsa." North Tulsa still contains some of the highest concentrations of Black people in Oklahoma. In 2015, ZIP code 74126, situated in North Tulsa, has a life expectancy of 10.7 years less than a majority-white community in Oklahoma located in ZIP code 74137.[41] Median household income in Tulsa shows that Black people earn nearly $15,000 less per year than their white peers.[42] In a town where Black people once earned significant sums

What Is Owed? 189

financially and owned property, only 32% of Black households own homes, compared to white Tulsan households, 57.9% of whom are homeowners. And Black adults are arrested at over twice the rate of whites in Tulsa.

Taken at its face without the context history so artfully provides, one could easily assume that these outcomes for Black people are outcomes they produced. Put another way, the social and material conditions of Black people, disparate and harmfully divergent they might be from our white counterparts, are the fault of Black people. That somehow, endemic to being Black leads to these divergent outcomes. Reading these outcomes absent the treasure of public memory replete with history does nothing but lead people to vacuous conclusions that we, Black people, are somehow flawed. And this ahistorical reading of present outcomes gives chase to racecraft.

Public memory reaffirmed the most viable pathway for dismantling racecraft. Racecraft is a term and theory created by historian Barbara Fields and sociologist Karen Fields. They describe racecraft:

> Racecraft encompasses the fact that the race that is pictured by the subjects as real in fact is not; it's made to be real and envisioned collectively as something real. People begin to think, "I have a racial identity, I have a race. As a black person or white person, I have certain characteristics: I'm smart; I deserve to be at the bottom, and so on." These things are programmed into people through the activity of doing that first thing, the act that is ostensibly based on heritage. That puts somebody in his or her place.

Karen Fields wrote,

> Racecraft shares characteristics with witchcraft, two in particular. First, there's no rational causality. We often speak as if black skin causes segregation or shootings. Second, there's (witting or unwitting) reliance on circular argument. For example, blood serves as a metaphor of race but is often taken as a feature of race, even by scientifically trained people. . . . If everyone takes race for granted, there's no reason that scientists would wean themselves from doing the same. Race is the category they start and end with.

Racecraft conjures the characteristics that are not naturally tied to race but are linked to race to define race categories and their subsequent treatment. Criminal tendencies are not naturally or intrinsically tied to race. But histories of over-policing, like in the case of Tulsa where the danger and violence on the part of Black people, are over-assumed, fuel the more over-policing and thus a greater propensity to misidentify criminality. Lack of labor force participation is not any more Black than it is with any other race nor home ownership, health, or life expectancy. History, and the fullness of it, interrupts the crafting of race narratives that might otherwise omit necessary complexities.

190   *Caleb Gayle*

But what reparations compel is a reconsideration of how what was owed might rectify not only what experiences people have had but also what unfair, inequitable experiences we have now and how it is linked to what once was.

Conclusion

This is what public memory replete with the good and the bad does for those who choose to remember it: it chastises American history but provides an impetus to rectify it. The fact that we do not readily recall these blatant acts of terror and destruction as well as the ongoing effects of that terror and destruction is not unintentional. Like Mayor TD Evans who wanted to ensure that the narrative about Tulsa was not one of naked racial violence and marginalization, America is loath to remember its acts of naked racial violence and marginalization. Because remembering the pain can potentially compel us to relieve that pain and provide the recompense necessary to begin to address it.

Perhaps if I knew what once was, I would not have assumed that reparations, as a high schooler, seemed beyond the scope of what should happen. Answering what is owed and framing this history within the context of what can be repaired reconstitutes our public memory as a long-term project to right wrongs that have historically caused significant damage to people whose ancestors have been historically brutalized and marginalized.

Notes

1 Erik Eckholm, "Using History to Mold Ideas," *New York Times*, May 4, 2011, https://www.nytimes.com/2011/05/05/us/politics/05barton.html?searchResultPosition=1

For additional reading about David Barton and the work of Wall Builders, consider the work of Nate Blakeslee, "King of the Christocrats," *Texas Monthly*, September 2006, https://www.texasmonthly.com/articles/king-of-the-christocrats/

and Paul Harvey, "Selling the Idea of a Christian Nation: David Barton's Alternative Intellectual Universe," *Religion Dispatches*, May 11, 2011, https://religiondispatches.org/author/paul-harvey/page/4/

For further consideration of the effect of Christian-based schooling on the teaching of American history and race, read Kathleen Wellman, *Hijacking History: How the Christian Right Teaches History and Why It Matters* (Oxford: Oxford University Press, 2021).

2 Text – H.R.3745–101st Congress (1989–1990): Commission to Study Reparation Proposals for African Americans Act. *Congress.gov*, Library of Congress, October 24, 1990, www.congress.gov/bill/101st-congress/house-bill/3745/text.

3 Ibid.

4 Rhett Morgan, "Go Inside the New Grocery Store Opening Today in a Tulsa Food Desert," *Tulsa World*, May 17, 2021, https://nam12.safelinks.protection.outlook.com/?url=https%3A%2F%2Ftulsaworld.com%2Fbusiness%2Flocal%2Fgo-inside-the-new-grocery-store-opening-today-in-a-tulsa-food-desert%2Farticle_fa8053d6-b274-11eb-a73b-f7bb8a932688.html&data=05%7C01%7Cm.blatt%40northeastern.edu%7C9479879451624df2ef2a08db19d42d30%7Ca8eec281aaa34daeac9b9a398b9215e7%7C0%7C0%7C638132171398518145%7CUnknown%7CTWFpbGZsb3d8eyJWIjoiMC4wLjAwMDAiLCJQIjoiV2luMzIiLCJBTil6Ik1haWwiLCJXVCI6Mn0%3D%7C3000%7C%7C%7C&sdata=Kd6fESHoajYzpKbXT5eowJB2%2B90JjaoOsBvLIhd3S%2BA%3D&reserved=0

What Is Owed? 191

5 "North Tulsa Grocery Store Breaks Ground," *Oklahoma Eagle Newswire*, June 25, 2020, https://theokeagle.com/2020/06/25/north-tulsa-grocery-store-breaks-ground/

6 Choc Phillips, "Murder in the Streets," Memoir of the Eyewitness Account of the 1921 Tulsa Race Massacre William 'Choc' Phillips, http://www.eakinpress.com/murder-in-the-streets.html

7 Kweku Larry Crowe and Thabiti Lewis, "The 1921 Tulsa Race Massacre: What Happened to Black Wall Street," *Humanities*, Vol. 42, No. 1 (Winter 2021).

8 Scott Ellsworth, Book 1: "1921," *The Ground Breaking: An American City and Its Search for Justice* (New York: Dutton, an imprint of Penguin Random House, 2021), p. 14.

9 "Unequaled advantages in the B.I.T.," *Muskogee Comet,* June 23, 1904, p. 2. B.I.T. stands for Beautiful Indian Territory, https://nam12.safelinks.protection.outlook.com/?url=https%3A%2F%2Fwww.newspapers.com%2Fimage%2F585127973%2F%3Fterms%3Dcreek%26match%3D1&data=05%7C01%7Cm.blatt%40northeastern.edu%7C9479879451624df2ef2a08db19d42d30%7Ca8eec281aaa34daeac9b9a398b9215e7%7C0%7C0%7C6381321713985181 45%7CUnknown%7CTWFpbGZsb3d8eyJWIjoiMC4wLjAwMDAiLCJQIjoiV2luMzIiLCJBTiI6Ik1haWwiLCJXVCI6Mn0%3D%7C3000%7C%7C%7C&sdata=hTe74VfCqpJzkpIbb%2F1s5uCqVS35CmhWhr%2B%2B5vMThIo%3D&reserved=0

10 Alexis Clark, "Tulsa's 'Black Wall Street' Flourished as a Self-Contained Hub in Early 1900s Greenwood Avenue Featured Luxury Shops, Restaurants, Movie Theaters, a Library, Pool Halls and Nightclubs," *History*, September 4, 2019, www.history.com/news/black-wall-street-tulsa-race-massacre.

11 Ellsworth, *The Ground Breaking*.

12 Larry O'Dell, "Senate Bill One," *Oklahoma Historical Society*, www.okhistory.org/publications/enc/entry.php?entry=SE017.

13 "Nab Negro for Attacking Girl in Elevator," *Tulsa Tribune*, May 31, 1921, https://thegrandarchive.wordpress.com/nab-negro-for-attacking-girl-in-elevator/

14 Ibid.

15 Scott Ellsworth, *Death in a Promised Land: The Tulsa Race Riot of 1921* (Baton Rouge, LA: LSU Press, 1982).

16 Ellsworth, *Death in a Promised Land*, p. 48.

17 Ibid.

18 Ibid.

19 Mary E. Jones Parrish, *Events of the Tulsa Disaster* (privately printed, 1922), https://digitalcollections.nypl.org/items/98261810-208d-013a-5279-0242ac110003

20 *Tulsa Race Riot: A Report by the Oklahoma Commission to Study the Tulsa Race Riot of 1921*, February 28, 2001.

21 Caleb Gayle, "100 Years After the Tulsa Massacre, What Does Justice Look Like?" *New York Times*, May 25, 2021, https://www.nytimes.com/2021/05/25/magazine/tulsa-race-massacre-1921-greenwood.html?searchResultPosition=1

22 Ibid.

23 James S. Hirsch, *Riot and Remembrance: The Tulsa Race Riot and Its Legacy* (Boston, MA: Houghton Mifflin, 2014), p. 134.

24 Ellsworth, *Death in a Promised Land*.

25 Steve Gerkin, "Beno Hall: Tulsa's Den of Horror," *This Land*, September 3, 2011, https://thislandpress.com/2011/09/03/beno-hall-tulsas-den-of-terror/

26 Chris Messer, Thomas Shriver, and Alison Adams, "The Destruction of Black Wall Street: Tulsa's 1921 Riot and the Eradication of Accumulated Wealth," *American Journal of Economics and Sociology*, Vol. 77, Nos. 3–4 (May–September, 2018).

27 Tulsa Race Riot Report, February 28, 2001.

28 For further study of Ta-Nehisi Coates' framework and considerations of reparations, review Coates, "The Case for Reparations," *Atlantic*, June 14, 2014, https://www.theatlantic.com/magazine/archive/2014/06/the-case-for-reparations/361631/

192 *Caleb Gayle*

29 Carla D. Pratt, "Tribes and Tribulations: Beyond Sovereign Immunity and Toward Reparation and Reconciliation for the Estelusti," *Washington and Lee Journal of Civil Rights and Social Justice*, Vol. 11, No. 1 (Winter 2005).

30 William Darity and Kirsten Mullen, "Black Reparations and the Racial Wealth Gap," *Brookings Institution*, June 15, 2020, https://www.brookings.edu/blog/up-front/2020/06/15/black-reparations-and-the-racial-wealth-gap/

31 William Darity and Kirsten Mullen, *From Here to Equality: Reparations for Black Americans in the Twenty-First Century* (Chapel Hill, NC: University of North Carolina Press, 2020).

32 Tracey Jan, "What Reparations Mean to One American Family," *Washington Post*, January 24, 2020, https://www.washingtonpost.com/podcasts/post-reports/what-reparations-mean-to-one-american-family/

33 Ibid.

34 "Evanston Local Reparations," *City of Evanston*, www.cityofevanston.org/government/city-council/reparations.

35 Julie Bosman, "Chicago Suburb Shapes Reparations for Black Residents: 'It Is the Start'," *New York Times*, March 22, 2021, https://www.nytimes.com/2021/03/22/us/reparations-evanston-illinois-housing.html?searchResultPosition=1

36 Redlining was and, in many cases, still is the denial of services, often, to Black residents or in their neighborhoods or in their communities. This has resulted in denying neighborhoods, communities, residents financial services such as mortgages, or raising prices such that they become prohibitive of insurance, or even locating healthcare services and groceries and stores distant from the very people who need them.

37 Annabelle Timsit, "The Blueprint the US Can Follow to Finally Pay Reparations," *Quartz*, October 13, 2020, https://qz.com/1915185/how-germany-paid-reparations-for-the-holocaust

38 "Agreement 3 Between the State of Israel and the Federal Republic of Germany," *United Nations Treaty Series*, Signed at Luxemburg, September 10, 1952.

39 Kriston McIntosh, Emily Moss, Ryan Nunn, and Jay Shambaugh, "Examining the Black-white Wealth Gap," *Brookings Institution*, February 27, 2020, www.brookings.edu/blog/up-front/2020/02/27/examining-the-black-white-wealth-gap/.

40 Patrick Sharkey, Keeanga-Yamahtta Taylor, and Yaryna Serkez, "The Gaps between White and Black America, in Charts," *New York Times*, June 19, 2020, https://www.nytimes.com/search?query=Patrick+Sharkey%2C+Keeanga-Yamahtta+Taylor++The+gaps

41 "Community Collaboration Helps Narrow Life Expectancy Gap in Tulsa," *Tulsa Health Department*, September 3, 2015, www.tulsa-health.org/news/community-collaboration-helps-narrow-life-expectancy-gap-tulsa.

42 "Annual Report 2020: Tulsa Equality Indicators," *Community Service Council*, 2020, www.csctulsa.org/wp-content/uploads/2021/03/EI-Report_Tulsa_2020.pdf.

9 Remembering Pulse

Lisa Arellano

In the early morning hours of June 12, 2016, Omar Mateen entered the Pulse Nightclub in Orlando, Florida, and begin firing rounds from a handgun and an AR-15 rifle.[1] Between 2 am and 5 am, Mateen alternately killed, injured, and threatened the 300-plus people inside the club.[2] At 5 am, police entered the building and, after exchanging gunfire with Mateen, shot and killed him. The incident left 50 people dead (49 victims plus the shooter) and another 53 injured.

> [Among the victims] nearly half were of Puerto Rican descent; while many more were Cuban, Dominican, Ecuadorian, Mexican, Salvadoran, Venezuelan, Afro-Latinx, and from other Latinx communities. Some were Black. Some were undocumented. Over half were under the age of 30, the youngest victims having just turned 18 years old.[3]

In July 2016, a month after the incident, The onePULSE Foundation was established by Pulse Nightclub proprietor Barbara Poma. The inaugural and primary goal of the foundation was, from its inception, to build a Pulse memorial to honor the event's victims and survivors, first responders and the larger community impacted by this event.

Though the intention to remember Pulse was immediate and absolute, narrative accounts about what happened that night reveal the slippery relationship between violent event and narrative description.[4] In some accounts, the event is described as "the deadliest terrorist attack in the United States since the September 11 attacks in 2001," an account that prioritizes Mateen's claimed allegiance to ISIS prior to, and during, the attack. In others' accounts, the violence at Pulse is remembered vis-à-vis its victims as "the deadliest single incident targeting the LGBTQ community in U.S. history."[5] This emphasis on victim identity rarely centralizes the fact that the victims were overwhelmingly Latinx.[6] And sometimes, focusing on the particular type of violence, the event is described as "the deadliest mass shooting in U.S. history up to that time"[7] or "the deadliest mass shooting by a single gunman."[8] Descriptively, each of these claims seeks to capture the scale of the event (measured largely through the

DOI: 10.4324/9781003217848-13

194 *Lisa Arellano*

sheer number of victims) but each of these claims also functions to make the Pulse shooting meaningful and legible in particular ways, alternately emphasizing and de-emphasizing various aspects of what happened.[9] These claims make reference to particularly resonant types of violence – terrorism, hate violence, and gun violence – and imply their distinction and separability.

The onePULSE memorial project necessarily emerges into this complicated space and is faced with the near-impossible challenge of metabolizing complex and sometimes competing understandings of what makes violence meaningful and significant. The enormity of the project's ambitions creates both procedural and formal challenges for those doing the work of building the memorial. Nonetheless, work on the memorial is well underway in Orlando; the preliminary plans for the multifaceted memorial offer a rich, multi-layered cultural text ripe for analysis. I am interested, of course, in how the memorial is taking shape and will attend here to both its process and formal aspects. But first, I want to consider the complicated narrative and historical space into which this memorial enters – a space defined by relationships among violence, national identity, queer citizenship, and race. My analysis of the national memorial project in Orlando emerges from this broader analysis. Ultimately, I am interested as well in an array of other memorial projects – less centralized (or less permanent) attempts to engage with and represent the Orlando shooting. I want to highlight, in particular, the way the interim Pulse memorial is able to do a different kind of memory work. While it is practically inevitable that there will be one centralized and primary Pulse memorial in Orlando, ephemeral and peripheral memory projects serve an important function in the ongoing project of remembering Pulse.

What and Why We Remember

The characterizations of the events at Pulse as terrorist violence, anti-gay violence, and/or gun violence inevitably draw on larger understandings of how and why we should remember particular forms of violence and what these forms of violence mean within larger ideas about queer community, race in the US, and the country's relationship to violence. In June 2021, President Joe Biden signed a law designating the Pulse Nightclub as a national memorial. At the signing, Biden attempted to articulate the place of Pulse memory within the larger national imaginary.

> Just over five years ago, the Pulse nightclub, a place of acceptance and joy, became a place of unspeakable pain and loss. And we'll never fully recover, but we'll remember. And we have to – what we're going to do is what the members of Congress here did, and enshrine in law – as a consequence of that law, enshrine, in perpetuity, literally a monument to the loss that occurred there, and an absolute determination that we're going to deal with this every single, solitary day and make sure that we're not in a position to see this happen again.[10]

The Orlando memorial project will need to, Biden suggests, offer a site-specific and centralized articulation of the unspeakable, represent the past, and offer a theory of a better, more utopian future – all in the name of a national "we" who share both an understanding of Pulse and inclusion in the nation itself. The federally recognized Orlando memorial project appears to emerge in singular response and relationship to Pulse, but there are a number of powerfully resonant ideological frames that preexist the 2016 shooting that informs how and why this memorial site is so resonant; these frameworks include constructions of legible gay vulnerability, US anti-terrorism rhetoric, anti-LGBT violence activism, and ideas about gun violence. Histories of these complex and intersecting issues powerfully inform the location of Pulse memory within the larger national imaginary.

In the wake of the Pulse shooting, many were quick to note the focus on gay victimhood alongside a de-emphasis on the fact that most of the victims were Latinx.[11] Miranda Joseph calls this "homosexism – that is, the prioritization of gayness over other identity features."[12] This tendency was fully evident in Biden's reference, at the time of the National Memorial signing to "the 49 lives lost: family members, parents, friends, veterans, students, young, Black, Asian, Latino – all fellow Americans."[13] The fact that Biden didn't mention the victims' gayness suggests that this aspect of their identity is both obvious, and central to the designation of the site. Indeed, the US government is newly interested in the preservation of LGBT history and in the designation of relevant memory sites. Beginning in 1999, the National Park Service (NPS) turned attention to the relative paucity of LGBT heritage sites leading, in June 2014, to an announcement of the National Park Foundation LGBTQ Heritage Initiative (along with an updated acronym).[14] By 2016, ten sites were added to the NPS National Register of Historic Places and a 1,262-page, multi-author theme study was published on the Park Service website. The theme study's authors – a remarkable assemblage of preeminent queer historians and scholars – are unrelenting in their attention to racial, gender, and sexual diversity and the study's individual chapters do remarkable work on attending to the varying complexities of queer life. But the initiative to remember LGBTQ history is embedded within larger and more far-reaching national projects – many of which de-emphasize the complexities of queer community in favor of an easily recognizable (and memorialized) version of LGBTQ life.

Arguably, such homogenizing national memory projects are animated by instrumentalist constructions of the gay subject and conceptualizations of the US nation. These instrumentalist constructions have been named most clearly by Jasbir Puar as homonationalism, which "ties the recognition of the homosexual subject, both legally and representationally, to the national and transnational political agendas of U.S. imperialism."[15] While the designation of the Pulse national memory site does, on the one hand, offer important recognition of the work being done by the multi-racial, Orlando-based organization actually building the memorial, the gesture is simultaneously embedded in other, wholly unrelated nationalist agendas.[16] The congressional and presidential

196 *Lisa Arellano*

endorsements of Pulse memory serve as a near-perfect expression of gay-inclusive democratic idealism scaffolded by larger historical constructions of the presumptively Muslim terrorist. In other words, a homonationalist agenda is optimally instantiated and expressed by the recognition of violence that is simultaneously "terrorist" *and* directed against the lesbian and gay subjects. It bears noting, as Puar's work might suggest, that the recognition of terrorist violence vis-à-vis gay vulnerability relies centrally on a constructed opposition between the terrorist as Muslim (presumptively brown-skinned and anti-gay) and the gay subject (presumptively white and secular).[17] This dichotomization of faith, geography, race, and sexuality inevitably and falsely precludes the existence of queer, brown-skinned Muslims. As a corollary, state-sponsored memory of gay vulnerability seems cast, no matter how inaccurately, as focused on an imaginary white gay subject.

Criticisms about the seeming singular emphasis on gay victimhood following the Pulse shootings, at least in the context of national memory, respond to this ideological context. There is a historically dense relationship between the *inclusion* of the putatively white gay citizen vis-à-vis the *exclusion* of the Muslim other always and falsely construed as the terrorist from elsewhere. The simultaneous failure to name the violence at Pulse as "racial violence" or "xenophobic violence" suggests a continuing and indelible link between violence and terrorism from "the outside" that renders a host of other and ongoing forms of violence invisible, including the state's own violence. The material vulnerabilities of Pulse patrons, or those who share their identities, to xenophobic immigration policies, carceral racism, and white nationalist domestic terrorism seem to recede: within homonationalist anti-terrorism rhetoric and logic, the state is rendered protective and state violence against queer people of color disappears. As Sima Shakhsari writes,

> Not only does this racist division of violence assume an inherent risk of terrorism to be hidden in Muslim and Middle Eastern bodies, but it also minimizes the terror that numerous mass shootings committed by white men (including those by the police in places like Ferguson) incite in many people's lives.[18]

The Pulse memorial is not only a site of national memory but also a project with thick connections to the actual LGBTQ community and ideas about violence against LGBTQ people. As Christine Hanhardt and Chandon Reddy have argued, constructions of gay vulnerability have developed in tandem with ideas about the safety of cities, neighborhoods, and the nation itself.[19] According to Hanhardt, "Violence and safety have been the not-always-spoken-about yet defining motors of mainstream LGBT political life since the 1970s."[20] Over the course of these years, Hanhardt argues, vulnerability to violence has become an increasingly legible, if not key, feature of gay political subjectivity. Concomitantly and even more crucially, official state protections from, and condemnations of, this vulnerability have emerged as an ideal expression of what Hanhardt calls "domestic urban governance."[21] The emergent safety of disproportionately white, commercial gay neighborhoods acts as the optimum expression of the evolving state – a formulation that inevitably serves to alibi and obfuscate state violence elsewhere (most typically directed against low-income communities of color – precisely the populations criminalized by much gay anti-violence movement). A historical monument that memorializes, first and foremost, violence against the LGBTQ community is necessarily informed by this history. Within this context, it is possible to see how the state's recognition of Pulse as a site of national memory is animated by both constructions of terrorist violence *and* ideas about gay (and lesbian) vulnerability. The posited relationship between a protective state and a vulnerable gay population augments and is supported by adjacent homonationalist formations.

Remembering the Pulse shooting in terms of gun violence conjures a third and related set of ideological relationships between violence, race, and citizen inclusion. Scholars such as Melissa Merry and Jennifer Carlson are drawing much-needed attention to the ideological and rhetorical frameworks that inform and animate organizing about (and against) gun violence. They agree that some particularly well-circulated rhetorical constructions can unintentionally obscure the real and material effects of guns, particularly with respect to state violence and other forms of race-based exclusion. In *Warped Narratives: Distortion in the Framing of Gun Policy*, Merry argues that "by emphasizing mass shootings, gun control organizations neglect the major causes of gun fatalities (suicides) and the most common victims of gun homicide (blacks and Latinos)."[22] In the case of Pulse, the contrast is complicated somewhat by the fact that a disproportionate number of shooting victims *were* Latinx – though the point still holds in that spectacular, public mass shootings are relatively rare in comparison to gun violence embedded within everyday structures of inequality.

In a similar vein, Carlson attends closely to the ways that gun rhetoric (both pro- and anti-) is deeply, if invisibly, embedded within constructions of state violence and criminality. She writes,

> While gun policy may often appear to center on color-blind questions about who can purchase guns, who can carry them, and what kinds of guns they can own, its foundation in racial presumptions about legitimate violence makes the promise of gun policy fundamentally different in the United States than in other places.[23]

This is most significantly the case when gun control's opposition to citizen possession and use of firearms implicitly (if rarely transparently) relies on the state's capacity for criminalization and enforcement (via the legitimate violence of the police). While gun control debate rhetoric can, on its face, appear morally unambiguous and race-neutral, any discussion of violence – its legitimacy, illegitimacy, and control – is necessarily embedded within larger, intensely

198   *Lisa Arellano*

racialized formations about violence, criminality, and the carceral state. Carlson writes:

> [I]n most gun debates in the United States, the significance of the police – both as a practice and as an institution – has been surgically removed and sanitized. Police, however, are not merely on the sidelines of the gun debate. This is not only because they contribute to a sizable portion of gun deaths that disproportionately harm already vulnerable communities. It is also because they are wrapped up – professionally, ethically, and practically – in the broader politics of legitimate violence, a politics that includes the gun debate but far exceeds it.[24]

An overly simplistic alignment of Pulse memory with gun opposition can unintentionally lend credence to pro-police logics that ultimately bring more, rather than less, violence to (queer) communities of color.

Terrorist violence, hate violence, and gun violence are each, and collectively, forms of violence defined through frameworks of race, nation, and gay and lesbian citizenship. Understanding how and why we think we understand these forms of violence can help us understand what it means to remember them and, more specifically, what it means to remember the violence at Pulse. "Remembering Pulse" must necessarily mean focusing on the vulnerability of queer bodies of color, larger frameworks that define these forms of violence function to render this vulnerability, and the state's central role in sustaining it, invisible.

Consolidated Memory: The Pulse Memorial in Orlando

Throughout the memorial-building process, the foundation has aspired to, as Biden's loftiest goals suggest, articulate the unspeakable, represent the past, and offer a theory of a better, more utopian future. Against all semiotic probability, the proposed memorial achieves each of these things. From the beginning, the foundation was committed to creating a Pulse memorial that would be maximally sensitive to victims and their families as well as the larger community; an aspiration made manifest through intricate feedback processes and carefully assembled advising teams. Drawing on the responses to a public survey, the foundation opened a design competition, seeking memorial proposals from design firms across the globe. Between March and October 2019, one-PULSE solicited and vetted memorial designs[25] leading to its ultimate selection of French firm Coldefy and Associates.[26] The winning design will include the Pulse Memorial (at the site of the club), the Pulse Museum (which will include objects from the nightclub), and the Survival Walk (which will trace the distance between the Nightclub and the Orlando Regional Medical Center, where victims were taken the night of the shooting). The design will be ambitiously embedded within the South Downtown (SoDo) neighborhood where the club once operated. The spaces will enable and facilitate the foundation's aspiration to "create and support a memorial that opens hearts, a museum that opens minds, educational programs that open eyes, and legacy scholarships that open doors."

Much is made, on the website, about how each phase of the project includes representatives of the victims and survivors as well as "experts" in the field of memorial work. In September 2017, the foundation sent out a community survey that asked a series of questions of family members, first responders, and survivors of the shooting.[27] The survey answers, along with every other aspect of the onePULSE memorial-building process, are available in full detail on the foundation website. The surfeit of documents and documentation reveals how conscientious the foundation is being about including the many, and varied, ideas of stakeholders.[28]

The call for design proposals included many specifications, including a mandate that the memorials incorporate the original nightclub building. While the onePULSE Foundation has a remarkably strong digital presence, this place specificity makes sense within a larger history of queer culture and nightlife. Scholars of queer history are well aware of what Hanhardt calls the "historically significant role of bars and other sites of leisure in fostering LGBTQ sociality."[29] Pulse memory frequently invokes this idea, emphasizing the jubilant, singular qualities of Pulse, and even more specifically, Latin night. Though gay bars can, also, serve to sustain and codify gender, racial, and class divisions within the queer community, the memorial favors a unified representation of queer community life.[30] The memorial at the club site will include a reflecting pool surrounded by 49 colored lines in an enhanced rainbow palette. The 43 additional colors gently expand the rainbow's hues without compromising its legibility as "a universally recognized, global emblem of the LGBTQ community and its proud legacy."[31] The rainbow's universalizing capacity is mirrored on the one-PULSE merchandise page which promises t-shirts in "the colors that everyone looks good in!"[32]

The memorial's design, with its emphasis on rainbows, emphasizes the place of this project within gay and lesbian monument-making and implicitly suggests that this event can be best understood as anti-LGBTQ violence. In its current form, the project makes no mention at all of Omar Mateen, an erasure that precludes remembering the event as terrorist. Without Mateen's expressed connections to ISIS, the violence is not legible as "terrorist violence" in the same way. The decision to de-emphasize terrorist violence does reveal a move away from the initial survey responses about the monument. When asked, "What place or memorial have you seen that you like?" respondents overwhelmingly cited the 9/11-Ground Zero memorial, with fewer scattered mentions of the Oklahoma City and Vietnam War memorials and virtually no references to LGBTQ memory sites. This does not, of course, mean that respondents do not consider Pulse an important LGBTQ memory site, but it could suggest that memories of terrorist violence are embedded in the scale of the nation and therefore resonate as more significant. "Liking" the 9/11-Ground Zero memorial can be understood as asserting a claim of equal significance for the Pulse

Figure 9.1 What the National Pulse Memorial will look like during the day
Source: Credit – Courtesy of Coldefy/RDAI with HCHP, Visualizations by Brick Visual/Coldefy

site. Despite this, because Mateen is absent from the memorial plans, this set of connections is absent as well.[33]

Though some scholars have attempted to reframe Mateen's violence as *domestic* terrorism – akin to other acts of violence and shootings motivated by racial animus – this reframing has not taken hold at the site of the memorial.[34] The repeating 49 motif (in number of colors and trees at the memorial site) grieves only those the project deems "angels." The refusal to remember Mateen as the fiftieth person who died at Pulse seems to function as the aesthetic and memorial expression of the project's larger aspiration to "refuse hate." But refusing to think about Mateen forecloses certain forms of (potentially much-needed) thought. In her work on 9/11, Judith Butler considers the challenges of thinking not only about victims but also about those who commit acts of violence.

> To condemn . . . violence and to ask how it came about are surely two separate issues. . . . Those who commit acts of violence are surely responsible for them; they are not dupes of mechanisms of an impersonal social force, but agents with responsibility. On the other hand, these individuals are formed and we would be making a mistake if we reduced their actions to purely self-generated acts of will or symptoms of individual pathology or "evil." . . . to take the self-generated acts of the individual as our point of departure in moral reasoning is precisely to foreclose the possibility of questions what kind of world gives rise to such individuals.[35]

To think critically about the kind of world that gave rise to Mateen's actions at Pulse requires a denser and more unruly set of ideas than those currently adopted by the memorial planners. The Pulse Museum's educational mission aspires to "educate, engage, inspire, and activate visitors and community members to advocate for change,"[36] but this will be difficult to do absent a thorough-going engagement with the racial, national, religious, and global conditions that produce and sustain violence. Neither terrorism nor (anti-LGBTQ) hate violence can be fully understood as "acts of will or symptoms of individual pathology or evil"; indeed, by definition both are embedded in political, cultural, and social systems. But to think about this larger complex of relationships requires thinking about Mateen as well – asking how, if at all, his demand that the United States "stop bombing ISIS in Syria"[37] can be understood as an effect of a particular kind of world.

The half-mile survivor's walk will include biographical information about the shooting's victims and the event's first responders. "First responders" is itself a complicated term, referring non-specifically to police officers, firefighters, and ambulance personnel – all of whom played essential roles the night of the shooting. Over the course of the three hours that Mateen spent inside the nightclub, police officers surrounded the venue, ultimately entering the club in an armored vehicle. Among the shooting's victims were an aspiring firefighter (Corey Connell, 21), an aspiring emergency medical technician or EMT (Luis Vielma, 22), and an army veteran (Antonio Brown, 29).[38] While there are good reasons to highlight the sometimes vexed relationships between a violent state and queer of color communities, simple binaries do not hold up when first responders *are* members of the queer community or are acting on its behalf. The memorial brackets these complications through the seamless incorporation of first responders into the memorial walk.

Figure 9.2 Orlando Health Survivors Walk design

Source: Credit – Courtesy of Coldefy/RDAI with HCHP, Visualizations by Brick Visual/Coldefy

202 *Lisa Arellano*

The survivor's walk will further embed the project in the SoDo neighborhood and, with its planned open green spaces, link the memorial to larger plans for the area. SoDo, a large commercial zone surrounded by Orlando's historic neighborhoods, is described by the City of Orlando as "an emerging market,"[39] by the *Orlando Weekly* as Orlando's most "up and coming neighborhood,"[40] and by the *Orlando Sentinel* as "a neighborhood on the rise."[41] The Pulse memorial will tap into this revitalization energy. According to one architect, the project will create:

> A connected SoDo . . . so that the district can grow in the future on a strong basis. . . . A new canvas, a new start . . . a better connected SoDo with new modes of mobility, with bike paths, pedestrian paths and a new shuttle that should connect the SoDo district with [the] high-speed rail station and the downtown to form a future loop that is all weaving and interconnecting in a smoother way than it is today. A healthy and sustainable place of living, a vibrant district that we will bring through culture and the exchange of ideas for future business and residents to interact in a human environment.[42]

The architects and foundation are not alone in their desire to improve this area of the city. A 2018 *Orlando Weekly* article on the SoDo district asserts the relevance of the city's area, acknowledging that the neighborhood first became legible following the nightclub shooting but claiming that SoDo is "much more than that." The article's list of 20 things to do in SoDo includes a recommended stop to pay respects at the developing memorial, right after a "doughnut fix" at a neighborhood bakery and before visiting a child-friendly trampoline park.[43] The Pulse memorial is beginning to manifest its ambitions for the area; early in 2019, the city of Orlando announced a 20 million dollar spending initiative to fund "streetscape improvements and civic spaces"[44] and in July 2022, Orlando-based developer Center Corp announced intentions to convert an industrial site across from the future memorial into a multiuse (commercial and residential) development.[45]

But just as the site has its boosters, so too do some critics question the conflation of memorial and profit. Pulse survivor Norman Casiano – no longer able to work as a result of his injuries – asserts, "They are trying to make money off a tragic situation and trying to make this a tourist attraction when I myself need a lot of financial help."[46] Casiano's concerns about economic disparity surely apply to both individuals impacted by the Pulse shooting and the neighborhood more broadly. Inevitably, the memorial will both tap into and increase tourist traffic to the city – this will be financially beneficial to some and increase economic disadvantage for others. Neighborhood "growth" often brings "future business" at the expense of existing, less "vibrant" commercial spaces. Biographical information about the Pulse victims reveals that they worked in occupations across the economic spectrum, including jobs in the service, tourism, and retail sectors; alongside jobs in finance, healthcare, and ententertainment.[47] In a town that relies heavily on tourist income, the long-term impact of the Pulse memorial project, and its impact on the surrounding area, will bring uneven effects.

Memorial projects need to distil and singularize complex stories, emotions, and narratives into coherent, legible sites and experiences. The onePULSE Foundation and Coldefy are well on their way to achieving this. The memorial promises to bring affective impact, the museum seems likely to encourage engagement from visitors, and the survivor's walk will connect the project to the city around it. The memorial will, in other words, articulate the unspeakable, represent the past, and offer a theory of a better, more utopian future. In order to do this, the project foregrounds some ideas about violence – for example, that the shooting can be best understood as violence against the LGBTQ community – and deemphasizes others – such as Mateen's complicated and muddy relationship to US imperial violence. These representational choices are unavoidable: as communications scholar Manuel Santiago points out in an essay about Pulse memory, "collective memory consists in producing memories as part of a group or community where some narratives are privileged over others."[48] Understanding these inevitable traits of national memorial projects, I would like to turn to a different memorial endeavor to consider how a less fixed and more contingent site can facilitate a different kind of Pulse memory.

Fragments of Memory: Public Grief and Resilient Love

Though the onePULSE project is the nationally designated, and arguable primary, site of Pulse memory work, there are a range of other post-Pulse memory projects. These projects range from "The Orlando Syllabus" on Queer theory's bullybloggers website[49] to a quilt drive sponsored by the Orlando Modern Quilt Guild.[50] In some cases, these projects emerged from more "official" historical sources (The University of Central Florida,[51] the Stonewall Museum,[52] The Orange County Regional History Center[53]) and in others from individuals personally connected to one (or more) of the victims (The Dru Project[54] and the Pride Fund[55]). The memorial projects are too numerous to consider comprehensively here, but I do want to pay attention to the interim memorial site in order to consider how a community-produced, multivocal site of public grief can express and materialize community resilience.[56]

While plans (and fundraising) proceed for the primary memorial, an interim memorial has been erected at the site of the nightclub. A central feature of this interim site is a two-sided memorial wall, with panels where visitors are encouraged to write their thoughts. Though in part regulatory, the panels invite visitors into the memorial process. A sign at the pillar reads: "The memorial is a place of love, hope, and healing. Please be respectful of the rest of the memorial and leave all messages and written notes on these panels." Many, many of these messages draw on one of the official memorial's key themes – *love*. Posts include "Love Everyone," "Love is Love," "Love wins," and "Love will always win!"[57] Of course, the official Pulse Memorial is centrally focused on love as

204 *Lisa Arellano*

well; upon entering the onePULSE website, one encounters a fundraising pop-up window with the tautological declaration, "To outlove hate is to win by loving." Love has been central to many other Pulse memorial projects as well, including the star-studded "Broadway for Orlando" YouTube video featuring a wealth of stars singing "What the World Needs Now is Love Sweet Love."[58] Love – or its antithesis "hate" – serves as a conceptual cornerstone of Pulse memorial projects.

"Love" has long been a keyword in gay and lesbian political patois, with uses ranging from Oscar Wilde-era references to "the love that dare not speak its name" to the marriage equality slogan that "love is love." In part, these formulations have deployed gay *love* as a strategic and cleaned-up replacement for gay *sex* – a substitution that reached its strategic zenith in the run-up to gay marriage legal battles. The 2003 Supreme Court decision in Lawrence v. Texas (which effectively ended State-level sodomy laws) relied centrally on replacing assessments of gay sex with a reverence for gay love. The justices wrote,

> When sexuality finds overt expression in intimate conduct with another person, the conduct can be but one element in a personal bond that is more enduring . . . the liberty protected by the Constitution allows homosexual persons the right to make this choice.[59]

Gay and lesbian citizens, the court decreed, should be free to love; a mere 12 years later, the court would extend this recognition of gay love in Obergefell v. Hodges to a recognition of gay marriage. By the time of Lin-Manuel Miranda's post-Pulse acceptance speech at the 2016 Tony Awards, love was indelibly resonant and recognizable as the slogan of gays, lesbians, and their allies. "Love is love is love is love is love is love is love" Manuel exhorted through tears as the audience cheered.[60]

Love sloganeering does not explain how, exactly, love will actually decrease homophobia or homophobic violence – except by simply positioning itself against both as expressions of "hate." Indeed, the primary slogan that appears on onePULSE merchandise declares, simply, "We will not let hate win." But perhaps the invocations of love at the site of the interim memorial, individually expressed and wholly uncoordinated, can be read together as a radical, and deeply political declaration of community. In some (almost overly obvious way), public expressions of love can seem embarrassing – overly sentimental and incurably trite. But bell hooks reminds us that this very aspect of love may be one source of its strength.

> Love knows no shame. To be loving is to open to grief, to be touched by sorrow, even sorrow that is unending. The way we grieve is informed by whether we know love. Since loving lets us let go of so much fear, it also guides our grief. When we lose someone we love, we can grieve without shame. Given that commitment is an important aspect of love, we who love know we must sustain ties in life and death. Our mourning, our

letting ourselves grieve over the loss of loved ones is an expression of our commitment, a form of communication and communion.[61]

Understood thus, the individual declarations of love at the site of the interim memorial can be read as both past-looking expressions of grief and as multivocal, future-facing demands from "we who love." Judith Butler reminds us, we grieve because we have desired; the declarations of love on the panels document not only the love of grief but also the love of queer desire.[62]

This understanding of love is distinct from strategic invocations of gay love that make queer desire palatable; rather, we could insist upon reading these invocations of love as distinctly and decidedly queer. According to David Halperin, queer love is "love that is socially inept, that threatens, rejects, ignores, or simply fails to correspond with established forms of social life." In this interpretation, love is not, in fact, love.[63] Halperin's point is a necessary one, if we are to remember more fully what happened at Pulse. The very existence of a gay club alongside the many, many references to the much-needed safety provided by the club reminds us that gay love often needs to hide from straight love. That the shooting took place on Latin night reminds us further that even gay love is not gay love – gay love is often distinguished by gender, race, class, and ethnicity. As Katie Acosta writes in an essay about Pulse memory:

> Latinx night at the gay bar is necessary. Yes, it is a safe space, but it is also a space for resilience, a home for the brave who do not experience unconditional love and support from *la familia* of origin, their colleagues or neighbors, and who dare to be present nonetheless. Even in death the Pulse victims speak: We are here, irrespective of your love, acceptance, or lack thereof. We are unapologetically here.[64]

We can read the voices and words at the interim memorial as evidence of this resilience – a continued insistence on presence, despite the many ways in which the world remains unsafe.

We might imagine the grief-stricken, future-mandating love at the interim memorial as a kind of queer family love that remembers not only the joys of the Pulse Nightclub's dancefloor but also the necessity of the nightclub's walls – a necessity that long pre-dated Omar Mateen's rampage. This love can acknowledge both the ephemeral and responsive community formations that emerged in the days, weeks, and months following the violence at Pulse while also acknowledging the divisions characteristic of every day queer life. These dissonant and more complicated truths cannot be made manifest at the national memorial site; the national memorial site is obligated to do a different kind of memory work. But a more fragmented form of remembering can acknowledge other forms of violence as well, including the violence of a larger city that did not always embrace its gay citizens, the violence of a nation that does not always welcome "outsiders," and the violence we sometimes, inevitably, do to each other.

206   Lisa Arellano

There is no doubt that the June 2016 shooting at Pulse was a tragedy of monumental, indeed monument-meriting, proportions. The onePULSE Foundation is achieving the near-impossible in figuring out how to create a memorial experience that honors this event. But this memorial project requires a clarification and codification of narrative – especially difficult in the context of Orlando, where so many narratives, both in content and in type, are at play. Understanding that consolidation is not the only or best way to remember complicated events, we should continue to pay attention to smaller, even temporary memory projects. "Remembering Pulse" must mean not only a large-scale, nationally recognized monument but also an insistence on smaller and less consolidated projects that persist in naming the ongoing and unruly conditions that create not only the horrors of violence but also the life-sustaining beauty of queer communities.

Notes

1 I thank Laura Saltz, Ben Lisle, Laura Sachiko Fugikawa, Amber Hickey, and Carleen Mandolfo for their critical and editorial feedback on earlier versions of this chapter.
2 This account draws on "What Happened at the Pulse Nightclub?" *New York Times,* broadcast October 31, 2016, www.nytimes.com/video/us/100000004740674/911 and John Berman, Kate Bolduan, Juliette Kayyem, Art Roderick, and Dana Bash, "Victim SnapChatted Video of Shooting," *At This Hour With Berman and Michaela, CNN,* broadcast June 13, 2016, http://www.cnn.com/TRANSCRIPTS/1606/13/ath.02.html
3 www.qlatinx.org/who-we-are.
4 On the relationship between violence and narrative, see Michel Foucault, *I, Pierre Riviere, Having Slaughtered My Mother, My Sister, and My Brother: A Case of Parricide in the 19th Century* (Lincoln, NE: University of Nebraska Press, 1975) and Lisa Arellano, *Vigilantes and Lynch Mobs: Narratives of Community and Nation* (Philadelphia, PA: Temple University Press, 2012).
5 www.britannica.com/event/Orlando-shooting-of-2016/The-motive-and-aftermath.
6 Doug Meyer, "An intersectional Analysis of LGBTQ Online Media Coverage of the Pulse Nightclub Shooting Victims," *Journal of Homosexuality*, Vol. 67, No. 10 (2020), p. 1349.
7 www.britannica.com/event/Orlando-shooting-of-2016. The Pulse shooting was superseded a year later, in number of victims, by the October 2017, shooting in Las Vegas.
8 Keri Watson, "Curatorial Statement," in Keri Watson, ed., *Resilience: Remembering Pulse* (Orlando, FL: University of Central Florida, 2017), p. 10.
9 Sima Shakhsari, "After Orlando," *Middle East Report Online*, June 17, 2016, https://merip.org/2016/06/after-orlando/
10 www.whitehouse.gov/briefing-room/speeches-remarks/2021/06/25/remarks-by-president-biden-in-bill-signing-of-h-r-49-to-designate-the-national-pulse-memorial-into-law/.
11 C. Winter Han, "The Deliberate Media Making #gaymedia So White," *Contexts*, Vol. 16, No. 4 (Fall 2017), pp. 70–71.
12 Mirando Joseph, *Against the Romance of Community* (Minneapolis, MN: University of Minnesota Press, 2002), p. 18.
13 www.whitehouse.gov/briefing-room/speeches-remarks/2021/06/25/remarks-by-president-biden-in-bill-signing-of-h-r-49-to-designate-the-national-pulse-memorial-into-law/.
14 www.nps.gov/subjects/lgbtqheritage/upload/lgbtqtheme-intro.pdf. This research was part of a larger Park Service initiative investigating civil rights commemoration.

Remembering Pulse 207

15 Jasbir Puar, *Terrorist Assemblages: Homonationalism in Queer Times* (Durham, NC: Duke University Press, 2007), p. 9. See also Darakshan Raja, "Almost Twenty Years Later," *Women's Studies Quarterly*, Vol. 47, No. 3/4 (Fall/Winter 2019), pp. 276–282. See also Holly Randell-Moon, "Mediations of Security, Race and Violence in the Pulse Nightclub Shooting: Homonationalism in Anti-immigrant Times," *GLQ*, Vol. 28, No. 1 (2022), pp. 1–28.

16 National memorial sites are typically managed by the National Park Service. The Pulse memorial will be one of a number of exceptions to this practice, in that the site will be run by an independent organization. This has raised some questions concerning individual profiteering, vis-à-vis tourist revenue, and increased property values at the memorial site.

17 Puar, pp. 13–15.

18 Shakhsari, "After Orlando."

19 Christine Hanhardt, *Safe Space: Gay Neighborhood History and the Politics of Violence* (Durham, NC: Duke University Press, 2013) and Chandon Reddy, *Freedom with Violence: Race, Sexuality, and the US State* (Durham, NC: Duke University Press, 2011).

20 Hanhardt, *Safe Space*, p. 31.

21 Hanhardt, *Safe Space*, p. 223.

22 Melissa Merry, *Warped Narratives: Distortion in the Framing of Gun Policy* (Ann Arbor, MI: University of Michigan Press, 2020), p. ix.

23 Jennifer Carlson, *Policing the Second Amendment: Guns, Law Enforcement, and the Politics of Race* (Princeton, NJ: Princeton University Press, 2020), p. 175.

24 Carlson, pp. 175–176.

25 https://onepulsefoundation.org/design-construction/#background-information.

26 The larger design team includes Coldefy & Associés with RDAI, Orlando-based HHCP Architects, Xavier Veilhan, dUCKS scéno, Agence TER, and Prof. Laila Farah.

27 https://onepulsefoundation.org/survey/.

28 Despite these many efforts, the project has its detractors – those who feel the 45 million dollar budget might be spent in better, more reparative, ways. See Graham Bowley, "At Pulse Shooting Site, a Plan to Remember Renews Pain for some," *New York Times*, December 15, 2019, www.nytimes.com/2019/12/15/arts/pulse-shooting-memorial-plan-renews-pain-for-some-html.

29 Christina Hanhardt, "Making Community: The Places and Spaces of LGBTQ Collective Identity Formation," in Mega Springate, ed., *LGBTQ America: A Theme Study of Lesbian, Gay Bisexual, Transgender and Queer History* (Washington, DC: National Park Service, Department of the Interior, 2016), https://www.nps.gov/subjects/lgbtqheritage/upload/lgbtqtheme-community.pdf
   See also Christina Hanhardt, "Safe Space Out of Place," *QED: A Journal of GLBTQ Worldmaking*, Vol. 3, No. 3 (fall 2016), pp. 121–125.

30 Jen Jack Gieseking, "LGBTQ Spaces and Places," in Mega Springate, ed., *LGBTQ America: A Theme Study of Lesbian, Gay Bisexual, Transgender and Queer History* (Washington, DC: National Park Service, Department of the Interior, 2016), www.nps.gov/articles/lgbtqtheme-places.htm.

31 www.glbthistory.org/rainbow-flag.

32 https://onepulsestore.com/.

33 Similar issues have been raised in the context of the 9/11 memorial; an interesting example can be found in the *The Outsider*, directed by Steven Rosenbaum and Pamela Yoder (Abramorama Entertainment). See also Erica Doss, "Fear: Terrorism Memorials and Security Narratives," in *Memorial Mania: Public Feeling in America* (Chicago, IL: University of Chicago Press, 2010), pp. 117–185.

34 Shakhsari, "After Orlando," and Darakshan Raja, "Almost Twenty Years Later," *Women's Studies Quarterly*, Vol. 47, No. 3/4 (Fall/Winter 2019), pp. 276–282.

35 Judith Butler, *Precarious Life: The Powers of Mourning and Violence* (London: Verso, 2004), pp. 15–16.

36 https://onepulsefoundation.org/onepulse-foundation-memorial/memorial-process/.

208   *Lisa Arellano*

37 *ABC News*, "Orlando Nightclub Massacre: A Timeline of What Happened," https://youtu.be/GMfuNIe33t4.
38 Ryan Murphy and Human Rights Campaign (HRC), "Stop the Hate," https://youtu.be/Nq6xRZlCSoM.
39 www.orlando.gov/Our-Government/Departments-Offices/Economic-Development/Business-Development/Orlando-Main-Streets/SODO-District-Main-Street.
40 www.orlandoweekly.com/orlando/20-things-everyone-should-do-in-sodo-orlandos-most-up-and-coming-neighborhood/Slideshow/30947742/30774929.
41 Michael Candelaria, "SoDo: An Orlando Neighborhood on the Rise," *Orlando Sentinel*, May 10, 2017, https://www.orlandosentinel.com/features/os-osig-june-community-20170510-story.html
42 "National Pulse Memorial Presentation-onePULSE foundation," https://onepulsefoundation.org/community-update/.
43 www.orlandoweekly.com/orlando/20-things-everyone-should-do-in-sodo-orlandos-most-up-and-coming-neighborhood/Slideshow/30947742/30774929.
44 https://onepulsefoundation.org/wp-content/uploads/2019/03/National-Pulse-Memorial-and-Museum-International-Design-Competition-Request-for-Qualifications.pdf.
45 Laura Kinsler and Dustin Wyatt, "SoDo Industrial Site Slated for Mixed-Use Development," *Orlando Sentinel*, July 2, 2022, p. 10b.
46 Graham Bowley, "At Pulse Shooting Site, a Plan to Remember Renews Pain for Some," *New York Times*, December 15, 2019, www.nytimes.com/2019/12/15/arts/pulse-shooting-memorial-plan-renews-pain-for-some-html.
47 Ryan Murphy and Human Rights Campaign (HRC), "Stop the Hate," https://youtu.be/Nq6xRZlCSoM.
48 Manuel Avilés Santiago, "Digital Pulse: Looking at the Collective/Cultural Memorialization of the Puerto Rican Victims of the Terrorist Attack in Orlando," *Journal of Latin American Communication Research*, Vol. 6, No. 1–2, p. 213.
49 https://bullybloggers.wordpress.com/2016/06/24/the-orlando-syllabus/.
50 http://theorlandomodernquiltguild.blogspot.com/2017/07/quilting-for-pulse.html.
51 https://cah.ucf.edu/citizencurator/project1/.
52 https://stonewall-museum.org/exhibitions/.
53 www.thehistorycenter.org/past-exhibits/.
54 http://thedruproject.org/about; The Dru Project was founded in remembrance of Christopher "Drew" Leinonen to support high school Gay Student Alliance organizations.
55 www.pridefund.org/about/boar; The Pride Fund is an LGBT organization working to combat gun violence.
56 For more on temporary memorials, see Erica Doss, "Grief: Temporary Memorials and Contemporary Modes of Memory," in *Memorial Mania: Public Feeling in America* (Chicago, IL: University of Chicago Press, 2010), pp. 61–116.
57 Notably, these and most other posts at the site are in English.
58 https://oneorlandocollection.com/broadway-for-orlando/.
59 *Lawrence* v. *Texas,* 539 U. S. 558 (2003).
60 www.youtube.com/watch?v=3frkqULr008. For an analysis of Miranda's phrase in the context of LGBTQ consumer campaigns, see Amy Corey, "Love Is Love Is Love Is Love: From Flaktivism to Consumer Activism in LGBTQ+ Communities," *Queer Studies in Media & Pop Culture*, Vol. 4, No. 2.
61 bell hooks, *All About Love: New Visions* (New York: William Morrow, 2001), pp. 200–201.
62 Judith Butler, *Precious Life: The Powers and Mourning and Violence* (London: Verso, 2004), pp. 23–24.
63 David Halperin, "Queer Love," *Critical Inquiry*, Vol. 45 (Winter 2019), p. 397.
64 Katie Acosta, "Pulse: A Space for Resilience, A Home for the Brave," *Queer Conversations: Fingers on Our Pulse: Engaging Orlando's Aftermath and Futurity, QED: A Journal If GLBTQ Worldmaking*, Vol. 3, No. 3 (2016), p. 108.

Part IV
Apartheid

10 The Art of Memory

Echoes of Apartheid Police Brutality in the 2012 Marikana Massacre

Leah Nasson, Sihle-isipho Nontshokweni, and Dylan Wray

Introduction

Milan Kundera wrote: "The struggle of man against power is the struggle of memory against forgetting."[1] During apartheid, the police force played a central role in upholding the totalitarian state. From the headquarters at John Vorster Square in central Johannesburg, the police brutally suppressed any resistance to apartheid – arresting, torturing, and murdering those who were believed to be against the state.

Efforts were made after the end of apartheid to reform the police from a militaristic force empowered to protect the state to a citizen force that served all of South Africa's people. But the new democratic dispensation did not bring about an end to police brutality nor did it mean that the police would never again be used to serve political and economic agendas. Eighteen years into democracy, echoing some of the most brutal events of apartheid, the South African police killed 34 striking miners. The Marikana Massacre, as it became known, has been the most lethal use of force by the South African Police against South African citizens in the post-apartheid period.

This chapter explores how police brutality, within the walls of John Vorster Square and against miners at Marikana, has been remembered and how the victims, have been memorialized. Both serve as valuable case studies of how dominant power shapes the memorialization of traumatic events, enabling palpable silence on accountability and justice when the state is implicated.

Within the Walls of John Vorster Square

Ahmed Timol (1971), Wellington Tsazibane (1976), Elmon Malele (1977), Matthews Mabelane (1977), Neil Aggett (1982), Ernest Dipale (1982), Stanza Bopape (1988), and Clayton Sithole (1990) all died in police custody in John Vorster Square. Sithole was only 20 years old, 12 days before Nelson Mandela was released from prison after 27 years on February 11, 1990. Sithole was found hanging from a water pipe in the shower, the cause of his death ruled a "suicide."

DOI: 10.4324/9781003217848-15

John Vorster Square police station was named after the notorious apartheid Prime Minister who served between 1966 and 1978, a time in which the above political prisoners died in "custody." It was Vorster who passed the 1967 Terrorism Act, which essentially legitimized state terror and allowed, inter alia, police officers to detain so-called suspects without trial – which had hitherto been limited to 90 days. As this chapter will demonstrate, police brutality in South Africa is unfortunately not limited to the apartheid epoch. Indeed, as the country approaches a decade since 34 miners were killed by the police force in the Marikana Massacre in 2012, 18 years into democracy, some national self-reflection over the legacy of police violence is overdue.

John Vorster Square was renamed Johannesburg Central Police Station in 1997. Despite attempts to sanitize the building and essentially cleanse its scars from the past, a writer for the Sunday Times Heritage Project (2021) writes that it still has "that smell unique to government buildings of a certain era – of linoleum, disinfectant and cold concrete."[2] Common torture practices enacted by police officers and members of the security forces at the prison included the use of electric shocks and what was known as the "money bag" method. This method involved soaking a cloth bag in water and placing it over the head of a prisoner, tightening the bag around the neck with a drawstring. With the oxygen supply almost depleted, prisoners would then be kicked in the stomach in an attempt to force them to reveal information or draw confessions. Other methods included suffocation, being forced to stand or squat for extended periods of time, and verbal abuse. In addition, both solitary confinement and sleep deprivation were used as tactics to induce confusion, "acute psychosis" and "toxic delirium."[3]

The WITS (University of Witwaterstrand, located in Johannesburg) Justice Project was established in 2008 to investigate human rights abuses in South Africa's criminal justice system. Its work reveals that police brutality did not die with the onset of democracy – the Independent Police Investigative Directorate investigated 259 allegations of police torture between 2018 and 2020.[4] An independently established website titled "Police Accountability Tracker"[5] reports that there were almost 48,000 complaints registered against the police between 2012 and 2020. Of these reported cases, only 1,553 police officers were convicted and there were a total of 194 dismissals. The nature of the cases ranges from murder (3,198) and assault (30,459) to torture (1,244) and rape (964). It is, however, important to remember that the figures represent *reported* cases: when the mechanism of registering complaints is controlled by the police, there is no doubt that many acts of brutality go unreported. It is clear that exploring the themes which emerge from John Vorster Square can also shed light on the violent legacy that persists in the post-apartheid era.

The apartheid government, 1948–1994, relied heavily on a militaristic police force to secure its control over the majority of South Africans. Renowned for its brutal repression of so-called enemies of the state, it was arguably the murder of 69 peaceful protestors at Sharpeville in 1960 that first catapulted the police's excessive and unnecessary use of force onto the international stage. From

1960 onward, after the banning of the Pan Africanist Congress (PAC) and the African National Congress (ANC), incidents of police violence continued to escalate, particularly after the passing of the 1963 General Laws Amendment Act, the precursor to the Terrorism Act of 1967. A series of laws introduced between 1976 (in the aftermath of the Soweto Uprising of the same year) and 1986 further expanded the powers of the police.[6] In many ways, John Vorster Square was the embodiment of the collective trauma experienced by the political activists whose arrests under these acts led them to the infamous ninth and tenth floors of the detention building.

The elevator in John Vorster Square did not reach the tenth floor, which housed the quarters of the nefarious Security Branch. Prisoners walked up a flight of stairs to reach their cells. It was from this floor that the first casualty of the regime of torture, Ahmed Timol – a political activist working underground for the South African Communist Party – "jumped" to his death in 1971, as a 1972 inquest into his death found.[7] It would take over 40 years of campaigning for justice until the truth surrounding Timol's death was revealed in 2017 when a judge ruled that he "died as a result of having been pushed to fall, an act was committed by members of the security branch . . . amounting to murder."[8] It is likely that Timol fell to his death after being dangled by his feet from a window in John Vorster Square in an attempt by the police to extract a confession.[9]

In 2021, advocates for the reopening of the investigation into the death of the trade unionist Neil Aggett – the first white man to die in detention – found success. Aggett died in detention in 1982, having been found hanging from the bars in his cell at John Vorster Square. The original inquest concluded that no one was to blame for Aggett's death, but the legal team representing the Aggett family has argued that responsibility for his death lies solely in the hands of the Security Branch at John Vorster Square. Lawyers representing the members of the Security Branch have responded by stating that the men responsible for Aggett's death should not be punished for the evils perpetuated by the establishment for which they worked. They further argued that facts should be separated from emotion and truth should be privileged over speculation.[10]

At the time of writing, no verdict had been issued on Aggett's death. Many are concerned that, as has been the case in other trials brought into the limelight since the conclusion of the Truth and Reconciliation Commission, the members of the Security Branch will evade prosecution. Indeed, almost 40 years since Aggett died in detention, no high-level officers or apartheid leaders have been prosecuted for his death.[11] The Aggett case is one of almost 400 cases handed over to South Africa's National Prosecuting Authority in 1998 for further investigation. Most of these cases have yet to see the light of day. A number of perpetrators who were responsible for the meting out of torture in John Vorster Square have died in recent years, having eluded accountability by "taking their secrets to the grave."[12] Members of victims' families, such as the sister of Neil Aggett, have thus been left without hearing the truth and finding closure to a disturbing and painful chapter in their lives.[13]

214   Leah Nasson, Sihle-isipho Nontshokweni, and Dylan Wray

There are palpable silences when it comes to the stories which emerge from John Vorster Square. One of these silences, namely the experience of women detained for resisting the apartheid regime, has been ruptured by the release of a two-hour documentary titled "Surviving John Vorster Square." The documentary, released in 2021, consists of interviews with nine female political activists who were arrested, detained, and tortured by the infamous Security Branch. In echoes of the stories of their male counterparts, the women also describe enduring the brutality of the officers. Unjinee Poonan, a student activist who took a leading role in protesting against the state during the height of the Black Consciousness movement, was arrested for organizing two protests in response to the death of Steve Biko in detention in 1977. She was held at John Vorster Square for 2 weeks under the Internal Security Act of 1956. While she was transported to a nearby police station during the day to face violent interrogations, her evenings were spent lying on the floor of a cold cell, with only lice-infested blankets stained with dried human excrement and vomit.[14] Poonan's experience is far from unique. There are dozens of other female activists who faced a similar fate: they too deserve to form part of a collective effort to remember.

Memorializing This Space

Memory is by no means a passive process – it requires active engagement with the past. Neither is it necessarily intangible. In post-apartheid South Africa, debates surrounding memorials have not been without controversy. In 2015, the Rhodes Must Fall movement at the University of Cape Town succeeded in its campaign to have the statue of the British colonialist and mining magnate, Cecil John Rhodes, removed from its central campus. Similar protests against a statue of Rhodes emerged at Oriel College at Oxford University around the same period, gaining momentum in the midst of the 2020 Black Lives Matter movement. The statue of Cecil John Rhodes is arguably most well known for the way in which it precipitated mass protests and reignited divisive conversations surrounding structural injustice in democratic South Africa. However, there remain a number of other monuments and memorials which belong to a centuries-old era of white economic and political domination.

It has been argued that the juxtaposition of new monuments which confront both the apartheid and colonial national legacy with preexisting monuments opens up a reconciliatory and constructive dialogue about both the present and the past.[15] This is certainly the case in Pretoria, the administrative capital of South Africa. Construction of the Voortrekker Monument began in 1937, almost a century after what was known as the Great Trek had concluded. The Great Trek saw the migration of Afrikaners from the Cape Colony into the interior in response to British imperial rule. These Afrikaners became known as Voortekkers ("moving forward"). The Great Trek and the monument erected in their honor became a symbol of nineteenth- and twentieth-century

Afrikaner nationalism. Once apartheid ended, instead of deconstructing the symbolic relic of white minority rule, the decision was made to construct a counter-memorial, namely Freedom Park, to honor those who had contributed to South Africa's liberation. The decision to erect the Freedom Park memorial, however, was not without its detractors. Part of the findings of the Truth and Reconciliation Commission in 1998 recommended that 21,000 victims of apartheid be awarded financial reparations of between R(Rand)102,000 and R138,000 and that symbolic reparations, such as memorials and monuments, be constructed. The government has delivered on the latter part of the recommendation, with Freedom Park costing more than R300 million.[16] The South African government's efforts to facilitate the payment of reparations, however, have been woefully inadequate.

It took three years after 1994 for John Vorster Square to be renamed Johannesburg Central Police Station and for the bronze bust of the ex-Prime Minister to be removed. It would take another nine years for a public memorial to the eight detainees who died in detention to be installed. Rather than being commissioned by the government, the memorial was installed as part of a heritage initiative pioneered by a national media outlet, the Sunday Times, in 2006. Subject to extensive debate and deliberations among the Heritage Project, the South African Police, and the City of Johannesburg, the initially proposed artwork – a sculpture of a man falling from a building – was rejected.[17] Entitled SIMAKADE (the isiZulu word for "forever standing"), the memorial sculpture – a large, imposing rock – is the only indication of the building's dark history. Although there was once a plaque contextualizing the monument and reflecting the names of the eight victims of the Security Branch's methods of torture, it no longer exists.[18] Thus, for the hundreds of people who walk past Johannesburg Central Police Station on a weekly basis, and particularly for those who did not grow up during apartheid, the building is no different from the blur of buildings surrounding it. It forms part of a nameless cityscape.

While SIMAKADE is a conventional monument insofar as it occupies a physical space, the South African History Archive has created a virtual memorial in the form of a "Google Arts and Culture" exhibit.[19] This interactive exhibit contains a collection of primary sources, artwork and multimedia resources – including interviews with male and female ex-detainees as well as clips from the Truth and Reconciliation Commission in 1996. The use of panoramic photographs of the present-day linoleum floors and the cells where detainees were held suggests that not much has changed since the building was named John Vorster Square. In some ways, it could be argued that the fact that the imposing building largely remains unchanged is problematic, particularly because it houses the South African Police force. According to the results of an Afrobarometer survey from 2021, public trust in the police has declined by 50% since 2011. Over 73% of the citizens who participated in the survey said that they do not trust – or have very little trust – in the police. The large majority of the surveyed citizens cited endemic corruption as the primary reason for distrust.[20]

The issue of police brutality has thus transcended the transition to democracy.

In 2012, 34 striking miners were gunned down by the police in what has become known as the Marikana massacre, while 78 were severely injured. In echoes of the 1960 Sharpeville Massacre, a number of miners were shot in the back. Ultimately, the memorial at John Vorster Square should serve as a reminder of what happens when police violence goes unchecked, but its abstract presentation renders murky what should be transparent. A lack of transparency and accountability, both of which are cornerstones of a successful democracy, threatens the very foundation upon which post-apartheid South Africa is built.

The Marikana Massacre

The massacre of striking mineworkers at the Lonmin mine in Marikana, Rustenburg, on August 16, 2012, has been the most lethal use of force by the South African Police against South African citizens in the post-apartheid period.

The protest action began at the platinum mine a week before the massacre took place. The miners were demanding a wage increase that would put them on a par with mineworkers at Lonmin's mines in other parts of the world, notably Australia, where the company paid miners almost double the wages of their counterparts in South Africa. Around 3,000 miners joined the strike which did not have the support of the miners' union – the National Union of Mineworkers (NUM).

On August 11, while attempting to meet with the union leadership to demand their support for the strike, a confrontation broke out between the striking miners and miners loyal to the NUM. Two people were injured after live ammunition was fired. Over the next few days, the situation became more volatile as the miners became increasingly frustrated that the union would not sanction the strike and the Lonmin management would not negotiate (let alone meet) with them. The growing number of police who had been called in to protect the mine added to the tension.

By August 16, the day of the massacre, ten people, including police officers, miners, and Lonmin security guards, had already been killed in violent skirmishes. The mine had already halted production. Discussions with the police had taken place, but the miners gathered on *koppie* (small hill), which they called "Thaba," refused to end the strike. Instead, they continued to request a meeting with the Lonmin management.

While the Lonmin management had refused to negotiate with the miners, they had been having discussions with the police. It is clear from recorded discussions, two days before the massacre, between North West Police Commissioner Zukiswa Mbombo and Barnard Mokoena, a Lonmin executive, that the police were squarely on the side of the mine owners and were facing political pressure to bring an end to the strike. Specifically, pressure came from Cyril

The Art of Memory   217

Ramaphosa, who was at that time a Lonmin shareholder and was on the African National Congress's highest decision-making body – the National Executive Council (NEC). He is now the current president of South Africa. An extract from the transcript reveals this political, and possibly personal, pressure from the current President to protect his financial interests.

MBOMBO: "But when I was speaking to Minister Mthethu [it's likely the transcriber meant Police Minister Nathi Mthethwa] he mentioned a name to me that is also calling him, that is pressuring him, unfortunately it is a political high."

MOKOENA: "It is Cyril."

MBOMBO: "Cyril Ramaphosa, yes. Now remember now when I was talking to the national commissioner last night she says to me, look General who are the shareholders here, so I said I do not know the shareholders but I know that when I spoke to the minister he mentioned Cyril. And then she says, now I got it. You know why she says I got it?"[21]

In an email to a Lonmin executive the day before the massacre, Ramaphosa wrote:

> *The terrible events that have unfolded cannot be described as a labour dispute. They are plainly dastardly criminal and must be characterised as such . . . there needs to be concomitant action to address this situation.*[22]

It is important to note that under South African law, the police may not use force to protect private property. However, later that evening police management decided to launch an operation the next day. Indeed, on August 16, it became clear that the police had decided that the protest would come to an end that day. More police arrived, bringing the total police force presence to 500.[23]

Police spokesman Dennis Adriao said at the time that attempts to negotiate with the miners and get them to disperse peacefully had failed. On two occasions he referenced that day as D-Day for the police. "It is an illegal gathering," he went on to say. "We've tried to negotiate and we'll try again, but if that fails, we'll obviously have to go to a tactical phase."[24]

The police rolled out razor wire to surround the miners who were gathered on Thaba, the small hill. Once the miners realized they were not safe, many decided to leave. As they descended, they found they were fenced in and the only way out was through a gap in the police perimeter leading them to the Tactical Response Team. At some point soon after, the police fired tear gas and rubber bullets causing panic. They then opened fire with live ammunition – firing "284 rounds of live ammunition at the miners within eight seconds."[25] Seventeen of the miners were killed in full view of the television crews and journalists who were stationed behind the police perimeter. The other 17 miners were killed fleeing or hiding from the police in a nearby rocky area.[26]

Even though the police had opened fire on and killed 34 miners, 270 miners were arrested for their murder under an apartheid law that is still in existence. The law of "common purpose" had been used by the apartheid government to arrest and convict groups of protestors for murder by simply being present when a member of the police force was killed.

Later that day, the South African government released the following statement.

> *Following extensive and unsuccessful negotiations by SAPS members to disarm and disperse a heavily armed group of illegal gatherers at a hilltop close to Lonmin Mine, near Rustenburg in the North West Province, the South African Police Service was viciously attacked by the group, using a variety of weapons, including firearms. The Police, in order to protect their own lives and in self-defence, were forced to engage the group with force. This resulted in several individuals being fatally wounded, and others injured.*[27]

This interpretation – that vicious, dangerous, and heavily armed miners (who had no right or permission to strike) attacked the police who could only engage with force – is the view that became etched in the South African psyche. This resulted largely from the way the miners and their grievances had been portrayed early on by most of the media outlets covering the story. How the events at Marikana were reported came to define, for many, how the events were and are remembered today.

The "Symbolic Annihilation" of the Miners by the Media

The early portrayal of the striking miners by most media outlets created an impression of a violent, disorganized, primitive mob who were a threat to the mine, the police and, importantly, a threat to the South African economy.

One image published early on showed a close-up of a miner licking the tip of a spear. It is likely that this image, given that it was repeatedly used in news broadcasts reporting on the events at the Lonmin mine, presented an image of the miners as a violent, possibly barbaric, threat which many South Africans accepted. In her article, *Colonial Tropes and the Media Coverage of the Marikana Massacre*, Gillian Schutte points to the confirming weight of this single image:

> *It was a sight that was likely to bring to the fore the deeply held beliefs on which white fear is premised – that of the black man as savage and a potential killer. Cut from that scene to a wide shot of thousands of men with various cultural weapons and we were given the message that masses of black men were on the loose, wild and uncontrollable and therefore needed to be contained, disarmed and suppressed.*[28]

Most media outlets at the time portrayed this view of the miners and, in so doing, generated support for the police and mine owners among South

The Art of Memory   219

Africans reading news accounts and watching televised reports. Jane Duncan analyzed 153 newspaper articles between August 13 and 22, 2012 – the "period that the media assisted in forming public perceptions about the massacre, including the events that took place, the causes and the blame apportioned to the various actors."[29] Her findings show that the media coverage of the Marikana massacre and the events leading up to it largely ignored the miners' voices.

Analysis of sources of information for the news articles shows that 41% of sources used were from business and mine management, 21% were from government, political parties, and the police, and only 3% were from the miners themselves. Tellingly, of this 3% of miners quoted, only one miner was quoted describing the massacre.[30]

> *[Of] all 153 articles, only one showed any attempt by a journalist to obtain an account from a worker about their version of events. There is scant evidence of journalists having asked the miners the simplest and most basic of questions, namely "what happened?" Overwhelmingly they relied on official sources of information and on business perspectives for information and analysis.*[31]

Not surprisingly, when analyzing the primary framers of the stories, which as Duncan argues, "is useful in assessing how social power is expressed through the media," business and the Lonmin mine management emerge loudest and strongest with 41%. The workers accounted for just 2%.[32]

Far from giving equitable space to the miners and the working and living conditions that drove their decision to strike, the miners, Duncan argues, were subjected to "symbolic annihilation" by the media. Through under-representation (and in many cases not being represented at all), "no alternative narrative emerged to challenge the dominant perception of events" that justified or at least sympathized with the view that the police faced a violent and threatening mass of striking miners.[33]

A Different Story

While early public opinion was shaped by the dominant narrative that portrayed the police as acting in self-defence, a few days after the killings, investigative journalists, and social scientists provided evidence supporting a different story. After 2 weeks of investigative journalism, Greg Marinovitch was able to counter the narrative that the police had been attacked and had responded in self-defense.

> *Some of the miners killed in the 16 August massacre at Marikana appear to have been shot at close range or crushed by police vehicles. They were not caught in a fusillade of gunfire from police defending themselves, as the official account would have it.*
>   *Of the 34 miners killed at Marikana, no more than a dozen of the dead were captured in news footage shot at the scene. The majority of those who died, according*

220 *Leah Nasson, Sihle-isipho Nontshokweni, and Dylan Wray*

> to surviving strikers and researchers, were killed beyond the view of cameras at a nondescript collection of boulders some 300 metres behind Wonderkop.[34]

The sociologist Peter Alexander and two researchers interviewed miners in the days after the massacre. Through the voices of the miners, they were also able to tell a different story.

> *Mineworker: It was late in the afternoon around five or [something] to five, we saw the razor wire and the Hippos were also drawing closer and closer . . . We tried to find an opening where we could escape; as we were about to get out a Hippo stood in front of us so we were trapped . . . Near the kraal that is where we tried to escape. The police used the Hippo to block the way while some were inside the Hippo and others outside behind it with guns pointing at people. If anyone tried to escape they were shot at. The first gun went off and the rest followed. There was a white police-man who said, "fire." It became chaos, people were stamped by the Hippo, water and teargas were used after the bullets which was pointless because whoever choked on the teargas was stamped by the Hippo. Most people who died were stamped by the Hippos. They used teargas to make them dizzy, then stamped on them. They lied about rubber bullets, they did not use them. There were also helicopters that were shooting at my fellow brothers.[35]*

Besides presenting a different view of the events of August 16, Alexander and his team were also able to do what the media had not done prior to the massacre – speak to, understand, and present the lives and motivations of the miners.

> *In South Africa, a typical working day lasts eight hours, but Lonmin workers we spoke to said they could not "knock off" until they had reached their target, which often meant working 12 hours, sometimes more (Mineworker 8 mentioned work-ing a 15-hour shift). Mineworker 7 complained: "They do not even give you time to eat lunch. They just say 'your lunch box must remain on the surface." Refer-ring to incessant pressure to reach targets, Mineworker 5 protested that "conditions in the mines are those of oppression." Moreover, it is taken for granted that mine labour also involves anti-social hours, with shifts starting at 05:30 or 21:00 and Saturday-working being a requirement. A group of wives that I spoke with agreed in chorus that their husbands always returned home exhausted. My sense is that today's Lonmin workers often slave for more hours a week than the 1920s colliery workers I studied, and they probably work harder.[36]*

While this work was important in countering the dominant narrative, the symbolic annihilation of the miners from the initial reporting on events had already shaped public understanding and opinion. In the absence of an imme-diate and deliberate attempt by the media to address the symbolic annihila-tion that they had subjected the miners to, changing public opinion would be difficult. Hence, there has not been a widespread public outrage, demand for justice, and, years later, a call for a dignified memorialization.

Modes of Remembrance

Mourning Needs No Approval, We Will Remember Marikana

It has been nine years and the memory of the Marikana Massacre is still contested. Some scholars view Marikana as a turning point in the post-Apartheid dispensation, a sentiment shared by current president, Cyril Ramaphosa, who described the occurrences of Marikana as "the darkest moment in the life of our young democracy." The dominant view among scholars, however, is that this moment marked "a rupture in a time of ongoing oppression" and "repetition of history," likened to the events of Sharpeville (1960), Soweto (1976), Boipatong (1992), and Durban Strikes (1973). These past atrocities act as a benchmark and continuation of terror in the present.

No one has been prosecuted for the deaths of the miners which occurred in broad daylight, as though – like the fictional characters in Chris van Wyk's poetry and Hugh Masekela music – they "slipped on a piece of soap while washing" or were "wantonly murdered in the dead of night by roving, marauding gangs of no particular origin."[37] What has followed, instead, is "a litany of injustices . . . lain like a ghoulish incubus on our nation's soul."[38] The families and surviving mine workers have shouldered the burden of loss and trauma compounded by "the police refusing to accept responsibility" and "governments lack of accountability or apology." In spite of repeated attempts by the families to seek justice, it still remains largely elusive. Only nine police officers have been charged for their role in the massacre. At the time of writing, six are currently on trial for murder. The trial is expected to last two years. The majority of the perpetrators have evaded prosecution. In spite of having been promised R1 billion (approximately $6,478,034 in 2022) under the Zuma presidency in 2016, many families of the affected victims, as well as those who were injured in the massacre, have yet to receive any financial compensation.

Selected and sensational narratives emerged from the Marikana Massacre. Media coverage was quickly dominated by the cultural mockery of strikers using "muti [traditional African medicine or magical charms] and traditional weapons." This primitive imagery undermined the strikers by delegitimizing their agency with their story presented in a questionable manner. This "anti-worker bias," as Peter Alexander noted, filtered into the Report of the Marikana Commission of Inquiry. Dispiritingly, the report drew parallels between the violence perpetrated by the state and that committed by miners, in an attempt to equate their roles, ultimately obfuscating any party from being held accountable. The "two sides of the story" narrative quickly manipulated the popular memory of Marikana.

In the interest of the dominant forces, it seemed urgent and necessary that the reportage on the series of events was manipulated and distorted from the moment it happened. While this popular memory sought to crystalize this hegemonic distorted view through the news medium and subsequently authorized reports, there were those who produced alternative modes of remembering Marikana. There is the Marikana Memorial to the victims of the massacre at Thaba and the design of the Mgcineni Noki Memorial Sports Centre. Cultural artifacts have included *Marikana the Musical*, *Man in the Green Blanket* series by Tokolos Stencils, and the chilling documentary depiction in *Miners Shot Down*. An interesting memorial that has continued to "erode, contradict or render mute the dominant narrative" has been the image of Mgcineni Noki (40 years old), known as Mambush – an iconic symbol of the Marikana Massacre, inscribed on walls, road signs, and bridges across the country. This powerful symbol has continued to interject "city texts into commercial and road signage to reveal the 'legibility' of the city as operating in the interests of capital and [current political power] while maintaining the segregationist spatial designs of apartheid."[39]

On Governance and Violence

The "Remember Marikana" stencil along with Ramaphosa's name in red is a direct rejection of the falsified narrative, holding true to the biblical scripture: "*their blood still cries out from the ground.*" In response to the injunction to remember Marikana, Thomas[40] asks this critical question, "*How is it possible to forget a massacre? How is it possible to forget a massacre?*" According to the Marikana Report, erasures of history and culpability seem to have been built into the very planning of the massacre. The erasure and culpability of mineworkers serve current power interests. This becomes particularly apparent when the Minister of Police at the time of the massacre subsequently becomes the Minister of Arts and Culture, and Cyril Ramaphosa, who was implicated in the massacre, ascends to the post of Deputy President of South Africa in 2014 and then President in 2018.

Ramaphosa's and Mthethwa's indictment in the case is at odds with championing a memorial for those whose lives were lost in Marikana. Given the "objectivation or crystallization" of popular memory, the counter archives from local artists can be read as a "dialectical interaction between popular and hegemonic discourses." The counter archives by local artists have been a struggle of memory against forgetting, while resisting acts of censorship[41] by public institutions pressured by corporations and political power "to maintain their profits and to undermine radical action."

Men of Flowers: A Creative Protest

Beyond symbolic accretions, Zakes Mda's commemoration, as presented in a series of paintings, has reconstructed the Marikana crime scene. Mda is a global literary figure with over 22 books, a painter and scholar, and also the firstborn son of AP Mda. His father was one of the founders of the African

National Congress Youth League, alongside Nelson Mandela, Walter Sisulu, Oliver Tambo, and Anton Lembede. These "Young Lions" came with a Programme of Action, which included the formation of the ANC's military wing, Umkhonto we Sizwe, and installed themselves as the new senior leadership of the ANC. However, when the YL Programme of Action was turned into the Freedom Charter in 1955, which would later become a cornerstone of the country's democratic constitution, AP Mda and others saw this change as a betrayal. He broke away from the ANC to establish Pan Africanist Congress of Azania in 1959.

Like his father, Zakes Mda's contribution to socio-political life in Africa is vast. His creative work has been translated into 20 languages, including Catalan, Dutch, German, Italian, Korean, Norwegian, Serbian, Swedish, and Turkish. He is a recipient of the Ikhamanga Order in Silver from the South African government. In October 2021, his long-awaited solo exhibition, *Mirrors and Washboards*, opened at the St. Lorient Art Gallery in Tshwane, South Africa. His paintings create a separatist orientation, a competitive view that humanizes and opens a space for potential transformative remembering, so that we can imagine Mambush not as a spear-chugging striker with murderous intent but as a kind man, who carries a bouquet of flowers instead. Mda's paintings are necessarily political, the green-blanketed man over the Nkandla homestead is interlinked to the political betrayal theme that Zakes Mda lifts in his work, revealing that the "lives of common people today are reminiscent of colonial rule."[42]

The artwork by Mda opens a set of new narratives linked to Black men, their stories, histories, and imaginings for a better future. Mda interrupts dominant stereotypes of Black violent masculinity commonly associated with mining, digging, and extracting hard metals from the ground. In his left hand, Mambush carries flowers, a weapon of kindness. This new softness introduced through flowers disrupts the paradigm of violent Black men, reminding us of their shared longing for liveable environments, in this case – better working conditions and a *living* wage. In this manner, art challenges the memorialization of mineworkers and questions "the habitual" imagery. We reopen to their humanity.

Mgcineni Noki (40 years old), known as Mambush, from Twalikhulu in the Eastern Cape, is standing over the Nkandla Homestead, the controversial[43] private home of former President Jacob Zuma, waving an item that could be a white flag but also a weapon with a wide blade on one hand. On the other hand, Mambush is carrying a bouquet of pink roses. On the horizon, the sky is pink, one mountain purple, and another just behind Nkandla is blood red. The lushness of green and yellow bloom abounds. The image of the Nkandla Homestead and that of Mambush in a green blanket are occurrences that occupied the public mind in the Zuma reign – matters of morality, mortality, and accountability. In an apparent bid for justice by the artist, a resistance to the manipulation of memory for nefarious reasons, Mda emphasizes grievance by creating his own view of the past, passing it in bits to form an archive

Figure 10.1 Zakes Mda, The Man in a Green Blanket #1, oil on canvas painting, 2015
Source: Credit – Permission granted by artist

of collective memory. The art lays bare the structures of domination that lie beneath the surface of political power and at once memorializes the moment. This image of a Black man with a bouquet of flowers in one hand and panga in another, overlooking Nkandla, intercepts the ongoing violence and structural oppression of Black people who continue to fight for material equality, a living wage, and decent conditions to live.

Beyond Nkandla, the "grand scale" extraction by Jacob Zuma for his singular gain intersects with the large-scale extraction from miners underground. Wealth gain remains unequally divided between workers and board members. This represents an ongoing crisis of systemic inequality and structural violence. Back in 2012, company reports showed that former Lonmin chief executive Ian Farmer earned R24 million ($1,553,000 in 2022), Gold Fields chief executive Nick Holland was paid R32.6 million ($2,109,491), and Anglo Platinum chief executive Neville Nicolau's pay was R21.5 million ($1,391,229). An ordinary mine worker earns less than R70,000 ($4,529) a year.[44]

This imagery counters the foundational story of "nation-building" which Murray (2012) argues is built on "imagined community." This imagery assaults

The Art of Memory 225

Figure 10.2 Zakes Mda, The Man in a Green Blanket #3, oil on canvas painting, 2016
Source: Credit – Permission granted by artist

our temptation to "nation-building" in the service of constructing a national identity.[45] Marschall further submits that the challenge in the current post-apartheid era "lies in creating a new, inclusive myth of origin or that can be shared by all and provide the basis of identification with the new nation."[46] Collective memory in this sense becomes a pivotal "mediating force" in the construction of national identity, according to Murray.

These Black men at the foot of the hill, except for a singular foreboding in Mambush's face, do not yet know that their resistance to power would soon mean the breaking of their own bodies. They're looking over leaps of land, reminding them too of "their lands, and their herds that they had been taken from." They have been deprived of their land of plenty. And they have underestimated the brooding hailstorm ahead of them, maybe because its root is hidden in the hopefulness of yellow underneath their feet. Their adversaries have come with barbed wire and mortuary vans. For a brief moment in Mda's art depiction with Mambush, we are "wrenched away" from the "clutches of Lonmin" that will soon, "*Dissect the miner's bodies bit by bit, likening their souls to that of Satan, declaring themselves the ultimate God!*[47]" over their labor and over their lives.

In this imagery, there is no bloodshed; instead, the miners march with bouquets of flowers.

This commemoration modulates the visual anger of Black miners holding pangas. We can begin to engage with their difficult reality and imagine them going underground in mines digging for platinum, diamonds, and gold underground where miners dig deep using spades. These pangas are the spades to a system that will not provide a "better life for all"[48] but only for a few. Yet they carry "flowers" as a request for a living wage. Flowers are commonly understood as a symbol of beauty; they soothe a heavy heart and bring peace. This is a peace that they do not experience with a better living wage; instead as seen in the second image they may attain it in the next life. As the miners walk away, it is here that they may enter into peace.

> *I have made your bed at the foot of the hill,*
> *your blankets are covered in buchu and mint,*
> *the proteas stand in yellow and white.*[49]
>
> – **Diana Ferrus**

Figure 10.3 Zakes Mda, The Man in a Green Blanket #4, oil on canvas painting, 2016

Source: Credit – Permission granted by artist

Finally, in this image, the miners depart as though entering into the next realm with pangas on one hand and flowers on the other, a duality of anger and kindness. With heads facing forward they pick up their weapons, "pick up the stones over which they stumble, to go build altars," almost to say "let a thousand flowers bloom," and "Aluta continua" the struggle continues.

Conclusion

Contemporary society has to contend with the critical questions of memorialization. To arrive at a more democratic valorization of collective memory, it is necessary for memory to be negotiable and contestable in order to guard against the social control of memory which likely produces an undesirable hegemonic narrative.

The case of John Vorster Square and the Marikana Massacre raises the necessary contestation of memory in the pursuit of fulfilling a just and socially cohesive society. While there is widespread agreement that the police actions during apartheid were wrong, remembering and memorializing the victims of police brutality then may turn the gaze toward police brutality today. It is telling that the memorial to the victims of the police brutality that took place within the walls of John Vorster Square headquarters today is just a rock. Their names vanished when the brass plaque memorializing them was stolen. Neither the *Sunday Times* nor the state has done anything to return their names to the rock. It is inevitable the interest of the Sunday Times would last only as long as their memory campaign would drive newspaper sales. The state, on the other hand, likely prefers a rock with anonymity, because returning names might also mean adding new names like Sitelega Meric Gadlela, Thembinkosi Gwelani, Mgcineni Noki, and the names of the other 31 miners who were brutally killed by police at Marikana.

In a post-apartheid society, whose collective imagination is founded on notions of "social cohesion" and "nation-building," Marikana assaults the image of a "constitutional democracy" where the rights of the individuals and minorities are respected. The involvement of the state has contradicted the paramount concern of human dignity, and the worth of individuals as provided by the constitution. Consequently, there is currently no plan by the state to create a memorial at Marikana. But as we have seen, through graffiti stencils and the work of artists like Zakes Mda, the victims of the police brutality in a democratic South Africa have been memorialized. Their names are returning.

Notes

1 From Milan Kundera, *The Book of Laughter and Forgetting* (1979), Part 1, Chapter 2, in Susan Ratcliffe, ed., *Oxford Essential Quotations* (Oxford: Oxford University Press, Online, published 2017).
2 South African Historical Archive, "Symbol of Past Horrors Holds Hope for the Future," n.d., https://sthp.saha.org.za/memorial/articles/symbol_of_past_horrors_holds_hope_for_the_future.htm [Accessed October 16, 2020].

3 F. Forbes, "Death in Apartheid Detention: Verdict Eagerly Awaited After Neil Aggett Inquest Ends," *The Daily Maverick*, 2021, www.dailymaverick.co.za/article/2021-07-12-death-in-apartheid-detention-verdict-eagerly-awaited-after-neil-aggett-inquest-ends/ [Accessed October 23, 2021].

4 V. Cruywagen, "Police Watchdog Playing a Losing Game When It Comes to Holding Rotten Cops Accountable," 2021, www.dailymaverick.co.za/article/2021-10-06-police-watchdog-playing-a-losing-game-when-it-comes-to-holding-rotten-cops-accountable/ [Accessed October 16, 2021].

5 Police Accountability Tracker, n.d., https://policeaccountabilitytracker.co.za/?fbclid=IwAR2LZyqvYbWGjI3WGeAWLsPWmh45xV3sAfdDc5DZaYfSJp8hjCS-gRYv3TkM [Accessed October 23, 2021].

6 The 1976 Internal Security Amendment Act no, 79, legalized "preventative" detention of political activists for 12 months. The 1982 Internal Security Act no. 74 allowed for indefinite "interrogatory" detention and 6 months "witness" detention. The Internal Security Act no. 66 allowed for 180 days "preventative" detention ("The Detention Weapon," www.sahistory.org.za/archive/detention-weapon [Accessed October 10, 2021]).

7 J. Mothle, "The Re-Opened Inquest Into the Death of Ahmed Essop Timol: The Johannesburg High Court Judgement," 2017, www.ahmedtimol.co.za/ [Accessed October 17, 2021].

8 "Inquest Resumed 46 Years After His Death," 2017, www.ahmedtimol.co.za/ [Accessed October 17, 2021].

9 South African Historical Archive, "Remembering a Darker Time," www.saha.org.za/news/2010/August/remembering_a_darker_time_when_john_vorster_square_was_opened.htm [Accessed September 17, 2021].

10 T. Smith, "Neil Aggett: The Reckoning," *New Frame,* 2021, www.newframe.com/neil-aggett-the-reckoning/ [Accessed October 23, 2021].

11 D. Forbes, "Detention, Torture Killed Neil Aggett," *The Daily Maverick*, 2021, www.dailymaverick.co.za/article/2021-07-12-death-in-apartheid-detention-verdict-eagerly-awaited-after-neil-aggett-inquest-ends/ [Accessed October 23, 2021].

12 Ibid.

13 U. Ho, "Security Branch Police in the Spotlight as Neil Aggett Inquest Resumes," *Daily Maverick*, 2021, www.dailymaverick.co.za/article/2021-01-18-security-branch-police-in-the-spotlight-as-neil-aggett-inquest-resumes/ [Accessed October 23, 2021].

14 T. Pillay, "Their Stories Behind Bars," *The Sunday Tribune*, 2021, www.pressreader.com/south-africa/sunday-tribune-south-africa/20210829/281509344281648 [Accessed October 24, 2021].

15 S. Marschall, "Transforming the Landscape of Memory: The South African Commemorative Effort in International Perspective," *South African Historical Journal*, Vol. 55, No. 1 (2006), pp. 102–123.

16 S. Marschall, "Gestures of Compensation: Post-Apartheid Monuments and Memorials," *Transformation: Critical Perspectives on Southern Africa*, Vol. 55 (2006), pp. 78–95.

17 C. Molele, "Memorial to Deaths in Detention," *Sunday Times Heritage Project*, n.d., https://sthp.saha.org.za/memorial/articles/memorial_to_deaths_in_detention.htm [Accessed October 26, 2021].

18 Associated Press, "Grim Apartheid Deaths," *Afro News*, 2017, https://afro.com/south-africa-case-opening-doors-grim-apartheid-deaths/ [Accessed October 26, 2021].

19 South African History Archive, "Detention Without Trial in John Vorster Square," *Google Arts and Culture*, n.d., https://artsandculture.google.com/exhibit/detention-without-trial-in-john-vorster-square-south-african-history-archive/gQ-1o9MM?hl=en [Accessed October 27, 2021].

20 Afrobarometer, "South Africans' Trust in the Police Drops to a New Low," 2021, https://afrobarometer.org/press/south-africans-trust-police-drops-new-low-afrobarometer-survey-finds [Accessed October 27, 2021].

The Art of Memory   229

21 G. Marinovich and G. Nicolson, "Marikana Massacre: SAPS, Lonmin, Ramaphosa & Time for Blood. Miners' Blood," *The Daily Maverick*, 2013, www.dailymaverick.co.za/article/2013-10-24-marikana-massacre-saps-lonmin-ramaphosa-time-for-blood-miners-blood/ [Accessed October 28, 2021].

22 G. Hosken, "Marikana Inquiry Shown Ramaphosa Emails," *The Sowetan Live*, 2012, www.sowetanlive.co.za/news/2012-10-24-marikana-inquiry-shown-ramaphosa-emails/ [Accessed October 28, 2021].

23 D. Bruce, "Commissioners and Commanders: Police Leadership and the Marikana Massacre," *South African History Online*, 2016, www.sahistory.org.za/sites/default/files/2019-05/commissioners_and_commanders_police_lead.pdf [Accessed October 23, 2021].

24 G. Marinovich, "The Murder Fields of Marikana. The Cold Murder Fields of Marikana," *The Daily Maverick*, 2012, www.dailymaverick.co.za/article/2012-09-08-the-murder-fields-of-marikana-the-cold-murder-fields-of-marikana/ [Accessed October 28, 2021].

25 K. Dyantyi and T. Masiangoako, "Marikana Massacre: The Devastating Impact of the Narrative Painted by Business, Police and the State," *The Daily Maverick*, 2020, www.dailymaverick.co.za/article/2020-08-26-marikana-massacre-the-devastating-impact-of-the-narrative-painted-by-business-police-and-the-state/ [Accessed October 28, 2021].

26 Ibid.

27 Marinovich, "The Murder Fields of Marikana."

28 G. Schutte, "Colonial Tropes and the Media Coverage of the Marikana Massacre," *French Journal For Media Research* (2018), https://frenchjournalformediaresearch.com:443/lodel-1.0/main/index.php?id=610 [Accessed October 23, 2021].

29 J. Duncan, "South African Journalism and the Marikana Massacre: A Case Study of an Editorial Failure," 2013, p. 5, www.polecom.org/index.php/polecom/article/download/22/197 [Accessed October 23, 2021].

30 Ibid., p. 6.

31 Ibid., p. 6.

32 Ibid., p. 7.

33 Ibid., p. 9.

34 G. Marinovich, "The Murder Fields of Marikana."

35 Peter Alexander, Luke Sinwell, Thapelo Lekgowa, Botsang Mmope, and Bongani Xezwi, *Marikana: A View From the Mountain and a Case to Answer* (Johannesburg: Jacana Media, 2012).

36 Ibid., p. 11.

37 A.M. Versola, "Jazz & Apartheid: An Analysis of the Life and Music of Hugh Masekela," 2018. Thesis submitted in partial fulfilmentof the requirements for the degree of Master of Music in Jazz Performance in the College of Arts and Communication William Paterson University, p. 38, www.proquest.com/openview/a44e47f7eb8e44b750a6429d3ce595a6/1?pq-origsite=gscholar&cbl=18750.

38 D. Forbes, "Marikana: The Unfolding of a Never-Ending Tragedy," *The Daily Maverick*, 2021, www.dailymaverick.co.za/article/2021-08-14-marikana-the-unfolding-of-a-never-ending-tragedy/ [Accessed November 1, 2021].

39 N. Makhubu, "Changing the City After Our Heart's Desire: Creative Protest in Cape Town," *Journal of Postcolonial Writing*, Vol. 53, No. 6 (2017), pp. 686–699, https://doi.org/10.1080/17449855.2017.1391741.

40 K. Thomas, "'Remember Marikana': Violence and Visual Activism in Post-Apartheid South Africa," *ASAP/Journal*, Vol. 3, No. 2 (2018), pp. 401–422, https://muse.jhu.edu/article/700570.

41 Ibid., p. 11.

42 "The Theme of Political Betrayal in the Plays of Zakes Mda," www.jstor.org/stable/40238979?seq=2#metadata_info_tab_contents [Accessed December 13, 2021].

43 M.L.J. Koenane, "Politics Without Morality and Accountability: The Nkandla Case From a Deontological Perspective," *The Journal for Transdisciplinary Research in Southern Africa*, Vol. 13, No. 1 (2017), https://doi.org/10.4102/TD.V13I1.383.

44 Ibid.

45 M.J. Murray, *Commemorating and Forgetting: Challenges for the New South Africa* (Minneapolis, MN: University of Minnesota Press, 2013), p. 1305.

46 S. Shall, *Landscape of Memory: Commemorative Monuments, Memorial and Public Statuary in Post-Apartheid South Africa* (Leiden: Brill, 2009), p. 172.

47 D. Ferrus, "I've Come to Take You Home," n.d., https://books.google.co.za/books/about/I_ve_Come_to_Take_You_Home.html?id=kSMRAwAAQBAJ&printsec=frontcover&source=kp_read_button&hl=en&redir_esc=y#v=onepage&q&f=false [Accessed November 5, 2021].

48 African National Congress Election Poster, "A Better Life for All," *South African History Online*, www.sahistory.org.za/archive/better-life-all [Accessed November 5, 2021].

49 Ferrus, "I've Come to Take You Home," n.d.

11 The Land of Milk and Honey (and Palestinians)

Eitan Bronstein Aparicio and Eleonore Merza Bronstein

Can a map describe a settler colonial project? Can a map account for its dynamic changes and continuity? Can a map reveal the power relations between the colonizer and the colonized? Can a map function as an "anti-map" in the sense of countering the (colonial) state hegemonic maps? Can a map reveal the hidden crimes of the colonizer? Can a map serve as an educational and a political and advocacy tool in the anti-colonial struggle?

It is demonstrably clear that shaping, plotting, and naming the space is a fundamental component of a colonial project. Signage has been used as an attempt to assert control and legitimize the occupier's sovereignty. In Hebrew, the words "sign" (*shelet*) and "control" (*shlita*) have the same root: can we use colonial tools in order to decolonize?

We believe the answer to all the above questions is affirmative. The map "Colonialism in Destru(A)ction"[1] is an attempt to expose the real dimension of the Israeli settler colonial enterprise. You can access the map on our website. We want to follow the famous call by Karl Marx, in that we know that it is not enough to describe correctly the political situation, but the challenge is also to change it.

This map can serve as a tool in the hands of those who take upon themselves the critical goal of bringing an end to the oppressive Zionist political regime. We see this map as a means to help promote social justice in Palestine/Israel.

The map is designed to be used in a printed format, 100 cm × 700 cm, rather than an online one. It aims to depict in one image the different layers of destruction of localities during Israeli and Zionist (pre-state) history. To define terms, by localities we refer to neighborhoods, communities, towns, and villages. De-Colonizer developed this project which is based on the work of Eitan Bronstein Aparicio (one of the authors) at Zochrot[2] and other organizations and researchers. Zochrot, an Israeli organization founded in 2001 by Eitan, works to educate Israelis about the Nakba, which was hardly addressed by Israeli Jews. De-Colonizer was established by the two authors in Tel Aviv and in Brussels. It aims to broaden the original scope of Zochrot beyond the Nakba and to look at different aspects of the Israeli regime as a colonial enterprise throughout Israeli history. This map is one of the tools De-Colonizer has created.

DOI: 10.4324/9781003217848-16

232 *Eitan Bronstein Aparicio and Eleonore Merza Bronstein*

This map is a direct development from the first Nakba map we published in Hebrew at Zochrot in 2013. A key difference is that we are targeting an international audience so our presentation is in English and French. Also, this is an attempt to compile all the different types of locality destructions in Zionist history and the contemporary moment. Though the Nakba represents the peak of the demolition, there were other important periods of destruction, both before and after 1948.

Mapping was one of the powerful tools we used at Zochrot. As people who were raised in a colonial state, we understood the efficacy and power of maps. In this post-truth world, maps still maintain their factual appearance and people tend to believe them perhaps more than written texts. In other words, their mythological power is still solid. Maps retain great credibility as many view them to be visually "true."

We first produced in 2007 a map of contemporary Tel Aviv that showed the remnants of different Palestinian localities in its territory and that are hidden so carefully from maps and physical space in the city. Even though the remains of Manshiyyah, Sumail, Jamain al-Gharbi, Salama, Abu Kabir, and Sheikh Muannis are still visible, they do not appear on official maps nor on the many indicative signs around the city. Now, in 2022, the remains on the ground of those localities are disappearing so this map functions as an important archive.

We undertook another mapping project in a workshop with Israeli Jews and internal Palestinian refugees from a village named Miska. Together we drew a map of a possible, imagined future after the return of the Palestinian refugees. This project was published in Zochrot's Sedek magazine with the aim to promote the discussion about the return of Palestinian refugees within the Israeli public. We showed how this return is possible, including the rebuilding of Palestinian localities destroyed at the Nakba, without removing Israeli Jews from their homes.

Zochrot performed a kind of "return" to destroyed localities by conducting many tours to destroyed localities, especially designed for the Israeli public. It was the first opportunity for thousands of Israeli Jews to learn about those places. Palestinian refugees from those villages and towns shared their stories about life in those places before they were destroyed in 1948 and also about the events of the Nakba. A special booklet about the village, in Hebrew and Arabic, was prepared for each tour. Signs with the names of the destroyed village and its different sites were erected at the tour site. They were removed a short time afterward by Israelis who do not want to see reminders of the Palestinian history of "their" country.

Zochrot was born in Canada Park, one of the most popular Keren Kayemet LeIsrael-Jewish National Fund, or Jewish National Fund (JNF), for short, parks in the country. The idea of posting simple signs next to remains of the destroyed Palestinian villages around the park came to mind at the end of a visit organized for Jewish school pupils. A few years later the organization filed a petition to the supreme court, demanding an order for the JNF to post signs indicating the destroyed Palestinian villages alongside the information about

The Land of Milk and Honey (and Palestinians)   233

the other histories (Roman, Mamluk, Jewish, and more) on the existing signs. The petition was successful and the JNF had to post signs with the new narrative. It was the first major public appearance and success for Zochrot but not the last encounter with this major Zionist organization.

The clearest proof of the impact and success of Zochrot was the Nakba Law passed by the government in 2011. This law aims to prevent any commemoration or educational activity regarding the Nakba. As an anti-democratic law which sought to curtail free and open discussion, it sparked a huge debate about its own reference and for many Israelis it was the first time they ever heard the word Nakba. The searches for the term Nakba (in Hebrew) on Google multiplied by a factor of three that year. The initiator of the law, former MK (Knesset or Parliament Member) Alex Miller explained the need for the law:

> At that time in Israel, 2006 and beyond, all those demonstrations that were around the State of Israel's Independence Day . . . also instances at Tel Aviv University to mark the Nakba Memorial; it was actually the trigger for the legislation, because for me it doesn't make sense that there is a situation in which the state's Independence Day is mentioned as a catastrophe . . . it is contempt for the emblem, so it makes sense and is reasonable to enact a law to prevent it.[3]

Since the law was enacted, the government tried time and again to prevent Zochrot's activities, but in fact, these (mostly failed) efforts kept the discussion of the Nakba alive within the Israeli mainstream media.

One relevant example of the authorities' attempts to suppress Nakba events happened in the book of the authors of this chapter. Their book Nakba, in Hebrew (נכבה בעברית),[4] is probably the only book in Hebrew compelled to survive two court proceedings in order to be launched. Barbur art gallery organized a conference to launch the book. Because the gallery is located in a Jerusalem municipal building, the cultural minister at the time, Miri Regev, together with the Jerusalem mayor addressed the Attorney General with a demand for "immediate intervention to promote legislation that would enable us, once and for all" to prohibit such programs. Regev characterized the event as one that would feature "incessant pro-Palestinian babble" that "undermines our very existence and cultivates Nakba fairytales." The municipality lawyer addressed the court to try to forbid the launch of the book but the court turned him down. The municipality appealed to a higher court with the argument that the event is not allowed according to the Nakba law but again, the court allowed the conference.

Zochrot remains the main resource in Hebrew for the Nakba and the only organization in Israel dedicated to educational work on that critical issue for Israelis. Journalists from a variety of media, liberals as well as nationalists, continue to make reference to Zochrot. Researchers and teachers at all levels are using educational tools produced by Zochrot. The map of De-Colonizer is

234 Eitan Bronstein Aparicio and Eleonore Merza Bronstein

a further tool that is having an impact all around the world. Five editions have been published for scholars, school and university teachers, activists, and organizations.

General Description of the Map

This map displays all the localities, or at least all that we have been able to identify, that were destroyed during Israeli colonial history from the first Zionist migration to Palestine until the present time and even projects into the future.

The title of the map indicates two notable ongoing characteristics of Israeli colonialism: (1) it is very active, and (2) it destroys many localities. Israel takes great pride in its reputation for building new localities or settlements since its inception. However, it is important for us to relate what Israel is trying to hide: the destruction of almost a thousand Palestinian, Syrian, and Jewish towns and villages. These localities have been destroyed since the beginning of Zionist immigration to Palestine in the last quarter of the nineteenth century and continue to this day.

To be very clear, the Zionist colonial enterprise has been very active in destroying historical Palestine (*depalestinizing*) while at the same time building (for Jews).

Contrary to regular mapping visual codes, the names in gray, which seem to be the background of the map, are localities in Israel and Palestine that exist today.[5] In contrast, the names in different colors represent the Palestinian, Syrian, and Jewish localities that were destroyed, almost all of them by Israel.

Our idea is to create a visual shock while looking at the map and its massive numbers of colored dots: all that you see which is foregrounded no longer exist.

Each color refers to a specific historical layer of the colonial *continuum* rather than "ethnic" belonging to the expelled population.

Localities indicated in blue were destroyed before 1948, the year Israel was established, the year of the Nakba. This is significant because it means that before Israel was born, Zionist immigrants had already destroyed dozens of Palestinian localities. These men and women were the pioneers of the Zionist movement that was developed in Europe and had mobilized Jews to settle in Palestine in order to found a Jewish state. The blue stars represent Jewish localities that were destroyed by Palestinians. Their resistance to the Zionist colonization of the land resulted in several violent revolts that caused destruction of Jewish localities.

The Black double-head flashes are connecting a Jewish locality with a Palestinian one. They represent non-aggression initiatives that existed between two neighboring communities from both sides following the deterioration into violence in December 1947 until the collapse of these Palestinian localities with the Nakba.

Red is the main color of the map. It indicates, mostly, more than 600 Palestinian localities which Israel destroyed during the Nakba.

The Land of Milk and Honey (and Palestinians) 235

"Nakba," an Arabic word meaning disaster or catastrophe, took root in the language of Palestinians and to a much lesser extent Israeli Jews to describe the expulsion of 750,000 Palestinians by Israel in 1948. The phrase Nakba today has great resonance internationally but is a highly contested term within Israel.

The red dots appear in three sizes: small for localities with less than a hundred inhabitants; medium for localities which had between 100 and 3,000 residents; and large for cities that had been populated by more than 3,000 inhabitants.

On the map can also be seen red stars. They depict Jewish settlements that were destroyed by Arab military units that intervened in the 1948 war. No Israeli settlements were demolished by Palestinians in 1948.

In green, we have four different types of localities destroyed by Israel since 1967. The triangles show the Syrian localities of the occupied Golan Heights which Israel destroyed during the war of 1967.

It is politically important to broaden the picture of the colonial project of the occupation. When talking about 1967, many still refer to the occupation of the West Bank and the Gaza Strip, erasing the occupied Syrian Golan as if it is a forgotten occupation. This "forgotten" narrative has influenced the way Israelis themselves refer today to Golan: no checkpoint to arrive there, they feel "at home," etc.[6]

The green dots indicate the Palestinian localities which Israel obliterated since the war of 1967. The green dots with a black cross in them are Palestinian localities threatened to be demolished by Israel in the future. Green and empty circles show Palestinian (Beduin) localities that Israel refuses to recognize.

In orange, we have two categories of localities that, although Jewish, Israel demolished as part of the colonial process. The first sub-category is for Jewish settlements built and then destroyed by Israel in order to facilitate better control over the Palestinians. The second includes localities that were inhabited by Mizrahi Jews, from Arab and Muslim countries.

Colonization Before 1948 and Its Destructive Results

In blue, we see the destruction that took place before the Nakba in 1948 and thus prior to the creation of the state of Israel. Zionist settlers, with the help of some complicit landowners, destroyed 58 Palestinian settlements. This destruction occurred in the midst of a process of land acquisition and settlement building by the Zionist movement. Several Jewish associations, mostly based not only in Europe but also in the United States, contributed money to buy land in Palestine to establish settlements. Many of the landowners were not Palestinians but Syrians or Lebanese. They had bought the land from the Ottoman government at a low price, so for them Zionist investments provided significant profit opportunities.

Before Zionist immigration, when someone acquired land, he received the land along with the Palestinian sharecroppers who lived there. The goal of the Zionist settlers was to establish settlements for Jews only, so it was essential for them that the land they acquired should be empty of Arabs. They called this process "land redemption" (an almost religious concept) and "land conquest." In other words, their aim was to make these lands purely Jewish.

Zionist landowners and settlers had a common interest in making the land empty of Palestinian farmers. The Ottoman government and its rule of law made it possible to conclude the purchase agreements, if necessary with the intervention of soldiers. Palestinian tenant farmers had no ownership rights on the land on which they lived and worked. Sometimes they received such a low level of monetary compensation for their evacuation that conflicts broke out between Jewish settlers and Palestinian farmers. These clashes led to violence and, in some cases, deaths.

This approach to developing the Jewish presence in Palestine embodied the colonial character of the Zionist movement. Similar to the United States, Canada, and others, the Zionist enterprise was and is a settler colonial project. Unlike resource-use colonialism, in settler colonialism, settlers live in the colonized country and dispossess the Indigenous population. In addition, this is an important feature in the Zionist case, and the settlers establish a regime which privileges them at the expense of the native population.

Interestingly, there were Zionists who warned in the early twentieth century of the dire consequences this policy would have. For example, Yitzhak Epstein, Zionist educator, warned in 1907 that "When we buy such an estate . . . we have taken the poor out of their poor nest, we have destroyed their livelihood."[7] Haim Margaliot Kalvarisky, an important Zionist who was active in land acquisition in Palestine as part of the Jewish Colonization Association, told the Zionist leadership: "When the Jews established a new settlement, there were clashes. We have not always been fair. The land was purchased from landowners in Beirut. The officials (Zionists) and the vendors (Arabs) were not interested in the plight of the farmers."[8]

The first case of displacement of Palestinians took place in 1878 in the area of the city of Petah Tikva. It was a small village named Mlabes.[9] A small group of Jews from Jaffa bought that land and sought to have it empty of non-Jews. This led to a legal conflict that resulted in the evacuation of the Palestinian farmers. This episode is the basis for a fascinating case study of collective memory and collective oblivion in Israel.[10] This mistreatment of Palestinians is immortalized in a well-known Israeli song, performed by the popular Arik Einstein. "The Ballad of Yoel Moshe Salomon"[11] tells the story of the Jewish pioneers' group, led by Salomon, and references that "Beside Umlabes they stopped"[12] but even after climbing on a hill "to see the surrounding" all that they saw around them was swamps with no birds. There are no people there and the land is hard and empty. One could argue that the writer instilled a subtle clue or warning by suggesting that if there are no birds singing then "Death rules here." But the fact is that the overwhelming majority of Israelis who know by heart the lyrics and join the singing have no idea about the price the local Palestinians paid for this first colonization event.

Understandably, Palestinians opposed settlement from the outset. Sometimes their reaction was expressed by armed resistance, which even caused the

The Land of Milk and Honey (and Palestinians)   237

destruction of 19 Zionist localities. On the map, these are marked with blue stars. Maps, by their nature, hide the differences between locations of different categories, as all locations appear as abstract graphic symbols. For us, therefore, it is important to underline the differences between Indigenous Palestinian localities and Jewish settlements, between the colonized and the colonizer. Even so, it is also our aim to recall the price of demolished localities that the colonizer extracts in the colonial process. In Algeria, Congo, and many other places, history has already taught us that the colonizer always pays a heavy price for participation in the colonial project: being a colonizer is not exempted from price.

There were two notable differences between Jewish-destroyed localities and the Palestinian-destroyed localities: (1) most Jewish settlements were established a short time before they were destroyed, whereas Palestinian settlements had already existed for hundreds of years and (2) most of the Jewish settlements were later rebuilt, while the Palestinian settlements were destroyed forever.

An exceptional and tragic event befell the Jewish population who lived for hundreds of years in Hebron, a Palestinian city 40 km south of Jerusalem. In 1929, as a result of a provocation by Jews against Palestinians in Jerusalem at the Western Wall, a site of great meaning to both Jews and Muslims, Palestinians attacked Jews in Hebron and massacred 67 of them. Many Jews were nevertheless saved by their Palestinian neighbors, but this massacre remained a trauma in collective Israeli memory. It is important to note that even after this terrible event, not all Jews left Hebron. This fact testifies to the good relations between Muslims and Jews at the time in the city. The Jews finally deserted Hebron following violent events during the Arab Revolt in 1936. The British government forced the Jews to leave the city because it was too difficult for them to provide security. This traumatic story served as a pretext for Israel to establish a Jewish settlement in the center of Hebron after the occupation of the West Bank in 1967. This settlement led to the expulsion of many Palestinians from their homes and to other forms of violence against them.

The destruction in 1948 embodies also an elimination of hope. It concerns the crushing of 48 non-aggression initiatives between Palestinian and Jewish neighbor localities.[13] These quasi-accords were concluded in 1947–1948 between neighbor communities from the two sides. On the map, they are marked by black two-headed arrows that connect between Jewish and Palestinian localities. Between each pair of neighboring localities, there was a relationship of a certain trust, which was built over the decades. These initiatives collapsed because of the Nakba. When Zionist military units attacked Palestinian localities, their good relations with neighboring settlements did not provide them with any protection or security.

One of the most symbolic cases is probably the nexus of Deir Yassin and Givat Sh'aul. Both communities were keeping cordial relations which did not prevent the massacre of 120 Palestinians in Deir Yassin on April 9, 1948, many of them women and children killed in their houses. Contrary to what we often hear in the Israeli narrative, the systematic expulsions of Palestinians from their

238 *Eitan Bronstein Aparicio and Eleonore Merza Bronstein*

villages and towns during the Nakba had nothing to do with the level of "hostility" of the villages with their Jewish neighbors.

For the first time on a map, we are reporting those non-aggression initiatives. We do so because the aim of this map is to show coloniality is not only about physical destructions, however massive those have been, but also features the destruction of human relations and of the previously existing social fabric.

Destruction During the Nakba

Red is the most notable color on the map because it represents the massive destruction of Palestinian localities in 1948 in order to establish Israel as a Jewish state. The expulsion of a huge number of Palestinians, indeed the majority living in what would become Israel, and the destruction of their communities by Zionist forces was carried out with the aim of having as much territory as possible for the Jews with the minimum number of Palestinian inhabitants.[14] Zionist aggressors destroyed 612 Palestinian localities through military operations against the Palestinian civilian population. Palestinian armed resistance was minor. This contradicts the myth in Israel that the Palestinians became refugees as a result of a war. Obviously, there was a war in 1948 but it did not play out as Israeli mythology and propaganda have led many Israelis Jews and others to believe.

We know that the Palestinians did not fight not only by their own testimonies but also by the testimonies of Zionist soldiers who fought in 1948. For example, Amnon Neumann, a fighter in the Palmach[15] in 1948, testified on the Nakba:

> we had already eliminated all Arab (Palestinian) resistance, which had not been difficult. You might think we fought against the Palestinians, but there were hardly any battles. . . . But there were no great battles. Why? Because they had no military capability. They were very poorly organized.[16]

On the map, we see a black dot inside 207 of the 612 red dots. These dots indicate Palestinian localities that were destroyed in the Nakba, but before the creation of Israel. The war between Israel and the Arab countries erupted on May 15, 1948, immediately after Israel declaration of independence at the end of the British Mandate. We want to emphasize that over a third of the Palestinian localities that Zionist forces destroyed during the Nakba were destroyed before the start of the war. In fact, the destruction and expulsion began at the end of 1947, following the violence that erupted after the UN decision on November 29, 1947, to divide Palestine into two states: one Jewish and one Arab.

As surprising and counter-intuitive as it may seem, the Israeli military was the first to use the word "Nakba" in reference to the Palestinian catastrophe. In July 1948, the Israel Defense Forces (IDF) distributed propaganda tracts to the Palestinian inhabitants of Tirat Haifa who were resisting their expulsion.

The Land of Milk and Honey (and Palestinians)   239

In excellent Arabic prose, the military urged them to surrender: "If you want to avoid the Nakba, avoid a disaster, and save yourselves from an unavoidable catastrophe, you must surrender."[17] It demonstrates that Zionists were well aware of where all this violence was leading and pushed for it.

As noted earlier, most of the expulsions were the result of Israeli military attacks. Palestinian residents had no defense, as Neumann said: "They had no weapons. Who would have given them?" Palestinians escaped to save their lives and Israel prevented their return. Another method of deportation was the carrying out of massacres by which we mean, the murder of many defenseless people. In a dramatic moment of his testimony, Neumann refuses to talk about it: "there was a massacre. No, I don't want to talk about it, forget it! this . . . these . . . there is nothing to say. Why? because I did."[18] The aim of dozens of similar massacres was not to exterminate the population but rather to create terror and fear and hence incite them to flee from their localities. Sometimes Israeli soldiers killed several Palestinians and left one of them alive so that that lone survivor could relate to other Palestinians what had happened. Such testimony often scared many and they decided to run away immediately.

In the work of Zochrot, several testimonies of Zionist fighters were collected and published. As we wrote in our book, *Nakba. The Struggle to decolonize Israel*, these eyewitness accounts can be very effective tools in educating the Israelis on the Nakba because those 1948 fighters are perceived as heroes in Israel. Their testimonies are not easily contested while in contrast Israelis believe, owing to their investment in the founding myth and their own racism, that they can refute Palestinian accounts of the Nakba "because they are against us."

As we termed it in our book, these fighters are exposing a type of family secret.[19] Though it is hard for the "Israeli family" to listen to these truths, some recognize that these 1948 fighters are not inventing this narrative but are speaking the truth. Due to the work of Zochrot, today many more Israelis know that Israel played a role in creating the Palestinian refugee problem in 1948. In the survey De-Colonizer conducted for the writing of the book *Nakba*, we found that 42.1% of Israelis hold that Israel played a role in the creation of the refugee population.[20] This is quite a distance from the Israeli hegemonic and official narrative that suggests that Palestinians were forced out as a result of a war that they, as part of "the Arabs," launched against Israel. In this distorted view, the outcomes are the sole responsibility of "the Arabs."

When we talk about destruction of localities, it is important to clarify our use of the word "destruction." The 612 localities destroyed in 1948 ceased to be Palestinian but were not necessarily physically destroyed. For example, in Jaffa, 70,000 Palestinians lived until 1948. After their deportation by the Zionists in April 1948, 3,000 Palestinians remained in the city. So obviously Jaffa as a Palestinian city ceased to exist, but it continued to exist physically.

There was also destruction of Palestinian homes in 1948 but many remained standing. Tens of thousands of empty houses were repopulated by Jews who had immigrated to Israel from many countries. So the emptied Palestinian houses helped Israel to solve the housing shortage problem but that was not the

240 *Eitan Bronstein Aparicio and Eleonore Merza Bronstein*

main reason for their repopulation. This was done with the aim of preventing the return of Palestinians to their homes. This was the main way to prevent the Palestinians from exercising their natural rights and returning to their homes. This act of Israel, of repopulating Palestinian homes, is the culmination of the Zionist settler colonial enterprise. It includes preventing the return of Palestinians and thus ensuring Jewish sovereignty over as large a territory as possible with a large demographic majority.

In 1948, 26 Israeli settlements were also destroyed, and we present them as red stars. Their destruction was carried out by Arab military units and not by Palestinians. Fifteen of them were in territory intended to be in the Arab state in accordance with the UN partition decision. This indicates that warring units from Arab countries, especially Jordanians and Egyptians, which were the most powerful, were trying to prevent Israel from expanding beyond the borders allotted to the Jewish state in the UN Partition Plan. This contradicts another Israeli myth that the Arab armies sought to eliminate Israel.

Destruction From 1967 to the Present Day

The green triangles depict the 195 localities in the occupied Golan that Israel destroyed during the 1967 war. A total of 120,000 residents were expelled. Most of them were Bedouin farmers (*Felahin*), and there were also Turkmens, Circassians, and Alawites. Israel only allowed the Druze to stay, with the intention that they would establish a quasi-country to be called "Jabl a–Druze" (Druze Mountain). The (failed) Israeli attempt was intended to help the Druze to establish in parts of Syria and Lebanon a sovereign government that would work with Israel. In 1981, Israel illegally annexed the Golan Heights, Syrian territory, and allowed the Druze to receive Israeli citizenship.

Green dots indicate the 11 Palestinian villages that Israel has destroyed since the 1967 war. The best-known case of destruction during this war took place in the region of Latrun, where three villages – Imwass, Yalu, and Bait Nouba – were destroyed within days after the war. In fact, they were the only villages Israel destroyed in this war. So the 1967 war was characterized mainly by occupation and expansion which multiplied four times the territory of the country.[21] The destruction of the three villages of Latrun and the expulsion of their inhabitants is similar to the strategy implemented by Israel in 1948. Indeed, they were leveled in a kind of perverse revenge for the failure of occupying that region in 1948.[22]

The empty green dots represent the 65 Bedouin villages that Israel did not recognize. Some of them have been in their current locations for many years before the establishment of Israel, and some of them were relocated by Israel after the Nakba. We have decided to include them on the map, even if they have not been destroyed in the usual sense of the term, because since the establishment of the state they live in conditions of neglect without proper infrastructure and under the constant threat of destruction. These are not just threats. Most of these villages are located in Israeli territory within the borders that were set in 1949. They often suffer from the destruction of houses they

The Land of Milk and Honey (and Palestinians)   241

built "illegally" due to lack of a construction plan on the part of the Israeli state. The largest and most famous of these home destructions occurred in the Negev in the south of the country, but some also took part in the north. The most important plan to destroy Palestinian-Bedouin villages is called the "Prawer Plan." The main idea behind this plan is to centralize the Bedouins in the big cities that Israel has built for them, and so dispossess them of land that had been theirs for centuries. Israel confirmed the plan in 2013 but had to suspend it after six months because of mass angry protests.

The green dots with a black cross in them represent 70 Palestinian localities threatened with abolition by Israel, mostly in the West Bank. This violent, threatening strategy is for the purpose of building or expanding Jewish settlements and military bases. Therefore, Israel will destroy these Palestinian villages. Indeed, cases of destruction in these villages by Israel are an almost daily affair. It is important to note that most of this population had previously been expelled by Israel in 1948 or after the 1967 war.

One village that has become notable owing to its planned destruction is Khan al Ahmar, 20 km east of Jerusalem. This project is aimed at expanding the Jewish settlement of Kfar Edomim at the expense of the Palestinian village. A large mobilization of Palestinians, international protesters, and even Israeli activists have succeeded for now in stopping the plan, but the danger that it will be implemented in the future exists all the time.

Another important village to note in this context is Al Araqib, a small Bedouin village in southern Israel. Unlike most of the other villages in this category on the map, Al Araqib is located in the territory of the State of Israel and not in the West Bank. In 1948, Israel expelled 90,000 Bedouins from the Negev outside its borders and pushed the remaining 10,000 into a restricted area. Al Araqib families, like other Bedouins, waged legal battles against the state in an attempt to return to Al Araqib but to no avail. At the turn of the millennium, inhabitants of the village decided to return to their land and since 2010 the Israeli security forces have destroyed the village 193 times, as of this writing. The case of Al Araqib (and two other Bedouin villages in Israel) demonstrates that Israel is destroying Palestinian localities in its territory just as it is doing in the West Bank.

The significance of this category on the map is to highlight the historical continuum of Zionist colonial destruction. This map is not (just) a document which keeps the memory of past events but a visual, cartographic testimony of the perpetual destruction of the localities which began more than 140 years ago and will not stop by itself. This map has not only an educational role but also an advocacy one: without worldwide pressure, Israel's colonial enterprise will not stop.

Destruction of Jewish Settlements by Israel

Strange as it may sound, Israel destroyed Jewish settlements in the course of its colonial enterprise. There are two categories of destroyed Jewish settlements.

242 *Eitan Bronstein Aparicio and Eleonore Merza Bronstein*

The first is the 28 settlements built and then destroyed to increase control over the Palestinians, marked on the map by orange stars. Most of them (21) are the settlements in the Gaza Strip, established since the 1970s, and Ariel Sharon (the former Prime Minister) decided to evacuate in 2005. The strategic thought behind this plan of "redeployment" was to save state resources and the endangered status of Jewish settlers that this colonization provoked. Yet Israel continues to control the Gaza Strip from the air, from the sea, on the ground, and even below it. So unlike the evacuation of settlements as a decolonial practice, as in the case of the evacuation of settlements from Sinai as part of the peace process with Egypt, the evacuation of settlements in the Gaza Strip was a one-sided Israeli tactical maneuver to preserve colonial control there.

The second category encompasses settlements of Arab Jews (often called "Oriental" Jews) that Israel destroyed. Not everyone is equally and fully Israeli in the settler colonial state of Israel. Not surprisingly, whiteness has importance, including within the Jewish component of the population. There are 15 localities marked with orange stars inside orange circles. These localities were destroyed in various contexts, but the similar feature in each of them was the racism of Ashkenazi Jews toward Mizrahi Jews.[23] This category of destruction underscores the European origin of the Zionist movement. They imported the orientalist and racist approach from the continent in which they have established their vision. While the Ashkenazi Zionists saw (and continue to see) themselves as an "outpost of civilization" in the midst of those "Arabs," they saw (and continue to see) Mizrahi Jews as "inferiors" because after all they remain "Arabs."

The first case is from 1912 or well before the establishment of Israel. Fourteen Yemeni families had settled by the Sea of Galilee. A year later Ashkenazi Jews settled nearby and formed the Kinneret Group, which became one of the most important settlements in the history of the Zionist movement. In this story its ugly part is hidden. The Yemenis lived in poor conditions, while the Ashkenazi, with their ties to the Zionist establishment, lived in significantly better conditions. They did not value their Yemeni neighbors, and tensions were created and escalated based on cultural and religious differences. The tension mounted and intensified to the point that the Ashkenazi settlers succeeded in having the Yemenis expelled in 1929.

The second case continues to this day in a district of Tel Aviv. Until the Nakba it was a Palestinian village called Jamasin al-Gharbi. In February 1948, its residents escaped fearing Israeli military activity against another nearby village. In 1949, Israelis populated the houses in the village to prevent the return of the Palestinians. These Jews were of Arab origin. Since then, the district has been called Givat Amal. In another part of the same Palestinian village, on its agricultural land, Israel founded a new neighborhood called Shikun Tzameret. It was built especially for city officials and activists from the Mapai party that ruled the country at the time. They were of Ashkenazi descent. A few years later the Ashkenazim of Shikun Tzameret bought the houses in which they lived and thus became their owners. Unlike them, across the road, the Arab

The Land of Milk and Honey (and Palestinians) 243

Jews were never given rights to the houses in which they lived.[24] For years they have fought against the state in court, and in recent years also against real estate companies, in order to receive proper compensation in return for leaving the neighborhood. Some of them had already been evacuated by violence, and the remaining families were forced out in November 2021. This case and others like it indicate clear racism against the Mizrahim in Israel. Several localities with a similar history, of Jews inhabiting Palestinian homes, exist in the Tel Aviv and Jerusalem areas to this day.[25]

The kibbutzim,[26] predominantly Ashkenazi, who also settled in Palestinian homes and land after the Nakba, were never forced to leave their homes and even took possession of them. This anti-Arab (even though those Arabs are Jews), Eurocentric, and Orientalist approach is central to the Israeli colonial regime: for white settlers, the Arabness of some makes them lesser Jews than others.

This map was created for the use of educators and activists who read English, French, and Hebrew, and who want to learn about and/or teach a lesser-known history of Israel/Palestine. It shows a continuing reality of destruction in the past, present, and future. It is a tool that allows us not only to remember the history but also seek to prevent more expulsions. The names are revealed, they are on this map, and the map provides full transparency, so no one will be able to claim you did not know.

Where there is constant destruction, there is also resistance, and a lot of violence also results, which is dismaying but totally understandable. Unlike other colonial settlement projects, such as New Zealand, the United States, and Canada, Israel continues to use daily violence against the natives of the country it colonized. The map "Colonialism in Destru(A)ction" helps us to understand that the hegemonic and empty discourse of "peace" between Israelis and Palestinians has no relationship to the reality on the ground. Those who hope for a better future must bring their moral outrage and activism against the continued destruction of Palestine. So long as there is no justice, we firmly believe that there will be no peace.

Notes

1 www.de-colonizer.org/map If you go to our website, you can access our complete map, the map legend, and accompanying compendium which lists the destructions of localities.

2 https://zochrot.org/en.

3 Yoav Kapshuk and Lisa Strömbom, "Israeli Pre-Transitional Justice and the Nakba Law," *Israeli Law Review*, Vol. 54, No. 3, p. 316; http://cambridge.org/core/about.

4 Eitan Bronstein Aparicio, Eléonore Merza Bronstein; *Nakba in Hebrew*, Pardes, 2018.

5 As a geographical place we rather name it Palestine. As a regime that established sovereignty it is Israel. We'll use both names.

6 On the specific work done by De-Colonizer on Syrian occupied Golan Heights, see www.de-colonizer.org/golan and in particular: www.de-colonizer.org/destroyed-localities-and-settlements.

7 In Alan Dowty and Yitzhak Epstein, "'A Question That Outweighs All Others': Yitzhak Epstein and Zionist Recognition of the Arab Issue," *Israel Studies*, Vol. 6, No. 1 (2001), pp. 34–54, www.jstor.org/stable/30245563.

8 In Tom Segev, *One Palestine, Complete: Jews and Arabs Under the British Mandate* (New York: Henry Holt and Company, 2000).

9 Commonly pronounced Umlabes.

10 Ernest Renan argues that "Forgetting . . . is an essential factor in the creation of a nation." From "What is a Nation?," text of a conference delivered at the Sorbonne on March 11th, 1882, in Ernest Renan, *Qu'est-ce qu'une nation?* (Paris: Presses-Pocket, 1992) (translated by Ethan Rundell), http://ucparis.fr/files/9313/6549/9943/What_is_a_Nation.pdf.

11 Lyrics by Yoram Taharlev.

12 Translation by Hebrew-Language.com, https://hebrew-language.com/songs-moshe-salomon/.

13 These 48 cases are mainly based on research conducted by Ariella Aïsha Azoulay for her movie "Civil Alliance": www.youtube.com/watch?v=lqi4X_ptwWw (with English subtitles).

14 On the eve of the Nakba, there were 1,300,000 Palestinians in Palestine, including the Gaza Strip and the West Bank, and 600,000 Jews. In 1949 within the Israeli borders (excluding the Gaza Strip and the West Bank), there were 150,000 Palestinians and 900,000 Jews.

15 The Palmach was the most combative part of the Zionist combat units.

16 Watch it here: www.youtube.com/watch?v=JIDPesq9ysc&t=205s.

17 Eitan Bronstein Aparicio and Eléonore Merza Bronstein, *Nakba, the Struggle to Decolonize Israel* (London: Nomad Publishing, 2022), pp. 212–213.

18 Ibid.

19 Bronstein Aparicio and Merza Bronstein, *Nakba*. See Chapter 8.

20 Ibid., pp. 240–241.

21 At the same time, a quarter of a million Palestinian refugees have been added as a result of this war, mostly workers in Gulf countries, whom Israel has prevented from returning to the West Bank.

22 To read more on that: https://zochrot.org/uploads/uploads/76f008b16810088acdd645 6a3f6eb0c5.pdf.

23 While all the other categories of destruction in the map are based on outside resources, this one is based on De-Colonizer's research and it is the only attempt known to the authors to assemble these destructions under one analytic category.

24 To read about the comparison between Givat Amal and Shikun Tzameret, please see Harel Nachmany and Ravit Hananel, *A Tale of Two Neighborhoods: Toward a New Typology of Land Rights*, Vol. 80 (Amsterdam: Elsevier, January 2019), pp. 233–245.

25 More on this: www.972mag.com/the-mizrahi-communities-destroyed-by-the-israeli-establishment/.

26 Kibbutzim is the plural of "Kibbutz," a type of settlement which is unique to Israel and is a collective, traditionally agrarian, community.

Part V

Fascism and War

12 Public Commemorations of Argentina's Histories of Violence

Marisa Lerer

On March 24, 2020, the 44th anniversary of Argentina's 1976 military coup and 5 days after the start of a nationwide lockdown in response to the coronavirus pandemic, the sound of the banging of pots and pans rang out from open windows and balconies in a cacophony of protest against Argentina's 1976–1983 military dictatorship and in commemoration to its victims. As Argentines were under shelter-in-place orders to prevent the spread of the coronavirus, public spaces were left empty. However, civil society found ways to continue to memorialize the events under the dictatorship through this auditory memorial and in virtual public spheres on social media. The commitment to widespread commemoration of the anniversary of the military coup after more than four decades had passed and during the onset of a global pandemic speaks to the lasting impact that the dictatorship and its human rights abuses had on the Argentine nation. It also highlights the importance that many in Argentina place on memorializing the victims of the dictatorship and in emphasizing the repercussions that the dictatorship had well into the twenty-first century.

As in the United States, a national reckoning on monuments erupted in Argentina. Social justice activists directly connected the violent human rights abuses perpetuated by the 1976–1983 Argentine military dictatorship to the Indigenous genocide of the nineteenth century and a series of current and past economic and political crises. They tied the last military dictatorship to multiple forms of contemporary violence, such as food and housing insecurity stemming from the country's economic collapse in 2001, which many scholars argue was directly linked to the military junta's neoliberal economic policies.[1] Argentine civil society continues to debate how to frame contentious leaders from the past and how to memorialize the victims of state-sponsored terrorism from the country's last military dictatorship.

Critically, the history of the Argentine dictatorship is one that spans beyond Argentina's borders to South America and the United States. The dictatorship was part of Operation Condor, a plot fomented by the United States in the Cold War climate (the 1950s–1980s political and economic conflict between the United States and the Soviet Union and their allies) to combat the perceived threat of communism. It was a web of espionage, murder, and severe human rights abuses conducted through a secret program of police cooperation

DOI: 10.4324/9781003217848-18

248   *Marisa Lerer*

across South American borders including Brazil, Argentina, Chile, Uruguay, Paraguay, and Bolivia. These Southern Cone neighbors all shared the detrimental experience of US intervention in their economy and politics as well as US-learned tactics of torture, political repression, assassination, and intelligence maneuvers to deter what they called "leftist subversives."[2] Realpolitik, politics imposed by means of physical violence, political extortion, or economic suppression, became the modus operandi for the Argentine and other Southern Cone dictatorships. Some countries were more supportive of and fervent about the operation than others. A cable from the US Federal Bureau of Investigation (FBI) explained, "Members of Operation Condor showing the most enthusiasm to date have been Argentina, Uruguay, and Chile."[3] Upon their return to democracy, all three countries' governments encouraged their populations to forget the human rights abuses committed through state-sponsored terrorism.

This chapter explores the legacy of state-sponsored violence in Argentina's public sphere and studies the memorials dedicated to the estimated 30,000 victims of the dictatorship, often referred to collectively as "the disappeared." Human rights activist Rita Arditti described them:

> Male and female, young and old, babies and teenagers; pregnant women, students, workers, lawyers, journalists, scientists, artists and teachers; Argentine citizens and citizens of other countries, nuns and priests, progressive members of religious orders – all swelled the ranks of the disappeared.[4]

Anyone could have been a target of the military forces, including high school students who organized to protest bus-fare hikes. Thousands of those victims were never linked to any political activities at all. Among the disappeared and those captives who were eventually released from clandestine detention, torture, and extermination centers were people from every social strata and career. The government statistics on disappeared persons included 30.2% blue-collar workers, 21% students, 17.9% white-collar workers, 10.7% professionals, 5.7% teachers, 5.0% self-employed, 3.8% housewives, 2.5% military conscripts and members of the security forces, 1.6% journalists, 1.3% actors and performers, and 0.3% nuns, priests, and religious leaders. Jews comprise 2% of the Argentine population but 10% of those disappeared.[5]

Memorials to these victims discussed here include typologies that range from former clandestine centers for detention, torture, and extermination (ex-CCDTE); cultural centers; monuments; public sculptures; and sidewalk tiles. The scale of these memorials extends from a 38-acre museum complex to small, modest mosaics. The sites of memory include both ephemeral imagery and memorials intended to maintain a permanent presence in public space. I argue that the use of public space to both memorialize the victims of state-sponsored terrorism and highlight the violence that occurred under the dictatorship is part of a territorial struggle by grassroots-led human rights organizations to interweave the history of the dictatorship into the very fabric of the urban landscape.

Public Commemorations of Argentina's Histories of Violence   249

The emergence of built memorials for the victims of state-sponsored terrorism grew out of the grassroots organizing of human rights and neighborhood organizations. These memorials functioned with multiple missions to commemorate the victims of state-sponsored terrorism and to carve out a place for families to mourn their lost loved ones, when they often didn't have the bodies to mourn over. The memorials also carried an inherent didacticism in order to create a counternarrative to the false historical claims that were perpetuated by the dictatorship, its supporters, and by subsequent democratic administrations.

Examining the political conditions that gave rise to the extremist right-wing violence perpetuated by the military junta as well as the protests against it brings into view the shifting attitudes of the nation's population and political leaders toward the dictatorship, which are reflected in the visual changes that occur in the country's commemorative practices. To contextualize the memorial projects in Argentina, it is important to understand how the military junta came to power, its method of rule and control, and the judicial processes during the post-dictatorship era.

A Brief History of the Junta

The early period of the 1970s in Argentina was marked by the return and death of President Juan Perón (in office 1946–1952, 1952–1955, 1973–1974) and the Alianza Anticomunista Argentina (Argentine Anti-Communist Alliance, Triple A) death squadrons. Political violence committed by left-wing urban guerrilla groups including the Montoneros and the Ejército Revolucionario del Pueblo (People's Revolutionary Army, ERP) was prevalent during this time. In response, the Triple A killed 66 young guerillas during Perón's last presidency, which forged a precedent for the violent and brutal actions of the 1976–1983 military dictatorship.

After President Juan Perón died in 1974, power was handed over to the vice-president, Peron's third wife, Isabel Martínez de Perón (in office 1974–1976). Martínez de Perón's administration was unable to control the extreme left and right fronts that were active at the time. On March 24, 1976, the Argentine military launched a coup against Martínez de Perón's government. As a result, there were three military juntas that ruled in succession from 1976 to 1983. The leaders of the first military junta were Navy Admiral Emilio Eduardo Massera, Army General Jorge Rafael Videla, and Air Force Brigadier General Orlando Ramón Agosti. Coups were not new in Argentine politics; they had taken place throughout the 20th century, in 1930, 1955, and 1966. In fact, the change in power was at first welcomed by many citizens and was supported by renowned personalities, such as the author Jorge Luis Borges. Like this internationally famed literary figure, many Argentine citizens mistakenly believed that the military coup would transform Argentina into a stable and safe nation.

The idea of a communist menace generated during the Cold War era penetrated deep into the dogma of the Argentine military dictatorship. Along with fighting the perceived communist threat, the military junta declared that

250 *Marisa Lerer*

it was firmly establishing and maintaining Western and Christian family values. Therefore, the Catholic Church aligned itself with the junta. In fact, the church, like the military, denied the existence of the military's practice of kidnapping, torture, slave labor, and forced disappearance. The military attempted to erase their violent acts through denying that kidnappings ever took place.

The junta leaders, who observed and learned from the earlier 1973 *coup d'etat* in Chile that perpetrated open repression, decided upon a secretive method of disappearance. The Argentine military used unmarked cars and men in plain clothes to conduct the kidnapping operations. Disappearance left no trace of the victim or the identity of the perpetrator; political anthropologist Jennifer G. Schirmer has explained that "disappearance then is a form of censorship of memory by the State."[6] Beginning in 1974, abduction was also used by the Triple A as a method of repression prior to the military coup of March 24, 1976. From 1976 on, forces that usurped power took absolute control of the resources of the state so that disappearance became a widespread practice, with the greatest number of disappearances occurring from 1976 to 1978. Art historian Andrea Giunta observed,

> Individuals and spaces that were previously immune now became not only the enemy but also "legitimate" targets for extermination. This presumed the denial of their situation as citizens within national borders. First, they "died" as citizens through the elimination of all their rights, which left them *deterritorialized* and finally, they were eliminated physically.[7]

One of the difficulties that citizens of Argentina faced is that, at the time, there was often no physical site of the remains, no publicly known site of death or burial, and thus no trace of many of the dictatorship's victims.

In addition, the junta's propaganda campaign circulated its ideology through newspapers, magazines, and posters, which successfully convinced a large part of Argentine citizens that the people whom the military targeted were extremists and terrorists. This was untrue and part of a playbook of falsehoods that totalitarian regimes like the Argentine junta generated. The military leaders identified the period of their rule as the "Dirty War" because the Argentine dictatorship established that there was an "internal enemy" without a specific known location, which had to be identified secretly among the population. The distinction in terminology for this historical moment is important to clarify. The "Dirty War" is a phrase that the military dictatorship invented to suggest that it was fighting a war with an equal but opposing faction. Leaders of the military wanted to emphasize that it was in the midst of a war, as opposed to terrorizing its own citizens.

In the dictatorship's view, actions of opposition included taking part in union or student activities. Opponents of the dictatorship were intellectuals who questioned state terrorism, or anyone who could be identified "simply because they [the victims of state-sponsored terrorism] were relatives, friends, or [had their] names included in the address book of someone considered subversive."[8]

Public Commemorations of Argentina's Histories of Violence   251

In fact, in 1981 when a journalist asked about the need for an investigation into the disappearances, General Roberto Eduardo Viola, who served briefly as president from March to December 1981, replied,

> I think you are suggesting that we investigate the [Argentine military] Security Forces – that is absolutely out of the question. This is a war and we are the winners. You can be certain that in the last war if the armies of the Reich had won, the war crimes trials would have taken place in Virginia, not in Nuremberg.[9]

Conversely, it should be noted that those who were victims of the military were not fighting a war. This period of armed hostility was one in which the government abused its disproportionate might to inflict human rights abuses on its own population. The dictatorship's "enemies" were victims of state-sponsored terrorism, and therefore it is critical to refer to this era as the last military dictatorship, or the era of state-sponsored terrorism, instead of the military's nomenclature of the "Dirty War."

Collective protests against the dictatorship to show the faces of the disappeared began with the formation of the Madres de Plaza de Mayo (the Mothers of the Plaza de Mayo, Madres). The group's first public march on April 30, 1977, took place at the Plaza de Mayo, a square in front of the Casa Rosada, the seat of the Argentine national government. The Madres de Plaza de Mayo took to the streets because the military had blurred the space between public and private by pillaging homes and kidnapping their children.[10] The Madres marched with enlarged photographs of their disappeared loved ones and covered their heads with white handkerchiefs that symbolized diapers. Hebe de Bonafini, president of the Asociación Madres de Plaza de Mayo (Association of the Mothers of the Plaza de Mayo), described the group's rationale for entering the public realm. "We made ourselves, our struggle and our pain public and collective and together we went to a public place, The Plaza [de Mayo], so that everyone could see us."[11] Their individual, private losses prompted them to enter into the public sphere. The government censored the media and did not allow families to file writs of habeas corpus (a legal report of unlawful detention). Therefore, the taking over of public space was paramount to making the disappeared present in the citizenry's daily view.

Public space is often equated with a democratic sphere for the people; under the dictatorship, it was one of prohibition, control, and restriction. The junta cleared the streets and plazas and placed them under surveillance; thus, Argentines had to relearn the concept of communal space.[12] The members of the Madres de Plaza de Mayo – many of whom were previously apolitical – applied nonviolent action to call attention to the disappearances which had tremendously impacted their private lives. Their actions find parallels in other countries, such as the United States, where mothers organize against violence inflicted upon their children by the state (discussed later in this chapter). It should be noted that, in Argentina, many other human rights organizations

252 *Marisa Lerer*

were active during this time, such as Centro de Estudios Legales y Sociales (Center for Legal and Social Studies, CELS) and Servicio Paz y Justicia (Service Peace and Justice, SERPAJ). Other organizations, such as Hijos por la Identidad y la Justicia contra el Olvido y el Silencio (Children for Identity and Justice Against Forgetting and Silence, HIJOS), formed after the dictatorship with the goal of seeking justice for their disappeared parents.

The Post-Dictatorship Era

In 1983, when the military lost power and Argentina returned to democratic rule, a series of laws was passed to protect perpetrators of crimes against humanity from legal punishment.

Raúl Ricardo Alfonsín of the Radical Party (in office 1983–1989) took over the presidency in 1983. In 1985, nine leaders of the military juntas were tried for crimes against humanity in a civilian court, but tensions between human rights organizations and the democratic government escalated during the trial. Despite the protests by human rights organizations, at the trial's end only some of the leaders of the dictatorship were given light sentences of five years in prison. In addition, the Alfonsín government passed a series of laws that protected violators of human rights abuses. Alfonsín's successor, Carlos Saúl Menem (in office 1989–1999), further impeded the realization of institutional justice for the victims of state-sponsored terrorism and their families. In 1990, Menem granted a presidential pardon to the members of the military who were indicted under the Alfonsín administration. Menem not only left the country void of the limited justice that it achieved, but in 1994 went so far as to publicly praise the military for fighting against subversion, thus perpetuating the military's own justification for its crimes against humanity over a decade after dictatorial rule had ended.[13] However, in a turn in favor of human rights, Argentina's Supreme Court overturned the amnesty laws in 2005, paving the way for prosecutions against the perpetrators of disappearance to begin in 2009. As of 2020, 3,329 people have been charged, 997 convicted, and 162 acquitted. The protests in Argentina that demanded that missing loved ones be brought back alive shifted to demanding the persecution of the perpetrators and commemorating the loved ones who were disappeared.

Commemorative Strategies

The memorials discussed here were created during a tumultuous time in the 1990s and early 2000s when many of the perpetrators of state-sponsored violence walked free. Therefore, these memorials function on multiple levels. They are didactic, therapeutic, and, importantly, they also function as physical testimonials of the lives and very existence of the victims of state-sponsored terrorism so that the perpetrators of crimes against humanity could be held in judgment – if not in a legal court at least in public opinion.

Public Commemorations of Argentina's Histories of Violence   253

There was much debate about the most appropriate type of commemoration strategy for the victims of state-sponsored terrorism. In the end, the multiple and varied paradigms of commemorations that exist speak to the fact that distinct types of memorials to the victims of state-sponsored terrorism allow for both a visitor's personal connection and historical comprehensibility. The memory work at all the sites functions in tandem with calls for justice. Argentina's multifaceted commemorative frameworks offer models for other nations grappling with how to explain, contextualize, and commemorate historical and contemporaneous state-inflicted violence. These frameworks include rewriting school curricula and textbooks, establishing archives, transforming Centers of Detention, Torture, and Extermination into museums, and creating sculpture parks dedicated to the victims of the dictatorship. What is critical to keep in mind when discussing these memory projects is that their creation and/or transformation was often met with resistance by various sectors of society who wanted to bury the history of the dictatorship, and by extension its crimes against humanity.

Ex-Centers of Detention, Torture, and Extermination

The dictatorship created Centers of Detention, Torture, and Extermination (CCDTE) throughout the country, and many of these sites were in the middle of neighborhoods in Buenos Aires, the capital city. After the dictatorship, the CCDTEs were occulted or, in some cases, demolished. Thus far approximately 750 CCDTEs have been uncovered. After years of legal and political battles, many of these spaces were transferred to the stewardship of organizations such as Memoria Abierta (Open Memory), an alliance of human rights organizations to promote democracy in Argentina dedicated to commemorating the human rights abuses of the military dictatorship and other human rights abuses. Before the former sites of CCDTEs were turned over, public artworks called attention to their sinister uses. For instance, at ex-CCDTE El Olimpo, life-size white figures were drawn on the ground, resembling police chalk outlines of murder victims. The layout of the white outlined figures surrounding the entire block of El Olimpo revealed to pedestrians the crime of political genocide that occurred at the site.

Similarly, *El Siluetazo II* was created by a group of artists in December 2004 to commemorate and conjure the presence of Argentina's disappeared. The artists hung silhouettes symbolizing the disappeared on the gates of one of the most notorious CCDTEs, Escuela de Mecánica de la Armada (The Navy Mechanics School for Officers, ESMA) to demand that the navy vacate the site (Figure 12.1). They scrawled "JUSTICIA YA" (Justice Now) across ESMA's gate. These types of silhouettes appeared in multiple manifestations beginning in 1983 (the last year of the dictatorship) and at different locations, and later functioned as recurring forms of remembrance at the actual space where the disappeared were detained. Some of the more well-known artists who contributed to *Siluetazo II* included Guillermo Kexel (b. 1955), Julio Flores (b. 1950),

Figure 12.1 Siluetazo II. 2004. ESMA, Buenos Aires
Source: Credit – Photo courtesy of Marisa Lerer, 2009

León Ferrari (1920–2013), Luis Felipe Noé (b. 1933), and Diana Dowek (b. 1942). The participating human rights organizations included Asamblea Permanente por los Derechos Humanos (Permanent Assembly on Human Rights), Asociación de Ex Detenidos-Desaparecidos (Association of Ex Detained-Disappeared Persons), Familiares de Desaparecidos y Detenidos por Razones Políticas (Relatives of Disappeared and Detained Persons for Political Reasons), and Fundación Memoria Histórica (Historic Memory Foundation), among many others. People living outside Buenos Aires were able to engage in the silhouette creation as well by submitting their designs via email for artists to recreate in an outdoor workshop in front of ESMA.

The work was created out of utilitarian, quotidian materials including cardboard, brown butcher paper, corrugated paper, and more durable materials such as colored plastic and metal. The *Siluetazo II* engaged the Madres de Plaza de Mayo and other participants who lay on the floor as artists traced their bodies to symbolize the silhouettes of their missing children and to embody their disappeared children through their own physical form. Names of the disappeared were written on the body tracings along with calls for justice, such as "My face is 30,000 faces, my name is 30,000 names." The collaborative, community-engaged art project served as indicators to passersby of the site's history and the proximity of the human rights abuses that occurred so close to their daily lives in the midst of a thriving neighborhood.

In 2002, the government handed over ESMA to the Instituto Espacio Para la Memoria (Space for Memory Institute). Several years after the transfer, the campus – where an estimated 5,000 people were detained, tortured, forced into slave labor, and assassinated – has been converted to include the Museum and Site of Memory ESMA. It now houses 15 interrelated sites of memory, human rights organizations, and civil society associations including the Space for Memory and for the Promotion and Defense of Human Rights; the Espacio Cultural Nuestros Hijos (Our Children's Cultural Center, ECUNHI), a cultural center and art gallery which hosts rotating exhibitions centered around social justice; and the Museum of the Malvinas and Islands of the South Atlantic, a museum dedicated to "Argentina's Vietnam War," started in 1982 under the dictatorship. This tying together of associations, organizations, and histories is effective in contextualizing the continued ramifications of the dictatorship's violence against the population and in promoting social justice in the contemporary moment.

By the same token, the archives from the National Commission on the Disappearance of Persons Report (CONADEP, published in 1984) and the offices of Memoria Abierta are located there. Memoria Abierta has both a physical and digitized archive that includes powerful oral histories and testimonies. It is part of the United Nations Education Scientific and Cultural Organization's (UNESCO's) Memory of the World Program and is considered cultural patrimony, emphasizing its importance on both national and international levels. In 2013, Memoria Abierta established the Museum and Site of Memory ESMA dedicated to remembering and framing Argentina's period of state-sponsored terrorism through written, firsthand testimonies, a tour of the cells that victims were held in, and a multimedia presentation on the history of the dictatorship.

A powerfully significant location at the Museum and Site of Memory ESMA is known as the "Casino" and is the site of the cells where victims were imprisoned, tortured, and forced into slave labor. This space has been strategically left bare in what sociologist Vikki Bell described as "scenes of abandonment and aesthetics of obsolescence." Visitors enter the cells with a guide; it is the guide's historical narrative that accompanies the visual bareness and invokes the history of the site. The exhibition is based on survivors' testimonies from the CONADEP Report and the 1985 Trial of the Juntas as well as declassified documents by state agencies for the trials specifically related to ESMA personnel. Rhetoric scholar Kristi M. Wilson aptly described the space as "active sources of factual or forensic truth."[14] Each guide is educated and trained, but the tour is not standardized. Eschewing rote monologues, the tours offer new insights into the period and the site, and they encourage repeat visits. Included in the bare "Casino" are labels with excerpts of survivors' testimonies about the cruel conditions and their personal experiences. Rather than simply a museum of the dictatorship's atrocities, the narrative features, excerpted testimonies, and

256　*Marisa Lerer*

sparseness work together to transform the "Casino" into a deliberately ruminative space.

The visually minimalist tour ends in a spartan room. Once visitors are situated, the lights dim, and projections light the walls with historic photographs that include photographic portraits of some of the perpetrators of crimes against humanity who worked at ESMA. Also included in the projections are perpetrators' identifying information (name, nicknames, rank, where they worked, etc.) and their status in the judicial system. The ephemeral and fleeting nature of the projections of the perpetrators is a novel strategy that allows for the display of their faces while simultaneously denying them an honorific place, which might unintentionally occur with more permanent and static forms of portraiture. Instead, the projections tie the images of the perpetrators with the text-based facts of their crimes at the site of the human rights abuses that they committed. This strategy of ensuring that the perpetrators, their names, their roles, and their crimes are not lost to history is a model for other sites that are reckoning with how to hold human rights abusers accountable in the midst of a civil society and institutions that often still support them, their innocence, and their version of historical events.

Parque de la memoria (Park of Remembrance)

Approximately 2.5 miles from the Museum and Site of Memory ESMA is the Parque de la memoria (Park of Remembrance), a memorial park next to the River Plate in Buenos Aires. Its construction began in 2001 after intense and layered debates around the creation of the park. Museum and Site of Memory ESMA's focus is on the sinister imprisonment and torture at the CCDTE, and the park's site is directly related to the river where the dictatorship "disappeared" many of the bodies of its victims. The Parque de la memoria is a place of remembrance and reflection that illuminates a dark chapter in Argentina's history through multiple sensorial experiences, including a somatic and tactile encounter of moving amid the landscape with views of the river, walking through and touching a monument dedicated to the victims of state-sponsored terrorism, and the visual experience of the park's artworks to engage with the history of the dictatorship. The park includes therapeutic and didactic commemorative strategies. The main focus is the *Monumento a las Víctimas del Terrorismo de Estado* (*Monument to the Victims of State Terrorism, MVTE*, Figure 12.2) by Baudizzone-Lestard-and-Varas Studio and the associated architects Claudio Ferrari and Daniel Becker. The monument lists names of the victims by year of disappearance and then alphabetically, and includes the age at which the victims were disappeared. Many were in their teens and early twenties. It is a sequential arrangement of four walls that zigzag in a minimalist design reminiscent of Maya Lin's (b. 1959) *Vietnam Veterans Memorial* (*VVM*, 1982) in Washington, DC. The wall of names memorial falls under what art historian Kirk Savage has described as "therapeutic memorials." Savage describes the *VVM* as the first therapeutic monument, defined as "a monument whose primary goal

Public Commemorations of Argentina's Histories of Violence 257

Figure 12.2 Baudizzone-Lestard-and-Varas Studio and the associated architects Claudio Ferrari and Daniel Becker. *Monumento a las Víctimas del Terrorismo de Estado (Monument to the Victims of State Terrorism)*, Parque de la memoria, Buenos Aires, Argentina, 2006

Source: Credit – Photograph by Orianna Gonzalez, 2018

is not to celebrate heroic service or sacrifice, as the traditional didactic monument does, but rather to heal a collective psychological injury."[15] The *MVTE* functions similarly to the *VVM* in terms of its minimalist aesthetic (geometric, abstract, serial forms), its listed names of the disappeared, and its therapeutic function for family members and visitors.[16] It is important to note that the *VVM* movingly commemorates the American war dead but says nothing about the huge number of Vietnamese military and civilian deaths.

Art historian Harriet F. Senie pointed out that "(A) memorial is rarely judged on artistic merit alone, if at all. Rather its relevance is determined by audience response."[17] In the case of the *MVTE*, its design and content are affective and shape visitors' understanding of the dictatorship. For example, members of the Madres de Plaza de Mayo Línea Fundadora – an organization that supported the construction of the park – emphasized that the monument was the only place that they had to mourn. While the monument was under construction, one member of this group, Tati Almeyda, explained, "I want to touch the name of my son. I want to touch it . . . It's going to be at a height so that everyone can touch it."[18] A Peruvian student studying in Buenos Aires sought out the space to learn about the dictatorship in Argentina and identified with

258   *Marisa Lerer*

his own country's national trauma under the violence inflicted by the Shining Path party in the 1980s.[19] Additionally, a journalist was deeply impacted by the *MVTE*'s zigzag design. She exclaimed that she originally thought that the monument just contained two walls and declared, "The fact that you turn a corner when walking to reveal even more walls made me really understand the enormity of just how many victims of state-sponsored terrorism existed."

At the end of the *MVTE*'s path, visitors are led to the art exhibition and archival space La Sala Presentes, Ahora y Siempre (Present, Now and Always Hall, PAyS, inaugurated 2010), which shares a building with the Centro de Documentación y Archivo Digital (Center for Documentation and Digital Archive). The latter contains a digital database accessible to visitors, which includes public and private documents, texts, photographs, drawings, and letters about the victims represented on the monument that encompass how they lived and how the military government disappeared them.[20] The text-based names on the *MVTE*, coupled with more personal visual data such as photographs and letters, humanize and individualize those who are listed on the monument beyond their identity as victims, and thereby tie together the therapeutic nature of the monument and the factual and personal information of the digital archive. La Sala PAyS hosts art exhibitions, talks, interviews, seminars, and workshops. It purposefully does not contain a permanent pedagogical display and therefore reflects the desire for an unfixed history of the dictatorship.

In addition to the *MVTE* and La Sala PAyS, displayed throughout the park to date are nine sculptures by renowned Argentine and international artists. Although many of the sculptures take into account the location of the River Plate and its symbolic and historical weight, Claudia Fontes's (b. 1964) *The Reconstruction of the Portrait of Pablo Míguez* (2010) is the only sculpture installed in the river itself. Fontes created a life-size full-body portrait of Pablo Míguez, who was disappeared in 1977 at the young age of 13 along with his mother. The artist was interested in depicting this particular victim of state-sponsored terrorism because they were born in the same year. *The Reconstruction of the Portrait of Pablo Míguez* is based on the testimonies of his father and the journalist Lila Pastoriza, who befriended Pablo while they were both detained at ESMA. Fontes stated,

> For me this is the representation of the condition of the disappeared: he's present, but we're prohibited from seeing him. A portrait is always a possible version . . . maybe it is the closest to reality that is possible because it's constructed on the basis of a collective memory from distinct angles.[21]

The sculpture's surface is made of highly polished stainless steel so that it reflects the river water and the sun. Fontes plays with the visual appearance and disappearance of the sculptural portrait. Depending on the weather conditions, the sculpture itself almost disappears from sight. A former curator at the Parque de la memoria, Florencia Battiti, noted that the sculpture is one of the most beloved by the public at the park. "There's a question of identification with

Public Commemorations of Argentina's Histories of Violence   259

Pablo because he was a child."[22] This ability to identify with victims of the dictatorship is crucial to the Parque de la memoria's commemoration strategy. The Parque de la memoria offers multiple vehicles for contemplating the dictatorship and remembering the disappeared through a somatic, tactile, and visual experience that transcends a detailed historical narrative.

Baldosas (Sidewalk Tiles)

Unlike the Parque de la memoria, which is located at the edge of the city, *Baldosas* (sidewalk tiles) are centrally situated in most neighborhoods in the Argentine capital and attempt to address a critical issue around the memory of the disappeared that Argentine historian Martin Capparós pointed out:

> Our companions became disappeared and in our stories without history we made them disappear a second time, we took their lives from them. We spoke of how they were objects of kidnapping, torture, and murder, and we barely spoke of how they were when they were subjects, when they chose to live destinies that included the danger of death, because they felt they had to do so. Those versions of history were among other things, a way to disappear the disappeared yet again.[23]

Baldosas textually illustrate the fight for social justice by many of the victims of state-sponsored terrorism and reconstruct their history before they fell victims to the dictatorship and the Triple A's covert kidnapping and assassination operations (Figure 12.3). *Baldosas* restore an identity to those disappeared persons who were popular activists through urban intervention, text, and a color-filled palette that contrasts with the gray cement sidewalk. The tiles look like official plaques, and examples of the texts include INES COBU STUDIED HERE/ACTIVIST/DETAINED DISAPEPARED/09–01–1976/BY STATE TERRORISM/NEIGHBORHOOD FOR MEMORY AND JUSTICE.[24] Barrios x Memoria y Justicia (Neighborhoods for Memory and Justice, Barrios x Memoria) produces and funds the tiles; it is organized by neighborhood and began as a formalized collective, community-based organization in 1996.

In some instances, sites for the installation of the *baldosas* were selected based on where activists were killed or disappeared. However, Barrios x Memoria also marks spaces where the disappeared lived, organized, protested, and studied so that pedestrians physically walk past the disappeared individual's personal history. Historian Pierre Nora proposed that private memory demands that its own history be made public; by encapsulating the private life of the disappeared in a few sentences the *baldosas* linked them to a public space.[25] Barrios x Memoria stated:

> The goal of this activity, represented in the largest quantity of neighborhoods possible, is to leave a mark of our companions amongst the traffic in each of their neighborhoods, because they are our fallen companions and

Figure 12.3 Barrios por Memoria y Justicia. *Baldosas (Sidewalk Tiles)*, n.d., Buenos Aires, Argentina

Source: Credit – Photo courtesy of Marisa Lerer, 2018

they experienced all possible forms of negation. Their lives were negated when they were kidnapped and they were denied their humanity. They were denied their identity and their rights. They were denied their bodies when they were assassinated and they were denied their social and political activism. They were denied justice. Today we attempt to create just reparations and recognition by rescuing their sociopolitical values. Through them we try to reflect that activism, their activism, is a living position worthy of imitation.[26]

Like many of the memorial projects discussed earlier, Barrios x Memoria simultaneously memorialized the victims of state-sponsored terrorism while seeking state-sponsored justice. The *baldosas* marked homes and institutions throughout neighborhoods in Buenos Aires, which encouraged reflection on the proliferation of the dictatorship's operations in the public sphere and critical reevaluation of the excuse of the collective declaration "We didn't know" by the Argentine citizenry under the dictatorship. In some cases, the *baldosas* also functioned as "therapeutic memorials" by allowing for the public grief of the relatives of the disappeared, leading to catharsis. For instance, a sister of a disappeared person revealed, "I feel that I socialized a living pain that I kept private for thirty years," and a mother stated, "Now I can return to stepping on this sidewalk."[27] The *baldosas* are an indexical sign of the disappeared and represent national trauma at a localized site.

The Violence of Historical Omission

A proliferation of other memorials have been and are being created across Argentina in the form of built and less physically tangible commemorations. For instance, on the 30th anniversary of the military coup in 2006, the National Day of Memory for Truth and Justice became an official public holiday celebrated annually on March 24. In 2021, on the 45th anniversary of the military coup, Argentina's Ministry of the Interior initiated the campaign #Planatamos Memoria (We Plant Memory) with the goal of planting 30,000 trees in honor of the detained-disappeared. To mark the initiative, grandchildren of the disappeared together with human rights organizations planted a tree at the Museum and Site of Memory ESMA.

Foundationally, in addition to the national developments around physical commemorations, scholars and social justice movements contextualized the dictatorship within the history of Argentina prior to the junta. This challenge to the dictatorship's official history has also shed light on the erroneous and untold histories of the nation from previous eras, including the human rights abuses committed in Argentina after the country gained its independence from Spain in 1816. Indigenous genocide and enslavement – which was not outlawed until 1853 – are part of a long history of violence imbedded into the founding of the nation. In 1983, human rights organizations publicly connected the dictatorship's crimes against humanity to the legacy of violence within the first century of the nation's founding by positioning the dictatorship's political genocide within the context of the genocide of Indigenous peoples including the Tehuelches, Pehuenches, Picunches, and Pehuelches. Previously celebrated "founding fathers" such as President Julio Argentino Roca (in office 1898–1904), who perpetuated the genocide against First Nations while serving as a general, were publicly framed in a new light. Reckoning with historic monuments dedicated to figures such as Roca began in 1983 with the call to remove a statue and street names dedicated to this former president. As in the United States, reexamining who is represented in the public sphere is paramount to the historical visual culture of Argentina.

Connecting the nineteenth-century history of the formation of Argentina as a nation with the military dictatorship is urgent to consider as well because of the violence of omission of Africans and Afro-descendants in Argentina in the visual public sphere. The variety of memorials to victims of state-sponsored terrorism which now proliferate throughout Argentine cities can serve as a model for revisiting the country's history of slavery. Memorials to enslaved people and Afro-Argentine contributions to the nation are rare, and as legal scholar Alí Delgado pointed out, "There are no black journalists or politicians,

262 *Marisa Lerer*

but Argentina's poor barrios [neighborhoods] are full of Afro-descendants. So are our prisons, just like in the United States."[28] The parallel to US prison practices that Delgado identifies, an extension of institutionalized racism, is significant when addressing the impact of Argentine human rights organizations' strategies on social justice movements in the United States and in other regions of the world.

Motherhood and International Solidarity

Argentina's grappling with legacies of violence in public space has had an impact beyond its own region. Social justice organizations around the world have adopted and adapted some of the strategies employed by organizations protesting Argentina's last military dictatorship, such as amplifying the role of motherhood in public space and marching with photographs of victims of state-sponsored violence. Organizations have embraced commemorative and protest strategies with origins in Argentina's family-based, grassroots human rights organizations for protesting disappearance. For example, in March 2011, in Cairo, in the midst of Egypt's Arab Spring, family members held aloft official passport photographs of their missing relatives outside of the Secret Police Headquarters. The My Right to Know Campaign organized by the Families of Lebanese Victims of Enforced Disappearance in Syria also emphasizes the status of motherhood and displays official photographs of disappeared loved ones. Mothers have been a potent and enduring force in international social justice movements for decades.

Geographer Ruthie Wilson Gilmore drew parallels between the Mothers of the Plaza de Mayo and the racial justice movement in the United States through women-led oppositional struggles. For example, the US-based Mothers Reclaiming Our Children (Mothers ROC) "was developed to support Black and Latino men who were arrested and incarcerated in Los Angeles on false or exaggerated charges" and to work against the militarization of the Los Angeles Police Department.[29] Mothers ROC "self-consciously identifies" with other activist mothers from the Global South and deliberately invokes "South American women's struggles."[30] The members echoed the Madres de Plaza de Mayo's amplification of the strength of motherhood as a public political presence and protected status. Like the Madres de Plaza de Mayo, Mothers ROC members mobilize "the power of motherhood to challenge the legitimacy of the changing state" in their protests against mass incarceration, and while protesting, hold aloft signs with their children's portraits.[31] The primacy of motherhood in protest is also centered in Mothers of the Movement (formed in 2013), which is an organization of women responding to the deaths of their Black children killed by police officers and gun violence in the United States.

Many other organizations and individuals have taken to marching with photographs and portraits of victims of police violence, echoing the photos of Argentina's disappeared that are featured in protest marches and commemorations to this day. One of many powerful instances of visual modes of dissent occurred in the "March With The Families" demonstration in New York on June 10, 2020, which was part of the uprising in support of Black Lives Matter across the United States in the wake of the murder of George Floyd by police officer Derek Chauvin and in response to the thousands of people killed by police and racist violence. Constance Malcolm, the mother of Ramarley Graham who, at 18, was killed by police in 2012 in New York, marched with a photograph of her son and his name on a placard just as the Madres de Plaza de Mayo began doing in the 1970s. Like the ephemeral and mobilized photographs of Argentina's disappeared, the photographs of victims of police violence bring their visual presence and memory into public space in an effort to demand justice, hold the perpetrators accountable, and advocate for systemic change.

Conclusion

Senie contended that "Permanent memorials are meant to last, to provide symbols and structures for public mourning and then for remembering. Formally and through usage over time, they may convey or distort actual events."[32] This is a caution that should be heeded when examining memorials to victims of state-sponsored terrorism across the globe and specifically in Argentina, given the contentious nature of the historical discourses. However, the multiple typologies, sites, and sponsors of memorials dedicated to the victims of state-sponsored terrorism offer diverse yet interconnected narratives that keep the complicated and complex history of the dictatorship and the personal lives of its victims in public view. The continued embrace of distinct memorial paradigms in contrastive contexts, spaces, and epochs in relation to the dictatorship counters the junta's misleading monolithic account. The memorials instead maintain space for multiple approaches so that people can come to understand that violent period in Argentine history and commemorate the victims in their own terms.

These memorials also have a larger significance beyond Argentina's borders and are part of late twentieth- and early twenty-first-century shift in international commemorative practices. Savage points out that when monuments became more prevalent in the nineteenth century, "disaster monuments were essentially unknown. Public monuments did not commemorate victims."[33] The monuments and memorials discussed here are part of a more recent trend in monuments that focus on the trauma of public violence. They diverge from earlier monuments, which were dedicated to proselytizing a positive national identity linked to progress.[34] The memorials to the victims of state-sponsored terrorism disrupt the narrative of a nation's forward movement and instead open up the horrors of the dictatorship while drawing connections to the violence perpetuated throughout Argentina's history from its very founding as a nation. The memorials also align with an international impulse to memorialize victims rather than perpetuating national origin myths around purported heroes.

264 *Marisa Lerer*

The violence by the dictatorship has a long reach into the contemporary moment and is countered with expanded notions of commemoration, which entail living memorials for activism and education such as ex-CCDTE El Olimpo's dedicated space for tutoring students and youth arts organizations. Perhaps the most gripping and galvanizing commemoration of this historical time period is the Madres de Plaza de Mayo – many of them in their nineties – who, along with their supporters, continued to march every Thursday in the Plaza de Mayo with the photographs of their children held high, demanding justice and commemorating their disappeared loved ones. During the coronavirus pandemic, these marches could no longer take place at the plaza; however, they were continued through online programming in the virtual public sphere. The proliferation of memory projects in Argentina speaks to the immense effort by the mothers of the disappeared, other human rights organizations, and various sectors of civil society to bring the dictatorship's crimes to light and honor its victims amid manifold types of public spaces.

Notes

1 Ronaldo Munck, "Argentina, or the Political Economy of Collapse," *International Journal of Political Economy*, Vol. 31, No. 3 (2001), pp. 67–88, www.jstor.org.www.library.manhattan.edu/stable/40470786 [Accessed July 9, 2021].
2 Cezar Mariano Nilson, *Operación Cóndor. Terrorismo de Estado en el Cono Sur* (Buenos Aires: Lholé-Lumen, 1998).
3 Chile and the United States: Declassified Documents Relating to the Military Coup, 1970–1976, FBI, Operation Condor Cable, September 28, 1976, George Washington University, www.gwu.edu/~nsarchiv/NSAEBB/NSAEBB8/ch23-02.htm [Accessed June 30, 2021].
4 Rita Arditti, *Searching for Life: The Grandmothers of the Plaza de Mayo and the Disappeared Children of Argentina* (Berkeley, CA: University of California Press, 1999), p. 14.
5 Conadep, "Part IV Recommendations and Conclusions," *Núnca Más Never Again Report of Conadep*, 1984, http://web.archive.org/web/20031019155334/nuncamas.org/english/library/nevagain/nevagain_283.htm [Accessed May 4, 2021].
6 Jennifer G. Schirmer, "'Those Who Die for Life Cannot Be Called Dead:' Women and Human Rights Protest in Latin America," *Feminist Review*, No. 32 (July 1, 1989), p. 5.
7 Andrea Giunta, "Bodies of History: The Avant-Garde, Politics, and Violence in Contemporary Argentinean Art," in *Cantos Paralelos: Visual Parody in Contemporary Argentinean Art* (Austin, TX: Jack S. Blanton Museum of Art, 1999), p. 153.
8 Conadep, "Part VI Recommendations and Conclusions," *Núnca Más Never Again Report of Conadep*, 1984, http://web.archive.org/web/20031019155334/nuncamas.org/english/library/nevagain/nevagain_283.htm [Accessed May 12, 2021].
9 *El Clarín*, Buenos Aires, March 18, 1981, cited in Conadep, "Part V The Doctrine Behind the Repression."
10 Diana Taylor, *Disappearing Acts: Spectacles of Gender and Nationalism in Argentina's "Dirty War,"* p. 198.
11 Hebe De Bonafini, interview with Juan Gelman and Mara la Madrid, *Ni El Flaco Perdón De Diós: Hijos De Desaparecidos* (Buenos Aires: Planeta, 1997), p. 55. "Nosotras, nuestra lucha y nuestro dolor, los hicimos públicos y colectivos y juntas fuimos a un lugar público, la Plaza, para que nos viera todo el mundo." All translations are by the author unless otherwise noted.

Public Commemorations of Argentina's Histories of Violence   265

12 Marguerite Feitlowitz, *A Lexicon of Terror: Argentina and the Legacies of Torture* (New York: Oxford University Press, 1998), p. 192.

13 "Menem elogió a los militares y advirtió contra el revanchismo," *Clarín*, Buenos Aires, June 21, 1998. revanchismohttp://edant.clarin.com/diario/1998/06/21/t-00801d.htm [Accessed February 11, 2020].

14 Kristi M. Wilson, "Building Memory: Museums, Trauma, and Aesthetics of Confrontation in Argentina," *Latin American Perspectives*, Vol. 43, No. 5 (2016), p. 114.

15 Kirk Savage, "Trauma, Healing, and the Therapeutic Monument," in Daniel Sherman and Terry Nardin, eds., *Terror, Culture, Politics: Rethinking 9/11* (Bloomington, IN: University of Indiana Press, 2006), p. 106.

16 To read more on the Parque de la memoria and the debates around its creation, see: Lerer, "Competing for Memory: Argentina's Parque de la memoria," *Public Art Dialogue*, Vol. 3, No. 1 (2013), pp. 58–77.

17 Harriet F. Senie, *Memorials to Shattered Myths: Vietnam to 9/11* (New York: Oxford University Press, 2016), p. 19.

18 Gustavo Bruzzone, "Quiero tocar el number de mi hijo: Conversación con Tati Almeyda de Madres de Plaza de Mayo, Línea Fundadora," *Ramona: Revista de Artes Visuales Argentina*, Vol. 9, No. 10 (2001), p. 12.

19 Interviews by author, Buenos Aires, August 2014.

20 The database can be accessed at http://basededatos.parquedelamemoria.org.ar/registros/2123/.

21 Claudio Fontes quoted in "Parque de la Memoria: detalles de la única obra que está en las aguas del Río de la Plata," *Buenos Aires Ciudad*, www.buenosaires.gob.ar/laciudad/noticias/parque-de-la-memoria-detalles-de-la-unica-obra-que-esta-en-las-aguas-del-rio-de-la [Accessed June 20, 2021]. "Para mí, esta es la representación de la condición del desaparecido: está presente, pero se nos está vedado verlo. Un retrato es siempre una posible versión . . . tal vez ésta es la más real posible porque está construida en base a la memoria colectiva desde distintos ángulos."

22 Florencia Battiti, "Parque de la Memoria: detalles de la única obra que está en las aguas del Río de la Plata," "Es una de las más queridas por el público de este lugar . . . Hay una cuestión de identificación con el personaje con este adolescente."

23 Martin Capparós, "Reappearances," in *Buena Memoria: A Photographic Essay by Marcelo Brodsky* (Buenos Aires: La Marca, 1997), p. 11.

24 AQUI ESTUDIO/INES COBU/MILITANTE POPULAR/DETENIDA DESA-PARECIDA/01–09–1976/POR EL TERRORISM DE ESTADO/BARRIO X MEMORIA Y JUSTICA.

25 Pierre Nora, Kritzman, and Goldhammer, *Realms of Memory: Rethinking the French Past: [the Construction of the French Past]. Vol. 1, Conflicts and Divisions.*

26 Barrios por Memoria y Justicia, *Baldosas x la Memoria* (Buenos Aires: Instituto Espacio para la Memoria, 2008), p. 221. "El sentido de esta actividad, en la cual promovemos estén representandos la mayor cantidad de barrios posibles, es dejar una huella del tránsito de los compañeros por cada uno de sus barrios, porque son nuestros caídos y tuvieron todas las negaciones posibles. Se los negó cuando los secuestraban y se negó su humanidad. Se les negó su identidad y sus derechos. Se les negó sus cuerpos cuando los asesinababan, se les negó su inserción social y política, su militancia. Se les negó su Justicia. Hoy intentamos justas reparaciones y reconcimientos, intentamos rescatar esos valores, intentamos reflejar a través de ellos que la militancia, esa militancia, es una actitud de vida digna de imitar."

27 Barrios por Memoria y Justicia, p. 24. "Siento que socialicé un duelo vivido como privado durante treinta años." "Ahora podré volver a pisar esta vereda."

28 Alí Delgado quoted in Uki Goñi, "Time to Challenge Argentina's White European Self-Image, Black History Experts Say," *The Guardian*, May 31, 2021, www.theguardian.com/world/2021/may/31/argentina-white-european-racism-history [Accessed May 31, 2021].

266 Marisa Lerer

29 Mothers Reclaiming Our Children, https://mothersroc.home.blog/ [Accessed July 14, 2021].
30 Ruthie Wilson Gilmore, "You Have Dislodged a Boulder: Mothers and Prisoners in the Post Keynesian California Landscape," *Transforming Anthropology*, Vol. 8, No. 1 (1999), p. 13.
31 Wilson Gilmore, "You Have Dislodged a Boulder," p. 14.
32 Senie, *Memorials to Shattered Myths*, pp. 9–10.
33 Savage, "Trauma, Healing, and the Therapeutic Monument," p. 103.
34 Savage, p. 103.

13 The Violence of the Vietnam War in the Memorialized American Landscape

Elise Lemire

The Vietnam Veterans Memorial is unusual in the history of American war memorialization. Not a soaring obelisk nor a heroic representational statue, it is in the form of a wound slashed into the national body that is Washington DC's memorial landscape. The names of over 50,000 American war dead engraved in the stacked granite tablets that comprise The Wall, as the memorial is popularly known, are at least a partial acknowledgment of the cost Americans paid for their government's global ambitions. But while between four and five million people visit this site of national mourning and regret in a typical year, virtually every American passes daily a very different memorial to the Vietnam War that presents the United States as the doleful victim, not of its own decisions, but of the Vietnamese. The POW/MIA (Prisoner of War/Missing in Action) flag flies in every town across America, often at multiple sites. This essay recounts the central role the organization Vietnam Veterans Against the War (VVAW) played in getting the American public to acknowledge that the Vietnam War was an American crime against both the American citizenry and the people of Southeast Asia, as well as the federal government's success in countering VVAW's narrative, first with the POW/MIA campaign and later with a return to traditional war memorialization practices.

American Technowar in Southeast Asia

In the largest air attack campaign launched in the nation's history, the United States dropped more bombs on Southeast Asia than were dropped on all of Europe by every side combined during WWII. The sophisticated technical means of delivery was also unprecedented in world history. The United States used fast and low-flying helicopters to fire grenades, rockets, and bullets as well as to spray herbicides, while it launched supersonic fighter-bombers from massive naval aircraft carriers four times the size of those the United States deployed in WWII. Equipped with on-board radar and capable of flying at unprecedented speeds and altitudes, these planes were used to fire air-to-air and air-to-ground missiles, as well as to drop various kinds of bombs, including precise television- and laser-guided bombs as well as cluster bombs, which release explosive bomblets over a wide area or disperse chemical or biological

DOI: 10.4324/9781003217848-19

268   *Elise Lemire*

weapons. While napalm, a petrochemical mixed with gel that causes fatal burns from temperatures 8 to 12 times the boiling point of water, had been used immediately after its development in the US lab as a weapon in WWII and was used by the US military again in Vietnam, herbicide and defoliant chemicals were first used by the United States in Vietnam. Despite Geneva Protocols regulating the use of chemical and biological weapons and scientists' concerns about the human side effects, the US military used Agent Orange and other chemicals to destroy the enemy's ground cover as well as civilian food supplies, in the process causing both immediate and inter-generational health problems for both the Vietnamese and exposed US personnel, including cancer and severe birth defects. And at the same time as the United States was reigning terror on the region from both the sea and the air, it was also deploying ground troops armed with new automatic weaponry that dramatically increased the number of bullets per second and the strength of propulsion over WWII levels. The M16 shot bullets that break into fragments on impact, causing devastating wounds.

VVAW Enters the Fray

In February 1971, six years after the United States first sent ground troops into Vietnam on the premise that communism would otherwise spread throughout Asia, 200 Vietnam veterans testified at VVAW's Winter Soldier Investigation in Detroit to what the US government did not want the American public to know, namely that by withstanding the unprecedented level of force levied by the United States, the Vietnamese had utterly demoralized American military personnel. Intent on ridding their country of an imperialist invader, the Vietnamese built a massive volunteer army, employed guerrilla tactics, and made full use of a terrain they knew far better than the Americans, even tunneling underground. Unable to accept that their new technology would not prevail against a country the size of California and with little regard for mounting causalities on both sides, American officials were refusing to alter their strategies. Every day, officers ordered American ground troops on search-and-destroy missions meant to attract engagement and thus reveal the enemy's position so that those under attack could relay the enemy's geographical coordinates to an American base that would then deploy massive air power. What this meant in practice was that American soldiers were being used as bait and with deadly results as they ran into landmines and endured relentless sniper fire. Typically, by the time air support arrived, the Americans had already suffered causalities with no hope of retaliation. The enemy had already vanished.

VVAW's national spokesman, a Yale-educated naval lieutenant named John Kerry, brought a summary of the veterans' testimonies to Washington, DC, where 1,200 Vietnam veterans joined him for a 5-day protest VVAW called Operation Dewey Canyon III (Operation DCIII) in a reproach of US Operations Dewey Canyon I and II, both secret and illegal missions the United States had carried out in the neutral country of Laos. Invited to address the Senate

The Violence of the Vietnam War 269

Foreign Relations Committee, Kerry appeared in his fatigues and reeled off a list of horrifically violent actions being carried out by American troops.

> They told stories that at times they had personally raped, cut off ears, cut off heads, taped wires from portable telephones to human genitals and turned up the power, cut off limbs, blown up bodies, randomly shot at civilians, razed villages in fashion reminiscent of Ghengis Khan, shot cattle and dogs for fun, poisoned food stocks, and generally ravaged the countryside of South Vietnam in addition to the normal ravage of war and the normal and very particular ravaging which is done by the applied bombing power of this country.[1]

It was an astounding list of 11 kinds of atrocities. Television news producers who had ignored the Detroit hearings were riveted by this Ivy Leaguer's rebuke of a country that, if not for the Vietnam War, would have provided him with a seamless transition from college to the halls of America's most powerful institutions. Kerry's report of widespread American war crimes against civilians was covered by each of the major networks in an admission that the My Lai Massacre, during which American troops murdered as many as 500 Vietnamese civilians and about which the public first learned in the fall of 1969, was, in VVAW's terms, "no unusual occurrence."[2]

While Kerry said that cattle and dogs were shot by US troops "for fun," he never allowed listeners to blame the soldiers whose atrocities he enumerated. The fault lay, he asserted, with the war's chief architects, "McNamara, Rostow, Bundy, Gilpatrick, and so many others." America's soldiers were the victims of what Kerry described as these men's racist and violent impulses, arguing that they forced American troops to use weapons against the Vietnamese that "I do not believe this country would dream of using were we fighting in the European theater." Appropriating American military parlance for VVAW's cause, Kerry explained that the organization had come to the nation's capital on "one last mission," namely "to search out and destroy the last vestige of this barbaric war, to pacify our own hearts, to conquer the hate and fear that have driven this country these last ten years and more." He fell short of calling the denial of another country its independence a crime, but he did insist the Vietnam War was "a mistake." And he closed by asking senators to imagine a time "thirty years from now" when "our brothers go down the street without a leg, without an arm, or a face, and little boys ask why."[3]

On the last day of the protest, VVAW underscored Kerry's message that America's troops had been morally injured by giving members an opportunity to throw away their war medals. One photograph of the more than 800 veterans who participated captures a veteran identifiable as a helicopter pilot by the wings pinned to his olive drab shirt and the Ugly Angels patch on his leather flight jacket in the act of throwing away a Silver Star. Hurled over a fence erected by the Nixon administration to keep the veterans distant from the usually open grounds of the US Capitol Building, the third-highest combat medal

270 *Elise Lemire*

awarded by the US military would land on a pile of other medals and commendations next to which the veterans had erected a sign lettered with a single word: "TRASH." The pilot's long curls signaled his rejection of the united front put on by American military personnel with its requirement of shortly clipped hair, while his anguished expression signified the emotional cost of realizing that what was an honor in WWI and WWII had become a symbol of American war crimes and, worse, that he had played his part in those crimes. Only by throwing away their medals could he and the other veterans attempt to disburden themselves of their guilt and teach their countrymen the necessity of ending the Vietnam War immediately.[4]

Other press photographs of Operation DCIII focused on the physical cost to American troops, which VVAW was careful to foreground by asking the wounded to lead the various marches and events they staged that week. As a result, no one, except for Kerry, was photographed more than 20-year-old Bill Wyman of Boston who had lost both of his legs when his jeep ran over a landmine toward the end of his tour in Vietnam. One of the several photographs of him that ran in newspapers across the country showed him sitting on the ground of the veterans' encampment, his stumps prominently sticking out toward the viewer.[5]

VVAW's insertion of the Vietnam veterans' experiences into the public's consciousness killed the WWII image of the heroic and impenetrable American soldier liberating the world from fascism and replaced it with two new images: those GIs who were going berserk in Vietnam and VVAW's new melding of fatigue-clad soldier, peace-loving, long-haired hippy, and grievously injured American. Horrified by the former, the public embraced the latter.[6]

Comparing the Vietnam War to the American Revolution

After the antiwar veterans' week-long occupation of the nation's capital finally secured VVAW the national appreciation that had eluded the organization since its founding in 1967, the New England chapter returned to its headquarters in Cambridge, Massachusetts, determined to keep up the pressure on the federal government to end the war immediately. VVAW-New England (VVAW-NE) invited local veterans, including those convalescing at area Veterans Administration hospitals, and the two nearest VVAW chapters, VVAW-Connecticut and VVAW-Rhode Island, to join their efforts over the upcoming Memorial Day weekend.[7]

Rather than repeat the multi-event protest that was Operation DCIII, VVAW-NE decided to stage a repeat of Operation RAW (so called because "war" spelled backward captured how the veterans were feeling while also serving as an acronym for what the veterans wanted, a "Rapid American Withdrawal"). The previous fall, antiwar Vietnam veterans had spent Labor Day weekend marching 86 miles from Morristown, New Jersey, to Valley Forge, Pennsylvania, both of which were Continental Army encampment sites during two brutally cold winters of the Revolutionary War. The purpose of that

The Violence of the Vietnam War   271

march route had been to establish that the veterans were not anything like those troops who, having deserted, Thomas Paine castigated as "summer soldiers." Rather, as the name they chose for the Detroit hearings underscored, they were, being indefatigable patriots, "winter soldiers." The New England veterans believed a multi-day march was the perfect means of displaying their commitment, while also giving them an opportunity to be seen protesting by as many people as possible. They repeated the selection of a route that would highlight their patriotism, this time determining to follow the one poet Henry Wadsworth Longfellow described Paul Revere taking on the night of April 18, 1775, to warn the towns to the west of Boston that the imperial troops occupying that port city were moving to destroy the defiant colonists' secreted military stores. It was a route that would have the added benefit of taking the veterans to Concord's Old North Bridge, the Battle Road, the Lexington Battle Green, and Bunker Hill. Each of these four Revolutionary War battlefields would be an opportune venue to perform the mock search-and-destroy missions VVAW had started staging the year before as a means of showing the public what was being done in its name. Staged at the nation's sacred birth sites, they would also show the citizenry how far the nation had veered from its founding ideals. One, perhaps unintended, consequence that resulted in their mass arrest was that the three participating VVAW chapters would end up revealing as mythic five narratives about war promulgated at these memorialized Revolutionary War sites.

Myth 1: War Is Creativity and Swiftness

What most Americans know about Paul Revere comes from Longfellow's popular and widely memorized 1860 poem "Paul Revere's Ride." The poet credits Revere's semaphore system in the form of signal lanterns flashed from Boston's Old North Church and his subsequent ride on horseback from Charlestown to Concord with giving the colonial militia enough advance warning to gain the upper hand that day and ultimately win the war. The truth is far more complicated: Revere was not the only alarm rider that night; the warning the colonists also spread through church bells and gunshots traveled faster than his or anyone else's speeding horse ever could; the King's troops were literally bogged down in a Cambridge swamp for so long that the speed of the alarm was largely irrelevant anyway; and Revere was captured in Lincoln, although another patriot did succeed in carrying his message the last few miles to Concord. Still, the myth of a single person using creativity and alacrity to outsmart the world's most powerful army has proven so appealing that it is far more widely believed than these historical facts.[8]

The memorialized landscape repeats Longellow's assertions. On Boston's Paul Revere Mall, for example, a monumental equestrian statue by Cyrus E. Dallin of Revere en route to Lexington and Concord also promotes the idea that creativity and alacrity are as efficacious as actual fighting. Dallin's Revere is dressed in clothes cut to look like a Continental Army uniform. He is far leaner and stronger than his 1768–1770 portrait by John Singleton Copley

272 *Elise Lemire*

indicates he actually was. And while Revere actually rode a mare on the night of April 18, 1775, Dallin shows him easily controlling a mighty stallion by standing up in his stirrups to arrest the stallion's course so he can shout his warning down to colonists who the statue thus imagines as far smaller than the strapping Revere in size. The public is asked to consider that Revere's invention of a signal system flashed from the nearby Old North Church's steeple and his ability to marshal the power of a massive steed over a long distance was just as, if not more, important than the Continental Army's efforts in winning the American Revolution.[9]

Rather than attempt access to the steeple of the Old North Church, a couple of New England Vietnam veterans began their protest by shooting flares into the sky over the church on the Friday afternoon before Memorial Day. "One if by land, two if by sea, and three if by air." By shooting off six flares in total, VVAW signaled that the United States was attacking Vietnam from all three directions and thereby declared that war is not a contest of speed or creativity. It is a contest in which combatants attempt to injure and kill each other.[10]

Myth 2: War Is Freeing

By early Friday evening, 60 or so veterans had converged at the Old North Bridge in Concord, having determined to cover Longfellow's version of Revere's route in reverse in order to underscore that the nation was traveling away from its founding ideals. They found the replica bridge flanked by a memorial obelisk on one side and Daniel Chester French's famous statue of a Minute Man on the other, the latter of which, like Dallin's statue, defines war in nonviolent terms.

French's statue picks up where the Revere myth leaves off. By pushing forward the actual arrival time of the warning in Concord from 2 am to several hours after sunrise, he was able to depict a farmer in his fields. Having received the alarm that British Regulars were marching to Concord to find and destroy the colonists' hidden military stores, the farmer stops his plow in its furrow, picks up his musket, and steps toward the direction of the oncoming troops, fully prepared at a moment's notice to risk his life protecting what the colonists claimed were their natural rights. By consulting photographs, French created a likeness of the descendants of 30-year-old Acton Captain Isaac Davis, who tirelessly trained and carefully outfitted his local militia in the weeks leading up to the encounter at the bridge and who volunteered to lead the approach to it. French depicts Davis on a warm spring day. The patriot has removed his coat and rolled up his sleeves, revealing what French imagines to be a well-muscled forearm and a broad chest. The sculptor makes no reference to the fact that Davis was shot in the heart and instantly killed nor to the private anguish of Davis' wife, their four young children, or his parents and siblings. Only those visitors steeped in local history are prompted by the statue to mourn the loss of this patriot. Everyone else is asked to focus on the farmer's great physical strength, his ready weapon, and the fact of his hand lingering on his plow. This last detail carries significant weight as it indicates that this man prefers peaceable pursuits over fighting. Like Cincinnatus, French's farmer will only leave his fields when called by his country and even then with every intention to return to his fields when his military work is done. What the memorialized landscape says, in other words, is that Americans won the war because they are peaceable people who only veer away from peaceable actions such as feeding their families for the purpose of defending themselves and their rights. It is an astounding calculus in which the act of tearing open flesh is elided so that war can be defined as the act of freeing, in this case freeing American colonists from the imperial and tyrannical British.

The veterans were already well aware that the Lexington Selectmen had denied their request to perform mock search-and-destroy missions in Lexington and to camp Saturday night on the Lexington Battle Green, even despite being asked to reconsider their stance by Lexington residents who wanted to support the veterans' efforts. After a dinner supplied to them by local Concord supporters on Friday night, the veterans decided to commence their weekend march by broadening their appropriation of Revolutionary War symbols. While they were still intent on carrying a message to the people as so many Paul Reveres, they also voted to commit civil disobedience in Lexington in what the press release they issued after the vote described as "the tradition of the Minute Men."[11]

To underscore their affiliation with those colonial militiamen charged by their peers with being ready at a moment's notice, the veterans orchestrated their departure on Saturday morning carefully, forming two lines under the Minute Man Statue and then proceeding eastward across the arched bridge toward the obelisk on the other side and, ultimately, Lexington. They asked the press to wait on the obelisk side such that when the veterans crested the bridge, French's statue appeared to march alongside them, being one of them.

However, when, as had been VVAW's practice, the war wounded were asked to lead the way in a display of what the Vietnam War had cost them, the myth that war is freeing was debunked. The *Boston Globe* ran a photo above the fold on its front page of a paralyzed veteran in a wheelchair being pushed over the bridge by another veteran with French's statue behind them (Figure 13.1). The photograph revealed the significant contrast between the veterans' wartime experiences and the statue's promise. While the statue creates the illusion that American soldiers are simultaneously inviolate and peaceable, the VVAW soldiers in the photograph have suffered irreversible injury serving in a violent and immoral war. In other words, even as the veterans meant to align themselves with the mythical farmer with whom they shared the imperative to resist injustice, they were also restoring to the statue the heartbreaking story of the young father who was shot in the chest by an imperial army. Their message about the war in Vietnam meant they had to dramatically and forcefully deconstruct some of the United States' most fundamental myths, first among them that Americans are the descendants of Cincinnatus and that, as such, they only engage in the act of freeing for a short period of time before returning to their fields, and that, because the United States is a country with a righteous cause, its soldiers are never physically hurt or emotionally traumatized by war.

Figure 13.1 Wounded Vietnam Veteran commences antiwar march at Concord's Minute Man statue

Source: Credit – Boston Public Library/United Press International

Myth 3: War Is Immortality

The veterans' first stop along their march route was at the second of the four memorial obelisks they would pass that weekend. In addition to the one at the Old North Bridge, another on the Lexington Battle Green, and the largest on Bunker (really Breed's) Hill in Charlestown, there is a 30-foot memorial obelisk in Concord's Monument Square raised in memory of those residents who died in the Civil War and which, by 1971, stood alongside other monuments, including a large granite boulder embedded with a plaque listing the town's WWI dead. Here, too, the veterans' goal was to write war's violence back into a landscape whose memorialization erases it.

An advanced group of veterans in fatigues and armed with very realistic-looking toy M16s rushed out into the grassy expanse in the middle of the square and began throwing civilians up against the war monuments while demanding to know if they were "VC" or Viet Cong. Locals out enjoying the spring morning or heading downtown to shop stopped to gape as fliers were pressed into their hands explaining that this is what happened daily in Vietnam. Within minutes, the captives, all of whom had rehearsed this mock search-and-destroy mission with the veterans and many of whom had performed with them the month before on Boston Common (Figure 13.2), were tied up and being questioned. None of their answers swayed the brutish soldiers who summarily pretended to execute them only to pick them up by their arms and legs and toss them into a growing pile of limp bodies at the base of the obelisk.

While obelisks were widely used as a funereal form in American cemeteries and fulfill this function as war memorials to those who died on the battlefield, they are also shrines to the nation itself and specifically to its expansionist efforts. Taken as trophies, they have long been a means for conquerors to mark their expanding power. In 10 bc, the Emperor Augustus erected in the Circus Maximus in Rome an obelisk originally installed by Ramesses II in Heliopolis. And after Napoleon's excursion to Egypt in 1798, the French took and installed in Paris a 3,000-year-old obelisk originally situated outside of Luxor Temple. The Bunker Hill Monument Association also seems to have chosen the obelisk shape as a means of claiming the title of world's greatest civilization. Addressing a crowd of 100,000 at the laying of the cornerstone for the ultimately 221-foot-tall Bunker Hill obelisk, Senator Daniel Webster made clear that Americans were also using the obelisk form to make a claim for their own greatness. "We wish," he intoned, "that the last object to the sight of him who leaves his native shore, and the first to gladden his who revisits it, may be something which shall remind him of the liberty and the glory of his country."[12]

With a pile of lifeless people pretending to be murdered Vietnamese civilians at its base, the Concord obelisk in Monument Square was revealed for what it is. While it reminds the community to always remember the war dead and in doing so does confer some version of everlasting life, it is also a reminder that the nation continues to ask the citizenry to express their patriotism with

Figure 13.2 Members of VVAW-NE perform a mock search-and-destroy mission on the Boston Common, April 14, 1971

Source: Credit – Jeff Albertson Photograph Collection, Robert S. Cox Special Collections and University Archives Research Center

The Violence of the Vietnam War 277

the gift of killing others and of their own violent deaths on the battlefield. Be "faithful unto death," demands the Concord obelisk into whose base these words are carved. In the Vietnam War era, this meant being faithful to a nation that had illegally invaded another. And thus, before the veterans left the square to resume their march to Lexington, one of them aimed his Mattel M–16 at the obelisk, pulled back the cocking lever, and let rip the sound of automatic gunfire in rejection of its demand to participate in the deadly imperialist aims the obelisk form embodies.

Myth 4: War Is Preparedness

The veterans' route from Monument Square in Concord to the Lexington Battle Green took them along the Battle Road, which like the Old North Bridge area is part of what was then still a very new national park.

By the 1950s, the federal government's military spending at the Massachusetts Institute of Technology and Harvard had significantly altered the greater Boston area. Small farm towns had been transformed into suburbs connected by multilane highways to industrial parks where computer memory, radar transmitting tubes, satellite antennas, guidance systems, and more were designed and manufactured by the thousands of well-educated newcomers who were delighted to work in modern glass and steel buildings nestled into a bucolic landscape with a storied history. While the road along which the colonists had engaged in an hours-long running battle with the retreating imperial troops on April 19, 1775, was already unrecognizable along its easternmost portion, it was still lined with stone walls and open fields in parts of Concord, Lincoln, and Lexington, although here too commercial and residential development was fast encroaching. This was particularly true where the Battle Road abutted the large Air Force base where the many weapons labs that had spun off from their academic birthplaces were located.

In 1959, the federal government decided to create a national park in this residential area and used the threat of eminent domain to acquire and raze modern homes and businesses so that the Battle Road could be returned to its colonial appearance. The local elite supported the initiative on account of the park serving as both a green and an ideological screen between their homes and the Air Force base. While the name the government gave to the new park, Minute Man National Historical Park, is something of a misnomer in that only a small percentage of colonial troops were designated as "minute men" always ready to arm themselves at a moment's notice, it assured Americans that the United States won the Revolution on account of their preparedness. Like the euphemistic name given to the "Defense Department," the park's name drains violence from the story of the nation's birth and its continued military endeavors at the park's periphery.

When the veterans walked and rolled through Minute Man National Historical Park in single file on both sides of the Battle Road, the public was forced to reconsider the idea, embedded in the park's name, that war is preparedness.

278 *Elise Lemire*

"They were on patrol in the jungle," a local reporter following the march later recalled surmising. "They weren't walking in twos or threes or fours. It was a straight line, all spread out."[13]

"It kind of reminded me of my Army days when you'd go out on the road for maneuvers," one Korean War veteran, a Lexington resident, remembered thinking as he watched the veterans go past. "They'd have you walk single file on each side of the road in case you got strafed or something."[14]

Here too VVAW was debunking a myth. War is not preparedness. War is being attacked with guns or machine gun fire.

Myth 5: War Is Restraint

While it is impossible to determine exactly why the Lexington Selectmen proceeded with plans to deter the veterans from using the Lexington Battle Green, it is clear they took seriously their role as its guardians. A 1923 town bylaw stipulates that the Selectmen may only permit those behaviors that are "quiet and orderly" and "in keeping with a respectful regard and reverence for the memory of the patriotic service and sacrifice so nobly rendered" on the Battle Green. Having monitored the growing number of veterans marching through Concord, Lincoln, and into Lexington, the Selectmen were aware of the ways in which VVAW was using memorialized battlefields to focus the nation's attention not on 1775 but on 1971 and that, in doing so, VVAW was debunking the myths celebrated on the Battle Green.[15]

Many of the markers on the Battle Green were authored by the Lexington Historical Society in celebration of the myths the veterans had already encountered. A large granite boulder affixed with an iron plaque designating its location "The Site of the Old Belfry from which the alarm was rung" is, for example, an assertion like Longfellow's that the colonists' ingenuity was the key to their military success. Additionally, another marker, showing exactly where 40 or so of the local militiamen who had responded to the alarm lined up to face the hundreds of oncoming British Regulars, insists the American colonists were a restrained people. The marker imagines the colonists' captain ordering them to "Stand your ground" but to refrain from violence unless provoked. "Don't fire," the boulder quotes him as saying, "unless fired upon. But if they mean to have war, let it begin here." Marked thus with what historians have since proven is an entirely fanciful version of what was actually said that day, this boulder promotes the idea that even though Americans are willing to use violence, they are inherently restrained. Lexington's own seven-foot-tall bronze statue of a colonial militiaman looking eastward toward the oncoming British troops has his musket down by his side, further helping visitors populate the 1775 landscape with these determined but restrained farmers.

Rather than allow the now 200 antiwar veterans to continue to debunk the myth of a peaceable country winning its independence with the colonists' preparedness, creativity, alacrity, and restraint, the Lexington Selectmen carried out the largest mass arrest in Massachusetts history. Their aim was to reset the

The Violence of the Vietnam War   279

Battle Green's clock from 1971, with its horrific truths about US imperial warfare, to the sacred birth time of 1775 when the American colonists outsmarted, outran, and outlasted the violently aggressive imperialist invaders.

But while the selectmen may have sought to repurify what they saw as a defiled sacred space, the outpouring of support for the antiwar veterans from the press and the hundreds of people who committed civil disobedience alongside them on the Green proved the nation had largely come to agree with VVAW. The United States was not restrained. Rather, it had become the violent imperialist aggressor it had once sought to vanquish.

The Vietnam Veterans Memorial

Having made clear to the American public that the nation's young combatants had sustained death and grievous bodily and moral injuries in Southeast Asia, VVAW set the course for a very different Vietnam War memorial than those erected in Massachusetts for the Revolutionary and Civil Wars.

In a radical departure from traditional American war memorials, the Vietnam Veterans Memorial is formed of stacked black granite blocks embedded into the side of an almost 500-foot-long V-shaped trench and etched with the names of the 57,939 American soldiers who were killed in Vietnam. (While more names of those killed during the war have since been added as records are revised, the names of those who died later from exposure to chemical weapons, posttraumatic stress disorder, or other lingering wounds do not appear.) One line of the V stretches toward the Washington Monument, a colossal obelisk dedicated in 1885 that dwarfs even the Bunker Hill Monument. The other stretches toward the temple-shaped Lincoln Memorial, inside of which sits a 19-foot-tall white marble statue of the Civil War-era president carved by the same artist who sculpted Concord's Minute Man Statue. In contrast to both of these, the Vietnam Veterans Memorial functions less as a source of pride about the nation's democracy and more as an expression of the nation's sorrow over the loss of so many in a war most Americans regret precisely because it did not reflect the ideals associated with the president who oversaw the nation's birth and the one who orchestrated its rebirth as a free country for all.[16]

Unfortunately, but perhaps not surprisingly, VVAW's success in helping shape a memorial that declines to mythologize war was short lived. Two years after The Wall's dedication, the Federal Commission of Fine Arts added to the site, because of pressure from members of Congress, the White House, and others, an American flag and a heroic representational statue of three 8-foot-tall soldiers titled variously *The Three Infantrymen* or *The Three Soldiers*. Whereas the antiwar veterans ended their Memorial Day weekend march by ceremoniously breaking their toy M16s into plastic shards that they angrily ground beneath their feet, these soldiers are hyper-militarized. The three bronze Vietnam-era soldiers may hold their weapons down by their sides, perhaps in a gesture toward the Cincinnatus tradition embodied by the Minute Men statues in Concord and Lexington, but the sheer number, size, and power of their weapons

280   *Elise Lemire*

is a celebration of the techno-military might the United States unleashed in Southeast Asia. In addition to an M16, the soldiers have a .45-caliber pistol, an M16A1 rifle, and an M60 machine gun with its massive accompanying bandolier. If The Wall seems to sink into the ground under the weight of the nation's sorrow for the losses incurred in an unjust war, *The Three Soldiers* suggests that the strength of the American firepower deployed in Vietnam should be appreciated regardless of the death and destruction it caused.[17]

The POW/MIA Flag

In their letter asking the Lexington Board of Selectmen for permission to protest and camp overnight in their historic town, the antiwar Vietnam veterans of New England had explained that they were calling their march Operation POW because "We Are All," the flier they distributed in advance of the march asserted, "Prisoners of This War."

But even as the war was arguably still holding everyone prisoner in the spring of 1971, the march's name was also a pointed attempt to counter President Nixon's rationale for continuing the war long after his election in 1968. In 1969, Nixon had insisted that the North Vietnamese account for all of the missing American war dead, even as the United States never would have been able to provide such a list of the Vietnamese killed by American forces. Nixon proceeded to change the official name of Veterans Day in November 1970 to Prisoner of War Day, after which he directed that soldiers shot down in enemy territory no longer be counted as "Killed in Action – Body Not Recovered," but as "POW/MIAs," a conflation of two categories, Prisoners of War and Missing in Action, that had thus far been separate. All of a sudden, those who were most likely dead could be imagined as possible POWs who might one day return home.[18]

Having settled on the principle that the war must be continued in order to make sure every American soldier made it home, officials from the State and Defense departments convinced a group of wives to organize the National League of Families of American Prisoners in Southeast Asia. Nixon pledged to them in a joint press conference that "this Government will do everything that it possibly can to separate out the prisoner issue and have it handled as it should be, as a separate issue on a humane basis." In other words, Nixon was going to continue the war and he was going to continue it for reasons that he insisted were not political or violent but purely "humane." In an effort to garner public support for this rationale, Nixon's administration allowed the League to set up a display in the Rotunda of the Capitol Building in which an American prisoner was shown sitting in a bare cell with a rat and several cockroaches, while a second American was shackled in another cage nearby. Who could argue that the American military should leave Vietnam when American men were enduring such horrific conditions there? To ensure that these purported conditions resonated on a personal level with as many American citizens as possible, the League began selling bracelets with the names of individual POW/MIAs on them. The ten million Americans who purchased these bracelets vowed never to remove them until the person named had been either returned home or found dead. Soon the League had enough money from bracelet sales to erect billboards and to manufacture and sell bumper stickers, t-shirts, lapel pins, and matchbooks. Jonathan Schell was prompted to write in a 1970 issue of the *New Yorker* that Americans were acting "as though the North Vietnamese had kidnapped 400 Americans and the United States had gone to war to retrieve them." Many had come to accept as true this lie.[19]

In 1970 and 1971, the League took the additional step of paying an advertising agency to design a POW/MIA flag that asserted, in counter distinction to VVAW's claims, that the US military was only acting in self-defense. A white circle at the center of a black field features the silhouette of a man held captive behind barbed wire. The captive's head is hanging because the only person paying any attention to him is a guard in a tall tower. He believes he has been "forgotten" by his countrymen. By depicting an American soldier as imprisoned and despondent, the flag erases the fact of American aggression in Southeast Asia. And by asking for every citizen's sympathy, the POW/MIA flag arguably perpetuates the most dangerous myth of all: that war is love.

Even despite the widespread and sympathetic news coverage of Operation POW, VVAW-NE was not able to break the hold the League had on the American people with its focus on victimized individual men whose futures seemed to rest in the amount of sympathy and resolve their corresponding bracelet wearer could muster for them. President Nixon was able to stall the peace talks until January 1973, which led to the deaths of many more Vietnamese and American military personnel.

The MIA/POW flag might have become a footnote after the Paris Peace Accords when all 591 prisoners of war were returned by the Vietnamese to the United States. Instead, the POW/MIA flag has been used to rationalize America's first war loss as well as the nation's continued military action around the globe. By putting the flag on permanent display inside the Rotunda of the Capitol Building in 1987 and, in 1990, establishing US Public Law 101–355, which designates the third Friday of every September "National POW/MIA Recognition Day," the federal government asserts that the Vietnamese were the powerful aggressors. Without acknowledging the many war crimes committed by the US military in Vietnam or elsewhere, this law recognizes the flag on the grounds that "many American prisoners of war were subjected to brutal and inhuman treatment by their enemy captors in violation of the international codes and customs for the treatment of prisoners of war." "[M]any of these Americans," this law insists, "are still missing." This law recognizes the POW/MIA flag "officially" as the "symbol of our Nation's concern and commitment to resolving as fully as possible the fates of Americans still prisoners, missing and unaccounted for in Southeast Asia, thus ending the uncertainty for their families and the Nation."[20]

Even after the Senate Select Committee on POW/MIA Affairs concluded in 1993 that "there is, at this time, no compelling evidence that proves that

282 *Elise Lemire*

any American remains alive in captivity in Southeast Asia," Congress decided to designate six national holidays when the POW/MIA flag must be flown over the Capitol Building, the White House (where it is the only flag ever flown other than the Stars and Stripes), every major military installation, the Korean and Vietnam Veterans Memorials, offices of the secretaries of State, Defense, Veterans Affairs, and of the Selective Service System, and at every post office and all Veterans Administration Medical Centers and national cemeteries. The designated holidays are POW/MIA Recognition Day, Armed Forces Day, Memorial Day, Flag Day, the Fourth of July, and Veterans Day. Virtually every state has additional statutes requiring the POW/MIA flag to be flown on certain days. In 2011, Idaho became the first state to require that the flag be flown over all state buildings at all times "until such time as all our unaccounted for and missing members of the Armed Forces return." Many municipalities, companies, and organizations also fly the POW/MIA flag regularly and without being required to do so. It has flown at the New York Stock Exchange, the Super Bowl, and countless other places and events. Many post offices now fly the POW/MIA flag all year long. Indeed, so many towns fly the POW/MIA flag that the director of the Flag Research Center in Winchester, Massachusetts, has been prompted to call it "a permanent feature of the landscape," and one reporter concludes of POW/MIA flags that "They've become so common we hardly even see them." In short, the lie that the United States was victimized by Vietnam is ubiquitous in the United States.[21]

Recent War Memorialization

In 2004, a massive World War II memorial was installed directly between the Lincoln Memorial and the Washington Monument. Whereas the two-acre Vietnam Veterans Memorial is unsettling in its design, black in color, and with a reflective surface that embeds visitors in a dialogue about war and its costs, the over seven-acre World War II Memorial is neoclassical, all-white marble and bronze, and triumphal in tone. While The Wall lists the names of all of the American dead and thereby makes explicit war's human toll, the World War II Memorial includes quotations from great men that erase war's trauma in favor of celebrating masculine leadership and winning at whatever cost. President Franklin D. Roosevelt, for example, is quoted asserting that "The American people, in their righteous might, will win through to absolute victory." And, of course, the break in the National Mall's east-west axis has reframed the meaning of the Washington and Lincoln memorials, which are now separated by this glorification of WWII. While the Washington and Lincoln memorials were originally intended as celebrations of the nation's first president, who refused to be king and thereby helped to birth a democracy, and of the nation's sixteenth president, who ended slavery and thereby theoretically expanded the scope of that democracy to all, they are now at risk of being understood as war memorials themselves, one to the American Revolution and the other to the Civil War. Finally, the location and size of the World War II Memorial, which

The Violence of the Vietnam War   283

was dedicated at the height of the Iraq War and thus seemed to justify it, take away from the ability of the public to gather on the Mall in expressions of dissent. There is now significantly less space for people to gather at the foot of the Lincoln Memorial as they did during the March on Washington for Jobs and Freedom when Dr. King gave his "I have a dream" speech in 1963, or to camp, as the antiwar Vietnam Veterans did, in 1971. Fifty years after Vietnam Veterans Against the War marched on Washington and its New England chapter organized a reversal of Paul Revere's ride in a bid to wake the nation, American memorialization practices as well as American overseas military incursions indicate that we have forgotten the lessons VVAW imparted.[22]

Notes

1 A transcript of John Kerry's remarks before the Senate Foreign Relations Committee on April 23, 1971, is available online from The Sixties Project: http://www2.iath.virginia. edu/sixties/HTML_docs/Resources/Primary/Manifestos/VVAW_Kerry_Senate.html [Accessed August 18, 2021].
2 Opening statement, Winter Soldier Investigation Transcript, http://www2.iath.virginia. edu/sixties/HTML_docs/Resources/Primary/Winter_Soldier/WS_02_opening.html [Accessed August 18, 2021]. In addition to the transcript, see the 1972 documentary film *Winter Soldier*.
3 Ibid., the Sixties Project.
4 This photograph is reproduced in Elise Lemire, *Battle Green Vietnam: The 1971 March on Concord, Lexington, and Boston* (Philadelphia, PA: University of Pennsylvania Press, 2021), Figure 26, p. 139.
5 See Lemire, p. 47.
6 On the sympathetic media coverage of Operation Dewey Canyon III, see Gerald Nicosia, *Home to War: A History of the Vietnam Veterans' Movement* (New York: Three Rivers Press, 2001), pp. 103–144, and Lemire, p. 14.
7 For a detailed account of Operation POW, see Lemire.
8 For an accurate account of Paul Revere's ride, see David Hackett Fischer, *Paul Revere's Ride* (Oxford: Oxford University Press, 1995).
9 On the clothes and horse Dallin imaginatively sculpted, see Fischer, p. 334.
10 On war as a contest of "mutual injuring," see Elaine Scarry, *The Body in Pain: The Making and Unmaking of the World* (Oxford: Oxford University Press, 1987).
11 VVAW-NE's press release was reprinted in an article titled "VVAW Gives Reasons for Green Bivouac," which begins by noting that "the following is a statement approved by the Vietnam Veterans Against the War after the group had voted Friday night in Concord to bivouac on the Battle Green" (*Lexington Minute-Man*, June 2, 1971).
12 Quoted in Boston National Historical Park, *Bunker Hill: Battle Monument, Memory* (Fort Washington, PA: Eastern National, 2007), p. 25.
13 Tom Curran Lexington Oral History Project Interview (January 26, 1994), p. 8, www. lexingtonbattlegreen1971.com/files/Curran,%20Tom.pdf [Accessed August 18, 2021].
14 Bruce Gordon Lexington Oral History Project Interview (August 24, 1992), p. 8, www. lexingtonbattlegreen1971.com/files/Gordon,%20Bruce.pdf [Accessed August 18, 2021].
15 Cited in Robert Cataldo Lexington Oral History Project Interview (August 24, 1993), pp. 17–18, www.lexingtonbattlegreen1971.com/files/Cataldo,%20Robert.pdf [Accessed August 18, 2021]. The bylaw dates back to 1923 or earlier according to the footnote in the Cataldo interview.
16 On how the Vietnam Veterans Memorial came into being, see Patrick Hagopian, *The Vietnam War in American Memory: Veterans, Memorials, and the Politics of Healing* (Amherst, MA: University of Massachusetts Press, 2009). There are numerous excellent

284 *Elise Lemire*

interpretations of the Vietnam Veterans Memorial. For a particularly good study that considers the memorial within the context of prior war memorials, see Robin Wagner-Pacifici and Barry Schwartz, "The Vietnam Veterans Memorial: Commemorating a Difficult Past," *American Journal of Sociology*, Vol. 97, No. 2 (September 1991), pp. 376–420.

17 On the controversy surrounding the design of the Vietnam Veterans Memorial and the decision to add a statue, see Hagopian.

18 On the Nixon administration's POW/MIA campaign, see H. Bruce Franklin, *M.I.A., or, Mythmaking in America* (New Brunswick, NJ: Rutgers University Press, 1992).

19 Quoted in Franklin, pp. 51, 60.

20 www.govinfo.gov/content/pkg/STATUTE-104/pdf/STATUTE-104-Pg416.pdf [Accessed August 11, 2021].

21 United State Senate, "POW/MIA's: Report of the Select Committee on POW/MIA Affairs," January 13, 1993, https://fas.org/irp/congress/1993_rpt/pow-exec.html [Accessed August 11, 2021]; Director of the Flag Research Center quoted in Craig Timberg, "Decades after Vietnam, States Embrace POW Flag," *Washington Post*, March 5, 2001, www.washingtonpost.com/archive/politics/2001/03/05/decades-after-vietnam-states-embrace-pow-flag/a859d288-0e87-4693-b5fe-9e01b82338f2/ [Accessed August 11, 2021]; Rick Holmes, "Take Down the POW/MIA Flags," *Metrowest Daily News*, April 26, 2015, www.rickholmes.net/take-down-the-pow-flags [Accessed August 11, 2021].

22 For an in-depth reading of the WWII Memorial, see Erika Doss, *Memorial Mania: Public Feeling in America* (Chicago, IL: University of Chicago Press, 2010), pp. 186–216.

Index

Note: Page numbers with f indicate photographs; n indicates a note

9/11 Memorial: critiques of 208n33; as model for the Pulse Memorial 199–200
54th Massachusetts Regiment memorial 2
1619 Project (*NY Times*) 90
1776 Commission 90
1807 Commemorated project, University of York 110
1811 Slave Revolt, commemorations of violence against freedom fighters at 95–96
1921 Tulsa Race Massacre Centennial Commission 182

Abolition of the British Slave Trade Act (1807): Agbetu's protest 108–109, 109f; Bicentenary celebrations 102, 107–111; and the "culture of abolition" 102–113, 117–118
Acosta, Katie 205
Adenauer, Konrad 187–188
Adriao, Dennis 217
Aegis Trust, Kigali Genocide Memorial 67, 69
African Diaspora, monuments and memorial plaques 87
African National Congress (ANC), AP Mda's role in 222–223
African Rights, report on Rwandan genocide 70
Afrikaner nationalism, countering symbols of 214–215
Agbetu, Toyin 108, 109f
Agent Orange 268
Aggett, Neil 212–213
Agosti, Orlando Ramón 249
Aje, Lawrence 95

Akoto-Bamfo, Kwame 164
Al Araqib Bedouin village, destruction cycles 241
Alexander, Peter 220
Alfonsín, Raúl Ricardo 252
Allen, James 156, 163
'*All the Real Indians Died Off': And 20 Other Myths About Native Americans* (Dunbar-Ortiz and Gilio-Whitaker) 133–134
American Civil War, the "Lost Cause" narrative 83; *see also* Confederate monuments
American Friends Service Committee 42
American Indian Movement (AIM), toppling of St. Paul Columbus statue 129–130
"American Jewish Commission on the Holocaust" report 48
American Jewish Congress, anti-Nazi rally 38
American Jewish Joint Distribution Committee 42
Am I Not A Man and a Brother? (Wedgewood medallion), influence 104
Amnesty International 2, 12
Anderson, James Craig, murder of 153
Anderson, Rhonda 138
Andy Warhol Museum, Pittsburgh, *Without Sanctuary* exhibit 159
Annual Deer Island Sacred Paddle and Run 147
anti-gay violence 194–195
anti-Latinx violence, and monosexism 195
anti-LGBT+ violence 194
anti-lynching laws 11

286 *Index*

anti-lynching movement 154
anti-Muslim stereotypes 195–196
anti-Nazi rally at Madison Square Garden 39f
anti-racism riots, UK 106
antisemitism: in Germany, after the defeat of the Nazis 26; and Israeli racist policies 12; at the January 6, 2001 insurrection 53; spike in, following Trump's election 52–53
anti-slavery societies, Britain, relics associated with 103–104
ant-Muslim stereotypes 196
Aparicio, Eitan Bronstein 12–13, 231
apartheid: defined 12; South Africa, and legitimization of state terrorism 212; as an UN-designed crime against humanity 12; violence associated with, challenges of commemorating 12
Arab Revolt, 1936 237
Arapaho people, Sand Creek Massacre 142–143, 145–146
Araujo, Ana Lucia: on the Jefferson portrayal at the National Museum of African American History and Culture 100n51; *Slavery in the Age of Memory* 92; on Washington denture souvenirs 80
Arditti, Rita 248
Arellano, Lisa 11
Argentina: commemorative strategies 252–253; death squadrons 249; human rights activism 252; the Junta, history 249–251; memorials for the disappeared 248; memory projects 13, 247, 263–264; National Day of Memory for Truth and Justice 261; Operation Condor 247; protection of perpetrators of crimes against humanity 252; protests against the Junta 251; state-sponsored violence 3, 248; *see also* the disappeared, Argentina
Arusha Peace Accords 60, 62, 64
Asociación Madres de Plaza de Mayo (Association of the Mothers of the Plaza de Mayo) 251, 254
assimilationism 144
Atlantic slave trade, British focus on 104–105
"atrocity materials" debates about displaying 110–111
Attwood, Bain ("Difficult Histories exhibit: The Museum of New Zealand") 137

Bailey, Anne 89
Baldosas (Sidewalk Tiles), Buenos Aires 259–261
"The Ballad of Yoel Moshe Salomon" (Einstein) 236
Barrios x Memoria y Justicia (Neighborhoods for Memory and Justice), Buenos Aires 259–260
Barton, David 172
Battiti, Florencia 258–259
Battle Road, Massachusetts: location 277–278; Operation POW at 271
Baudizzone-Lestard-and-Varas Studio, *Monumento a las Víctimas del Terrorismo de Estado (Monument to the Victims of State Terrorism, MVTE)*, Buenos Aires 257f
Bauer, Fritz 22
Becker, Daniel 256, 257f
Bedouin communities in Israel, status 240–241
Beech, John 104–115
On Being with Krista Tippett (podcast) 169
Bell, Vikki 255
Bellow, Saul 47
Beloved (Morrison) 87
Bender, Melissa 7
Berg, Mary 44
Bergen, Germany, Wehrmacht crimes in 30
Bergen-Belsen concentration camp: identifying perpetrators 31; memorials at 20–22; survivor's association 20–21
Berger, Maurice 157
Berkeley Plantation, VA: backtracking about slavery 100n56; narratives at 92
Berlin wall, falling of 23
Berry, Daina Raima 82
Biden, Joe 194–195, 198
Black Americans: activism by 45–46, 106–107; persistent violence against 170, 173; racial wealth gap 183–184, 188–189; reactions to the *Witness* exhibit 158; reparations for 40, 173, 183; and representations of slavery 80–81; solidarity with Palestinians 46; stereotyping of 104, 189, 223–224; violence against the Vietnamese 3; *see also* lynching; reparations; slavery
Blackbear, Eugene Jr. (Southern Cheyenne Sundance) 146
Black Lives Matter (BLM) protests: and changes in public memory 118; coalitions with Indigenous peoples 130; discontinuing of UGGRs and other

Index 287

slavery simulations 86–87; focus on anti-Black violence 79, 169; invocations of the Holocaust during 53; toppling of Colston's statue 9–10, 102, 111–112, 112f

Black Wall Street, Greenwood area, Tulsa 173, 175, 178–181, 188; *see also* Tulsa Massacre, 1921

Blake, William (*Flagellation of a Female Samboe Slave*) 104

Blight, David 4

boarding schools, for Native children 143–144

Bonafini, Hebe 251

Boone Plantation, SC, weddings at 86

Bopape, Stanza 212

Borges, Jorge Luis 249

Boston, MA: Boston National Historical Park 2; toppling of monument to Columbus 130, 131f

Botbaum, Betsy 158–159

Brady, Tad 179

Breitman, Richard 39, 53

Brexit 118–119

Bristol, UK: anti-racist riots in 106; removal of Milligan's statue 111–112; *A Respectable Trade? Bristol and Transatlantic Slavery* exhibit 106–107; toppling of Colston's statue 5, 10, 102, 111–115, 112f

British Slave Trade Act, bicentenary of 9

Bronstein, Eleonore Merza 12–13

Brookes Slave ship design, popularity of 104

Brown, Antonio 201

Brown, Michael, murder of 79, 162

Bruyneel, Kevin: erasure/elimination practices 144; on "settler memory" 134; team names and mascots 139–140

B'Tselem, "A Regime of Jewish Supremacy From the Jordan River to the Mediterranean Sea: This is Apartheid" report 12

Buchenwald concentration camp: and the GDR's approach to memorialization 24; memorial at 28, 33n12

Buenos Aires, Argentina: *Baldosas (Sidewalk Tiles)* 259–261, 260f; *El Siluetazo II* commemoration 243–255, 254f; Museum and Site of Memory ESMA, Buenos Aires 255–256; Parque de la memoria (Park of Remembrance) 256–257; *see also* the disappeared

Bundy, McGeorge 269

Bunker Hill Monument Association 275

Butler, Judith 200, 205

Buxton, Thomas Fowell 102

Bynum, G.T. 174

Byrd, James, murder of 157–158

Cabot, John 120n18

Caledonia Farm 1812 Bed and Breakfast, VA 85

Calhoun, John C. 79

Calhoun College, Yale University, renaming 79

Canada Park (Jewish National Fund park), markers of destroyed Palestinian villages 232–233

cancel culture, and memorial destruction 114–115

Cannonball House, GA, minimalized slave history at 85

Capparós, Martin 259–260

the Caribbean, the enslaved in, British "forgetting" of 105

Carlson, Jennifer 197–198

Carter, Jimmy 49

"Case for Reparations" (Coates) 183

Casiano, Norman 202

the "Casino" (Museum and Site of Memory ESMA, Buenos Aires) 255–256

Caste: The Origins of Our Discontents (Wilkerson) 167

Centers of Detention, Torture, and Extermination (CCDTE), Argentina, transforming into museums 253

Central Square Theater 2

Centro de Documentación y Archivo Digital (Center for Documentation and Digital Archive), Buenos Aires 258

Charleston, SC: markers at slave auction sites 88f, 89; massacre at AME Church in 79, 82; memorial statue to Vesey 95

Chase-Ribaud, Barbara 91

chemical warfare, Vietnam, health impacts 268

Cheyenne people, Sand Creek Massacre, Colorado 142–143, 145–146

Chicago Tribune, efforts to provide aid to Greenwood residents 178–179

Chivington, John 142

Christian nation, America as a 172

Churchill, Winston 117

Cincinnatus tradition 279–280

Citizen: An American Lyric (Rankine) 153

Clarkson, Thomas 102–103

288   *Index*

Clinton, Hillary 135
Coates, Ta-Nehisi 188
Coldefy and Associates, design for the Orlando Pulse Memorial 198
Colonial Countryside project (National Trust) 117
"Colonialism in Destru(A)ction" map (De-Colonizer): areas of Palestinian-Jewish accord 237; description 234–235; destruction in 1948 238–240; exposure of Israel settler colonialism 231; general description 234; non-aggression initiatives, sites of 238; origin and goals 231–232
Colonial Tropes and the Media Coverage of the Marikana Massacre (Schutte) 218
Colonial Williamsburg, interpretive program on slavery 80–81
Colston, Edward, toppling of monument to 4–5, 9–10, 102, 111–112, 112f
Columbus, Christopher: monuments to, purpose 140–141; toppling of monuments to 129–130, 131f, 190f
Columbus Day, creation of 141
commemorative *vs.* historical voices 5–6
"Commitment to End Structural Racism and Achieve Racial Equality" (Resolution 58-R-19), Evanston, IL 185–186
Community Remembrance Project (Equal Justice Initiative) 166
concentration camps: application to broad range of detention sites 36; comparison of Trump's detention camps with 35; use for displaced persons, and forgetting the Holocaust 20; *see also* Germany; the Holocaust
Concord, MA, war memorial obelisk 275–277
Confederate monuments, identifying and removing 79, 82–85
Conference on Jewish Material Claims Against Germany 186–187
conquest, obelisks as symbols of 275
Conyers, John 173, 183
Copley, John Singleton 271–272
Cornell, Corey 201
COVID pandemic, memorialization during 247
Creek Nation, reparations for Black slaves of 183
crimes against humanity 33n14, 246, 252–253, 261

Crossfire (film) 43
Cubitt, Geoffrey 110
culpability/complicity/perpetrators: addressing in remembrances 22, 25, 27, 31–32, 221–222; ignoring 8, 160, 188, 252
culture of remembrance: and addressing culpability as well as victimhood 31; after the fall of the Berlin wall 34n42; categories of culpability 33n15; and the complexity of facing the past 30; and continued ambivalence about culpability 31; and crimes by the Wehrmacht 30; and debates about the location of memorials 23–24; and discussions of underlying history 22; diversity of approaches 19–20; Enquete Commission 22; and "Hitlerisation" 31; initial reluctance of German people to discuss the past 24–25; Memorial to the Murdered Jews of Europe (Holocaust Museum), Berlin 23; staffing and memorial maintenance 22; sustaining, challenges 20; and understanding needs of survivors' descendants 31; 27; victim and perpetrator site designations 22; victim-centered, *vs.* culpability/responsibility of perpetrators
culture of remembrance (Germany): government support for 19; turn to research of historical sites 22
"culture wars": and changes in public memory 118; and debates over public history 114–117; in the UK, and the mythologizing of imperialism 113–114
Cummings, John 93

Dachau concentration camp: Comité International de Dachau 21; memorial at 21–22; use of barracks for displaced persons 21
Daily Mail (London), role in culture wars 116
Daily Telegraph (London), role in culture wars 125n80
Dallin, Cyrus E. 271–272
Danticat, Edwidge 3
Darity, William "Sandy" 183–184
Davidson, Osha Gray 135
Davis, Isaac 272–273
DCIII protest *see* Operation Dewey Canyon III protest (VVAW), Washington, DC

De-Colonizer: founding and purpose 231; map, importance 233–234; original research by 243n23; *see also* "Colonialism in Destru(A)ction" map

Deer Island, MA, forcible removal of Nipmucs to 147

Defense Department, name of as euphemism 277

Deir Yassim massacre 237

Deloria, Philip (Lakota) 134

Democratic Republic of the Congo (DRC, formerly Zaire): and regional instability 60, 71; RPF/Ugandan invasions 64

denazification: in the Communist context 28, 33n22; in Germany 25–27; and trials of Nazi leaders 26

depalestinizing 234

Des Forges, Alison 59

designating memory sites 3, 11, 87, 89, 194–195, 278, 282

detention centers: in Argentina 253; for immigrants on the US border 35; *see also* concentration camps

The Diary of Anne Frank (film) 45

difficult histories, dealing with: challenges of 149, 150n5; Equal Justice Initiative efforts 162–163; focusing on people not optics 166; reinventing, pseudo-radical implications 149, 150n5; scholarship related to 137; using new language to describe old violence 167; *Without Sanctuary: Lynching Photography in America* 158–162; and work of acknowledgement and repair 166; *see also* historical justice movement; lynching, the disappeared, Argentina

"Difficult Histories: The Museum of New Zealand Te Papa Tongarewa and the Treaty of Waitangi Exhibit" (Attwood) 137

digital memory projects 6–7, 89, 199, 258, 265n20

Dipale, Ernest, murder of 212

"Dirty War" period (Argentina) 250

the disappeared, Argentina: as an act of memory erasure 250; commemorations at past torture sites 254f; efforts to memorialize, commemorative strategies 13, 252–253; *El Siluetazo II* commemoration 253–255; memorials to in Buenos Aires 253–261, 254f, 257f, 260f; memory projects honoring memory of 263–264; National Day of

Memory for Truth and Justice, Argentina 261; numbers of 248; protection of perpetrators of crimes against 252; victims, characteristics of 250–251

domestic terrorism 196

domestic urban governance 197

Dones, Chali'Naru 130, 131f

Doss, Erika 4

Dowden, Oliver 115

Drakeford, Kark 115

Druze, Israeli treatment of 240

Du Bois, W. E. B. 164

Dunbar-Ortiz, Roxanne 6, 133–135

Duncan, Jane 218–219

Dyson, Michael Eric 163

East Germany, denazification efforts 28

educational sites/programs: about the disappeared 68, 264; about the Holocaust 22–23, 25, 31, 36, 46, 49, 51; about Israeli settlements 231, 233–234, 241; "The Orlando Syllabus" 203; about the Pulse nightclub shooting 199, 201; about slavery and lynching 90–91, 158, 166; and reexamining understandings of history 10, 33n13, 173–174; *see also* public memory

Eichmann, Adolf 31, 44

Einstein, Arik ("The Ballad of Yoel Moshe Salomon") 236

Ellsworth, Scott 175

El Olimpo CCDTE, memories of genocide at 253

El Siluetazo II commemoration: fence 254f; involvement in 253–254; scope of project, participants 253–255

Emancipation Acts (Britain): compensation and conditions attached to 105–106; as focus of British public memory 102–103

Emmett Till Anti-Lynching Act 11

Enola Gay exhibit controversy 5

Enquete Commission (Germany), rules for funding memorials 22

the enslaved: ignoring of, in British public memory 103, 118; long-term impacts of slavery 3; and Lost Cause ideology 4; microtargeting reparations for slaves 183; role in Northern manufacturing 2; and the sanitizing of slavery 108; *see also* lynching; plantation tourist sites; slavery

enslavers: British, compensation paid to 105–106; monuments to, toppling of 5; public debates about in the UK

290   *Index*

112–113; trans-Atlantic slave trade 9–10, 102; *see also* slavery
epistemic impeachment 90–91
Epstein, Leslie (King of the Jews) 47
Epstein, Yitzhak 236
Equal Justice Initiative (EJI): Community Remembrance Project 166; exposing the history of lynching 162–164; identifying links between past and present 4; internet website 165; Legacy Museum, Montgomery, AL 94; *Lynching in America: Confronting the Legacy of Racial Terror* 11, 163–164; memorial markers 87–88, 88f; mission 156, 164–166; role in passage of anti-lynching law 11
Equiano, Olaudah 103
erasure/elimination: of history, countering 113–114; and homosexism/homonationalism 196; in imperialist memorials 3; of Native Americans, process of 130, 132–133, 136–137, 144, 149; the official view of the Marikana Massacre as 222; *see also* the disappeared, Argentina; genocide
Erbelding, Rebecca 41
Escuela de Mecánica de la Armada (The Navy Mechanics School for Officers, ESMA) CCDTE: *El Siluetazo II* commemoration 253–255, 254f; transfer to Insituto Espacio Para la Memoria 255
eugenics 40
Evans, T.D. 177
Evanston, Ill, structuring reparations in 186
"The Evil of Silence" (Wilkerson) 167
Exodus (film, Preminger) 45
"Exterminate All the Brutes" documentary (Peck) 5–6

Facing History and Ourselves office (NYC) 158
Farmer, Ian (Lonmin CEO) 224
fascism, acknowledging and countering 13, 19, 29, 32n7, 37, 52, 270
Faust, Drew Gilpin 81–82
Fayetteville, NC, removal of slave market building 84
"February 26, 2012/In Memory of Trayvon Martin" (Rankine) 169
Ferrari, Claudio 256, 257f
Ferrari, León 254
Ferrus, Diana 226
Fields, Barbara 189
Fields, Karen 189

Firsting and Lasting: Writing Indians out of Existence in New England (O'Brien) 132
first responders, acknowledging at the Pulse Memorial 201
Flagellation of a Female Samboe Slave (Blake) 104
Floyd, George, murder of, impacts 4, 10, 84, 130
Foner, Eric 157
Fontes, Claudia 258–259
food deserts, North Tulsa as 174
Foote, Kenneth: *Shadowed Ground* 87; on sites of violence in the United States 3
Forges, Alison Des 70
forgetting *see* erasure/elimination; public memory
Fossey, Dian 69
Fowler, Corinne 117
Frank, Leo 160
Frank Anne 44, 48
Freedom Park, Pretoria 215
French, Daniel Chester: Lincoln Memorial 279; Minute Man statue 272–273
Freund, Henry 1
Friedman, Philip 44
Friedman, Saul S. 48

gacaca dispute resolution system, Rwanda 66, 71
Garrison-Feinberg, Tracy 158
Gayle, Caleb 11
gay victimhood, skewed focus on white men 195–196
Gaza Strip: destruction of early Jewish settlements in 242; Israeli occupation and control 235, 242; Palestinian population 244n14
Geneva Protocols 268
genocide: and confronting Nazi violence 8; definitions 8; the disappeared in Argentina 250; elimination of Native American peoples 136, 139, 142, 144; against First Nations in Argentina 261–262; insufficiency of monetary reparations for 188; international awareness of 44; Peck's examination of 6; in Rwanda against the Tutsis 57; *see also* the Holocaust; the Pulse nightclub shooting; settler colonialism; the Tulsa massacre
Genocide Against the Tutsi Memorial Day, Rwanda 67
Gentleman's Agreement (film) 43

German Democratic Republic (GDR, East Germany): anti-fascist emphasis 27–29, 34n34; denazification efforts 26, 28–29; memorials and memorialization process 24, 28; reuse of concentration camps 22; role of Jewish survivors 34n41

Germany: and accepting culpability, challenges of 27, 29–30, 81; confronting Nazi violence 8, 24–25; culture of remembrance 19, 22–24; denazification efforts 25–26, 33n13; evolution and devolution of memorialization in 20; impact of Cold War on denazification efforts 26; as model for addressing difficult histories 137, 162; Nuremberg Trials 25; ongoing antisemitism in 26; reparations for Holocaust survivors 186–187; resurgent Nazism in 22; superior command and "clean Wehrmacht" myths 30–31; West German vs. GDR approaches 20

Gilio-Whitaker, Dina 133–134

Gilmore, Ruthie Wilson 262

Gilpatrick, Roswell 269

Giunta, Andrea 250

Glaude, Eddie Jr. 167

Glover, Danny 152–153

Golan Heights occupation 235, 240

"Google Arts and Culture" exhibit (South Africa History Archive) 215–216

Gorillas in the Mist (film) 69

Gourevitch, Philip 70

Graham, Ramarley, murder of 263

Great Britain see United Kingdom

Great Swamp Massacre 143

Greenberg, Cheryl Lynn 46

Greensboro Truth and Reconciliation Committee 81

Greenwich, UK, Trade and Empire Exhibit 107

Greenwood area, Tulsa, OK: arrested Black residents 182; destruction of 176, 176f, 180–181; temporary return of Black Wall Street 180; white redevelopment in 178–180; see also Black Wall Street; Greenwood area, Tulsa, OK

The Ground Breaking: An American City and Its Search for Justice (Ellsworth) 175

Gryglewski, Elke 8

Gulag Museum of Perm Russia 2

"GULAG: Soviet Forced Labor Camps and the Struggle for Freedom" 2

gun violence, framing 194–198, 208n55, 262

Haaland, Deb (Laguna Pueblo) 149

Habyarimana, Juvénal 57, 59–60, 62–63

Hale, Grace Elizabeth 160–161

Haley, Nikki 83

Halperin, David 205

Hamburg, exhibits on Wehrmacht crimes 30

Hanhardt, Christine 196–197, 199

Harvard University: Boston National Historical Park 2; Vietnam war spending at 277

Heart of Darkness (Conrad) 5–6

Hebron, Palestine, massacre of Jews in 237

Heffner, Simon 114

Heidelberg, Germany, memorial programs for former Jewish citizens of 1

From Here to Equality: Reparations for Black Americans in the Twenty- First Century (Darity) 183–184

Heritage Project, Johannesburg 215

Heuss, Theodor 21

Hickenlooper, John 143

Hilberg, Raul 44–45

Hill, Joby 89

Hill, Karlos K. 10–11

historical narratives: acknowledging all of 4–5; bias in museum exhibits 5; and changing views of public history 81; coming to terms with the past 81, 83; communicating the horrors of slavery 91–93; confronting past violence, approaches to 6; and correcting the historical record 153–154, 166–167; countering Confederate memorials 83; and healing 82; oral histories 29, 89, 255; political and policy impacts 97n9, 183–184; reckoning/ reconciliation approaches 81, 83; reframing understanding of slavery 79–80, 82, 90–91; responsibility to promote historical justice 82; and settler myth-making 134–135; transformation goal 93; see also difficult histories; the disappeared; memory and specific types and sites of violence

the Holocaust: comparing with other historical events 36–37, 58, 70, 75n63, 158, 168; confronting violence of 8; emigration of Jews forced by 38; as historically unique, sacrosanct 36–37, 52; Jewish survivors of in Germany 26; as symbol of depth of anti-Jewish hatred 41–42; in US public memory 8; see

292   *Index*

also antiemitism; Germany; Holocaust memorialization

Holocaust memorialization: during the 1980s 47; and American Jews' self-perception 37–38; early focus on the murdered and displaced 37; the establishment of the USHMM and the release of *Schinder's List* 38; expansion of awareness beyond the Jewish community 37–38; films 45; genocide awareness programs 52; "Hitlerisation" of 31; Holocaust/Genocide Studies 51; as an internal Jewish affair in early post war years 43; literary approaches 44, 47; President's Commission on the Holocaust 49; recommitment to by American Jews in the 1960s-1980s 46–47; reparations discussions and policy 11; and reparations for survivors 186–187; state memorials and formal commemorations 50–51; *Stolpersteine* ("stumbling stones") project 88; and the USHMM 49–50, 50f; varied approaches to repair 37, 187; *see also* Germany; Jewish Americans

The Holocaust (TV miniseries) 47
homonationalism 195–196
homophobia, homophobic violence 3, 204
homosexism 195–196
Hoover, Herbert 40–41
Hotel Rwanda (film) 70
Hotton, Julia 163
House Resolution 40 (HR 40 reparations study proposal) 173, 183
House of the Wannsee Conference memorial and educational site 22–23
Housing Act of 1949 180–181
housing discrimination/redlining *see* redlining
Human Rights Watch 12
Hutchins, Louis 2
Hutu ethnic group (Rwanda): inequitable taxation of 58; memorialization of successful takeover 59; organizing of and challenge to Tutsi domination 59; and the Tutsi genocide 57, 59–63, 72

"I Am Not Your Negro" documentary (Peck) 5
Ibuka ("remember"), Rwanda 68
imperialism: British, link with abolition memorialization 103; and monuments to enslavers in the UK 113; Peck's examination of 6; in the US, and homonationalism 195; *see also*

enslavement; Indigenous Americans; Israeli settler colonialism; settler colonialism; Vietnam War
Independent Police Investigative Directorate 212
Indians in Unexpected Places (Deloria) 134
Indigenous Americans *see* Native American/Indigenous Peoples; settler colonialism
Indigenous People's Day, Boston, MA 130, 131f
Ingando (RPF camps) 66–67
Instituto Espacio Para la Memoria (Space for Memory Institute) 255
International Convention on the Suppression and Punishment of the Crime of Apartheid 12
International Criminal Tribunal for Rwanda (United Nations) 74n33
International Festival of the Sea, Bristol 106
International Historic Site Museums of Conscience 2
International Memorial Society 2
International Slavery Museum, Liverpool 107
Interpreting Difficult History at Museums and Historic Sites (Rose) 137
Israeli settler colonialism: 1967 war 46; 1973 Arab-Israel War 46; apartheid policies 12; Bedouin communities 240–241; blaming the Palestinians approach 239; destruction associated with 232, 235, 237–239, 243; early Zionists 234–236; exposing history of 231–232; expulsions of Palestinians 239–240; kibbutzim 243, 244n26; map exposing 231; Nakba Law 233; "Prawer Plan" 241; providing housing for European refugees 239–240; US support for 48–49; the West Bank and the Golan Heights 235; *see also* Palestinians; Zionist movement

Jaffa, Israel, deportation of Palestinians from 239
Jamasin al-Gharbi. Palestine, intra-Jewish conflicts 242
Jan, Tracey 185
Japanese-Americans: imprisonment and relocation of during World War II 11, 184–185; Reagan's formal apology to 185; reparations for internment 11, 81, 184–185
Jefferson, Thomas, National Museum portrayal 91, 100n51

Jewish Americans: changing identities of 46; civil rights activism 45–46; criticisms of Israeli Palestinian policies 53; discrimination against 40; emphasis on victimhood in Holocaust memorials 49; increasing identification with the Holocaust and Israel in the 1980s 49; and the initial expulsion of Palestinians from Palestine/Israel 45–46; middle-class status, prosperity 43, 45; phases of relationship with the Holocaust 37; post-war impacts of the destruction of Eastern European Jews 42; pre-war efforts to help refugees from Nazi Germany 38–39, 48; private mourning and memorialization 37; religious discrimination against 40; self-criticisms for passivity during the Holocaust 48; self-perception and identification with Israel and Soviet Jewry 37–38; status following immigration 40; tension between antisemitism and pride in American identity 42–43

Jewish DPs (displaced persons) 43–44

Jim Crow South: dispossession and violence associated with 4; as structural racism 39; talking about, exposing 162; use of Confederate monuments in 83–84; violence associated with 3

Johannesburg Central Police Station 215

John, Maria 10

Johnson, Boris: exacerbation of "culture wars" 117; and the resistance to memorial destruction 114

John Vorster Square police station, Johannesburg: brutality/torture tactics 211–212; commemorations of violence at 12, 215; contesting official memories of 227; endurance of, despite efforts at change 215; naming and renaming of 12, 212, 215; Security Branch 213

Jones, Serene 169

Joseph, Miranda 195

Judaism, and Zionism 12

Judgment at Nuremberg (film, Kramer) 45

Just, Gustav 29

Kagame, Alexis 73n10

Kagame, Paul 57, 66, 69–70

Kalvarisky, Haim Margaliot 236

Kambui, Kamau 80

Karamehic-Muratovic, Alina 6

Kasumu, Samuel 114

Kayibanda, Grégoire 59

Keating, Frank 182

Kelman, Ari 143

Kerry, John 268–270

Khan al Ahmar, Israel, planned destruction of 241

Kigali, Rwanda: attacks and siege of 62–63; forced labor in 66; Kigali Genocide Memorial 67, 69

King, Dana 164

King, Martin Luther Jr. 164

King Philip's War: erasure of 132–133; Great Swamp Massacre 143; removal of Nipmucs to Deer Island 147

Kirshenblatt-Gimblett, Barbara 5

Kissling, Benjamin 1

Kohl, Helmut 23

Kojak, Laura 6

Kook, Hillel ("Peter Bergson") 42

Kosinski, Jerzy 44

Kramer, Stanley 45

Kristallnacht 27, 41

Ku Klux Klan 179

Kundera, Milan 211

Lancashire cotton workers 103

Landsberg, Germany, sympathy for convicted war criminals 26

land theft 41, 90, 136–137, 235–336; *see also* Israeli settler colonialism; Native American/Indigenous Peoples; settler colonialism; Tulsa, OK

language, as tool for reinforcing settler memory 134–135

Lanzmann, Claude 47

Laos, Dewey Canyon I and II missions 268

La Sala Presentes, Ahora y Siempre (Present, Now and Always Hall, PAYS, inauguration), Buenos Aires 258

Latinx people, victimization in Orlando 193

Latrun region, Israel, expulsion of Palestinian inhabitants from 240

Lee, Robert E. 83f

Lee, Sheila Jackson 173

Legacies of British Slave Ownership project 105–106

Legacy Museum, Montgomery, AL 94

Lemire, Elise 13

Lemkin, Raphael 8

Lerer, Marisa 13

Lexington, MA, Battle Green: civil disobedience by Operation POW participants 271, 273, 283n11; mass arrest of veterans on 278–279; memorial markers and boulder at 279

LGBTQ history: distortions of 195–196; and gay vulnerability stereotype 196;

294 *Index*

importance of community 203–206; and the role of bars in the queer community 199; US government focus on preserving 195; *see also* Pulse nightclub shooting

Liberation Day, Rwanda 67

Lichtman, Allan J. 39, 53

Ligali (Pan-African organization, UK) 108, 121nn28–29

Lincoln, Abraham 141–142

Lincoln Memorial 279

Linenthal, Edward: commemorative *vs.* historical voice 5; writings about violence and public memory 14–15n12

Liverpool, UK: anti-racist riots in 106; International Slavery Museum 107; memorial panel text 120n17; Slavery Remembrance Day 107; slave sales 105; *Transatlantic Slavery: Against Human Dignity* exhibit 106; *Transatlantic Slavery Gallery* 104

Longfellow, Henry Wadsworth 271

Longman, Timothy 9, 57–58

Lonmin platinum mine, Marikana, strike at 216–217

Lookstein, Haskel 48

Loosen the Shackles report 106

Lost Cause argument 4

L'Ouverture, Toussaint 3

Lowell National Historical Park 2

LPC proviso, 1929 40

Lübeck police battalion 307; post-war celebrations of comradeship 33n17

lynching: Allen's photograph collection 156; atoning for 156; current day parallels 162, 170; Douglass's campaign against 164; exposing and memorializing 3, 10–11, 157, 158–159; living legacy of 164; naming victims of, importance 157; national lynching museum and memorial 4; numbers of, 1880–1950 155; perpetrators, anonymity of 160; Rankine's double lynching photo remake 10, 153; recontextualizing white supremacism 153–154; role of law enforcement 155; souvenir postcard photos, dissemination 156–157, 168; Wells's campaign against 164

Lynching in America: Confronting the Legacy of Racial Terror (Equal Justice Initiative) 11, 163–164

Mabelane, Matthews, murder of 212

Madres de Plaza de Mayo, Argentina *see* Mothers of the Plaza de Mayo (Madres de Plaza de Mayo), Argentina

Magnolia Plantations and Gardens, SC, limitations of narratives at 92

Malcolm, Constance 263

Malele, Elmon, murder of 212

Manifest Manners: Narratives on Postindian Survivance 145

The Man in a Green Blanket #3 (Mda) 225f

The Man in a Green Blanket #4 (Mda) 226f

The Man in the Green Blanket #1 (Mda) 224f

maps: as memorials 241; as political tools, effectiveness 232

Maracle, Lee 134

March Against Death, 1969 1

Marikana Massacre, 2012: contested memories of 221, 227; events leading to 216–219; media coverage 218–219; memorializing 12, 211, 222, 223–226; mine worker perspectives 219–220; perpetrators, honoring of 221–222; police actions during 217; role of media in memorializing 218–222

Marikana the Musical, Man in the Green Blanket series (Mda) 222

Marinovich, Greg 219–220

Marion, Indiana, double lynching photo 10–11

maritimization of heritage sites associated with British slave trade 104, 106–107, 118–119

markers, historical 165–166, 165f

Marschall, S. 225

Martin, Trayvon, murder of 162, 169

Martínez de Péron, Isabel 249

mascots/team names 140

Massachusetts Institute of Technology, government war spending at 277

massacres: Great Swamp Massacre 143; of Jews in Hebron 237; My Lai Massacre 269; of Palestinians in Deir Yassin 237; reparations for 188; Rosewood, FL 81, 155–156; Sand Creek Massacre 142–143, 145–146; *see also* erasure/ elimination of history; genocide; Marikana Massacre; Native American/ Indigenous people; Tulsa Race Massacre, 1921; Tutsi ethnic group (Rwanda)

MASS Design Group 164

Massera, Emilio Eduardo 249

mass incarceration, and racial injustice 162

Mateen, Omar 193, 199–200

Mauriac, Francois 23

Maus (Spiegelman) 47

Mbombo, Zukiswa (North West Police Commissioner) 216, 222

Index 295

McConnell, Mitch 183
McGill, Joseph 89
McLeod Plantation, SC: memorializing of Gullah culture at 101n60; Roof's visit to 86
McNamara, Robert 269
Mda, AP 222
Mda, Zakes: anti-colonial perspective of 223–224; awards and honors 223; *Mirrors and Washboards* exhibit 223; nation-building imagery 224–227; paintings memorializing the Marikana Massacre 12, 222–23, 224f, 225f, 226f, portrayals of Zuma 222f, 223–224
Memoria Abierta (Open Memory) 253, 255
memorialization: acknowledging and addressing violence associated with 157; Argentina, diversity of 248; art as tool for remembering 12, 222–226, 222–223, 224f, 225f, 226f; the "Casino" (Museum and Site of Memory ESMA, Buenos Aires) 255–256; centralized *vs.* ephemeral and peripheral memorialization 194; "Colonialism in Destru(A)ction" map 231, 234–235, 243; combining with calls for justice, Argentinian examples 252–253; continuum for 3; digital memory projects 6–7; and the evocation of traumatic memories 6; and homonationalism 195–196; for the Marikana Massacre 222; memory projects 263–264; Museum and Site of Memory ESMA, Buenos Aires 255; and pseudo-history 149, 172; and remembering the forgotten 227; Rwandan commemoration days 67–69; tendency towards homogenized views of history 195; and Zochrot signage 232–233; *see also specific memorials*
Memorial Mania (Doss) 4
Memorial to the Murdered Jews of Europe (Holocaust Museum), Berlin 23
memory. *See* memorialization; public; public memory
Memory and Justice in Post-Genocide Rwanda (Longman) 57–58
Menem, Carlos Saúl 252
Merry, Melissa 197
Merseyside Maritime Museum, Liverpool, *Transatlantic Slavery: Against Human Dignity* exhibit 104, 106
Mgcieni Noki Memorial Sports Centre 222

Michel-Rolph Trouillot 6
Middle Passage 89, 104–105
Miles, James 137
Miles, Tiya 93
military junta, Argentina: characteristics of the disappeared 250–251; goals and methods of disappearance 250–251; human rights abuses, commemoration of 247; prosecutions of under Alfonsín 252; rise and establishment of 249–250; *see also* Rwandan Patriotic Front; settler colonialism
Miller, Alex 233
Milligan, Robert 111–112
Miners Shot Down (documentary) 222
mineworkers, South Africa, police massacre *see* Marikana Massacre, 2012
Minnesota, toppled Columbus statue in 4
Minute Man National Historical Park (Concord, Lincoln, and Lexington, MA), Operation POW at 277–278
Minute Man statue, Concord, MA 272–273, 274f
Mirrors and Washboards exhibit (Zakes Mda) 223
Miska, Israel, imaginary map of equitable future in 232
A Misplaced Massacre: Struggling over the Memory of Sand Creek (Kelman) 143
Mizrahi Jews, displacement of 242
Moehringer, J. R. 163
Mokoena, Barnard 216
Montgomery, Alabama: Equal Justice Institute memorial markers at sites of racial violence 87; national lynching museum and memorial 4, 164
monument destruction/removal: Confederate monuments 4, 82, 84–85, 141; debates about 114–115; monuments to British slave traders 4–5, 9–10, 102, 111–112, 112f, 129f, 130, 141; monuments to Columbus 129–130; reactions to 85, 87
Monumento a las Víctimas del Terrorismo de Estado (*Monument to the Victims of State Terrorism, MVTE*), Buenos Aires 256–258, 257f
monuments and memorials: alternatives to, Pulse nightclub example 203–204; in Argentina, funding and purpose 247, 249, 253–261; importance of audience response 257; in Johannesburg 215; multi-level purposes 252; permanence

296   *Index*

of 83; political use of in Africa 58; and public spaces "for all" 31, 251; and simplification of complex narratives 83, 203; temporary, in Orlando 203–206; therapeutic memorials 256–257; transforming sites of terror into 253; and variable responses to 94; war memorials 267, 275–279; *see also* culture of remembrance; monument removal and *specific monuments, memorials, and museums*

Moody, Jessica 9

Morgan, Jennifer 82

Morrison, Toni 87, 164

Morse, Arthur D. 48

mothers, activism by 262–263

Mothers of the Movement 262–263

Mothers of the Plaza de Mayo (Madres de Plaza de Mayo), Argentina 251, 254, 257, 262, 264

Mothers Reclaiming Our Children (Mothers ROC), United States 262–263

Murphy, Karen 10–11, 158

Murray, M.J. 224–225

Museum and Site of Memory ESMA, Buenos Aires 255–56

museum exhibits: biases in 5; using shocking optics 166; *see also specific museums*

Museum of African American History (Boston) 2

Museum of London Docklands, "London, Sugar Slavery" gallery 107

Muskogee Comet, on Tulsa as the Black Eden 175

My Lai Massacre 269

NAACP (National Association for the Advancement of Colored People), lynching investigations 10–11, 160

Nakba (catastrophe): and collapse of Arab-Jewish accords 237; destruction prior to 1948 235; educating Israelis about 13, 231; Israeli efforts to suppress knowledge of 233; Nakba Law (Israel) 233; numbers of communities destroyed during Palestinian populations before and after 243n14; *see also* "Colonialism in Destru(A)ction" map; De-Colonizer *Nakba. The Struggle to decolonize Israel* (Aparicio and Bronstein) 233, 239

naming, and humanization 157

Narragansett people, Great Swamp Massacre 143

Nasson, Leah 12

Nataraja Church Genocide Memorial 65f

Nathaniel Russell House, Charleston, SC, tour narrative 93

National Black Tourism Network 85

National Commission on the Disappearance of Persons Report (CONADEP, 1984) 255

National Commission for the Fight Against Genocide, Rwanda 66

National Commission for Human Rights, Rwanda 66

National Congress of American Indians (NCAI) 139

National Day of Mourning 147–148, 148f

National Heroes' Day, Rwanda 67

National League of Families of American Prisoners in Southeast Asia 280–281

National Maritime Museum, Greenwich, UK, gallery devoted to the slave trade 107

National Memorial for Peace and Justice, Montgomery, Alabama: centerpiece, structure and purpose 165; creation and opening 164; daytime view 201f; exposing the context for racial violence 164–165; focus on lynching 11, 201; survivor's walk 201, 201f; *see also* lynching

National Memorial to the Victims of War and Tyranny, Berlin 23

National Museum of African American History and Culture 51, 91

National Museum of the American Indian 51

National Negro Business League 180

National Park Service (NPS): "GULAG: Soviet Forced Labor Camps and the Struggle for Freedom" 2; LBGT heritage sites 195; "Roots of Liberty: The Haitian Revolution and the American Civil War" 2; Sand Creek Massacre National Historic Site 143

National Prosecuting Authority, South Africa 213

National Pulse Memorial, Orlando, FL: critiques of 207n28; design competition 198–199; downplaying terrorist aspects of the event 199–200; embedding in the SoDo neighborhood 202; as an example of consolidated memory 198; operation of 207n16; as a simplification of a complex narrative 203

National Register of Historic Places, addition of LGBT sites 195
National Summit on Teaching Slavery 79–80
National Trust (UK), public history of slavery and empire 116–117
National Union of Mineworkers (NUM), South Africa 216
National Unity and Reconciliation Commission (NURC), Rwanda 66
"nation of immigrants" myth 135
Native American/Indigenous peoples: in Argentina, memorials to 261–262; and assimilationist boarding schools 4, 143–144; coalitions with BLM 130; denial of political agency 134; dispossession and erasure 4, 10, 130, 136, 139–140, 144; genocide/elimination strategies 136–137, 142–143; the myth of Indian extinction 132–133; Native American and Indigenous Studies (NAIS) 132–133; resistance, and confronting colonial violence 10; revealing "difficult histories" 137; and settler memory/myth-making 134, 137–138, 149; stereotyping 134, 138; survivance and counter-memory 132, 144–145; toppling of Columbus statue 129–130; *see also* settler colonialism
Native American mascots/team names: historical and contemporary political function 140; impacts on native Americans 138–139; inherent racism of 139–140; ubiquity of 138; and the warrior stereotype 138–139
Nazi Holocaust *see* the Holocaust; Holocaust memorialization
Neiman, Susan 6, 19
Neue Wache (New Guardhouse), Berlin, redesign and rededication of 23, 32n7
New Orleans, LA: markers at slave auction sites 89; Take 'Em Down NOLA 84–85
Newsome, Bree 82
New York Historical Society (NYHS), *Without Sanctuary: Lynching Photography in America* 158–159
New York Times: 1619 Project 90; policy on weddings performed at plantations 86; review of the *Witness* exhibit 157
Niethammer, Lutz 29
Niles, Alva 179
Nipmuc Indians, forcible removal of 147
Nisei generation of Japanese-Americans, silence about internment 184–185

Nixon, Richard 280–281
Noki, McGinn (Mambush), as symbol of the Marikana Massacre 222–224
None Shall Escape (film) 45
Nontshokweni, Sihle-isipho 12
Nora, Pierre 58
Northeastern University, public history program 3
North Tulsa, OK, Black community in 174–175
Northup, Lauren 93
Not a Nation of Immigrants: Settler Colonialism, White Supremacy, and a History of Erasure and Exclusion (Dunbar-Ortiz) 135
Nuremberg Laws and Trials 25, 40, 44, 187

Oasis Fresh Market, Tulsa, OK 174
Obama, Barack, election of 183
obelisks 275–277, 279
Obergefell v. Hodges decision 204
O'Brien, Jean M. (White Earth Ojibwe) 132
Ocasio-Cortez, Alexandria 35, 53
Ohlendorf, Otto 26
Okemah, OK, lynching photograph 169
Oldfield, John 82, 103
Old North Bridge, Concord, MA: memorials at, mythic content 272–273; Operation POW at 271
Old North Church, Boston: and the initial event of Operation POW 272; and mythic glorification of Revere's signal system 271–272
Old South: mythologized nostalgia about 79; and romanticized portrayals of slavery 79
Olusoga, David 5, 115, 117
Omaar, Rakiya 70
onePULSE Foundation: aspiration for the Pulse Memorial 199; challenges faced by 11–12; design competition 198–199; goal 193; memorial-building process 199; *see also* National Pulse Memorial; Pulse nightclub shooting
Operation Condor, Argentina 247
Operation Dewey Canyon III protest (VVAW), Washington, DC 268–270
Operation POW (VVAW-NE): choice of route for 271; march over the Concord bridge 273, 274f; mass arrests 271; mock search-and-destroy mission 275–277; overshadowing by the POW/MIA campaign 281

298   Index

Operation RAW (VVAW-NE) 270
optics, shocking 166
oral history projects 29, 89, 255
Oriel College, Oxford University, Rhodes
    Must Fall/Fees Must Fall campaign
    (RMFO) 113–114
Orlando, FL: National Pulse Memorial
    194–201; one PULSE Foundation
    193–194; Pulse nightclub shooting
    193; smaller, life-affirming memorial
    to the Pulse shooting 203–206; SoDo
    Neighborhood development 201–202
Orlando Modern Quilt Guild 203
Orlando Sentinel, on the SoDo
    neighborhood development 202
"The Orlando Syllabus" 203
Orlando Weekly, on the SoDo
    neighborhood development 202
Ortiz, Ryan (Northern Arapho) 146
"Other Half Tour" (Colonial Williamsburg)
    81
Ottoman government, role in early
    Palestinian land sales to Zionists 235–236
Owens-Thomas House, Savannah, GA,
    narrative changes at 91–92
Ozick, Cynthia 47

Paine, Thomas 271
Paland, Hugo 28–29
Palestine, historical; repopulation of
    Palestinian cities 239–240; see also the
    Nakba (catastrophe)
Palestinians: Black American solidarity
    with 46; deportation methods 238–239;
    destruction of Jewish settlements 234,
    237; dispossession and violence against
    4, 234–236; Israeli apartheid policies
    12–13; lack of resistance to Zionist take-
    overs 236–238; population in Palestine
    and Israel, before and after the Nakba
    243n14; as refugees 232, 238–239;
    returning former land, proposal for 232;
    settlement near Tel Aviv, map showing
    232; see also "Colonialism in Destru(A)
    ction" map; De-Colonizer; Israeli settler
    colonialism; Nakba
Parque de la memoria (Park of
    Remembrance), Buenos Aires: Centro
    de Documentación y Archivo Digital
    (Center for Documentation and Digital
    Archive) 258; La Sala Presentes, Ahora
    y Siempre (Present, Now and Always
    Hall) 258; Monumento a las Víctimas

del Terrorismo de Estado (Monument to
    the Victims of State Terrorism, MVTE)
    256–258, 257f; purpose 256; The
    Reconstruction of the Portrait of Pablo
    Míguez (Fontes) 258–259
Patel, Priti 114
Paul Revere statue (Dallin), Boston, as a
    myth-based portrayal 271–272
Peck, Raoul 5–6
Peltier, Leonard 147
the Pequot, settler attacks against 142
Péron, Juan 249
"Pero's Bridge" Bristol, UK 107
Peru, Shining Path violence 258
Petah Tikva area, first displacement of
    Palestinians in 236
photos of lynchings 154, 156–158
Pilgrims, and Thanksgiving myths 133
Pinney, John 106, 107
plantation tourist sites 85–86, 91–93, 92f
Playing Indian (Deloria) 134
Plymouth, MA, National Day of Mourning
    147–148, 148f
Pocock, J.G.A. 149, 150n5
Poliakov, Leon (Harvest of Hate) 44
police, South Africa: brutality of, under
    apartheid 211–212; Marikana Massacre,
    2012 211, 221; ongoing brutality and
    distrust of 215–216; prosecutions/
    convictions for torture and murder
    212–213; state sanctioned violence
    197–198; torture tactics 212
Poonan, Unjinee, torture of 214
post-apartheid South Africa 225, 227
postcards as lynching souvenirs 157, 168
Pottier, John 70
POW/MIA (Prisoner of War/Missing in
    Action) flags campaign 267, 280–282
Pratt, Carla D. 183
Preminger, Otto (Exodus) 45
Prescott, William 107
President's Commission on the Holocaust,
    findings 49
Pretoria, South Africa, Voortrekker
    Monument 214
Prisoner of War day, 1970 280
Prisoners of War/Missing in Action
    (POW/MIA) campaign 13
pseudo-history 149, 172
Puar, Jasbir 195
public memory: active engagement
    required for 214; and addressing
    complicity and culpability as well

as victimization 31; Bicentenary celebrations 107–111; changing 6; commemorative *vs.* historical voices 5–7; and contested public spaces 4; and conversations about racist past 185; and "culture wars" 113; culture wars and the culture of abolition in the UK 118; and dealing with difficult histories 149; debates about following the British BLM protests 113; defining 5; and discussions about reparations, challenges of 172–173; explorations of violence in, and taking a position 5–6; and the goal of the onePULSE foundation 193; human rights abuses in Argentina 247, 261; identifying sites of violence 9; and incorporating "atrocity materials" 110; loss of, example of the Tulsa Massacre 177–179; mourning sites 13; and Native American counter-narratives 142, 149; and ongoing challenges of 3, 188; and pseudo-history 149, 172; reclaiming through reparations 183; and reeducation 173–174; and stereotyping 104; and the struggle against forgetting 10, 20, 105, 113–114, 137, 144, 165–166, 165f, 190, 211, 222; studies of meaning and nature of 6; survivance and counter memory 145, 154; as tool for rectification 3, 190; transformative 223; and trauma 4–7; United Kingdom, shifts in 102–104, 106–107; *see also* erasure/elimination; *specific events and locations*

Pulse Museum, Orlando, FL 201

Pulse nightclub shooting, Orlando, FL: the attack 3; centralized *vs.* noncentralized memorials 194; the importance of remembering 194; interim memorial wall 203–204; memorializing, issues associated with 11–12, 194, 199, 201; post-Pulse memory projects 203–204; as racial, xenophobic and homosexist 195–197; smaller, life affirming memory projects 203–206; victims 193

queer love 205
quota system, US 40–41

racecraft 189
racial justice: efforts to promote in Palestine/Israel 13; and justice politics 97n9; and lack of accountability for lynchings 155; ongoing challenges 94–95; racial wealth lynching gap 183; reckoning 157–158; *see also* Equal Justice Initiative (EJI)

racism, structural, in the US 3–4, 39–40, 139–140, 172–173; *see also* Jim Crow South; racist violence

racist violence: acknowledging and recuperating from 87, 164; anti-Asian, and the atrocities of the Vietnam War 269; in early 20th century Tulsa 175; and focusing on victims *vs.* perpetrators 160–161; historical markers 165–166; against Indigenous peoples in Argentina 261–262; in Israel 242; as the legacy of slavery 82; murder of James Byrd 157–158; need for public conversation and institutional reforms 166; numbers of lynchings, 1880–1950 155; ongoing effects of 173; and parallels between current day anti-Black violence and lynchings 162; the Pulse nightclub shooting 193; and reckoning with the past 173–174; and resistance to removal of Confederate monuments and symbols 84; and rethinking American public history 79; violence of, retrieving memories of 5–6; *see also* genocide; the Holocaust; lynching; massacres

rainbow symbolism 199
Ramaphosa, Cyril 216–217, 221–222
Rankine, Claudia 10, 153–154, 156–157, 167–169
Ravensbrück concentration camp, GDR approach to memorializing 23
Reagan, Ronald 47, 185
The Reconstruction of the Portrait of Pablo Míguez (Fontes) 258–259
rectification and repair: and active re-remembering 170; importance of dialogue 166; and memorializing images of violence 10, 157; varied approaches to 186–187; *see also* reparations
Red Cross response to Tulsa massacre 177
Reddy, Chandon 196
redlining 186, 192n36
Redress: The Inside Story of the Successful Campaign for Japanese American Reparations (Tateishi) 184
"A Regime of Jewish Supremacy From the Jordan River to the Mediterranean Sea: This is Apartheid" (B'Tselem) 12
Reichmann, Eva 44

300   *Index*

the Reichsführung SS (Reich Leadership SS) history site 23
Reichssicherheitshauptamt (Reich Security Main Office) history site 23
Reitlinger, Gerald (*The Final Solution*) 44
Remembering Pulse 198
"Remember Marikana" stencil 222
renaming sites of violence 12, 23, 32n7, 79, 84, 212, 215
reparations: direct payments to individuals, rejection of in Evanston 186; efforts to commit the US to studying 172, 182–183; and emotional loss 185; and the establishment of the Tulsa Race Riot Commission 182; Gayle's evaluation of 11; for Holocaust survivors 186–187; and identifying what is owed 190; for Japanese-American 81, 185; for lynchings 155; micro-targeting 183; monetary, insufficiency of 186; and the ongoing effects of racism 173; as a policy decision, pros and cons 186; and the question of what is owed 173; for the Rosewood massacre 155–156; symbolic 82; as tool for reclaiming history 183; for the Tulsa Massacre, failure to issue 182
repentance, and weak apologies for slavery 162
re-remembering 154
Revere, Paul: ride of, memorialization of as myth; route taken by, adoption by the winter soldiers for protest march 271
Revolutionary War, myths about: Operation POW (VVAW-NE) 271; as revealed by the VVAW-NE's Operation POW 271–272; war as freeing, peaceable 272
Rhodes, Cecil 113–114, 214
Rhodes Must Fall/Fees Must Fall campaign (RMFO) 113–114, 214
Rice, Susan 70
Richmond Indigenous Society, alliance with BLM 130
Ridgley, Gail (Northern Arapaho) 145–146
Ridley, Caleb 179
Riedel, Heinz 28
Rise and Fall of the Third Reich (Shirer) 44
Roberts, Andrew 117
Robertson, James B.A. 177
Roca, Argentina 261
Roediger, David R. 40

Romano, Renee C. 9
Rome, ancient, obelisk symbols in 275
Rome Statute, 2002, International Criminal Report 12
Roof, Dylann 82, 86
Roosevelt, Franklin D.: combining of quotas for Germany and Austria 41; contradictory stances towards American Jewry 53; creation of Columbus Day 141; and the decision to intern Japanese-Americans 184; as focus of Jewish activism pre-war 38–39; limited efforts to counter German anti-Jewish activities 39–40; sustaining of Hoover's isolationist policies 41
"Roots of Liberty: The Haitian Revolution and the American Civil War" 2–3
Rose, Julia (*Interpreting Difficult History at Museums and Historic Sites*) 137
Rosenthal, Hans 27
Rosewood, Florida, massacre 81, 155–156
Ross, Don 181–182
Rostow, Walt 269
Roth, Philip (*The Ghose Writer*) 47
Roth Horowitz Gallery, NY 157–158
Rowland, Dick 175–176
Rudahigwa, King 67
Rusesabagina, Paul 71
Rwanda: focus on international acceptance 69–71; foreign assistance 57; gacaca dispute resolution system 66; genocide memorialization, intent of 9, 71, 72; Habyarimana government 57, 59; Hutu takeover 59; Kayibanda government 59; pre-colonial 58, 68; role of missionaries and priests in 58; *see also* Rwandan Patriotic Front (RPF)
Rwandan Patriotic Front (RPF): and the Arusha Peace Accord 60; attacks on the Hutu 62, 63–64; authoritarian rule 57; focus on international acceptance 64, 69–70; founding 62; human rights abuses 71; invasion and takeover of Rwanda 57, 63–64, 66; memorialization of the Tutsi genocide 58, 64, 65f, 66–72; pretense of shared power 64; self-portrayal as heroic 68; ties with Israel 75n63; use of genocide memorialization to retain power 67–69; violence by, prohibitions of discussions of 68; *see also* Tutsi genocide
Rwigyema, Fred 62, 67

Sachsenhausen concentration camp: GDR memorializing of 24; importance 32n10

Saint-Gaudens, August 2

St. Paul, MN, toppling of monument to Columbus 129–130, 129f

Sancho, Ignatius 103

sanctification 3

Sand Creek Massacre, Colorado: annual commemorative activities 145–146; mischaracterization as a battle 142–143; Sand Creek Massacre National Historic Site 143

Sansei generation of Japanese-Americans, desire for reparations 184–185

Santiago, Manuel 203

Savage, Kirk 256–257

Save Our Statues campaign (UK) 114

Saving Slave Houses project 89

"Scattered Memories of Difficult History and Museum Pedagogies of Disruption" (Miles) 137

Schindler's List (Spielberg) 38, 51

Schirmer. Jennifer G. 250

Schutte, Gillian 218

Scotland, sites in associated with slavery and colonialism 115

"The Second World War and German Occupation in Europe" on 32n9

Security Branch, Johannesburg police 213

Seghers, Anna 28

Senate Foreign Relation, Kerry's testimony about soldier-committed atrocities during the war 269

Senie, Harriet F. 257, 263

settler colonialism: acknowledging and addressing violence of 149; Columbus Day and Thanksgiving holidays 142; destroyed locations, returning to 232; dispossession and erasure policies 136–137, 139; monuments to Columbus 140–141; Peck's examination of 6; reinforcing through stereotypes 140; resisting and rethinking 148, 150n5; and settler memory/myths 132, 134–135, 137–138; and violence 3, 137–138, 143–144; *see also* erasure/elimination; Israeli settler colonialism; Native Americans/Indigenous people

Settler Memory: The Disavowal of Indigeneity and the Politics of Race in the United States (Bruyneel) 134

Shadowed Ground (Foote) 87

Shakhsari, Sima 196

Shaw, Robert Gould 2

Shipp, Thomas, lynching of 153

Shirer, William L. 44

Shoah (Lanzmann; documentary) 47

Shuttlesworth, Fred 95

Silencing the Past: Power and the Production of History (Trouillot) 137–138

SIMIKADE monument, Johannesburg 215

Simmons, Robin Rue 186

Simon, David 6–7

Sithole, Clayton, murder of 212

Slave Dwelling Project 89–90

slavery: 1619 Project 90; British role in, bringing to light 9–10, 102–103; dismantling pro-slavery narratives 9, 80, 89–90; education about, new narratives 82, 90; exposing the horror and violence of 9, 79–80, 82, 92–93; links between past and present 80, 82, 95; memorial markers 87–89; preserving slave dwellings 89; recuperating and marking sites of violence 6, 81, 87; simulations of, in school environments 86; slave auctions, catalogue and markers of 88–89, 88f; *see also* the enslaved; enslavers; reparations

Slavery in the Age of Memory (Araujo) 92

"slavery question" (Great Britain) 103

Slavery Remembrance Day, Liverpool 107

Smith, Abram, lynching of 153

Smith, Clint 6

Smith, Matthew Paul 93

The Smithsonian, contradictions in public history 95–96

Smithsonian National Air and Space Museum, Enola Gay exhibit 5

SoDo neighborhood, Orlando, FL, development of 202

Soros, George 52

South Africa: apartheid 12; law of "common purpose" 218; legitimization of state terror 212; as model for addressing difficult histories 162; police violence 12, 211–213, 216; punishment of activists 213–214, 228n6; systemic inequality and violence in 223–224; Truth and Reconciliation Commission, South Africa 66

South Africa History Archive, "Google Arts and Culture" exhibit 215–216

Southeast Asia, chemical warfare, bombings in 267–268

302 *Index*

Southern Poverty Law Center: documented removal of Confederate monuments and symbols 84; improving education about slavery 82
Soviet Union, Jews in 46
Spain, culture of remembrance 19
Spence, David 108
Spiegelman, Art 47
Spielberg, Stephen (*Schindler's List*) 51
"States of Incarceration" exhibit 3
Stefani, Anne 97n9
Stern, Marianne Winter 27
Stevenson, Bryan: Equal Justice Initiative (EJI) 162; Equal Justice Institute 3–4; on the importance of marking sites of violence 87–88; on link between slavery and contemporary racial violence 82; role in passage of anti-lynching law 11
Stolpersteine ("stumbling stones") project 88
Stone Mountain, white-supremacist copy in ad for 96
The Stranger (film, Welles) 45
Stuckart, Wilhelm 26
Sullivan Island, SC, memorial bench 87
"summer soldiers" 271
Sunday Times (Johannesburg), Heritage Project 215
survivance: National Day of Mourning 147–148, 148f; reclamation of Native American history and agency 10, 132, 145, 147–148
Syphax, Ginny Yamamoto 185
Szlezak, Klara Stephanie 7

Take 'Em Down NOLA 84–85
Tateishi, John 184–185
Taylor, Gideon 186–187
Tel Aviv, markers of Palestinian settlements near 232
Tenenbaum, Joseph (*Race and Reich*) 44
terrorism: assumptions and false narratives about 196; downplaying in the National Pulse Memorial 199–200; framing through race, national origin, and queer citizenship 193, 195–198; identifying roots and complexities of in memorials 200–201, 208n33; state-sponsored 7, 13, 71, 164, 212, 250–253; *see also* the disappeared, Argentina; genocide; the Holocaust; lynching; massacres; violence
Terrorism Act of 1967 (South Africa) 212
Thälmann, Ernst 24

Thanksgiving: creation of 141–142; myths about 132–133
Thomas, Hank Willis 164
Thomas, K. 222
Three Infantrymen (*Three Soldiers*) statue 279–280
Timol, Ahmed, murder of 212–213
Topography of Terror Foundation 23
torture, examples of 102–103, 110, 160–161, 168, 212–215, 248, 250, 255–256, 259
totalitarian attitudes and language *see* fascism
Trachtenberg, Barry 8–9
Trade and Empire exhibit, Greenwich, UK 107
Transatlantic Slavery: Against Human Dignity exhibit, Liverpool 106
Transatlantic Slavery Gallery, Liverpool 104
traumatic memories: public memorials evoking 6; and regaining presence and agency 147–148
Tree of Life (L'Simcha) Synagogue, Pittsburgh, shooting at 52–53
Tremont Temple, Boston, "Roots of Liberty" exhibition 3
Trouillot, Michel-Rolph 137–138
Trump, Donald 35–36, 52–53, 90
Truth and Reconciliation Commission, South Africa 66, 213, 215
Tsazibane, Wellington 212
Tulsa, OK: Black neighborhoods, 1920s 175, 189; departure of Black Tulsans from the city 181; and the impacts of the Housing Act of 1949 180–181; impact of urban renewal projects on 180–181; Jim Crow laws 175; the Ku Klux Klan in 179; Oasis Fresh Market opening 174; population growth by 1921 174–175; reduced incomes and life expectancy of Blacks in 189; response to Rowland's arrest 176; *see also* Tulsa Race Massacre, 1921
Tulsa Race Massacre, 1921: casualties and property destruction 176; and the destruction of the Greenwood neighborhood 176f; investigative commission 81; lack of accountability for perpetrators 188; official silence about 177–178; the questions of reparations for 173; reexamining story of, challenges 173; rejection of outside aid for massacre victims 177–179; relocation of Black population following massacre 178–180;

Tulsa Race Riot Commission 181–182; and US reparations policies 11

Tulsa Tribune: 1921 headline about Rowland's alleged attack on girl in elevator 175; rationale for relocating Blacks to new area of Tulsa 179–180

Tuscaloosa County, AL, historical marker 165f

Tutsi ethnic group (Rwanda): anti-Hutu ethnonationalist policies 71–72; Hutu characterizations of as evil 60–62; limits placed on by the Kayibanda government 59; mythologized memories of life in Rwanda 62; refugees in Ugandan refugee camps 62; *see also* Rwandan Patriotic Front (RPF); Tutsi genocide

Tutsi genocide, 1994: activities leading to 57–61; African Rights report 70; assigning blame for 63; conflating with the Holocaust 58; explanations for within Rwanda 61; manipulation of public memories of 9; memorializing of, strategic purposes 58, 66; modes of violence 61–62; negative impact on Hutu military 63; numbers killed and ongoing attacks 61–62; preservation of massacre sites 64, 65f, 67–69; use of to court international support 58, 70–71

Twa ethnic group (Rwanda) 58

Twain, Mark 155

Uganda, founding of the RPF in 62

Uganda Heroes' Day 74n42

Underground Railroad Reenactments (UGRRs) 80, 86

Unger, Katrin 8

United American Indians of New England (UAINE), National Day of Mourning 147

United Daughters of the Confederacy, memorialization project 83–84

United Kingdom: bicentenary celebrations of the Abolition and Slave Trade Acts 107–111; Black Lives Matter protests 111–112, 112f, 115–116; culture of abolition 110; efforts to bring realities of slavery into public view 105, 116–117; maritimized view of slave trade 102, 104–105; "millennial reckoning" with slave past 107; myths about empire 113, 118–119; recognizing links between slavery, industry, and capitalism 105

United Nations: definition of genocide 8; International Criminal Tribunal for Rwanda 74n33; Memory of the World program 255; Partition Plan 240

United States: activism by mothers 251; antisemitism in 37; changing understanding of slavery in 6, 81; Congressional anti-lynching bills 155; and efforts to commit the government to study reparations to Black Americans 162, 182–183; foundational myths, challenging contradictions in 19, 90–91; Holocaust memorialization, phases of 41–51; immigration quota system 40–41; increasing efforts to aid war refugees 42; intervention in Argentina 247; isolationist policies 40–41; "manifest destiny" myth 135; "nation of immigrants" myth 135; pre-war responses to Nazism 38; racial anxieties among white Americans 40; racism in the justice system 3–4; refugee advocacy, hostility towards 42; reparations paid interned Japanese Americans 81; the Senate's formal apology for lynching 161–162; settler colonial myths 132; support for Israel 48; traditional misrepresentation of Native American history 130; war memorialization 13–14; War Refugee Board (WRB) 41–42; xenophobia in, and nation of immigrants meme 135; *see also* lynching; slavery; structural racism; Tulsa Race Massacre, 1921; Vietnam War

United States Holocaust Memorial Museum (USHMM): "Americans and the Holocaust" exhibit 53; condemnation of AOC for use of term concentration camps 35–36; criticism of insistence on uniqueness of the Holocaust 36; opening of 49–50, 50f

"Unite the Right" rally, Charlottesville, VA 37, 52

University of Cape Town, Rhodes Must Fall/Fees Must Fall campaign (RMFO) 214

Uris, Leon 44

Uwilingiyimana, Agathe 67

Vergangenheitsaufarbeitung ("working-off-the-past"), German *vs.* US approaches 6

Vesey, Denmark 95

304 *Index*

victims: focusing on 8, 27, 52

Videla, Jorge Rafael 249

Vielma, Luis 201

Vietnam Veterans Against the War (VVAW): early protests against the Vietnam War 13; mock search-and-destroy mission on Boston Common 276f; Operation Dewey Canyon III protest 268–270; Operation RAW 270; recognition of war as a crime against both the Vietnamese and the American citizenry 267; war medals, declaring as TRASH 270; Winter Soldier Investigation 268

Vietnam Veterans Memorial (The Wall Lin), Washington, DC 13–14, 256, 267, 279, 282

Vietnam War: American casualties in 268; atrocities committed by soldiers 269; deaths from toxic exposures and PTS 279; extensive US bombing during 267–268, 272; health problems among veterans 268; memorial projects 267, 280–282; Nixon's rationale for continuing 279; resistance to by the Vietnamese 268; as technowar 267–268; use of napalm and defoliants 268; violence/ massacres against the Vietnamese people 3, 269; as Western imperialism 279; "winter soldiers" 271; *see also* Vietnam Veterans Against the War (VVAW); Vietnam Veterans Memorial, Washington, DC

Villa ten Hompel History Site 23

Viola, Roberto Eduardo 251

violence, memorializing: and debates about depicting violent realities 110; ethical concerns and promotion of social justice 7; identifying sites of violence 3; multiple definitions for violence 4; and public memory 2–3; re-remembering as essential for repair 170; rethinking 132, 153, 195–198; and revealing perpetrators 200–201

Vision 2020 (Kagame) 66

Vizenor, Gerald (Anishnabee) 10, 130–132, 145

Voortrekker Monument, Pretoria 214–215

Voster, John 212

VVAW *see* Vietnam Veterans Against the War (VVAW)

"Waldheim Trials" 33n23

Wales, markers of slavery and imperialism in 115

The Wall *see* Vietnam Veterans Memorial

Wallace, Elizabeth Kowaleski- 107

Wall Builders 172

Walvin, James 105

Wampanoags, and King Philip's War 134

war: brutality of, downplaying in traditional military monuments 272–273; death and conquest as goals of 278; memorialization of 272, 282; *see also* Vietnam Veteran's Against the War; Vietnam War

war myths: war as freeing, essentially peaceable 272; war is immortality 275–277; war is preparedness 277–278; war is restraint 278–279; was as creativity and swiftness 271–272

Warped Narratives: Distortion in the Framing of Gun Policy (Merry) 197

War Refugee Board (WRB, 1944) 41–42

Warsaw Ghetto: A Diary (Berg) 44

Washington, D.C.: National Museum of African American History and Culture 91; Operation Dewey Canyon III protest (VVAW) 268–270; US Holocaust Memorial Museum (USHMM) 49–50; Vietnam Veterans Memorial (The Wall), Washington, DC 267; Vietnam Veterans Memorial, Washington, DC 13–14, 256, 279, 282; Washington Monument 279; World War II memorial, 2004 282

Washington, George, denture souvenirs 80

Webster, Daniel 275

Week of Mourning, Rwanda 67–68

Wehrmacht, crimes committed by 30

Welles, Orson (*The Stranger*) 45

Wells, Ida B. 164

"We Need to Talk about an Injustice" (Stevenson TED talk) 162

West Bank, Israeli occupation 235, 237, 241

"West India Interest" 103

We Wish to Inform You That Tomorrow We Will Be Killed With Our Families (Gourevitch) 70

white supremacy: and the celebration of lynching 168–169; Confederate monuments and symbols 83–84; Peck's examination of 6; in photos of lynchings 156–157; and plantation tours 85, 93; recontextualizing through lynching

photographs 153–154; and settler memory 134–135; and stereotyping violence as non-white 196; use of monuments to buttress 82, 130
Whitman, James Q. 39–40
Whitney Plantation memorial 92f, 93
Wiesel, Elie (*Night*) 44, 47
Wiesenthal, Simon 47
Wilberforce, William 102–103
Wilberforce Museum, Hull, redesign of 107
Wilkerson, Isabel 167–168
Williams, Eric 105
Wilson, Kristi M. 255–256
Winter Soldier Investigation (VVAW) 268
Wise, Stephen 42, 48
Without Sanctuary: Lynching Photography in America: Black *vs.* white responses to 158–159; criticisms of 163; goal of correcting the historical record 156, 166; goal of encouraging conversations 158; Hale's critique 160–161; long-term impacts 11, 161; move to Pittsburgh and expansion 159; planning for 158–159; public response to 159–160
Witness exhibit, attendance and impacts 157–158
WITS (University of Witwaterstrand) Justice Project, purpose 212
Wolfe, Patrick 136
Wood, Marcus 105
working-off-the-past 6
World War II memorial, Washington, D.C. 282–283
Wray, Dylan 12

Wulf, Joseph 22–23
Wyman, Bill 270
Wyman, David S. 48

Yad Vashem, criticism of Ocasio-Cortez for her invocation of concentration camps 35
Yale University, renaming of Calhoun College 79
Yemeni Jews, displacement of 242
YMCA, Underground Railroad Reenactments (UGRRs) 86
Young, Alfred 5

Zimmerman, George 168–169
Zionist movement: and the early pioneers 234; imperialist nature 236; and Judaism 12; support for Jewish refugees 42
Zionist settlers: destruction of Palestinian settlements prior to 1948 234–235; and the initial expulsion of Palestinians from Palestine/Israel 13
Zochrot: early mapping projects 232; founding and purpose 13, 231; government efforts to suppress 233; importance to public education and policy 13, 233; origins 232; tours to destroyed localities 232; *see also* Israeli settler colonialism; Nakba
Zucker, Eve Monique 7
Zuckerman, Lawrence 48
Zülsdorf- Kersting, Meik 31
Zuma, Jacob 223–224, 224f

Taylor & Francis eBooks

www.taylorfrancis.com

A single destination for eBooks from Taylor & Francis with increased functionality and an improved user experience to meet the needs of our customers.

90,000+ eBooks of award-winning academic content in Humanities, Social Science, Science, Technology, Engineering, and Medical written by a global network of editors and authors.

TAYLOR & FRANCIS EBOOKS OFFERS:

- A streamlined experience for our library customers
- A single point of discovery for all of our eBook content
- Improved search and discovery of content at both book and chapter level

REQUEST A FREE TRIAL
support@taylorfrancis.com

Printed in the United States
by Baker & Taylor Publisher Services